FATHERHOOI
THE NORDIC WELF/

Comparing care policies and practice

Edited by Guðný Björk Eydal and Tine Rostgaard

First published in Great Britain in 2016 by

Policy Press
University of Bristol
1-9 Old Park Hill
Bristol BS2 8BB
UK
t: +44 (0)117 954 5940
pp-info@bristol.ac.uk
www.policypress.co.uk

North America office:
Policy Press
c/o The University of Chicago Press
1427 East 60th Street
Chicago, IL 60637, USA
t: +1 773 702 7700
f: +1 773 702 9756
sales@press.uchicago.edu
www.press.uchicago.edu

British Library Cataloguing in Publication Data
A catalogue record for this book is available from the British Library

Library of Congress Cataloging-in-Publication Data
A catalog record for this book has been requested

ISBN 978-1-4473-1048-8 paperback

Cover design by Policy Press
Front cover image: istock
Printed and bound in Great Britain by CMP, Poole

Contents

Theme 1: Fathers, families and family policies

Theme 2: Fathers in everyday life – culture, work and care

Theme 3: Constructing fatherhood in different family settings

List of tables and figures

Tables

—

Figures

Notes on contributors

Arnfinn J. Andersen, Head of Research at the National Centre on Violence and Traumatic Stress Studies (NKVTS), Oslo, Norway. His research interests have until now been on family, fatherhood, friendship and intimacy in the context of citizenship. In his current position he is responsible for a research programme on the survivors after the terrorist attack in Norway in 2011. His recent publications include 'Sexual citizenship in Norway', in *International Journal of Law, Policy and the Family* (2011).

Lotte Bloksgaard, Associate Professor at the Department of Culture and Global Studies, Aalborg University, Denmark. Her primary research interest areas are work–life, work–life balance, fatherhood, masculinity and gender in organisations. Her recent publications include 'No, gender doesn't make a difference...? Studying negotiations and gender in organizations', in *Qualitative Studies* (2012), and 'Masculinities, femininities and work – the horizontal gender segregation in the Danish Labour market', in *Nordic Journal of Working Life Studies* (2011).

Berit Brandth, Professor of Sociology at the Department of Sociology and Political Science, Norwegian University of Science and Technology, Trondheim, Norway. Her research focuses on gender, work and family reconciliation, and welfare state policies. One central area of study has been fathers' use of parental leave; another is family, work and gender in a changing rural context. She is the co-author of the books, *Flexible fathers* (2003) and *The father's quota and the father friendly welfare state* (2013), both with E. Kvande (in Norwegian).

Ann-Zofie Duvander, Associate Professor at the Department of Sociology, Demography Unit, Stockholm University, and Senior Researcher at the Swedish Inspectorate of Social Insurance, Sweden. Her research interests include family policy and family and work connection, in particular fathers' use of parental leave and childcare effects on childbearing. Her recent publications include 'Earner-carer model at the cross-roads: reforms and outcomes of Sweden's family policy in comparative perspective' with T. Ferrarini, in *International Journal of Health Services* (2010).

Guðný Björk Eydal, Professor at the Faculty of Social Work, University of Iceland, Reykjavik, Iceland. Her main fields of research are the welfare state and social policy, with an emphasis on family policies, care policies, social services, poverty, child policies, and crisis management. Her recent publications include: *Parental leave, childcare and gender equality in the Nordic countries* (2011), with I.V. Gíslason (eds); 'Child maintenance policies in Iceland – caring mothers and breadwinning fathers?', with H. Friðriksdóttir, in *European Journal of Social Security* (2012); and 'Caring families – policies and practices in Nordic countries', with T. Rostgaard, in M.H. Ottosen and U.B. Björnberg (eds) *Challenges for future family policies in the Nordic countries: Reassessing the Nordic welfare model* (2013).

Hrefna Friðriksdóttir, Associate Professor of Family Law, Faculty of Law, University of Iceland, Reykjavik, Iceland. Her main research focus is the field of family law and succession law on inheritance, including research on marriage, non-marital co-habitation, sexual orientation and children's rights. Her recent publications include *Handbók: Barnalög nr 76/2003* (*Commentary on the Act on Children*) (2013), and 'Úrræði vegna umgengnistálmana' ('Enforcement of contact orders') in *Icelandic Law Journal* (2012).

Ingólfur V. Gíslason, Lecturer in Sociology, School of Social Sciences, University of Iceland, Reykjavik. His main fields of research are gender roles, masculinities, parental leave, violence, individuality and crowds. His recent publications include 'Polarization among Icelandic women in the aftermath of the crisis?' in G. Jónsson and K. Stefánsson (eds) *Retrenchment or renewal? Welfare states in times of economic crisis* (2013), and 'Gender display in a lifestyle magazine in Iceland 1978 to 2009', with B. Jóhannsdóttir, in *Arctic and Antarctic* (2013).

Janet Gornick, Director of LIS and Professor of Political Science and Sociology, The Graduate Center, City University of New York, US. Most of her research is comparative and concerns social welfare policies and their impact on family well-being and gender equality. She is the co-author or co-editor of three books: *Families that work: Policies for reconciling parenthood and employment* (2003), *Gender equality: Transforming family divisions of labor* (2009) and *Income inequality: Economic disparities and the middle class in affluent countries* (2013).

Anita Haataja, Senior Researcher in the Research Department of the Social Insurance Institution Finland (Kela), Helsinki, and Adjunct

Professor of Social Policy in the University of Turku, Finland. Her recent research interests include evaluating impacts of family and tax-transfer policies, especially on mothers' labour market situation and income distribution. She has also specialised using micro-simulation models and international comparisons as methods for assessing outcomes of alternative policies in the Nordic countries. Her recent publications include *Fathers' use of paternity and parental leave* (2009).

Mia Hakovirta, Director of the Social Insurance Expert Training Programme at the University of Turku, Department of Social Research, Finland. Her research interests include lone parenthood, child maintenance policies, post-divorce family life and child poverty. Her recent publications include 'A comparative analysis of child maintenance schemes in five countries', with C. Skinner and J. Davidson, in *European Journal of Social Security* (2012).

Mats Johansson, Senior Researcher at the Swedish Social Insurance Agency, Stockholm, Sweden. His research focuses on the fields of gender, income distribution, poverty and social security. His current research covers the effects of reforms in Swedish parental leave insurance and the distributional effects of Swedish family policy. His recent publications include 'What are the effects of reforms promoting fathers' parental leave use?' with A. Duvander, in *Journal of European Social Policy* (2012).

Elin Kvande, Professor of Sociology at the Department of Sociology and Political Science, Norwegian University of Science and Technology, Trondheim, Norway. Her research focuses on gender, work and family reconciliation and welfare state policies. One central area of study has been fathers' use of parental leave; another is internationalisation and the Nordic model of work and the welfare state. She is the co-author of *Flexible fathers* (2003) and *The father's quota and the father friendly welfare state* (2013), both with B. Brandth (in Norwegian).

Johanna Lammi-Taskula, Senior Researcher and Head of Unit in the National Institute for Health and Welfare (THL), Helsinki, Finland. Her research is focused on family policy, reconciliation of work and family life, and parental leave from a gender perspective. Recent international publications include a book on fathers and parental leave and chapters on parental leave policies in publications around gender, the labour market and welfare state. Her publications include 'Job quality, work–family tensions and well-being: the Finnish case' in S. Drobnič and A.M. Guillén (eds) *Work–life balance in Europe. The role of job quality* (2011) and 'Parental choice and the passion for equality in Finland' in A.L. Ellingsæter and A. Leira (eds) *Politicising parenthood in Scandinavia: Gender relations in welfare states* (2006), both co-authored with M. Salmi.

Mette Lausten, Senior Researcher at SFI – The Danish National Centre for Social Research, Copenhagen, Denmark. Her research interests span from balancing family and work over child well-being and parental employment to vulnerable children and children in out-of-home care. Her recent publications include 'Medium-term consequences of low birth weight – is there a catch-up effect?', with N.D. Gupta and M. Deding, in *Economics & Human Biology* (2013), and *Fathers' leave, fathers' involvement and child development: are they related? Evidence from four OECD countries*, with M. del Carmen Huerta et al, an OECD Social, Employment and Migration Working Paper (2013).

Anika Liversage, Senior Researcher and Programme Director for integration and migration research, SFI – the Danish National Centre for Social Research, Copenhagen, Denmark. Her research interests are immigrant family relations, attending specifically to issues of gender and power. Much of her work concerns changes in Turkish immigrant families in Denmark. Her recent publications include 'Gender, conflict and subordination within the household – Turkish migrant marriage and divorce in Denmark', in *Journal of Ethnic and Migration Studies* (2012).

Rasmus Juul Møberg, Assistant Professor, Department of Sociology and Social Work, Aalborg University, Denmark. His research interests are work, work–life balance, care obligations, and gender roles seen in a life course perspective with special attention to possible marginalisation processes. With P.H. Jensen, he wrote 'Tensions related to the transition of elderly care from an unpaid to a paid activity', in B. Pfau-Effinger and T. Rostgaard (eds) *Care between work and welfare in European societies* (2011).

Steen Baagøe Nielsen, Associate Professor at the Department of Psychology and Educational Studies, and Head of Centre for Research on Welfare, Profession and Everyday Life, Roskilde University, Denmark. His primary research interests lie in the intersection of knowledge and competence, learning, and gender/masculinities within education, care and social work. His recent publications include 'Danish daycare institutions and their changing political mandate: discourse fluctuations between labour market, family and educational politics' ['Danske daginstitutioners skiftende politiske mandat: Om bevægelse i diskurserne mellem arbejdsmarked, familie- og uddannelsespolitik'], in *The struggle over the daycare institution* [*Kampen om daginstitutionen*], edited by J.B. Krejsler, A. Ahrenkiel and C. Schmidt (2014).

Mikael Nordenmark, Professor at the Department of Health Sciences, Mid Sweden University, Sweden. His main research interests are relationships among working life, family life, gender and well-being. Most of his research has a longitudinal and/or comparative approach. His recent publications include 'Division of labour, perceived labour-related stress and well-being among European couples', with E. Hagqvist and K.G. Gillander, in *Open Journal of Preventive Medicine* (2012) and 'The importance of childhood and adulthood aspects of gendered life for adult mental ill-health symptoms – a 27-year follow-up of the Northern Swedish Cohort', with A. Månsdotter and A. Hammarström, in *BMC Public Health* (2012).

Margaret O'Brien, Professor and Director of the Thomas Coram Research Unit at the Institute of Education, University of London, UK. Her key research is in the field of fathers, work and family life, with a policy and parenting support focus. Her recent publications include 'Fitting fathers into work-family policies: international challenges in turbulent times', in *International Journal of Sociology and Social Policy* (2013).

Mai Heide Ottosen, Programme Director and Senior Researcher at SFI – The Danish National Centre of Social Research, Copenhagen, Denmark. Her research interests cover the sociology of childhood and the sociology of the family. Her current research projects are dealing with post-divorce family life, child well-being, family policies and child poverty. Her recent publications include *Challenges for future family policies in the Nordic countries: Reassessing the Nordic welfare model*, co-edited with U.B. Björnberg (2013).

Hannu Pääkkönen, Senior Researcher at Statistics Finland, Helsinki, Finland. Her key research interest is the investigation of time use data. Her recent publications include *Time use changes in Finland through the 2000s*, with R. Hanifi (2012) and 'Total work allocation in four European countries' in *Social indicators research* (2009).

Tine Rostgaard, Professor at the Centre of Comparative Welfare Studies (CCWS), Department of Political Science, Aalborg University, Denmark. She has written widely on care policies and practice for children and older people. Her recent publications include 'Nordic care and care work in the public service model of Denmark: ideational factors of change', in M. Leon (ed) *Care regimes in transitional European societies* (forthcoming); 'Nordic childcare – a response to old and new tensions?', with G. Eydal, in B. Pfau-Effinger and T. Rostgaard (eds) *Care between work and welfare in European societies* (2011); and 'Fathers' rights to paid parental leave in the Nordic countries: consequences for the gendered division of leave' in *Community, Work & Family*, with L. Haas (2011).

Minna Salmi, Research Manager, National Institute for Health and Welfare (THL), Helsinki, Finland. Her key research interests are family policy, gender equality policy, working life, and the well-being of families with children. She has written on work–family balance, parental leave and family policy outcomes in Finland, and on child poverty and the well-being of children and their families. Her publications include 'Job quality, work–family tensions and well-being: the Finnish case' in S. Drobnič and A.M. Guillén (eds) *Work–life balance in Europe. The role of job quality* (2011) and 'Parental choice and the passion for equality in Finland' in A.L. Ellingsæter and A. Leira (eds) *Politicising parenthood in Scandinavia: Gender relations in welfare states*, 2006, both co-authored with J. Lammi-Taskula (2006).

Allan Westerling, Associate Professor in Social Psychology at Roskilde University, Denmark. He works in the field of social psychology and family research, and is currently focusing on fatherhood, parenthood and everyday family life. His recent publications include 'Intergenerational care in the Danish welfare society: ethnic majority and ethnic minority families' with A. Singla, in *Fokus paa Familien* (2014).

Minna Ylikännö, Senior Researcher at the Social Insurance Institution of Finland (KELA), Helsinki, Finland. Her research interests include studies of unemployment and time use research. Her recent publications include 'Away from daily routines – holiday as a standard of prevailing society and manifestation of unequal society' in L. Minnaert, R. Maitland and G. Miller (eds) *Social tourism* (2006), and *Perspectives and potential and allocation of time between paid and non-paid work in Nordic families* (2011).

Acknowledgements

This book marks the end of three years of productive cooperation on our research project examining Nordic fatherhoods. We would like to thank all of the authors for choosing to publish their results in this book, and for their kind cooperation. We would also like to thank our English editor Jon Jay Neufeld, as well as Lea Graff, Research Assistant, Aalborg University, Cynthia Lisa Jeans, Assistant Professor, University of Iceland, and Eva Rós Sveinsdóttir, Research Assistant, University of Iceland, who assisted with the final editing of the typescript. We also send our appreciation to the team at Policy Press for all their support and advice, and to the nameless reviewers of our book proposal and typescript for their good advice, for which we have done our utmost to follow. Furthermore, we would like to thank Professor Ann Sheila Orloff for commenting on the chapters at an earlier stage, Professor Emeritus Peter Moss and Professor Emeritus Ulla Björnberg for commenting on the book proposal and for their kind guidance. Last, but not least, we would like to express our gratitude to REASSESS (Nordic Centre of Excellence in Welfare Research) for their assistance and for funding the English editing, and in particular, to the Director of REASSESS, Bjørn Hvinden, for his continuous support and encouragement, and to NOS-HS (The Joint Committee of Nordic Research Councils in the Humanities and Social Sciences), for funding the exploratory network on Nordic fatherhood policies and practice.

ONE

Introduction

Guðný Björk Eydal and Tine Rostgaard

Aim and background

In 2007, an Icelandic play entitled 'The Dad' held its world premiere in Reykjavik, Iceland, and was well received by audiences and critics alike. Since then, the play has been translated into 10 languages and performed in 20 European countries. What prompts people in so many different cultures and countries to watch a one-man show about the male perspective on parenthood? One attraction seems to be its precise depiction of modern fatherhood. As playwright Bjarni Haukur Thorsson sees it, fatherhood practices are changing without any clear instruction manual, 'We young fathers know so little, as our own fathers practised fatherhood in a very different way compared to what is expected of us. Women, on the other hand, seem to know what they're doing. At least that's what it feels like' (SVD Kultur, nd, authors' translation).

Young fathers are less likely to model themselves on their own fathers; instead they must build their own fatherhood practices on what they as individuals believe is suitable. However, as the quote from Thorsson reveals, there are also certain societal expectations of the appropriate role and behaviours of these young fathers and how they should father their children. This book is about the practice of fatherhood and how expectations of fathers are formed in Nordic policymaking.

The aim of this book is to provide an insight into contemporary policies and practice of fatherhood in the five Nordic countries of Denmark, Finland, Iceland, Norway and Sweden. It may be no coincidence after all that a country in this region gave birth to such a widely acclaimed play on fatherhood. The Nordic welfare model is known in academic literature for its explicit support of and achievements regarding gender equality in both family and gender equality policies. An important part of the Nordic gender equality model is the facilitation of the labour market participation of both parents often referred to as the 'adult worker model' (see Lewis, 2001), where men and women are considered equally employable, working full time. This includes the Nordic emphasis on both parents sharing in the care of their children, as expressed in the dual earner/dual carer model (see, for example, Leira, 2006; Gornick and Meyers, 2009). Therefore, the focus of this book is on how the Nordic model has implemented care policies that enable both parents to care for their children. Studies have not only shown that Nordic fathers participate in household chores; they have also established that Nordic fathers use their individual non-transferable 'use-it-or-lose-it' entitlement to paid parental leave, also known as the 'father's quota' (Duvander and Lammi-Taskula, 2011; Gálvez-Muños et al, 2011). Yet at the same time, our knowledge of policy outcomes, that may have ensured fathers' opportunities in becoming active parents involved in the care of their children, remains fragmented.

Therefore, this book analyses those policies that set out to support fathers in caring for their children, and examines if the outcomes of such policies are in line with the goals set out in Nordic family and gender equality policies. In addition to family law and policies on family benefits, it explores parental leave schemes as these policies are most likely to structure the time available for each parent to care for their new-born child and, more implicitly, contribute to the creation of norms in parental practices. Furthermore, the book investigates how Nordic men practise fatherhood in diverse family settings and how norms, policies and institutional frameworks contribute to shaping these practices. Thus, this book seeks to create an insight into the complex construction of fatherhood – how it is shaped in the interaction between policies, cultures and the daily practices of fathers – highlighting both similarities and differences within the Nordic region, and highlighting the diversity in Nordic populations, including ethnicity, class, sexual orientation and parental status. Therefore, the authors critically examine the idea of a common, universal Nordic model, and contest the idea of homogeneity in contemporary Nordic societies, investigating whether the men in these countries are equally provided with the opportunity to become fathers and to care for their children, and whether the outcomes are in fact in alignment with the goals set out in Nordic family and gender equality policies.

Likewise, the book sets out to investigate critically the conceptualisation of a Nordic model of active fatherhood policies and practices with regards to intra-Nordic differences and similarities. Last, but not least, the Nordic countries – and other European countries – have witnessed an increase in policies aiming to ensure the right of children to care from and access to both parents. As part of this phenomenon, changes have been made to Nordic family law in recent decades in order to make it possible for children to enjoy care from both of their parents, even if they do not live together with the child in question. The book investigates this theme from the perspective of the father, focusing on policy and legal developments, and whether they place the father, as a parent, on an equal footing with the mother.

The book and its themes are highly relevant, not least due to international interest in how to create societal structures and family settings that largely facilitate the 'adult worker model' so that both men and women may participate in the labour market, but also the increasing interest in how men can become better integrated into and share tasks related to the family and household. At the European Union (EU) and national levels across Europe, the political project is to increase women's full-time participation in the labour market, and there is great interest in gender equality and a strengthening of the rights and position of men in the family as a means to achieve this, with the Nordic countries pointed out as a regional setting where this seems to have been better achieved (see Table 1.1). A growing willingness to address how state policies support greater parity in the distribution of care has been evident insofar as this impinges on female labour market participation (see, for example, Lewis, 2001, 2002). This offers a good example of how Matta and Knudson–Martin (2006) and others have forwarded that fathers and fatherhood must be studied and understood in the context and intricacies within their relationships with mothers and families.

Another international policy concern has been the falling fertility rates witnessed in many countries, which the Nordic countries, via the family policy framework, appear to have been able to avoid, to some degree (d'Addio and d'Ercole, 2005) (see Table 1.1). There is also

Table 1.1: Employment rate (15–64 years) and employed part-time, by gender, and total fertility rates, Nordic countries and EU-27, 2012

	Denmark	Finland	Iceland	Norway	Sweden	EU-27
Female employment rate	72.2	72.5	79.1	77.3	76.8	62.4
Male employment rate	78.6	74.7	89.9	82.4	81.9	74.6
Women working part-time**	36.4	20.1	32.0	42.2	39.6	32.6
Men working part-time	16.0	10.3	11.3	15.4	14.6	9.5
Total fertility rate	1.73	1.80	2.04	1.85	1.91	1.56

Note: Data from EU Labour Force Survey. Part-time hours may vary between the Nordic and EU region.

Source: Eurostat, nd.

great interest in promoting and supporting a more active fatherhood role as part of the reconciliation of work and family, a policy that the Nordic countries – Sweden especially – have been a forerunner for.

Organisation of the book

With the overall aim of providing insight into contemporary policies and practices of fatherhood, this book is organised into a number of themes. Under the first theme, 'Fathers, families and family policies', Tine Rostgaard and Rasmus Juul Møberg discuss men's fertility and European men's attitudes towards becoming fathers. Next, Hrefna Friðriksdóttir outlines the legal provisions in regards to establishing fatherhood, as well as the legal rights and duties of fathers according to Nordic family law. In Chapter Four, Mia Hakovirta et al provide an overview of fathers' entitlements to family benefits.

The following chapters explore the practices of fathers in different contexts, as well as how fathers themselves construct fatherhoods. Under the theme 'Fathers in everyday life – culture, work and care', Minna Ylikännö et al and Mikael Nordenmark apply data from time use studies in order to analyse the part fathers play in care, and the factors that influence their caring roles. Berit Brandth and Elin Kvande emphasise the differences between working- and middle-class fathers, and the value they place on paid parental leave and on their construction of fatherhood. Lotte Bloksgaard examines how fathers negotiate leave in three different workplaces.

Also exploring practices, but under the theme 'Constructing fatherhood in different family settings', Steen Baagøe Nielsen and Allan Westerling focus on fathers' practices by examining innovative fathers and their learning process. Anika Liversage discusses whether there is an ethnic dimension in the practice of Danish fathers that is in some way related to origin. Arnfinn Andersen investigates how gay fathers in Norway create a space for fatherhood, and Mai Heide Ottosen accounts for paternal involvement after divorce.

Finally, four chapters examine the policies on paid parental leave, focusing on both policymaking and outcomes, under the theme 'Caring fathers and paid parental leave policies'. Tine Rostgaard and Mette Lausten discuss the take-up of leave in Denmark, Minna Salmi and Johanna Lammi-Taskula investigate Finnish policies and their outcomes, while Guðný Björk Eydal and Ingólfur Gíslason concentrate on the case of Iceland and the effects of the economic crisis on both policies and take-up of leave. Then, Ann-Zofie Duvander and Mats Johansson discuss the impact of three reforms in Swedish leave policies, as well as if and how these reforms affected fathers' take-up in 1995-2008.

To acquire a non-Nordic perspective, the American-based Professor Janet Gornick and UK-based Professor Margaret O´Brien, with their extensive empirical and theoretical knowledge of family policy and fatherhood research respectively, were also asked to comment on the findings of the book, which is presented under the theme 'International reflections on findings'. Following this, in a short conclusion, the editors highlight and discuss the main findings of the book.

Before discussing the content of the chapters in more detail, we look at the theoretical and conceptual understanding of fatherhood and fatherhood practices, involvement and regimes, which will be applied in the book.

Concept of fatherhood

The concept of fatherhood is applied in this book as it is believed to reach beyond daily practices and relations in individual families by also including the social constructions of expectations towards fathers. As Hobson and Morgan (2002, pp 9-10) note, the term 'fatherhood' can be seen as the 'cultural coding of men as fathers. Here, we are dealing with the rights, duties, responsibilities and statuses that are attached to fathers, as well as the discursive terrain around good and bad fathers.' As Collier and Sheldon (2008, p 20) point out, however, 'given the variety of contexts for fatherhood it may now seem paradoxical to attempt to characterise contemporary fatherhood as anything but a collection of fatherhoods.' In the belief that many forms of fatherhood exist, and that fathers in different social contexts take different routes towards fatherhood, the authors in this book apply the conceptualisation of fatherhood in its plural form.

As stated earlier, the book and its various themes focus on fatherhood. As Brannen and Nielsen (2006) note, however, there are conceptual slippages between the concept of fathering and fatherhood, and that the two terms are used interchangeably in contemporary research literature. They associate the concept of 'fatherhood' with the role of breadwinning, as has been common for previous generations of men. In acknowledging that contemporary fathers are more involved in family life, particularly in the everyday lives of their children, they advocate, instead, for the use of the concept of 'fathering', which to them better speaks to the practice and relational aspects of parenting. Likewise, Morgan (1996) associates 'fathering' with the set of practices carried out by a father, even those that may not require the presence of the child, such as applying for paternity leave.

Growing interest in fathers

In a historical perspective, fatherhood has generally attracted less attention than motherhood, although discussions about fathers and their (non-)involvement in family life have been increasing in the public and political debates in recent decades. Throughout Western societies, there is evidence of increasing research and political interest in fatherhood. The research literature on fathers has proliferated correspondingly (see, for example O'Brien, 1992; Marsiglio et al, 2000; Featherstone, 2009), including an increasing body of comparative studies (Lamb et al, 1987; Pease and Pringle, 2001; Hobson, 2002; Duyvendak and Stavenuiter, 2004; Gregory and Milner, 2008). This also applies to the Nordic countries, where there has been an increase in country-specific research (see, for example, Brandth and Kvande, 1998, 2002, 2003; Johansson, 2004; Johansson and Klinth, 2010; Holter, 2012; Lorentzen, 2012). Much of this interest has been sparked by what can be viewed as a fundamental shift in family life and gender relations, which has led to more diverse family formations and residency patterns. This has helped highlight the complexity of the rights and obligations of mothers, biological fathers and social/household fathers (Hobson, 2002). Moreover, structural changes, such as the increasing female participation in paid work and less secure labour market relations for men, have increased the interest in the role of the man in the family. Brannen and Nielsen (2006) point out how the literature has included frequent references to the 'crisis of the breadwinner father' since the 1970s, as men have lost their role as the sole breadwinner and must now establish a new role for themselves in the family.

Recent research has focused on the normative understanding of fatherhood by investigating its representations and discourses across generations, family forms and cultures, sometimes in comparison to motherhood. Much of this research has centred on the phenomenon of the 'new' or 'modern' father, arguing that social and cultural changes have unlocked a new image of fatherhood, but that men's behaviour is also changing, that is, they are 'fathering' differently than was the case just a generation ago (see, for example, Collier and Sheldon, 2008; Featherstone, 2009). Family-oriented, child-centred attitudes and the increased allocation of time towards more intense contact with their children is now expected and desired. Brannen and Nielsen

(2006) point out that the 'involved father' discourse is commonplace in the Nordic countries, whereas it is more 'fluid' in the UK. In the Nordic countries, interest in fatherhood has revolved around the male parenting role and state-legislated reforms encouraging men to assume greater responsibility in family life, going back to Alva Myrdal's pioneering work from 1938, 'Vart tar papa vägen?' ['Where did daddy go?'], where she discussed how fathers should take a more active role in the daily lives of their children (Carlsson, 1990), to the more recent introduction of gender-equality incentives in policies, promoting active participation of fathers in caring for their children (see, for example, Brandth and Kvande, 1998; Johansson, 2004; Skevik, 2006; Holter and Gíslason, 2007; Gíslason and Eydal, 2011; Lorentzen, 2012; Júlíusdóttir and Sigurðardóttir, 2013).

Fathers and their role and involvement in families

The fact that fewer men are entering into fatherhood both in Europe and the US represents a demographic as well as social concern (see, for example, Eggebeen, 2002; Olah et al, 2002), partly caused by the continuing importance of educational homogamy, that is, that people mainly marry or find a partner from within their own social class (Brannen and Nielsen, 2006). This is a consequence of women seeking to form partnerships with people of similar social opportunities – so-called 'positive assortative mating' (Blossfeld and Timm, 2003) – in order to pool economic and social-cultural advantages, and also in order to avoid asymmetrical and oppressive gender relationships. With the increase in female educational attainment levels, however, young women are now more likely to have a higher level of educational attainment than their male counterparts (OECD, 2011). Therefore they stand in a poorer competitive situation in finding a(ny) partner than men with a higher level of education because women look for a partner with an equal or higher educational level (Blossfeld and Timm, 2003).

The father's role in the breakdown of the family has also produced some concern: the increasing divorce and parental break-up rates in recent decades has increased the proportion of sole parenthood, and in most cases, children share legal residency with their mothers (Bradshaw et al, 1999; Hobson and Morgan, 2002; Levin, 2004; Skevik, 2006). Across the OECD countries, 15 per cent of all children today, on average, live with only one parent, whereas nearly 84 per cent of all children live with two married or cohabiting parents (OECD, 2010). In the Nordic countries, this is slightly higher: around one-fifth of all children live with a lone parent, although most still live with two adults, in most cases married parents (see Table 1.2).

Although divorce rates may have stagnated in recent years, the general expectancy among OECD countries is that the number of lone-parent families will increase in the coming years, for example by 27 per cent in Norway (OECD, 2011). Part of the reason for this may be the establishment of less traditional family forms, including LAT (living-apart-together) families, where couples establish non-residential relationships (Levin, 2004). Such relationships are difficult to trace in the statistics, and even though fathers may take an active part in raising their children, we know too little about their involvement in the family and how they practise fatherhood. Likewise, even when fathers have joint custody and spend as much time with the child as the mother, these fathers are not accounted for in the statistics. As the statistics neither document this diversity in parental arrangements and child–parent relationships nor changes over time, they therefore only provide a limited and static image of Nordic family diversity.

Another source of interest in the father's position in the family comes from the political discussion about 'absent fathers'. As welfare state support for lone-parent families is being cut back, the tendency – at least outside the Nordic countries – is to focus more on getting so-called 'deadbeat dads' to contribute to the costs of raising their children (Bradshaw et al, 1999; Lewis, 2002; Orloff and Monson, 2002). Many Western countries have recently addressed this issue by subsequently revising their system of advanced maintenance payments (see, for example, Skinner et al, 2007, 2012).

Other – and more darker – sides of fatherhood have been investigated in the literature focusing on fathers as a threat, such as in the research on sexually abusing or violent fathers (see, for example, Scourfield, 2002). This is, however, outside the scope of this book.

Table 1.2: Families with children, Nordic countries, 2011

	Denmark	Finland	Iceland	Norway	Sweden
No. of families with children (1,000)	771	581	51	629	1,110
Married couples (%)	60	61	57	54	77
Cohabiting couples (%)	17	18	23	24	–
Lone parents (%)	23	20	20	22	23

Note: Children aged 0–17. Denmark: From 2007, children aged 0–24 2009 data. Sweden: Married couples include cohabitating couples.

Source: Nordic Statistical Yearbook, 2013, Table 3.5

Theoretical and analytical perspectives

The contributors to this book apply different theories and address various topics on the micro, meso and macro levels. While some chapters explore the policy development by applying theories on actors and structures, others investigate the perspective of involved fatherhood at the workplace level, and others explore the everyday lives of fathers in the families and how they 'carve out their space for fatherhood' (Hobson and Morgan, 2002, p 5). While the theoretical and analytical perspectives differ, there are nevertheless some common understandings on which the authors base their work and frame their analytical reasoning and results.

Practising fatherhood

First, as already mentioned, fatherhood is conceptualised in the book in its plural form, as 'fatherhoods', thus assuming that groups and individuals have different ideas about what fatherhoods consist of. Second, the book is based on the understanding that fatherhoods are constantly created in everyday lives, framed by the normative, legislative and political premise. Fathers practise fathering in social contexts, as they must interact with others, in particular the mother/other parent. Fatherhood is created and recreated, 'in the shared goings-on between people in the course of their lives through intervals of negotiating, competing, compromising and rearranging' (Matta and Knudson-Martin, 2006, p 20). Cabrera et al (2000, p 133) point out that there is no longer an ideal of the father's role that can claim universal acceptance. Thus, each father must create his own ideas: 'Family practices are reflective practice, in being enacted they simultaneously construct, reproduce family boundaries, family relationships and possibly more discursive notions of the family in general' (Morgan, 2011, p 163).

'Practices' can be used both as a descriptive term and as a concept based on Morgan's (2011) definition of 'family practices'. The family practices concept originally proposed the re-conceptualisation of family studies and, as Collier and Sheldon (2008, pp 24) point out, it,

> ... refers not only to specific activities carried out by family members but also the wider behaviours, for example of politicians, which construct our idea of family: a term which shifts the focus to 'doing' as opposed to 'being' and conveys both a sense of regularity and fluidity. In fatherhood

studies adopting this approach avoids the problem of labelling particular activities as 'involved' or 'new'.

As Morgan (2012, p 2) points out, while there is an emphasis on the doing, the action is usually a matter of 'routinised, taken-for-granted attention to practicalities' rather than a matter of rational calculation. This concept captures the multidimensional nature of fatherhood and links history and biography. And as Morgan also emphasises, the concept encompasses the public and private, recognising:

> ... that individuals do not start from scratch as they go about family living. They come into (through marriage or parenthood, say) a set of practices that are already partially shaped by legal prescriptions, economic constraints and cultural definitions. This is in part what is meant by structuration as a set of processes rather than fixed external structures. (Morgan, 2011, p 7)

As Brandth and Kvande (2002, 2003) note, fatherhood practices are never solid and static; instead they are fluid and continuously constructed and negotiated in relation to different structures in society and organisations – fatherhood ideals, work–life demands and policies such as parental leave entitlements. So fatherhood practices may represent the *outcome* of the various negotiation processes within these different structures. As this book shows, practices can certainly be 'classed', typically accounted for in the classed difference in parental leave take-up (see Chapter Six, this volume). Addressing the critique of the 'middle-class' father model and its claim that the predominant fathering discourse and the organisation of parental leave represents a middle-class conception of 'good parenting', Brandth and Kvande (Chapter Six) investigate how Norwegian fathers (belonging to different social classes) incorporate leave rights into their fatherhood practices. They find that while middle-class fathers make more use of their entitlements compared to working-class fathers, working-class fathers also use the opportunity which the father's quota represents to transform their gendered – and classed – father practices. Likewise, in her account of minority ethnic fathers' practices, Liversage (Chapter Ten) points out that fathering possibly also has an ethnic dimension – minority ethnic fathers are more inclined to understand the roles of fathers as complementary to the mother rather than equal, which is otherwise the dominant understanding in Denmark, and may find themselves challenged as their children steer towards a family and gender practice which is very different from their own.

When fatherhood is arranged between friends, the parents are both gay, or the child is not living with the father, a whole new set of rules and arrangements must be negotiated, as described in Andersen's analysis (Chapter Eleven). Based on interviews with gay fathers, he unravels how they base their fatherhood on contemporary ideas of the involved father, but are nevertheless challenged by their less secure position in the family and having to negotiate their own mental and physical space for the child's upbringing.

Nielsen and Westerling (Chapter Nine) also investigate the practices of fathers by focusing on their learning processes. They argue that modern family life means new types of social participation, practices and a learning process, and the fathers in their study – who all represent pioneering and highly committed fathers – have had to find and negotiate new ways of 'doing fatherhood', primarily by being preoccupied with the concrete and practical challenges of everyday family life.

While 'project fatherhood' may provide an opportunity for reflection for the individual father regarding his role and practices as a father, and be an important part of male adulthood, the status of fatherhood on the societal level may be less certain. Chapter Two, by Rostgaard and Møberg, at least suggests that the notion of the importance of becoming a father is in flux. Their analysis illustrates that although most men become a father at some point in their lives (although as other chapters in the book bear witness, they do not always live with their children), there is widespread (and increasing) acceptance of the active choice of not having children, and this is particularly so in the Nordic countries. Men in these countries are generally more tolerant towards voluntary childlessness, as well as to what the right age is to have a child. Thus, in the European context, the Nordic men have more flexible attitudes to what the right fatherhood practice is in terms of *if* and *when* to become a father and *how many* children to have. As the analysis shows, however, such relaxed attitudes are closely associated with lower male fertility. These results depict another aspect in the practice of fatherhood, and that is the choice of whether or not to become a father.

Paternal involvement and time use

As well as examining fatherhood practices, scholars have also looked into the conceptual and empirical analyses of the diverse dimensions of fatherhood and father involvement, including the time use accounts that are now common for many countries. Parental, and paternal, involvement with the child can be defined as including the three major components: engagement, accessibility/availability and responsibility, as defined by Lamb et al (1987). Engagement is the positive or negative contact between father and child, defined as sharing activities or spending time together, on a one-to-one basis or together with the mother or other people. Accessibility (or availability) denotes that the father may be engaged in other activities but remains available for the child and is able to respond to the child's needs. And finally, assuming responsibility for the child involves being accountable for their welfare and care, overall and in daily routines (Lamb et al, 1987). Palkowitz (1997) later extends this so as also to include more cognitive manifestations of paternal involvement. As Coltrane (2004) points out, two further distinctions are often made within each of these three categories, particularly in time use research; the first is distinguishing the amount of time versus the quality of the involvement of the father, while the second is to construct relative (in relation to the mother) as well as absolute indices of paternal involvement.

This book includes two such studies of time use, drawing on the absolute account of fathers' time involvement relative to mothers. Both studies find that, over time, Nordic (as well as non-Nordic) fathers spend more time with their children, which is consistent with international studies (O'Brien and Shemilt, 2003; Gauthier and DeGusti, 2012). In Chapter Five by Ylikännö, Pääkkönen and Hakovirta, Finnish fatherhood is approached from the time use perspective, arguing that sufficient understanding of the realms of gendered practices in the families can only be achieved by investigating their everyday lives. Their study shows that the Nordic model, with its strong emphasis on gender equality, has been somewhat successful: Finnish fathers now spend considerably more time with their children than was the case two decades ago. Mothers also spend more time with their children, however, reflecting that parenthood has become a more important life project for both genders. On the whole, there is a clear trend towards a less unequal division of care responsibilities in the Finnish families. In Chapter Eight Nordenmark also investigates time use, now comparing the Nordic and Southern European gender policy regimes. His study confirms a relationship between the gender policy regimes and the time fathers invest in their families and homes, where Nordic fathers are more time-involved, but mainly with respect to housework. The driving factor appears to be attitudes: regardless of policy regime, gender-equality inclined fathers are more likely to spend time on housework and childcare. But socio-economic factors also remain significant: older fathers spend more time and fathers with a partner with a higher education are more likely to share in the family responsibilities. This suggests that if gender equality is to be achieved with respect to family responsibilities, welfare policies are well invested in creating more egalitarian attitudes among fathers, and more indirectly, perhaps, in investments in women's education.

In Chapter Twelve Ottosen presents a study on fathers' involvement in her account of post-divorce fathers' participation in the care of their children. First, she finds that if the father is not involved in the care of a young child, then there is a greater risk of family dissolution. Perhaps more surprising is that her analysis also confirms that a divorced man at the top of the occupational hierarchy is more likely to maintain contact with a child later in life if he was involved in their early childcare. This suggests that social classes are masked in the construction of modern fatherhood, not least when the family breaks up.

Fatherhood regimes, institutions and policies

A number of the chapters in the book address welfare policies, analysing the intersection of fatherhood regimes, institutions and actual policies. Using the fatherhood concept also makes it possible to incorporate the intersection of cultural meaning and the ideology of fatherhood at the micro level between parents, the family at large and men in-between, but also at the macro level, in the larger community, at the workplace, in the labour market, and in policy formulation and implementation. Hobson and Morgan (2002) initially emphasise the importance of institutions in the shaping of fatherhood and that the position of men must be viewed within the two triangles of market–state–family (institutional regime) and husband–wife–parent/child (domestic organisation). Gregory and Miller (2008) later extend this notion of the fatherhood regime to include references to national employment policies and working time regimes, finding that, with the introduction of statutory and organisational work–life balance in particular, measures may be successful in changing the gendered order of the division of labour in the home. Other scholars have pointed out the international institutional framing, which, for example, takes place at the EU level, and the regulation of the participation of women and men in the family (European Commission, 2000; Duncan, 2002; Walby, 2004), or the new EU Directive on a father's quota – but all of these are outside the scope of this book.

This book addresses the policies and legal framework of families and fatherhood in several chapters that specifically examine how national policies and legislation frame modern fatherhoods. For instance, Friðriksdóttir, in Chapter Three, accounts for how developments in Nordic family law have contributed to the construction of fatherhood. She concludes that Nordic family law is inconsistent in regards to the legal rights to be a father and in the juxtaposition of marriage and cohabitation regarding legal fatherhood and parental responsibilities. She also raises concerns about whether the growing number of legal provisions regarding post-separation parenting have enabled fathers and mothers to fulfil the ambitious aims of the reforms.

The macro-policy approach is also taken in Chapter Four by Hakovirta, Haataja, Eydal and Rostgaard, investigating how the Nordic welfare states support fathers through cash and fiscal family benefits to provide economically for their children, and whether the rights of fathers to these family benefits are in accordance with the dual earner/dual carer model. Very importantly, they find that only Swedish, and to some extent Norwegian, family policies provide the same rights for both parents independently of their family model. In the other Nordic countries (Denmark, Finland and Iceland), family policies support the mother to a greater degree, as she is considered the primary parent. Thus, there are some significant inconsistencies between and within the Nordic countries where policies actively support fathers in caring for their children, while supporting mothers (or resident parents, most often mothers) in a way that emphasises a gendered division of labour between parents that contradicts the dual earner/dual carer model mentioned above.

In Chapter Seven, Bloksgaard addresses how workplace settings and institutional factors in the labour market frame fatherhood. She addresses the meso level by investigating how fathers negotiate their leave rights in three Danish workplaces in the private sector. She finds that despite seemingly identical entitlements for fathers and mothers, fathers nevertheless must negotiate with their superior when to take the leave. Her conclusions indicate that, 'workplace norms, including masculinity ideals, and "what other fathers do" in relation to leave in the workplace seems to be significant for masculinity constructions and leave use among fathers'. Combined with the lack of a father's quota – Denmark is the only country in the Nordic region without a father's quota – and with a cultural ideal of fatherhood that provides little room for 'a father on parental leave', Danish fathers face obvious challenges when constructing leave practices and negotiating leave rights.

Several of the chapters argue that the father's quota has actually provided an efficient policy means with which to increase the number of fathers on parental leave and their share of the overall parental leave days. In Chapter Sixteen Duvander and Johansson thus investigate the introduction of the father's quota (currently eight weeks) and the tax gender bonus available in Sweden, finding that only the quota has had any gendered effect in leave take-up, with fathers in more precarious work positions changing their leave practice the least. Rostgaard and Lausten, in Chapter Thirteen, take a different perspective, examining the consequences of abolishing the father's quota in Denmark, and find that here, again, the quota offered a very efficient policy means to motivate more fathers to take leave. As a consequence of the abolishment of the father's quota, they find that Danish fathers are now positioned differently in their possibilities for taking parental leave, thus working against the Nordic principle of universalism. Consequently, fathers' leave take-up now depends on socio-economic status. Salmi and Lammi-Taskula, in Chapter Fourteen, account for the changes to parental leave schemes in Finland, where the tripartite policymaking process has obstructed the introduction of the father's quota, which was first introduced in 2013. However, they find that the main predictor preventing a father from taking leave is ultimately his individual view on men as the main breadwinner, for which reason the policies of and entitlements for parental leave must be gendered if any change is to be achieved. Finally, Eydal and Gíslason, in Chapter Fifteen, discuss the father's quota in Iceland introduced in 2000 and the development of both the policies and practices during the aftermath of the 2008 financial crisis in Iceland. Although austerity measures were taken, the father's quota was not cut; furthermore, the long-term goal according to new legislation from 2012 is to extend the quota from three to five months for each parent.

To acquire a non-Nordic perspective, American-based Professor Janet Gornick and UK-based Professor Margaret O'Brien were asked to comment on the findings on the basis of their extensive empirical and theoretical knowledge of family policy and fatherhood research, respectively (in Chapters Seventeen and Eighteen).

As Gornick points out in her comment on the conclusions and lessons emerging from the book – and in particular, with respect to the book's contributions to the research on parental leave – gendered expectations continue to be functioning at both the micro and meso levels; this also applies to the Nordic countries. And a persistency regarding the gendered division of paid and unpaid work frames the roles men and women assume in the family. Men and women at the individual and family levels thus continue to 'do gender'; and even in a welfare regime promoting universalism, there continues to be substantial variation across class and ethnicity. Workplace actors and workplace practices also appear to remain a barrier to the full application of gender-equal practices in terms of leave take-up. And as the Danish case illustrates, even at the macro-policy level it is not always politically favourable to work for gender equality policies – even when there is evidence that this should favour the male position in the family and workplace.

Margaret O'Brien points out that while all Nordic governments promote a dual earner/dual carer social democratic welfare state model, great variation exists in the policy and family practices between the countries. As she sees it, these differences are connected to historical and cultural legacies, but international factors are also among the driving forces. O'Brien discusses the challenges that migration, separation and sexual orientation pose for both practices and policies, stating that the study testifies:

> ... to the problems with a theory of change in the institution of fatherhood from a patriarchal past to an equal present. A future challenge as Nordic countries become more multi-ethnic and multi-faith is to explore if gender equality can co-exist with different ways of doing fathering and mothering. (O'Brien, Chapter Eighteen, this volume)

Thus, this book contributes to the critical discussion of the remaining hindrances and challenges facing fathers when entering fatherhood. While the results of the chapters confirm that the policies on gender equality, families and the labour market are aimed at the equal rights of both parents to earn and to care, structural and cultural hindrances remain that must be recognised and defined in order to make it possible to eliminate these obstacles. At the same time, the book shows that fathers in the Nordic countries are constructing a variety of fatherhoods building on their cultural heritage, but at the same time, being innovative in creating new practices.

References

Blossfeld, H.P. and Timm, A. (eds) (2003) *Who marries whom? Educational systems as marriage market in modern societies*, Dordrecht: Kluwer Academic Publishers.

Bradshaw, J., Stimson, C., Skinner, C. and Williams, J. (1999) *Absent fathers?*, London: Routledge.

Brandth, B. and Kvande, E. (1998) 'Masculinity and childcare: the reconstruction of fathering', *The Sociological Review*, vol 46, no 2, pp 293-313.

Brandth, B. and Kvande, E. (2002) 'Reflexive fathers: negotiating parental leave and working life', *Gender, Work and Organization*, vol 9, no 2, pp 186-203.

Brandth, B. and Kvande, E. (2003) *Fleksible fedre. Maskulinitet, arbeid, velferdsstat* [*Flexible fathers*], Oslo: Universitetsforlaget.

Brannen, J. and Nielsen, A. (2006) 'From fatherhood to fathering: transmission and change among British fathers in four-generation families', *Sociology*, vol 40, no 2, pp 335-52.

Carlsson, A.C. (1990) *The Swedish experiment in family politics: The Myrdals and the interwar population crisis*, Piscataway, NJ: Transaction Publishers.

Cabrera, N., Tamis-LeMonda, C., Bradley, R., Hofferth, S. and Lamb, M. (2000) 'Fatherhood in the twenty-first century', *Child Development*, vol 71, no 1, pp 127-36.

Collier, R. and Sheldon, S. (2008) *Fragmenting fatherhood: A socio-legal study*, Portland, OR: Hart Publishing.

Coltrane, S. (2004) *Fathers*, Sloan Network Encyclopedia Entry (https://workfamily.sas.upenn.edu/static/encyclopedia).

d'Addio, A.C. and d'Ercole, M.M. (2005) *Trends and determinants of fertility rates: The role of policies*, OECD, Social, Employment and Migration Working Papers, No 27, Paris: OECD.

Duncan, S. (2002) 'Policy discourses on reconciling work and life in the EU', *Social Policy and Society*, vol 1, no 4, pp 305-14.

Duvander, A. and Lammi-Taskula, J. (2011) 'Parental leave', in I. Gíslason and G.B. Eydal (eds) *Parental leave, childcare and gender equality in the Nordic countries*, Copenhagen: Nordic Council of Ministers, pp 31-64.

Duyvendak, J. and Stavenuiter, M. (eds) (2004) *Working fathers, caring men*, Hague and Utrecht: Dutch Ministry of Social Affairs and Employment and Verwey-Jonker-Institute.

Eggebeen, D. (2002) 'The changing course of fatherhood: men's experiences with children in demographic perspective', *Journal of Family Issues*, vol 23, no 4, pp 486-506.

Eurostat (nd) 'Labour market' (http://epp.eurostat.ec.europa.eu/portal/page/portal/labour_market/introduction).

European Commission (2000) Resolution of the Council and of the Ministers for Employment and Social Policy, Meeting within the Council of 29 June 2000 on the balanced participation of women and men in family and working life, *Resolution 2000/C218/02*, Brussels: European Commission.

Featherstone, B. (2009) *Contemporary fathering: Theory, policy and practice*, Bristol: Policy Press.

Gauthier, A. and DeGusti, B. (2012) 'Time allocation to children by parents', *Europe International Sociology*, vol 27, no 6, pp 827-45.

Gálvez-Muñoz, L., Rodríguez-Modroño, P. and Domínguez-Serrano, M. (2011) 'Work and time use by gender: a new clustering of European welfare systems', *Feminist Economics*, vol 17, no 4, pp 125-57.

Gíslason, I. and Eydal, G.B. (eds) (2011) *Parental leave, childcare and gender equality in the Nordic countries*, Copenhagen: Nordic Council of Ministers.

Gornick, J. and Meyers, M. (eds) (2009) *Gender equality transforming family divisions of labour*, New York: Verso.

Gregory, A. and Milner, S. (2008) 'Fatherhood regimes and father involvement in France and the UK', *Community, Work and Family*, vol 11, no 1, pp 61-84.

Hobson, B. (ed) (2002) *Making men into fathers: Men, masculinities and the social politics of fatherhood*, Cambridge: Cambridge University Press.

Hobson, B. and Morgan, D. (2002) 'Introduction', in B. Hobson (ed) *Making men into fathers: Men, masculinities and the social politics of fatherhood*, Cambridge: Cambridge University Press, pp 1-21.

Holter, Ø.G. (2012) 'Towards a new fatherhood: fathering practices and gender equalities in recent Nordic research', in M. Oechsle, U. Muller and S. Hess (eds) *Fatherhood in late modernity: Cultural images, social practices, structural frames*, Opladne: Verlag Barbara Budrich, pp 273-94.

Holter, Ø.G. and Gíslason, I.V. (2007) 'Välfärdsstat i könsklämma: kön, ekonomi och livskvalitet' ['Welfare state in gender-squeeze: gender, economy and quality of life'], in Ø.G. Holter (ed) *Män i rörelse. Jämställdhet, förändring och social innovation i Norden* [*Men in movement. Gender equality, change and social innovation in the Nordic region*], Oslo: Gidlunds Förlag, pp 22-61.

Johansson, T. (2004) *Faderskapets omvandlingar. Frånvarons socialpsykologi* [*Fatherhood conversions. The social psychology of absence*], Gothenburg: Daidalos.

Johansson, R. and Klinth, T. (2010) *Nya svenska fäder* [*New Swedish fathers*], Umeå: Boréa

Júlíusdóttir, S. and Sigurðardóttir, S. (2013) *Eftir skilnað um foreldrasamstarf og kynslóðatengsl* [*After divorce parental cooperation and generations*], Reykjavík: Háskólaútgáfa.

Lamb, M., Pleck, J., Charnov, E. and Levine, J. (1987) 'A biosocial perspective on paternal behavior and involvement', in J. Lancaster, J. Altmann, A. Rossi and L. Sherrod (eds) *Parenting across the lifespan: Biosocial dimensions*, New York: Aldine de Gruyter, pp 111-42.

Leira, A. (2006) 'Parenthood change and policy reform in Scandinavia 1970s-2000s', in A. Ellingsæter and A. Leira (eds) *Politicising parenthood in Scandinavia*, Cambridge: Cambridge University Press, pp 27-52.

Levin, I. (2004) 'Living apart together: a new family form', *Current Sociology*, vol 5, no 2, pp 223-40.

Lewis, J. (2001) 'The decline of the male breadwinner model: the implications for work and care', *Social Politics*, vol 8, no 2, pp 152-70.

Lewis, J. (2002) 'Gender and welfare state change', *European Societies*, vol 4, no 4, pp 331-57.

Lorentzen, J. (2012) *Fra farskapets historie I Norge: 1850–2011* [*From the history of fatherhood in Norway: 1850-2011*], Oslo: Universitetsforlaget.

Matta, D. and Knudson-Martin, C. (2006) 'Father responsivity: couple processes and the co-construction of fatherhood', *Family Process*, vol 45, no 1, pp 19-37.

Marsiglio, W., Amato, P., Day, R. and Lamb, M. (2000) 'Scholarship on fatherhood in the 1990s and beyond', *Journal of Marriage and the Family*, vol 62, no 4, pp 1173-91.

Morgan, D. (1996) *Family connections*, Cambridge: Polity Press.

Morgan, D. (2011) *Rethinking family practices*, Basingstoke: Palgrave Macmillan.

Morgan, D. (2012) 'Locating "family practices"', *Sociological Research Online*, vol 16, no 4.

Nordic Statistical Yearbook (2013) *Nordic Statistical Yearbook*, Copenhagen: Nordic Council of Ministers.

O'Brien, M. (1992) 'Changing conceptions about fatherhood', in U. Bjørnberg (ed) *European parents in the 1990s: Contradictions and comparisons*, Piscataway, NJ: Transaction Publishers, pp 171-80.

O'Brien, M. and Shemilt, I. (2003) *Working fathers: Earning and caring*, Manchester: Equal Opportunities Commission.

OECD (Organisation for Economic Co-operation and Development) (2010) *Doing better for families*, Paris: OECD.

OECD (2011) *Education at a glance*, Paris: OECD.

Olah, L.S., Bernhardt, E.M. and Goldscheider, F.K. (2002) 'Coresidential paternal roles in industrialised countries: Sweden, Hungary and the United States', in B. Hobson (ed) *Making men into fathers: Men, masculinities and the social politics of fatherhood*, Cambridge: Cambridge University Press, pp 25-57.

Orloff, A.S and Monson, R.A. (2002) 'Citizens, workers or fathers: men in the history of US social policy', in B. Hobson (ed) *Making men into fathers: Men, masculinities and the social politics of fatherhood*, Cambridge: Cambridge University Press, pp 61-90.

Palkowitz, R. (1997) 'Reconstructing "involvement": expanding conceptualizations of men's caring in contemporary families', in A.J. Hawkins and D.C. Dollahite (eds) *Generative fathering: Beyond deficit perspectives*, Thousand Oaks, CA: Sage.

Pease, B. and Pringle, K. (2001) *A man's world? Changing men's practices in a globalized world*, London: Zed.

Scourfield, J. (2002) *Gender and child protection*, London: Palgrave Macmillan.

Skevik, A. (2006) '"Absent fathers" or "reorganized families"? Variations in father–child contact after parental break-up in Norway', *The Sociological Review*, vol 54, no 1, pp 114-32.

Skinner, C., Bradshaw, J. and Davidson, J. (2007) *Child support policy: An international perspective*, DWP Research Report No 405, Leeds: Department for Work and Pensions.

Skinner, C., Davidsson, J. and Hakovirta, M. (2012) 'Special issue child maintenance schemes in five countries: introduction to child maintenance schemes across five countries', *European Journal of Social Security*, vol 14, no 4, pp 222-31.

SVD Kultur (nd) www.svd.se/kultur/islandsk-vanda-i-papparollen_1972341.svd

Walby, S. (2004) 'The European Union and gender equality: emergent varieties of gender regime', in social politics', *International Studies in Gender, State and Society*, vol 11, no 1, pp 4-29.

Theme 1:
Fathers, families and family policies

TWO

Fathering: the influence of ideational factors for male fertility behaviour

Tine Rostgaard and Rasmus Juul Møberg

Introduction

The falling number of children being born is a concern throughout Europe, with total fertility rates well below the reproduction rate of 2.1 children per woman in every country. Some see this failure of the population to reproduce itself as a crisis at the very foundations of European society (European Foundation, 2004). With the three major demographic trends of fertility decline, increased family diversity and ageing societies looming, 'demographic renewal' has therefore become a key impetus for several European governments (Commission of the European Union, 2005; O'Brien and Moss, 2010).

Demographic analyses argue that the low fertility rates are not due to less desire to have at least one child (Kohler et al, 2002), but rather the postponement of fertility from early to later adulthood, implying lower overall fertility (Kohler et al, 2006; Billari and Borgoni, 2005). The postponement transition towards late childbearing regimes is believed to be a common pattern characterising many European countries, and a phenomenon which is seen as a further step in a long-term transformation of fertility and related behaviours (Kohler et al, 2002).

Postponing the first child therefore, in accordance with the theory of postponement, is generally considered to be a most important event in what has been labelled the 'second demographic transition' (van de Kaa, 1987) in that the postponement of fertility not only leads to delayed childbearing patterns, but also has a negative affect on the number of children born and thus the completed fertility. The increase in the mean age of first-birth mothers is often used to characterise this phenomenon, with an average increase in OECD countries from 23.8 to 27.2 years for mothers for the timing of first birth in the years 1970-2000 (d'Addio and d'Ercole, 2005). Important factors for this increase in the age of first childbirth include changes in women's education, employment patterns and career orientation (Martin, 2000; Gustafsson, 2001).

However, it is increasingly recognised in accordance with the theory of planned behaviour that men's – just as women's – childbearing desires and intentions influence the birth rate, and with equal force (Thomson and Hoem, 1998), just as there is also a discrepancy between men's desired number of children (2.39 at age 55+, EU25; European Commission, 2006) and their realised number of children (2.11 at age 55, EU25; European Commission, 2006).

Yet with very few exceptions, the existing literature on fertility decisions has focused on women, while it is argued here that in order to fully understand fertility behaviour, it is also important to include the male perspective. Whenever men appear in the analysis of fertility patterns, the focus is primarily on their breadwinning role and how employment instability and associated loss of male income may have a negative affect on reproduction decisions (see, for example, Schmitt, 2012); or how fertility decisions are affected by men's lack of fully changing their involvement and commitment to family and housework to the same degree that women have changed their involvement in paid labour, as argued in the theory of the incomplete gender revolution (McDonald, 2000).

As Kemkes-Grottenhalser (2003) argues, this narrow focus on female reproductive issues misconstrues many aspects of low fertility and childlessness. When not taking into account male fertility choices, one risks overlooking that the decision to have a child is usually a decision couples make together. Attitudes and norms also concerning the desirability for men of having children and when to have them are thus important to investigate in order to understand fertility patterns, as is pointed out in many of the chapters of this book, as fatherhood has taken on a new role and meaning, with men increasingly identifying themselves as fathers. This chapter thus investigates the importance of individual attitudes and social norms in relation to the fertility behaviour of individual fathers across Europe, using European Social Survey (ESS) data.

However, as recent research has pointed out, fertility decisions are also shaped by the relationship between social policies and the gender contract in the sense of the division of responsibility for care between state and family, and the division of paid and unpaid labour between men and women (Crompton et al, 2007; McDonald and Meyers, 2009). Here, the Nordic countries are characterised by a more gender-equal division of work and extensive family policies. This is investigated in this chapter by dividing the countries into regimes, in this manner implicitly taking into account variations in family policy configurations.

The contribution of this chapter is thus to be able to understand whether and at what age men enter into fatherhood, and whether the number of children they have fathered by age 40+ is affected by individual attitudes and social norms regarding male fertility, also controlling for a number of socio-economic variables and attitudes to gender roles. In doing so, the chapter draws on the theory of planned behaviour in contrast to the theory of postponement as the sole explanatory dimension, and in applying the regime typology, the analysis indirectly takes into account variations in family policy configuration.

The chapter is structured in the following manner: first, there is an account of the theoretical framing of the factors explaining female fertility, considering whether and how they may also apply in an analysis of male fertility. This is followed by a methodology section, presenting the dataset and outlining the variables included in the analysis. Descriptions of variables are then presented, followed by the regression analysis. Results indicate that while postponement theory may explain some fertility outcome, the inclusion of ideational factors contributes to a fuller picture of what drives male fertility behaviour. Especially relaxed attitudes to the proper age of fathering, to childlessness and also to the importance of fathering for being considered an adult seem to be important mediators for male fertility behaviour – all attitudes that are widely supported in the Nordic countries.

Fertility decisions: structural, situational and cultural explanations

Across Europe, fertility patterns have undergone profound changes in the latter half of the 20th century (see Figure 2.1). Whereas the 1950s and 1960s witnessed high fertility in most of Europe, apart from the CEE (Central and Eastern European) countries, the 1970s saw a general decline in childbearing, with fertility rates being particularly low in the Nordic, Western and Southern European countries. Since the 1990s, a general decline in fertility is evident across Europe, and fertility in the 21st century continues to be low in the Continental and Southern European countries, with extremely low levels at present (below 1.4 children per woman), well below the reproduction level (2.1 children per woman). Fertility rates, on the other hand, have stabilised and even increased in recent years in Western European countries, with fertility levels slightly below the level of reproduction. In the Nordic countries, the decline in fertility came to a halt in the early 1990s, stabilising since then at around 1.87–1.98, although with some decline from 2010–11 (see Figure 2.2).

Figure 2.1: Trends in total fertility rates (TFR), 1960–2011, regimes

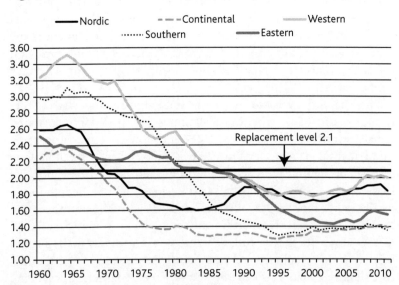

Notes: Total fertility rate is the mean number of children that would be born alive to a woman during her lifetime if she were to pass through her childbearing years conforming to the fertility rates by age of a given year. A rate of 2.1 is considered the replacement level fertility rate.

Countries divided into regimes consisting of Nordic: DK, FIN, N, S. Continental: AT, BE, CH, DE, FR, NL. Western: IRE, UK. Southern: CY, ES, PT. Eastern: BG, EE, HU, PL, RU, SI, SK, UA

Source: EUROSTAT, Fertility indicators (http://epp.eurostat.ec.europa.eu)

The question is, then, which factors possibly explain the decline in female fertility and whether any of these factors are also relevant in a study of male fertility? The cause of the low female fertility rate is often believed to be due to the postponement of first childbirth by women – being older when giving birth to one's first child leaves a narrower, biologically defined time gap to give birth to subsequent children. For each birth cohort, a much larger proportion of childbearing thus takes place today when women are in their thirties (d'Addio and d'Ercole, 2005). Studies have confirmed that at the aggregate level, a higher first-birth mean age correlates with lower fertility (Billari and Borgoni, 2005; Morgan and Taylor, 2006).

Figure 2.2: Trends in total fertility rates (TFR), 1960–2011, Nordic countries

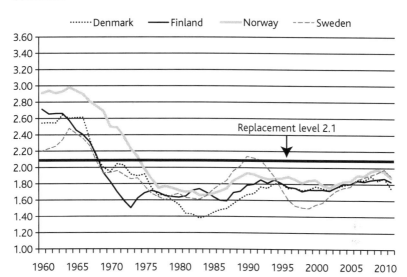

Notes: Countries divided into regimes consisting of Nordic: DK, FIN, N, S. Continental: AT, BE, CH, DE, FR, NL. Western: IRE, UK. Southern: CY, ES, PT. Eastern: BG, EE, HU, PL, RU, SI, SK, UA

Source: EUROSTAT, Fertility indicators (http://epp.eurostat.ec.europa.eu)

Although some recuperation is evident, analyses of different cohorts suggest that full recuperation over time is unlikely. According to *postponement theory*, female fertility postponement thus lowers overall fertility and the level of fertility under replacement rates is considered to remain the trend across OECD countries (d'Addio and d'Ercole, 2005). As is the focus of this study, the question then becomes whether male postponement in fertility has the same effect.

Other studies have challenged postponement theory, however, arguing that fertility postponement might not be the only factor leading to lower overall fertility. Despite the tendency in Eastern European countries to have children at a relatively younger age, this has not led to changes in the low fertility rates in these countries (Billari and Kohler, 2004). This suggests that other, less instrumental factors, may also be important, including *structural*, *situational* and *cultural* explanations, the latter being promoted in the theory of planned behaviour.

Structural determinants

As for structural explanations, the changes in childbearing have long been believed to be caused in particular by aggregate level changes in women's labour force participation. From the micro-economic theory perspective, the opportunity cost of giving birth to a child and subsequently losing wage income has been held to explain why increases in women's labour force participation have been accompanied by falling fertility rates (see, for example, Becker, 1991; Cigno, 1991).

Other studies have, however, pointed at the changes since the mid-1980s and early 1990s, witnessing a positive correlation between female labour force participation and total fertility (see, for instance, Esping-Andersen, 1990). Part of the explanation has been that accompanying the increase in women's labour force participation, family policy has also been rolled out, supporting the reconciliation of work and family life. And as recent research has pointed out, fertility decisions are in fact also shaped by the relationship between social policies and the gender contract in the sense of how the division of responsibility of care is between state and family, but also the division of paid and unpaid labour between men and women (Crompton et al, 2007; McDonald and Meyers, 2009).

The Nordic countries are often cited as examples of countries that have achieved a dual earner/dual carer model with high female labour force participation, while still maintaining a relatively high fertility rate (see, for example, d'Addio and d'Ercole, 2005). There is therefore interest in the Nordic case, not only because gender equality constitutes an institutional and cultural foundation in these countries (Eydal and Rostgaard, 2011a), but also because, as shown above, fertility rates in the Nordic countries have remained at a relatively high level and have rebounded since the drop in the early 2000s – despite Nordic fathers having a high mean age similar to the other countries for the birth of the first child and most women being active in the labour market. Generous family policies, such as parental leave, childcare and subsidies for children care, as are generally found in the Nordic countries (Eydal and Rostgaard, 2011a, 2011b), are also often considered independent levers to higher childbearing (d'Addio and d'Ercole, 2005). As regards the gender contract, studies have also shown that men with gender egalitarian attitudes not only have higher fertility aspirations, they also seem more successful in realising these aspirations (see, for example, Kaufman, 2000). And as is shown elsewhere in this book (see Chapter Eight, this volume), Nordic fathers not only share such attitudes but are also particularly involved in both housework and childcare.

The analysis is therefore carried out as a comparison of the Nordic countries as well as country regimes, drawing loosely on the familiar categorisation of social models by Esping-Andersen (1990) and in addition to his three ideal-types (Nordic, Anglo-Saxon and Continental), adding a fourth, distinctly Southern European social model (Leibfried, 1992; Ferrera, 1996) and a fifth, Eastern European social model (Keune, 2006).

By applying these country regimes, it is recognised that each regime has its own particular family policy model with a more traditional male breadwinner model and medium support for families in countries belonging to what we refer to here as the Continental countries, and lower support for families in countries in the Western model, while the family is traditionally responsible for welfare in the Southern model (Gauthier, 2002). There is greater variation in the Eastern European countries (Manning, 2004), although it may also be argued that a separate East European/post-Socialist model is emerging, combining characteristics from both the Western and Continental regimes (van Oorschot and Arts, 2005; Kääriäinen and Lehtonen, 2006).

Other explanations drawing on the structural approach have argued that fertility behaviour is also a response to actual and expected unemployment opportunities as well as general economic conditions, encouraging or discouraging the individual to take breaks from the labour market (see, for example, Butz and Ward, 1979; Ahn and Mira, 2002; Adsera, 2005). Recognising this, and given the traditional male role in securing the family income, labour market inactivity is included in the analysis as a possible explanation for lower or non-fertility, as well as education.

Situational determinants

Some studies consider the situational constraints caused by shifting family forms to be influential, such as the tendency to cohabitate rather than marry, or living in less committing 'living-apart-together' (LAT) relationships. Fertility rate trends do seem affected by the marital status of mothers, with married women having more children than unmarried women. However, the childbirth–marriage tie has loosened over many years. It is now evident that high fertility also occurs within cohabitating couples, with around half of all births in the Nordic countries and France taking place outside marriage. The marriage–childbearing link remains stronger in Southern Europe (d'Addio and d'Ercole, 2005).

Another situational factor of perhaps greater importance is whether unions between men and women are in fact formed. Here, the significance of educational homogamy seems especially important, as men and women seem to choose partners based on educational backgrounds. Studies thus indicate that women are more likely to marry men of the same educational level, which becomes all the more important as a consequence of women's increasing educational attainment, but men with lower education stand in a poorer competitive situation (see, for example, Oppenheimer, 1988; Blossfeld and Timm, 2004). Taking this into account, the analysis of male fertility in this chapter includes information on the partner situation from the assumption that men without stable partner relationships will, for instance, be less likely to have fathered a child.

Cultural determinants

While none of the above factors has really fully managed to explain women's fertility decisions, recent studies have instead taken a cultural approach, pointing to the notion of ideational factors such as norms and attitudes as an explanation for reduced fertility. This is also the main focus in this chapter. In recent years, the importance of attitudes and norms has been emphasised, in particular by proponents of the life course paradigm, believing that culturally based individual attitudes and societal norms on life course events affect the decision on *occurrence* (whether or not to have children), *timing* (when to have children) of childbirth, and *male fertility rate* (number of children) (see, for example, Liefbroer and Billari, 2009).

Drawing on the theory of planned behaviour, where individual attitudes and societal norms surrounding childbearing are considered an important mediator in the relationship between economic context and fertility outcomes (Ajzen, 1988, 1991), an individual attitude refers here to the individual behavioural belief, and can be defined as 'the degree to which a person has a favorable or unfavorable evaluation or appraisal of the behavior in question' (Ajzen, 1991, p 188). Social norms, on the other hand, refer to beliefs outside the individual, 'concerned with the likelihood that important referent individuals or groups approve or disapprove of performing a given behavior' (Ajzen, 1991, p 195).

While it is accepted that the dynamics may be the other way around – that actual fertility might trigger changes in attitudes and norms – in this chapter it is assumed, in accordance with the theory of planned behaviour, that attitudes and norms prescribe and thus affect subsequent behaviour. According to Surkyn and Lesthaeghe (2004), it should be possible to find the *footprints* of lifestyle preferences on actual fertility, that is, that preferences are likely to affect fertility outcomes. Given that the data available here for the study of the association between ideational factors and actual fertility behaviour is not longitudinal panel data, however, such dynamics are not possible to ascertain. Acknowledging that relationships between current attitudes and past behaviour are possibly spurious, the intention is to unfold the underlying associations between individual behaviour, attitudes and norms, but without claiming the course of direction of any relationships. For example, one of the explanations for the discrepancy between potential and achieved childbearing after age 40 is believed to be the so-called social age deadline, that is, the individual attitudes and social norms prescribing the oldest acceptable age for giving birth (Setterstein, 2003). As found by Billari et al (2011), there is considerable variation across Europe in terms of whether people feel that such a deadline exists and if so, which age they indicate is the oldest acceptable. They argue that this difference indicates that the social age is 'intimately conditioned by the social context' (Billari et al, 2011, p 620), suggesting that it is important to take into account variation in national as well as individual perceptions about the appropriate childbearing age. They also find that the social norms regarding the oldest age of childbearing are positively and significantly correlated with the actual rate of late fertility (Billari et al, 2011). This not only suggests that a social age deadline is one of many factors determining childbearing, but also that attitudes regarding social age should also be central in any analysis of male fertility, including attitudes to the ideal age of becoming a father.

Other important ideational factors conditioning fertility decisions are the attitudes and norms regarding whether or not to become a parent. As argued by Billari, Philipov and Testa (2009), the transition to parenthood is driven in particular by the existent normative pressure and individual personal attitudes towards childbearing. Not only do we witness increasing rates of childlessness across Europe (Frejka and Sardon, 2006), childlessness is also becoming more socially acceptable, and as a declared and intentional choice (Hoem et al, 2006; Sobotka and Testa, 2008). This suggests that parenthood has become just one among multiple competing choices (van de Kaa, 1987).

As pointed out in many of the chapters in this book, however, social and cultural changes throughout Western societies have unlocked a new image of fatherhood, not only emphasising the importance of fatherhood as a natural event in the life course, but also stressing the importance of a particularly involved and intense child–father relationship. This might place certain societal and individual expectations on men, expectations which possibly pull in different directions. Fatherhood may increasingly be seen as a necessary part of adulthood – but also as craving a devoted father who is willing to sacrifice other life projects.

The intention of this chapter is, thus, to unravel the importance of individual attitudes as well as social norms of entering into and timing of fatherhood in relation to the fertility decisions of individual fathers, contrasting the Nordic regime with other regime types. This takes place by investigating whether the *timing* and *occurrence* of fatherhood as well as the *male fertility rate* by age 40+ is affected by individual attitudes and social norms pertaining to male fertility, also controlling for social-economic variance and attitudes to gender role equality. This takes place in the form of a between-model analysis, contrasting the Nordic regime model with the other models, and thus more implicitly situating the analysis within different family policy models.

Data and methods

The analysis builds on data from the third round of the ESS 2006/07 in which 24 countries participated (ESS, 2006). The Nordic regimes are represented by Denmark, Finland, Norway and Sweden. In each country, a representative sample of approximately 1,500 respondents was interviewed.

The ESS includes individual attitudinal questions such as, 'At what age would you say a man is too old to father?'; 'In your opinion what is the ideal age for a man to have become a father?'; 'To be considered an adult, how important is it to have become a father?' and 'Do you approve/disapprove if a man chooses not to have children?'; as well as the individual's perceptions of societal norms as to whether one agrees with the statement 'Most people would react if a man chooses not to have children'.

The dependant variables used are whether the respondent is childless at age 40+ (*occurrence*), the age of transition into fatherhood (*timing*), and the number of children (*male fertility rate*).

Three regression analyses are applied. As occurrence is dichotomous, a logistic regression is applied while a linear regression is applied in the analysis of timing and male fertility rates. These analyses control for a number of background characteristics, including education, age, having previously had a partner for more than three months, and periods of unemployment exceeding 12 months at any time during

—

their working life. Finally, a question concerning individual attitudes about women having full-time employment while having children under the age of three is applied to understand the respondent's attitudes to gender roles.

The analysis applies a sample of men aged 40+ only in order to come close to completed fertility. This includes men of different generations and up to 96 years of age at the time of the interview; 87.1 per cent of the 40+ men in the sample had a child.

Bearing in mind that this book is about Nordic fathers, initial descriptive analysis includes data on each individual Nordic country, while the regression analysis is conducted on the regime level only.

Characteristics of fathering

As Table 2.1 illustrates, fatherhood is a common phenomenon across the Nordic countries as well as across regimes. Most of the 40+ men (87.1 per cent) in the sample had thus fathered a child at the time of the survey, while there were statistically significant differences between regimes. Men from the Eastern regime report the highest *occurrence* rate (92.9 per cent) of all regime types, the Continental regime the lowest (82.1 per cent), with the Nordic regime well situated in the middle, at 84.6 per cent.

Looking at the *timing* between the regimes, that is, the average age when these men first become a father (Table 2.1), men from the Eastern regime have the lowest mean age (26.4 years), distinguishing them from all of the other regime types. No other statistically significant differences between the other regimes can be ascertained. Nordic fathers on average become fathers at the age of 27.9.

Finally, regarding *male fertility rate*, that is, the average number of children being born to each father, it is remarkable that while more men in the Eastern regime report to have fathered a child, they have also fathered at a younger age, yet they have a statistically significant lower number of children (2.0 children) than fathers in the other regimes. Fathers in the Nordic regime have on average 2.4 children, which places them on a level with fathers in the Southern and Western regime, but also significantly higher than fathers in the Continental regime.

Apart from the fact that Norwegian men have a lower mean age at the time of their first born, there is no statistically significant differences *within* the Nordic regime in fatherhood characteristics.

Table 2.1: Occurrence, timing and male fertility rate: percentage of men who have a child (men 40+), average age of becoming a father and number of children (fathers 40+)

	Child	No child (n)	Age when fathering(n)	No. of children (n)
Nordic regime				
Denmark	84.8%	15.2% (257)	28.0 (217)	2.4 (218)
Finland	82.4%	17.6% (273)	28.1 (225)	2.5 (225)
Norway	87.4%	12.6% (262)	27.1 (228)	2.4 (229)
Sweden	84.1%	15.9% (290)	28.3 (242)	2.4 (243)
All regimes				
Nordic	84.6%	15.5% (1.082)	27.9 (912)	2.4 (915)
Continental	82.1%	17.9% (1.838)	27.9 (1449)	2.3 (1.453)
Southern	84.2%	15.8% (638)	28.4 (548)	2.4 (555)
Eastern	92.9%	7.1% (1.725)	26.4 (1552)	2.0 (1.556)
Western	85.4%	14.6% (564)	28.6 (432)	2.4 (437)
Total	87.1%	12.9% (5.847)	27.3 (4893)	2.2 (4917)

Note: Unweighted n (total) presented in parentheses. Average number of children is based only on men who have fathered, not to be compared with Total fertility rate.

Attitudes towards fatherhood

In line with the theory of planned behaviour, and the understanding that attitudinal factors are pivotal for understanding fertility, the question becomes, what opinions do these men hold about fatherhood? Table 2.2 depicts male respondents' views on the ideal age and the oldest acceptable age to become a father. Among the Nordic countries, there is general agreement that the ideal age for becoming a father is around age 25–26. There is more – and significant – variation between the regimes, with the oldest ideal age in the Southern European region (27.0 years) and youngest in the Eastern region (25.3 years).

Men from different regimes also vary in their opinions on when a man is too old to have a child. Within the Nordic regime, there is considerable variation in the social age deadline, Finnish fathers giving a significantly higher age (50.5 years) than the other countries (ranging from 45.5 to 47.4 years). And across the regimes, the tolerance towards older fathers is significantly higher in the North and lower in the South. Most respondents also find that there exists such a thing as a social age deadline (89.5 per cent) (not shown in Table 2.2).

Including respondents' attitudes to the youngest acceptable age for becoming a father in Figure 2.3, we can also see the 'window of opportunity' across regimes, illustrating that despite the differences in attitudes to youngest and oldest fathering ages, the range of years is

Table 2.2: Attitudes towards ideal age and social age deadline of fatherhood, all men (40+)

	Ideal age	Social age deadline
Denmark	26.3 (233)	45.5 (241)
Finland	24.6 (244)	50.5 (237)
Norway	25.6 (253)	47.1 (243)
Sweden	26.2 (255)	47.4 (259)
Nordic	25.8 (985)	47.4 (980)
Continental	26.8 (1582)	47.1 (1636)
Southern	27.0 (560)	45.8 (516)
Eastern	25.3 (1502)	46.9 (1285)
Western	25.5 (472)	47.3 (451)

Note: Not including 'no ideal age' and 'never too old'. Unweighted n (total) presented in parentheses.

similar between the regimes, but with some differences in attitudes to ideal age.

Other ideational factors included in the following analysis are questions of how important becoming a father is for being considered an adult. As Table 2.3 shows, this is more important in Denmark than in the other Nordic countries, while across the regimes it is particularly important in the Eastern regime. Here, the Nordic regime stands out, with significantly lower values attached to fatherhood as a precondition for adulthood.

Figure 2.3: Attitudes towards youngest, oldest and ideal age of becoming a father, all men (40+)

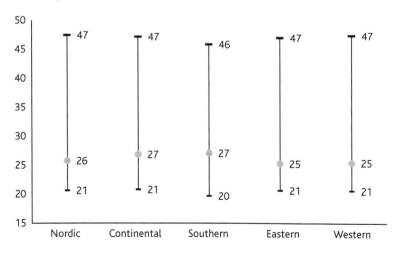

Table 2.3: Attitudes towards importance of fathering for adulthood and towards choice of childlessness, all men (40+)

	Fathering important for adulthood (1=not important at all, 5=very important)	Individual acceptance choice of childlessness (1=strongly approve, 5=strongly disapprove)	Perception of societal acceptance choice of childlessness (1=strongly approve, 4=strongly disapprove)
Denmark	2.9 (254)	4.2 (254)	3.4 (253)
Finland	2.5 (271)	3.1 (269)	2.9 (264)
Norway	2.3 (263)	3.8 (263)	3.5 (263)
Sweden	2.1 (286)	3.3 (279)	3.0 (275)
Nordic	2.4 (1.082)	3.6 (1065)	3.2 (1.055)
Continental	2.9 (1.827)	2.8 (1.811)	2.7 (1.790)
Southern	2.7 (623)	2.9 (633)	2.6 (617)
Eastern	3.5 (1.693)	1.9 (1.674)	2.0 (1.617)
Western	2.4 (559)	3.2 (555)	2.9 (548)

Table 2.3 also presents the final ideational factor including men's attitudes towards voluntary childlessness. The Northern countries are more inclined to accept the decision to remain childless, both regarding the individual acceptance of childlessness and perception of the norm in society, where there would appear to be less acceptance of this position in the societies in the Eastern regime, both from the individual perspective and as perception of whether people in society would generally accept the choice to remain childless. Disapproval rates for voluntary childlessness for men thus vary in extremes, between 6 per cent in Denmark and 86 per cent in the Ukraine (not shown in Table 2.3).

Overall, the variations between regimes are greater when looking at attitudes towards importance of fatherhood and attitudes to voluntary childlessness (Table 2.3) than variations in the perception of ideal age and social deadline for fathering (Table 2.2). These initial findings are in line with theories critical of the theory of postponement, which argues that a multitude of explanatory variables must be taken into account when analysing male fertility behaviour, such as ideational factors.

Relationship between ideational factors and male fertility: regression analysis

Turning to the question of the relationship between these ideational factors and male fertility, three regression analyses were carried out, with indicators of fertility behaviour as dependent variables and controlling for a number of socio-economic and attitudinal variables, as outlined in the section on methodology above.

Becoming a father

Starting with the question of what may explain whether or not men become fathers at all, Table 2.4 reports on the results from the regression analysis of factors explaining *occurrence*. Looking first at the overall difference between regimes, there is no overall difference between the regimes apart from the men living in the Continental regime having an odds ratio (= 1.62) of being childless than those in the Eastern regime.

As for the influence of ideational factors, several variables proved to be significantly associated with actual fertility. Regime differences are accordingly minimised when attitudes and socio-economic variables are included in the regression model (see models 1–3 in Table 2.4).

Across regimes, it seems as though attitudes towards childlessness go hand in hand with the respondent's own situation. If a man disapproves of childlessness, he is more likely to have fathered a child (odds ratio of childlessness of 0.42 compared to men who neither approve nor disapprove). Conversely, if he approves of individuals never having children, he has an odds ratio of 1.63 of being childless himself.

His odds of being childless also relates to whether or not he finds it *'important to become a father in order to be considered an adult'*. If he is indifferent, his odds ratio of childlessness is higher (1.47). This clear association between attitudes and actual behaviour necessitates caution when interpreting the results, especially regarding claims of causality. Recent research of fertility behaviour shows that individuals experiencing involuntary childlessness alter their attitudes towards parenthood according to their particular situation. Potentially, this constitutes a reversion of causality from situation to attitude (Gray et al, 2013). However, the problem of reverse causality is primarily a potential problem when the individual does not achieve his/her desirable goal, in this context the transition into fatherhood.

The effect on childlessness by the respondent's perception of *ideal age* of becoming a father is only significant for those men reporting that the ideal age is 30+. For this group, the odds ratio is 1.54 compared to those who think that the ideal age is between ages 25–29.

An almost identical result can be found regarding the male perception of when a man is too old to become a father. Here, we see that men answering *'you can never be too old'* also have an odds ratio of 1.55

Table 2.4: Logistic regression – occurrence

	Model 1	Model 2	Model 3
Regimes:			
Nordic	2.22***	0.92	1.14
Continental	2.78***	1.67**	1.62*
Southern	2.42***	1.28	1.27
Eastern (baseline)	–	–	–
Western	2.44***	1.14	1.36
Approve if person chooses never to have children			
Strongly disapprove/disapprove		0.41***	0.42***
Neither approve nor disapprove		–	–
Strongly approve/approve		1.76***	1.63**
To be considered an adult, how important is it to have become a father?			
Not important		1.50**	1.47**
Neither important nor unimportant		1.47*	*1.46*
Important (baseline)		–	–
Become father, ideal age (grouped)			
No ideal age		1.29	1.3
15–24		1.02	1.01
25–29 (baseline)		–	–
30 or more		1.56**	1.65**
Consider having more children, age too old			
Never too old		1.67*	*1.55*
39 or less		1.03	1.14
40–49		–	–
50–59		1.01	0.97
60 or more		1.27	1.29
Age, grouped			
40–49 (baseline)			–
50–59			0.96
60–69			0.58**
70–79			*0.63*
80 or more			0.65
Ever lived with a partner (min. 3 months)			10.99***
Previous history of unemployment			1.58**
Constant	0.07***	0.08***	0.04***
Goodness of fit[1]	1	0.837	0.29
N	5171	5171	5171

*Italic: <0.1; *<0.05; **<0.01; ***<0.001*

Note: 1=no children, 0=children

for being childless. In both cases, greater acceptance of postponing fatherhood thus increases the odds ratio of being childless.

As regards the socio-economic variables, a certain generational effect was expected in the fertility behaviour, and this is also visible regarding occurrence. Men in the 60-69 and 70-79 age groups (significant at a 10 per cent level) are less likely to be childless than those aged 40-49. As a consequence, childlessness is becoming more common in the younger generations, a result that can be contributed to the de-standardisation of the life course and a development that is especially predominant in family formation (Brückner and Mayer, 2005).

Unemployment history also has a negative effect on the possibilities of becoming a father. Men who have experienced at least one 12-month spell of unemployment have an odds ratio of 1.58 of not becoming a father. Economic instability may influence the attractiveness of these men as potential breadwinners. In addition, men in this particular situation tend to distance themselves from the idea of becoming a father (Gray et al, 2013).

Finally, the analysis indicates, not surprisingly, that living with a partner or spouse is highly influential (odds ratio of 10.99) on whether or not a man ever becomes a father.

When to become a father

Turning to the *timing* of fatherhood and the discussion of what can potentially lead to postponement of the first child, as already became apparent in the initial descriptive analysis, the timing of fatherhood is highly influenced by regime (see Table 2.5). Men from the Eastern regime are on average more than two years younger than those from the Southern and Western regimes and more than a year younger than men from the Nordic and Continental regimes when becoming a father for the first time. This is in line with the findings of Billari and Kohler (2004). These strong differences between regimes are affected, only to a minor extent, by the inclusion of attitudinal and socio-economic characteristics of the individual.

Considering the ideational factors, first, if a man does not find fatherhood important for being regarded an adult, his transition into fatherhood is on average delayed by six months compared to men who regard fatherhood as important in this regard.

How the ideal age of becoming a father is perceived also has a high impact on the timing – men who think that the ideal age for becoming a father is 30 or above were on average 1.4 years older than the baseline (ideal age 25–29).

Table 2.5: Linear regression – timing[2]

	Model 4	Model 5	Model 6
Regimes			
Nordic	1.55***	1.29***	1.31***
Continental	1.59***	1.17***	1.26***
Southern	2.13***	1.66***	2.17***
Eastern (baseline)	–	–	–
Western	2.37***	2.13***	2.24***
To be considered an adult, how important is it to have become a father?			
Not important		*0.55*	0.59*
Neither important nor unimportant		0.31	0.2
Important (baseline)		–	–
Become father, ideal age (grouped)			
No ideal age		–0.38	–0.62
15–24		–1.40***	–1.28***
25–29 (baseline)		–	–
30 or more		1.44***	1.42***
Consider having more children, age too old			
Never too old		1.15*	1.16*
39 or less		–0.44	–0.39
40–49 (baseline)		–	–
50–59		0.74*	0.74**
60 or more		1.17**	0.96*
Education			
ISCED 0–1			–1.99***
ISCED 2			–1.54***
ISCED 3			–0.99**
ISCED 4–6 (baseline)			–
Age, grouped			
40–49 (baseline)			–
50–59			–0.47
60–69			0.22
70–79			1.13**
80 or more			2.04**
Ever lived with a partner (min. 3 months)?			–0.80
Previous history of unemployment			–0.81*
_cons	26.30	25.87	26.6
N	4414	4414	4414
R-squared	3.3%	7.6%	10.9%[3]

Italic: <0.1; *<0.05; **<0.01; ***<0.001

Along the same lines, it can be seen that the higher the attitude of the social age deadline, the older the men were themselves when transitioning into fatherhood. Both the questions of ideal age and socially acceptable deadline are thus clearly linked to own experience. This can be interpreted as the footprint of lifestyle preferences, indicating that men to some extent are guided by norms regarding appropriate age of becoming a father in their actual behaviour. Regardless, the implication of the result is that acceptance of a broader 'window of opportunity' will potentially lead to postponement of fertility.

When interpreting the findings for all three ideational factors, caution must be applied. Since we have access to cross-sectional data only, causality is at best difficult to determine. The implication of de-standardisation of the life course is, however, that loosening of the age when fathering and importance of fatherhood contributes, to some extent, to postponement of fatherhood. The result stresses the importance in including attitudes towards fatherhood in order to grasp the complexity of fertility behaviour.

Turning to more structural factors, education is also a clear factor in postponing fatherhood – the longer the education, the higher the age of transition into fatherhood. A man with an ISCED (International Standard Classification of Education) level 0–1 is on average two years younger when becoming a father for the first time than an academically educated man. As the level of the education attainment in the Western societies increases, this may add to the general postponement of fertility, and potentially lower the general birth rate of the population.

Regarding age, the two older age groups have a significantly higher average age of transition into fatherhood compared to the baseline, which is men aged 40–49. Seen in a larger historic perspective, this indicates that the age of transition has decreased rather than increased.

Contrary to what might be expected due to the previous analysis on occurrence, the transition age for men who have experienced at least one 12-month spell of unemployment is lower than men who have not been unemployed for such a period of time.

Finally, living with a partner or spouse at any point in time for a minimum of three months lowers the age of transition into fatherhood. The effect is only significant at a 10 per cent level.

Influence on the number of children

Finally, the analysis turns to the male fertility rate and what influences the number of children men have. Even though on average men in the

Eastern regime become fathers at an earlier age than the other men, they have a significantly lower fertility rate than the men from all other regimes. For instance, the coefficient for men from the Nordic regime is 0.53 and highly significant. Again, this male fertility behaviour pattern among the Eastern men is consistent with the findings of Billari and Kohler (2004).

Again, the inclusion of ideational factors largely explains this conundrum, as there is clear evidence of an association between a number of these factors and the male fertility rate.

There is thus a positive correlation between number of children and disapproval of people who choose never to have children; in other words, men who view fatherhood as important have on average more children. The opposite attitude is insignificant.

Regarding the perception of societal attitudes towards those who choose never to have children, the effect is less obvious. There is a negative correlation between the male fertility rate and the answer *'Most people would secretly disapprove'*, implying that covert societal pressure results in more men having children, although in fewer numbers. Analysis not shown here indictes that this effect is particular strong in the Eastern regime, suggesting that a more repressive view on fatherhood exists in these countries. The effect of ideal age becomes insignificant when controlling for actual age of transition into fatherhood in the model, apart from 'no ideal age'. This indicates that especially age-related questions regarding fatherhood, is, to a large extent, correlated with own experience.

Therefore, caution must be applied when interpreting, since data available for the analysis are cross-sectional, making it impossible to determine which way causality runs.

As for the attitude that no ideal age exists, there is a negative correlation, that is, these men are more likely to father fewer children.

The perception of the social age deadline is also positively correlated with the male fertility rate. Men answering that *'39 years of age or less'* is too old have on average fewer children than those stating that the limit is 40–49 years of age. Beyond that, *'Between 50–59 years of age'* and *'Never too old'* is positively correlated with the number of children, although only at the 10 per cent level of significance.

This indicates that men who accept postponement as a viable strategy experience a slight increase in the number of children themselves. Therefore a less strict perception of appropriate age can potentially increase the number of children per person, even though this involves a postponement of fertility.

Turning to the socio-economic factors, as seen previously, higher education levels increase the age of transition into fatherhood. Regarding the male fertility rate, a similar tendency can be identified. Men with ISCED 0-1 and ISCED 2 on average have more children than men with ISCED 4-6. Not only does enrolment in education seem to result in postponement, it also has a negative effect on the male fertility rate. Once again, this negative effect on the fertility rate may only increase as the enrolment in education increases.

In connection with men's age, we previously saw that the older age groups have a higher age of transition into fatherhood; however, this does not result in lower fertility for these particular age groups. Male fertility increases on average with age, as seen in Table 2.6. The result indicates that postponement does not necessarily affect fertility in a negative direction. Considering the last variable included in the model, there is a clear, negative correlation between increasing age of transition and a lower male fertility rate, which is in line with the theory of postponement: men who have their first child before turning 25 have on average more children than those who first become a father after age 30. The inclusion of the 'age of transition' variable in the analysis is by far the biggest contribution to the explanation of the variance in the model, indicating the importance age of transition has on fertility rate, as stressed by the theory of postponement. However, the results in the analysis also suggests that attitudes towards fatherhood must be included in the explanation of male fertility behaviour.

Table 2.6: Regression analysis – male fertility rate[4]

	Model 7	Model 8	Model 9
Regimes			
Nordic	0.35***	0.49***	0.53***
Continental	0.22***	0.35***	0.40***
Southern	0.36***	0.49***	0.42***
Eastern (baseline)			–
Western	0.34***	0.48***	0.50***
Approve if person chooses never to have children			
Strongly disapprove/disapprove		0.30***	0.27***
Neither approve nor disapprove			–
Strongly approve/approve		0.01	0.02

(continued)

Table 2.6: Regression analysis – male fertility rate (continued)

	Model 7	Model 8	Model 9
Most people react if person chose never to have children			
Most people would openly disapprove		–0.12	*–0.14*
Most people would secretly disapprove		–0.19**	–0.18**
Most people would not mind either way			–
Most people would approve		–0.03	–0.06
Become father, ideal age (grouped)			
No ideal age		*–0.16*	–0.18*
15–24		0.15*	0.03
25–29 (baseline)			–
30 or more		–0.14*	–0.02
Consider having more children, age too old			
Never too old		0.09	*0.18*
39 or less		–0.23*	–0.28**
40–49 (baseline)			–
50–59		0.06	*0.10*
60 or more		–0.01	0.07
Education			
ISCED 0–1			0.31**
ISCED 2			0.20*
ISCED 3			–0.01
ISCED 4–6 (baseline)			–
Age, grouped			
40–49 (baseline)			–
50–59			–0.01
60–69			0.06
70–79			0.18*
80 or more			0.41**
Age of transition			
<20			*0.36*
20–22.49			0.20*
22.5–24.99			0.17*
25–27.49 (baseline)			–
27.5–29.99			–0.11
30–32.49			–0.26**
32.5–34.99			–0.58***
35–37.49			–0.68***
37.5–39.99			–0.74***
40–68			–1.02***
_cons	2.04***	1.89***	1.83***
N			
R-squared	1.7%	4.1%	13.6%

*Italic: <0.1; *<0.05; **<0.01; ***<0.001*

Conclusion

Across Europe, fatherhood is taking a new shape and it is therefore important to understand what is underscoring the changes. The results confirm a strong relationship between attitudes and behaviour regarding male fertility. As specified earlier, it is not possible with the available data to ascertain the dynamics between attitudes and actual fertility behaviour. However, the results confirm that in addition to structural and situational factors, it is important to include cultural factors to understand male fertility behaviour.

As stated elsewhere in this book, fatherhood has acquired new meaning. We see how the *occurrence* of fatherhood is, in fact, a common experience, and thus one that most men experience. This is evident in the Nordic countries and the other regimes, especially in the Eastern regime. Between 7 and 18 per cent of men had, however, not fathered a child at the time of the interview. Some of these men may potentially over time father a child; at least it is more common for the 40–49 age group to be childless than the older age groups. Unsurprisingly, becoming a father is related to whether one has had a stable partner relationship, which significantly increases one's chances of becoming a father. However, it also seems as though the chance of fathering a child relates to a man's economic position – men who have experienced long periods of unemployment have a higher odds of remaining childless, suggesting that a man's breadwinning role remains influential for his chances of reproducing.

While fatherhood may have acquired new meaning, it does seem as though the choice not to have children is also widely accepted. This suggests that, on the individual level, fatherhood may be an important life project for those who happen to be fathers, but the status of fatherhood on the societal level may be less certain. What *is* certain is that voluntary childlessness is accepted (and, as other studies point out, increasingly so). And that higher tolerance of childlessness is highly associated with actual childlessness. This could be due to the state of childlessness being a deliberate choice. It may, of course, also reflect some later attitudinal adjustment. Nevertheless, the clear attitude–childlessness association suggests that this is generally an acceptable situation.

Yet as was evident from the descriptive tables, there are significant differences in the acceptance of voluntary childlessness between the regimes, with far more tolerance in the Nordic than in the Eastern regime. Likewise, men in the Eastern regime feel more that becoming a father is important for being considered an adult, whereas the Nordic men are more indifferent. As the regression analysis shows, there is a clear association between this stand and actual fertility, again suggesting that a more relaxed attitude to fatherhood is related with higher odds of not entering into or at least postponing fatherhood. As also shown, the window of opportunity regarding attitudes to the lower and upper ages for becoming a father does not differ between the regimes, with the clear convention that there is a social age deadline around age 46–47. And here it seems again that having a more relaxed attitude to the social age deadline is also associated with actual childlessness. However, caution must be applied when interpreting these findings, since attitudes towards ideal age and social deadline is correlated with the individual fertility behaviour and could, in fact, be the result of reverse causality.

While there seems to be agreement across the regimes in attitudes as to when one is too young to father (20–21 years), actual fertility behaviour regarding the *timing* differs. And again, we find that men in the Eastern regime display a particular fertility behaviour in that they are significantly younger when having their first child. Again, we find the ideational factors to be strongly associated with actual fertility behaviour. Postponement of fatherhood is more likely if one does not think fatherhood important for being considered an adult, and also if one has a high ideal age and social age deadline for fathering. Unsurprisingly, and as is also the case for women, situational factors, such as pursuing an education, also tend to postpone fatherhood.

Turning to the last dependent variable, *the male fertility rate*, some of the findings confirm the theory of postponement: men who become fathers at a later stage in their lives generally have fewer children. This is also the case for men who get an education and who thus – as argued above – tend to postpone fathering; they also end up having fewer children.

However, the findings also confirm that fertility behaviour cannot be understood just from the theory of postponement: even though men in the Eastern regime tend to be younger when they first father, they tend to have fewer children than fathers in other regimes. Again, ideational factors as brought forward in the theory of planned behaviour help explain fertility behaviour: men who are more tolerant of voluntary childlessness and those who are more relaxed about the ideal age of fathering have fewer children. However, men who are more open to postponing fathering actually also tend to have slightly more children, suggesting that they leave the window of opportunity open for slightly longer.

More research and elaborated and not least longitudinal data is necessary to advance further in the analysis of the reproductive behaviour of men. However, the analysis confirms that ideational factors contribute significantly to the understanding of the framing of fatherhood. While acknowledging that some (traditional) explanations are still at play, such as partner situation, educational status and labour market attachment, the inclusion of attitudes and norms contribute to our understanding of what underscores fertility decisions. Conversely, the perception of gender roles did not turn out to be significant. It seems in particular that more relaxed attitudes to the proper age, importance of fatherhood and voluntary childlessness – as is particularly widespread in the Nordic regime – are associated with actual childlessness and having fewer children. While the results confirm the postponement theory to some degree, the inclusion of ideational factors thus helps better explain what frames male fertility behaviour.

Notes

[1] This is Hosmer and Lemeshow's test adapted to weighted data. The relative high p-value indicates that the model fits the data well.

[2] In order to control for selection bias, since the regression analysis only includes men who have had at least one child, a Heckman Selection model was used. However, there was no evidence of selection bias.

[3] Approximately 11 per cent of the variance is explained by the variables included in the regression analysis.

[4] In order to control for selection bias, since the regression analysis only includes men who have had at least one child, a Heckman Selection model was used. However, there was no evidence of selection bias.

References

Adsera, A. (2005) *Where are the babies? Labour market conditions and fertility in Europe*, IZA Discussion Paper 1576, Bonn: Institute for the Study of Labor.

Ahn, N. and Mira, P. (2002) 'A note on the changing relationship between fertility and female employment rates in developed countries', *Journal of Population Economics,* vol 15, pp 667-82.

Ajzen, I. (1988) *Attitudes, personality and behavior*, Milton Keynes: Open University Press.

Ajzen, I. (1991) 'The theory of planned behavior', *Organizational Behavior and Human Decision Processes*, vol 50, no 2, pp 179-211.

Becker, G.S. (1991) *A treatise on the family*, Cambridge, MA: Harvard University Press.

Billari, F.C. and Borgoni, R. (2005) 'Assessing the use of sample selection models in the estimation of fertility postponement effects', *Statistical Methods and Applications*, vol 14, no 3, pp 389-402.

Billari, F.C. and Kohler, H.-P. (2004) 'Patterns of low and lowest-low fertility in Europe', *Population Studies*, vol 58, no 2, pp 161-76.

Billari, F.C., Philipov, D. and Testa, M.R. (2009) 'Attitudes, norms and perceived behavioural control: explaining fertility intentions in Bulgaria', *European Journal of Population*, vol 25, pp 439-65.

Billari, F.C., Goisis, A., Liefbroer, A.C., Settersten, R.A., Aassve, A., Hagestad, G. and Spéder, Z. (2011) 'Social age deadline for the childbearing of women and men', in *Human Production*, vol 26, no 3, pp 616-22.

Blossfeld, H.-P. and Timm, A. (2004) *Who marries whom? Educational systems as marriage markets in modern societies*, Boston, MA and Dordrecht: Kluwer Academic Publishers.

Butz, W.P. and Ward, M.P. (1979) 'The emergence of countercyclical US fertility', *American Economic Review*, vol 69, no 3, pp 318-28.

Brückner, H. and Mayer, K.U. (2005) 'De-standardization of the life course: what it might mean? And if it means anything, whether it actually took place?', *Advances in Life Course Research*, vol 9, pp 27-53.

Cigno, A. (1991) *Economics of the family*, New York and Oxford: Oxford University Press and Clarendon Press.

Commission of the European Communities (2005) *Confronting demographic change: A new solidarity between the generations*, Green Paper, Brussels: Commission of the European Communities.

Crompton, R., Lewis, S. and Lyonette, C. (eds) (2007) *Women, men, work and family in Europe*, Houndmills: Palgrave.

d'Addio, A.C. and d'Ercole, M.M. (2005) *Trends and determinants of fertility rates: The role of policies*, OECD Social, Employment and Migration Working Papers, No 27, Paris: OECD.

Esping-Andersen, G. (1990) *The three worlds of welfare capitalism*, Cambridge: Polity Press.

European Commission (2006) *Childbearing preferences and family issues in Europe. Special Eurobarometer edition*, Brussels: European Commission.

European Foundation (2004) *Fertility and family issues in an enlarged Europe*, Dublin: European Foundation.

Eydal, G.B. and Rostgaard, T. (2011a) 'Gender equality re-visited: changes in Nordic childcare policies in the 2000?', Regional issue, *Social Policy & Administration*, vol 45, no 2, pp 65-97.

Eydal, G.B. and Rostgaard, T. (2011b) 'Nordic childcare – a response to old and new tensions?', in B. Pfau-Effinger and T. Rostgaard (eds) *Care between work and welfare in Europe*, Houndmills: Palgrave, pp 147-78.

Ferrera, M. (1996) 'The "Southern model" of welfare in social Europe', *Journal of European Social Policy*, vol 6, no 1, pp 17-37.

Frejka, T. and Sardon, J.-P. (2006) 'First birth trends in developed countries: persisting parenthood postponement', *Demographic Research*, vol 15, no 6, pp 147-80.

Gauthier, A.H. (2002) 'Family policies in industrialized countries: is there convergence?', *Population*, vol 57, no 3, pp 447-74.

Gray, E., Evans, A. and Reimondos, A. (2013) 'Childbearing desires of childless men and women: when are goals adjusted?', *Advances in Life Course Research*, vol 18, no 2, pp 141-9.

Gustafsson, S.S. (2001) 'Optimal age at motherhood: theoretical and empirical considerations on postponement of maternity in Europe', *Journal of Population Economics*, vol 14, pp 225-47.

Hoem, J.M., Neyer, G. and Andersson, G. (2006) 'Education and childlessness: the relationship between educational field, educational level, and childlessness among Swedish women born in 1955-59', *Demographic Research*, vol 14, no 15, pp 331-80.

Kääriäinen, J. and Lehtonen, H. (2006) 'The variety of social capital in welfare state regimes: a comparative study of 21 countries', *European Societies*, vol 8, no 1, pp 27-57.

Kaufman, G. (2000) 'Do gender role attitudes matter? Family formation and dissolution among traditional and egalitarian men and women', *Journal of Family Issues*, vol 21, no 1, pp 128-44.

Kemkes-Grottenthaler, A. (2003) 'More than a leap of faith: the impact of biological and religious correlates on reproductive behaviour', *Human Biology*, vol 75, pp 705-27.

Keune, M. (2006) 'The European social model and enlargement', in P.A. Serrano and M. Jepsen (eds) *Unwrapping the European social model*, Bristol: Policy Press, pp 167-88.

Kohler, H.-P., Billari, F.C. and Ortega, J.A. (2002) 'The emergence of lowest-low fertility in Europe during the 1990s', *Population and Development Review*, vol 28, no 4, pp 641-81.

Kohler, H.-P., Billari, F.C. and Ortega, J.A. (2006) 'Low fertility in Europe: causes, implications and policy options', in F.R. Harris (ed) *The baby bust: Who will do the work? Who will pay the taxes?*, Lanham, MD: Rowman & Littlefield, pp 48-109.

Leibfried, S. (2000) 'Towards a European welfare state?', in C. Pierson and F.G. Castels (eds) *The welfare state reader*, Cambridge: Polity Press, pp 190-206.

Liefbroer, A.C. and Billari, F.C. (2009) 'Bringing norms back in: a theoretical and empirical discussion of their importance for understanding demographic behaviour', *Population, Space and Place*, vol 16, pp 287-305.

Manning, N. (2004) 'Diversity and change in pre-accession central and eastern Europe since 1989', *Journal of European Social Policy*, vol 14, no 3, pp 211-33.

Martin, S.P. (2000) 'Diverging fertility among U.S. women who delay childbearing past age 30', *Demography*, vol 37, pp 523-33.

McDonald, P. (2002) 'Sustaining fertility through public policy: the range of options', *Population*, vol 57, no 3, pp 417-46.

McDonald, P. and Meyers, M.K. (2009) 'Social Policy Principles Applied to Reform of Gender Egalitarianism in Parenthood and Employment', in J.C. Gornick and M.K. Meyers (eds) *Gender Equality: Transforming Family Divisions of Labor*, New York, NY: Verso, pp 161-75.

Morgan, S.P. and Taylor, M.G. (2006) 'Low fertility at the turn of the twenty-first century', *Annual Review of Sociology*, vol 32, pp 375-99.

O'Brien, M. and Moss, P. (2010) 'Fathers, work and family policy in Europe', in M.E. Lamb (ed) *The role of the father in child development* (5th edn), Hoboken, NY: John Wiley & Sons, pp 551-77.

Statistical database (nd) (http://epp.eurostat.ec.europa.eu/portal/page/portal/population/data/main_tables).

Oppenheimer, V.K. (1988) 'A theory of marriage timing', *American Journal of Sociology*, vol 94, pp 563-91.

Schmitt, C. (2012) 'A cross-national perspective on unemployment and first births', *European Journal of Population*, vol 28, pp 303-35.

Settersten, R.A. (2003) 'Age structuring and the rhythm of the life course', in J.T. Mortimer and M.J. Shanahan (eds) *Handbook of the life course*, New York: Springer-Verlag, pp 81-98.

Sobotka, T. and Testa, M.R. (2008) 'Attitudes and intentions towards childlessness in Europe', in Ch. Höhn, D. Avramov and I. Kotowska (eds) *People, population change and policies: Lessons from the population policy acceptance study, Volume 1*, Berlin: Springer, pp 177-211.

Surkyn, J. and Lesthaeghe, R. (2004) 'Value orientations and the second demographic transition (SDT) in northern, western and southern Europe: An update', *Demographic Research*, Special Collection 3, article 3, pp 45-86.

Thomson, E. and Hoem, J.M. (1998) 'Couple childbearing plans and births in Sweden', *Demography*, vol 35, pp 315-22.

van de Kaa, D.J. (1987) 'Europe's second demographic transition', *Population Bulletin*, vol 42, no 1, pp 1-57.

van Oorschot, W. and Arts, W. (2005) 'The social capital of European welfare states: the crowding out hypothesis revisited', *Journal of European Social Policy*, vol 15, no 1, pp 5-26.

THREE

Nordic family law: new framework – new fatherhoods

Hrefna Friðriksdóttir

Introduction

Family law regulates the formal relationship between children and parents and between adults in close emotional relationships (Herring, 2009). It thus provides a definition of what constitutes legal families and legal relationships as in between fathers and their children. Historically, legal ties between children and parents constituted links to rights, property and power, and for decades the legal notions of fatherhood concerned biology and the economic contributions from father to child. In modern times, fatherhoods are strongly related to care and the rights of children in a broad sense. Family law thus deals with the framing and reframing of concepts such as marriage, cohabitation, mother, father, parentage, parental responsibility, residence, contact and child support.

Social and legal studies are currently grappling with the legal status of fathers in connection with often contradictory notions of rights, responsibilities, nurture, care and welfare, and family law reform has been widely noted as limited in dealing with the growing complexities of family life (Collier and Sheldon, 2006; Wallbank, 2010). Legislators are faced with the difficult task of trying to create a rational, unified system based on general principles, bound up with contradictory notions of evolving family ties, presumptions regarding the roles of fathers, the needs of children and gendered realities. Fatherhoods vary 'across historical epochs and subcultural contexts' (Lamb and Tamis-Lemonda, 2004, p 2), and many authors have contributed to the redefining and conceptualisation of fatherhoods and the status of fathers in family law in different jurisdictions (Dowd, 2000; Collier and Sheldon, 2008; Collier, 2010; Bridgeman et al, 2011). The Nordic countries share a culture based on common democratic and social values, and are 'remarkably similar to each other as regards the fundamental perception of the legal system, its design, methodology and basic principles' (Bernitz, 2007, p 28). This shared culture provides a basis for a legal study of how fatherhoods are understood, constructed and regulated in the context of Nordic family law.

The main aim of this chapter is to examine the development of contemporary Nordic family law and the extent to which common trends can be identified in the defining and redefining of fatherhoods; a further aim is to examine the inconsistencies, contradictions and competing interests in the basic arguments underlying the legal provisions regulating the relationship between fathers and their children, with a special emphasis on the child's perspective. The chapter begins by considering Nordic cooperation and the complex interrelationship between the developments in family law and social change in the Nordic countries in the 20th century, followed by a closer look at the common basic principles that have guided law reforms. The chapter then provides an analysis of fatherhoods in different settings, including the legal provisions on becoming a father and the status of fathers in 'legal families'. There is also a special focus on post-separation fathers. The analysis presented here does not provide in-depth information on the step-by-step legal reforms or laws in each of the countries. Rather, the aim is to give an overview of the most important aspects of Nordic legislation, and to draw out interesting or illuminating examples. The chapter concludes by drawing together common trends and contradictions. The findings will show that ideals surrounding shared parenting have in general become a presumed social good for children in the Nordic countries. Tensions are revealed, however, when actual law reforms in different contexts come under closer scrutiny. One of the biggest challenges is how law manages to balance the perspective of the child on the one hand, and presumptions of shared parenting or equal care on the other. The main data used in the analysis are national laws, major legislative policy documents and research reports.

Nordic family law and social change

Nordic legislation is often regarded as a legal system of its own (Therborn, 1993; Bernitz, 2007). Based on their commonalities, the Nordic countries have a long history of legislative cooperation, prominently in core private law areas such as family law. There is no unified Nordic family law, but the aim of cooperation has been to attain the greatest possible uniformity (Ludvigsen, 2005).

Law always develops in a social context, but the link between law and social change is bidirectional and complex. Laws are sometimes predominantly reactive, sometimes more proactive; this is a dynamic process in which legal norms are 'generated, selected, interpreted and implemented' (Fineman, 1995, p 16). Dey and Wasoff (2006) have drawn distinctions between the different functions played by family law; the first is the protection of the interests of family members at risk, most notably protecting the best interests of children, and the second is to resolve disputes. Other important functions of law involve regulating and guiding conduct. Family law thus plays a regulatory role associated with a symbolic purpose, both normative and instrumental.

Law reform is considered more likely to succeed in its regulatory and symbolic role if it goes with rather than against the grain of contemporary opinion and practice (Dey and Wasoff, 2006). This raises sensitive questions as to how well laws resonate with the social and cultural experiences of different groups in society, such as fathers in general, fathers with different backgrounds, and fathers with different family ties. Research has an important role to play here. In the last few decades, social scientists have gone from doubting that fathers significantly shape the experiences and development of their children to having amassed a solid body of evidence regarding the benefits of positive father involvement for the well-being of their children (Lamb and Tamis-Lemonda, 2004).

Family law often strives to set or refigure normative values. This begs the question to what extent a society shares an ideology, or how certain groups may perceive reform as unrealistic or as legal coercion (Bridgeman et al, 2011). Svenson and Pylkkänen (2004) point out how trust in the ability of law and politics to improve the situation of individuals has occurred quite naturally in the Nordic context, the state being understood as virtually identical with society as a promoter of the interests of its citizens. They also argue, however, that this legitimacy has come into question in recent times, concomitantly with increasing cultural multiplicity and individualism.

In analysing family law reform in the Nordic countries, it becomes evident that legislation is considered both normatively and ideologically powerful (Ottesen and Stage, 2011). This is evident in the changes made to marriage laws in the first decades of the 20th century, with a focus on gender equality, and in the development of rules for shared parenting and contact in the second half of the century. It is much more difficult to perceive if, or the extent to which, broad attempts at social engineering run parallel or counter to the complex realities of fathers and the needs of children.

Principles guiding family law reform

Equality

Taking a closer look at the common basic principles that have guided law reforms, the Nordic countries clearly link the modern ideas on fathering and fatherhoods primarily to the development of gender equality as a fundamental ideology, with its embedded questions about traditional gender roles (Annfelt, 2009; Collier, 2010). Gender equality has long been a key part of the Nordic identity. As later discussed, the revolutionary changes to the marriage laws at the beginning of the 20th century established formal equality between husband and wife. These changes were instrumental in redefining fatherhood in the Nordic countries. Since the early 1980s, the Nordic countries have seen a wave of legislative reforms on many fronts that actively promote gender equality, placing great emphasis on the father as carer (Eydal and Rostgaard, 2010).

The Nordic countries have all ratified (legalised in Norway and Finland) the United Nations (UN) *Convention on the Elimination of All Forms of Discrimination Against Women* (CEDAW) from 1979, which symbolises common principles that the states are committed to respect. The Nordic countries were instrumental in shaping Article 5 of CEDAW (Rehof, 1993), which demands all appropriate measures to modify the social and cultural patterns of conduct with a view to achieving the elimination of prejudices and all practices based on stereotyped roles for men and women. However, family law systems require a detailed understanding of the complex interrelationship between formal equality for fathers and mothers and the child's perspective.

The child's perspective

The legal status of fathers is greatly influenced by the development of the rights of the child. Since the early 20th century, the Nordic countries have strived to make children and their needs the axis of family law instead of the parents (Therborn, 1993; Schwenzer, 2007). The European Convention on Human Rights from 1950 established the principle of equality between children born within and outside of marriage, which greatly enhanced the status of fathers. This issue had already been a key element in legislative reforms in the Nordic countries, and in the following decades the growing focus on the child as a rights subject signalled the emergence of specific laws, or integrated legal provisions regarding children and on parental status and responsibilities in all the Nordic countries. These laws, in respect of children, have been under almost constant revision in Sweden, Denmark, Norway and Iceland since the beginning of the 1980s (Danielsen, 2003).

Important fundamental values that have guided family law reform and the construction of fatherhoods in the Nordic countries are enshrined in the UN Convention on the Rights of the Child (UNCRC) from 1989, which the Nordic countries have all ratified (legalised in Norway, Finland and Iceland) (Danielsen, 2003; Friðriksdóttir, 2011).

The preamble to the UNCRC emphasises the family as the natural environment for the growth and well-being of children, and Article 2 demands that children are protected against all forms of discrimination, including discrimination on the basis of the status of parents or other family members. The Nordic countries have generally accepted a dynamic, functional approach to the definition of families, as evident in the recognition of unmarried cohabitation and validation of same-sex partnerships (Friðriksdóttir, 2012).

The principle of the best interests of the child (Article 3) has been the guiding compass for the development of all family law reforms in the Nordic countries in the 20th century. How best to apply this principle to serve the needs of children can be controversial, however; this is a legal principle 'concealing all kinds of value assumptions' (Schiratzki, 2007, p 479). As such, the principle has been interpreted and used to legitimise both claims for legal reform for fathers, such as presumed equal parental care, and to criticise such claims (Haugli, 2008; Annfelt, 2009). Social and psychological sciences have been instrumental in developing the best interest principle (Eekelaar, 2010). On the one hand, such sciences provide important tools to determine individual cases; on the other hand, extensive research provides necessary knowledge, which can be used to legitimise the legal dimensions that directly affect the relationships between fathers and children. Both uses are sensitive to historical and cultural biases and moral value judgements. The assertion made by Freud and Solnit (1979, p 6) that all children need the 'unbroken continuity of affectionate and stimulating relationship with an adult' is generally accepted, for example, but its interpretation may rely on ideas on the traditional gendered roles of fathers and mothers.

The UNCRC emphasises the right of a child to, as far as possible, know and be cared for by their parents (Article 7) without providing a definition of what constitutes a parent in this respect. Hodgkin and Newell (2007) use concepts such as genetic parents, birth parents and psychological parents, and they distinguish between the right to know one's background from the right to be cared for. The UNCRC goes further in identifying the primary and common responsibilities of parents for the upbringing and development of the child (Article 18). The child's right to be cared for implies some form of active involvement on behalf of the parents, but the concept of common parental responsibilities is not synonymous with the equal status of fathers and mothers, and does not demand specific types of legal regulation of parental responsibilities, residence, contact and child maintenance. As a general principle, however, Article 18 has been a foundation for the development of all child law reform in the Nordic countries in recent decades and, as such, has specifically benefited fathers.

Fatherhoods in different settings

Becoming a father

Biologically, the conception of a child always results from the merging of genetic material from a woman and a man. Historically, our ideas of mother and father have been linked to the conception of the child, but how children actually enter families has changed radically and fuelled debates about the meaning of fatherhood, motherhood, parenting and families (Twine, 2011). Dey and Wasoff (2006) argue that the shifting boundaries of family life present awkward challenges for legal reforms, not least because different aims have been pursued across different boundaries. This can be tested by looking more closely at the legal position of three types of fathers: the biological father, contractual father, and social father.

The biological father emerges as a legal concept when fatherhood is traced to conception resulting from his sexual intercourse with the mother. The principle of the importance of biological ties is often linked to financial support and the child's right to know their origins. Construction of fatherhood can be closely related to sexual and procreative activity and to regulations surrounding contraception, abortion, pregnancy and childbirth, which can mark the beginning of sharply gender-differentiated patterns of the involvement of fathers and mothers with their children (Dowd, 2000). The medical understandings of the difference between male and female reproductive biology relates directly to different treatment in family law on the issues of paternity and maternity.

In the Nordic countries, as in most legal systems, legal maternity is a consequence of the fact that a woman has given birth to a child (Schwenzer, 2007). Legal paternity is quite different. The legal principle of paternal affiliation by presumption is fundamental to the establishment of paternity. Presumed legal paternity, pater est, is based solely on the status of the parents, the most common presumption being that the mother's husband is automatically established as the child's father (Snævarr, 2008). Since 1981, Iceland has been the only Nordic country to also apply pater est to unmarried registered cohabitation.

In cases where the pater est principle does not apply, all of the Nordic countries place a duty on the mother to identify the father and to allow voluntary recognition of paternity by the named father. This is usually a simple procedure that often takes place when the child is born, especially when the parents are cohabitating. In Norway, for example, the father can acknowledge paternity before a midwife or doctor, even before the child is born, and in Denmark paternity can be established by the mother and the father signing a Care and Responsibility Declaration provided by a midwife. In principal, these procedures also assume a biological link between the father and child, but are, in fact, consensual by nature. In the absence of such formal recognition, legal parenthood can be established through court procedures, relying almost exclusively on DNA testing (Lørdrup, 2003).

The pater est principle is based on the need to secure a social and legal framework from the start of a child's life, assuming that this framework is usually in accordance with the biological facts. This presents a contradiction. There is no direct correlation between a legal framework and secure circumstances for children. There is also clear tension between attaching legal parenthood to biological facts versus aiming to secure a child's stable attachment to caring and responsible adults. All of the Nordic countries allow proceedings to challenge already-established paternity. Historically, there were strict time limits for adults entitled to institute such proceedings, based on the child's need for stability. These time limits remain applicable in Denmark and Finland but were abolished in Sweden in 1976, Norway in 2002 and Iceland in 2003, emphasising the accuracy of modern DNA testing and the presumed need of a child to know their biological origins (Lørdrup, 2003). Interestingly, Norway reintroduced such time limits in 2013, generally requiring parents to instigate court proceedings within a year after receiving knowledge that raises doubts about the paternity of a child. Norway also introduced an interesting provision in 2013 giving a child the right to know the identity of their biological (genetic) father without this entailing a change in paternity. These changes are based on the need for secure and stable attachments and the grave consequences that changes to legal paternity can have for a child (NOU, 2009:5).

The contractual father emerges first and foremost through the use of reproductive technologies. Here, legal fatherhood can be established through a formal contract stipulating fertilisation with donor sperm. This legal bond between father and child completely overshadows the status of the provider of biological or genetic material. The status of the donor is viewed almost exclusively through questions pertaining to the interests or right of the child to receive information on donor identity. Legislation regarding donor anonymity differs in the Nordic countries, but there seems to be growing belief that knowledge regarding one's genetic paternity is important and does not disrupt the relationship with one's legal/social family (Collier and Sheldon, 2008). The status of the contractual father relies on assisted reproduction being performed in accordance with legal regulation. The legal status of all of the involved therefore changes dramatically if individuals negotiate reproduction outside the realm of formal legislation on assisted reproduction (see also Chapter Eleven, this volume). In such cases, the general rules of paternity apply, and a sperm donor can become the legal father through voluntary recognition of paternity or by court order.

The social father is someone who practises fathering independently of the presence of a biological or legal relationship with a child (Collier and Sheldon, 2008). This is the most fluid concept. A social father's bond to a child is usually contingent on his relationship (marriage or cohabitation) to the other parent; he can exist alongside a legal father for a shorter or longer period in a child's life and the fathering practices may vary accordingly. Step-parenting is not generally associated with legal rights or responsibilities in the Nordic countries, apart from Iceland. According to the Icelandic Act on Children, step-parents can have parental responsibilities for their step-child in certain circumstances.

It is worth noting that fatherhood is often not continuous and singular, but can be serial or multiple (Lind and Hewitt, 2009). A father may thus be involved in different types of fatherhoods simultaneously or that change over the course of a lifetime.

Being a father

Regulations on how men become fathers have been influenced by social and psychological research on fathering and the impact of fathers on child development. Questions of impact of fathers are often related to normative ideas on presumed differences between fathers and mothers as caregivers. This also relates to latent ideas on the connections between the inherent abilities of fathers and actual involvement. Research has thus often been misrepresented and led to 'overly stereotypic and uni-dimensional portrayals of fathers' (Lamb, 2010, p 3). Lamb suggests that the roles played by fathers are not informed by their inherent abilities but by a web of complex historical, cultural and familiar ideologies in constant interaction with formal family law constructs.

Fathers in legal families

Marriage

How may fatherhoods be constituted, and what is the status of fathers in 'legal families'? One such setting constituting fatherhood is marriage, which is universally recognised as the most revered social institution within family law (Agell and Brattstöm, 2011).

In the first decades of the 20th century, marriage went from being an institution in which the husband (father) ruled over his wife (and children) to an institution of two equal individuals with mutual obligations to support the family in all the Nordic countries (Bradley, 2000; Wetterberg and Melby, 2009). The Nordic countries were forerunners in this respect. The marriage law reforms from early 1910 to the late 1920s went further in establishing gender equality than most other marriage laws in Europe, and these ideals still form the foundations for the rights and obligations of married couples in the Nordic countries (Snævarr, 2008). The reformed legislation was a turning point from the patriarchal family pattern towards an *equal family*, declaring 'an explicit basic equality between husband and wife, father and mother' (Therborn, 1993, p 258). Despite the emphasis on joint responsibility, the new laws on marriage presumed a division of obligations between fathers and mothers, underlining the value of different forms of contributions, such as monetary payments, domestic work or other support within the family. Wetterberg and Melby (2009) argue that, in this sense, equality was based on the assumption of different gender roles, and in the decades to come this equality ideology was enmeshed in the stark reality that the gendered division of labour was the 'dominant casting script for family stories' (Fineman, 1995, p 176).

The Nordic countries have moved away from the breadwinner model toward an individual earner regime, which becomes evident in provisions on spouse maintenance and the dissolution of matrimonial property (Lund-Andersen and Nørgaard, 2012; Chapter Four, this volume). However, caring for children has increasingly become both an individualistic role, representing fathers as capable carers, and a joint undertaking, both in intact families and post-separation (see also Chapters Eight and Twelve, this volume). Legislative reforms in recent decades have increasingly centred on co-parenting ideals. Special measures have been designed to strengthen these ideals and to modify gendered behaviour, most notably the regulations on parental leave discussed elsewhere in this volume (see also Chapters Six, Thirteen, Fifteen and Sixteen, this volume). Simultaneously, post-separation reforms mirror a special tension between the familial and individualistic role that reflect interrelated notions of the rights and needs of children and the responsibilities of fathers and mothers, including if or how these responsibilities can be shared or individualised and divided. Co-parenting ideology has even surpassed the marital union itself, signalling a radical shift in the construction of fatherhood (Bergman and Hobson, 2002).

Registered partnership and gender-neutral marriage

Abolishing discrimination based on sexual orientation is very important, not just for gay men but for all fathers. Many have pointed out the insidious links between heterosexism and gender roles in general, and how heterosexism in the marriage debate has reinforced 'the social meaning of gender by affirming a sex-differentiated, patriarchal conception of marriage' (Law, 1998, p 232). Law reform for same-sex couples can thus be linked to the refiguring of men as fathers (see also Chapter Eleven, this volume). The Nordic countries are considered world leaders in recognising same-sex relationships (Scherpe, 2007); however, closer scrutiny of the developments reveals contradictions and persistent gender stereotyping (Friðriksdóttir, 1996, 2003).

In 1989, Denmark became the first country in the world to introduce registered partnerships for same-sex couples (Lund-Andersen, 2003). Norway followed in 1993, Sweden in 1994, Iceland in 1996 and Finland in 2001 (Scherpe, 2007). These laws offer a clear example of proactive legislation openly meant as political statements, equating homosexual and heterosexual couples in order to facilitate acceptance and modify values, attitudes and behaviour (Friðriksdóttir, 2003). Simultaneously, the laws excluded gay men and lesbians as parents, thus sending a very mixed message. The Nordic reasoning was based on the principle of the best interests of the child, linked to a presumption that children need both father and mother images. These justifications stand in stark contrast to the general Nordic policy on gender equality (Friðriksdóttir, 1996, 2003). Significant legislative reform has occurred as the Nordic countries have gradually abolished the limitations denying same-sex couples the right to parent.

Table 3.1 shows important milestones from the introduction of registered partnership to the recognition of marriage open to two individuals regardless of gender. The arguments for accepting parenthood for same-sex couples were generally founded on notions of equality and consistent research demonstrating homosexuals as good parents. Policy documents also contain references to shifts in traditional gender roles and how same-sex couples as parents can be instrumental in reflecting such changes (Friðriksdóttir, 2010). Law reforms have thus contributed to new understandings of fathering in general while providing new opportunities for gay fathers. The changes inevitably place gay fathers in a unique position, as legally assisted reproduction is open to single women and lesbians, which can effectively preclude any legal fatherhood. Same-sex partners also have and continue to create families in various forms, which can raise numerous questions regarding the legal status of all of those involved (see also Chapter Eleven, this volume).

Table 3.1: Same-sex relationships – important milestones

	Denmark	Norway	Sweden	Iceland	Finland
Registered partnership laws	1989	1993	1994	1996	2001
Joint parental responsibility	2010	2009	2003	1996	2002
Step-parent adoption	1999	2001	2003	2000	2009
Full adoption	2010	2009	2003	2006	NA
Formal access to reproductive technologies	2006	2009	2005	2006	2006
Gender-neutral marriage	2012	2009	2009	2010	NA

Information based on laws on registered partnerships and marriage in the Nordic countries.

Cohabitation

Growing recognition of unmarried cohabitation has been evident in all of the Nordic countries in recent decades (Friðriksdóttir, 2012). Nevertheless, a clear distinction remains between cohabitation and marriage, which affects the legal status of fathers.

The recognition of cohabitation as a status, referring rights and duties between the partners, has mainly been in the area of social and welfare rights and less prominent in family law (Friðriksdóttir, 2012; Lund-Andersen, 2012). Recent developments reveal marked differences between the Nordic countries. Sweden passed laws on joint residence in 1987 and laws on cohabitation in 2003, confirming certain important rights and obligations for cohabitants (Agell and Brattström, 2011). Norway provided limited protection in laws on joint residence in 1991, legislated certain inheritance rights for cohabitants in 2008 (Lørdrup and Asland, 2012), and have introduced ground-breaking proposals in 2014 for equal inheritance rights for married couples and cohabitants (NOU, 2014:1). Finland adopted laws on cohabitation in 2011, providing yet another form of protection on the dissolution of cohabitation (Kangas, 2010).

Historically, children born out of wedlock (illegitimate children) had fewer rights than children born in wedlock (legitimate children). Children were considered illegitimate regardless of whether their parents lived together or not. Even though these concepts have been abolished, marriage still retains its unique position in the Nordic countries when it comes to presumed legal paternity, except for Iceland, as mentioned before. The other Nordic countries have referred to the practical problems associated with the registration of cohabitation, and the fact that cohabitation is less legally binding than marriage and thus presumed less stable (Eriksson and Saldeen, 1993; NOU, 2009:5). In Iceland, cohabiting parents also enjoy automatic joint parental responsibility. Norway adopted rules on joint parental responsibilities for cohabitants in 2005, and Denmark to some extent in 2007, but the cohabiting father in the other Nordic countries must take certain legal steps to ensure parentage and joint parental responsibilities.

Fathers post-separation

It has been argued that the emergence of new politics of fatherhoods and law has become increasingly significant in family policy debates in the area of separation and divorce (Collier and Sheldon, 2008). This relates to the statistical fact that most children in the Nordic countries live with their mothers and have regular contact with their fathers post-separation (Schiratzki, 2007; Andersen and Ravn, 2009).

As mentioned earlier, post-separation reforms reflect a tension surrounding the needs of children and the responsibilities of fathers and mothers. It is thus important to look at the status of fathers post-separation in connection with the legal concepts of parental responsibility, residence, contact and child maintenance. In recent decades, most of the Nordic legislators have made effort to define these concepts more precisely in order to provide more detailed legislation that helps parents navigate their contentious rights and responsibilities, and to better protect children in the post-separation arena (Betænkning 1475, 2006; NOU, 2008:9, p 9). Issues surrounding principles and presumptive choices, such as joint parental responsibility, joint residence or equal care, are of particular importance to the legal status and role of fathers post-separation.

The following sections offer examples on how recent developments in family law have gradually constricted the use of presumptions in the process of imposing a post-separation parenting or contact regime (Collier and Sheldon, 2006; Gilmore, 2006; Backer, 2008; Haugli, 2008; Singer, 2008; Wallbank, 2010; Friðriksdóttir, 2011; Ottesen and Stage, 2011). Masardo (2011, p 131) suggests that a major challenge arises in the regulation to 'resist the temptation to become overly prescriptive in setting definitions that favour a particular pattern of care, however attractive an option this might seem'. He also warns against imposing any subjective judgements on one type of arrangement over another. This area also raises persistent questions about the 'very possibilities, and limits, of using law reform to regulate and change family practices' (Collier and Sheldon, 2008, p 140).

Table 3.2 maps out recent law reforms in order to give an overview of the details and complexity of the legislation and differences in developments in each of the Nordic countries. Some of these core issues are then defined and discussed further in the following sections.

Table 3.2: Regulation of the rights and responsibilities of parents

	Denmark	Norway	Sweden	Iceland	Finland
Laws on parental responsibility (PR), residence and contact	Forældre-ansvarsloven 499/2007	Barnalova 7/1981	Föräldrabalken 1949:381	Barnalög 76/2003	Lag angående vårdnad om barn och umgängesrätt 361/1983
Laws on child support	Lov om børns forsørgelse 352/2003	Lov om barn og foreldre 7/1981	Föräldrabalken 1949:381	Barnalög 76/2003	Lag om underhåll för barn 704/1975
Agreed joint PR after separation	1986	1981	1976	1992	1983
Agreed joint residence after separation	NA	1981	1976	NA	1983
Presumed joint PR after separation	2002	1981	1982	2006	1983
Adjudication of conflicts under joint PR regarding contact	1995	1981	1992	2003	1983
Adjudication of conflicts under joint PR regarding residence	2007	1981	1998	2013	1983
Joint PR by court order	2007	1981	1998	2013	1983
Joint residence by court order	NA	2010	1998	NA	NA
50/50 contact by court order	2007	1981	1998	2010/ 2013	1983

Information based on laws in the Nordic countries.

Parental responsibility

Parental responsibility (or custody) is a core legal concept used to explain the formal relationship between parent and child. From the perspective of the child, the analysis of the father–child relationship demands careful scrutiny of the balance of rights, responsibilities, care and welfare. Freeman (2008, p 23) thus suggests that 'parents still have parental rights, but these are subsumed in parental responsibilities.' Backer (2008) underlines caring and decision making as the two main themes characterising parental responsibility in modern families.

Until quite recently, as reflected in Table 3.2, Nordic family law reflected an emphasis on the interrelationship between duty and care; joint parental responsibility (or joint custody) was therefore only possible for parents living together with their child. Since 1992, all the Nordic countries have an option for parents living apart to agree on joint parental responsibility, and this is the preferred legal arrangement after parents separate. The explicit objective is to secure the parent-child (in practice, father–child) relationship, as this is presumed to be in the best interests of the child. This reform in fact modified the concept of parental responsibility, signalling a separation of actual care from aspects of legal responsibility involving status and decision making (Singer, 2008; Friðriksdóttir, 2011).

Allowing courts to order joint parental responsibility has proven a contentious subject. This option has been available in Norway since 1981, Finland since 1983 and Sweden since 1998. The supposed positive aspects of joint parental responsibility rendered this the presumed solution in practice in both Sweden and Norway (NJA, 1999, p 451; Rt, 2003, p 35). Criticism soon followed, and critics argued that this interpretation overlooked the actual needs of each child (Singer, 2008; Friðriksdóttir, 2011). The law was amended in Norway and Sweden in 2006, specifically rejecting any presumptions in adjudicating parental responsibilities but instead underlining the need for individual assessments, protection of children from harm and a focus on the ability of parents to cooperate on fundamental issues regarding the welfare of the child (Odelsetingsproposisjon [Ot prp] 103, 2004/05; Proposition 2005/06:99). Denmark legalised court-ordered joint parental responsibility in 2007 as the presumed solution for parents post-separation (Christensen, 2009). After extensive studies of the effects of the new law, the presumptive solution was effectively alleviated in 2012, and the current legislation places greater emphasis on necessary parental cooperation in individual cases, and an evaluation of the situation and needs of each individual child (Lovforslag 157, 2011/1). Court-ordered (but not presumptive) joint parental responsibility has been an option in Iceland from 2013, similarly requiring a careful scrutiny of the best interests of the child, protection from harm and the ability of parents to cooperate (Alþingi 2011-12, A: 328, A: 1529).

Formal residence

Formal residence is a concept that developed alongside joint parental responsibility post-separation. In real life, this gives resident mothers the power to make many important decisions regarding the child, directly testing the limits of the rights and obligations of the non-resident fathers (see, for example, NOU, 2008:9; Betænkning 1475, 2006).[1]

As evident from Table 3.2, Sweden, Norway and Finland each have a lengthy history of allowing parents to practice joint formal residence (or dual residence), which effectively assumes that fathers and mothers must agree on all matters concerning the child. The possibility of courts ordering joint residence has existed in Sweden since 1998. To avoid presumptive or arbitrary use of this possibility, some necessary prerequisites for such an arrangement have since been incorporated into legislative policy (Singer, 2008). Court-ordered joint residence was introduced in Norway in 2010, although only in special circumstances, explicitly to avoid over-interpretation and presumptive use (Ot prp 104, 2008/09). Haugli (2008) has argued that the reform rested on tenuous truths lacking a focus on the needs of the children. This resonates with Newnham's analysis of shared residence orders in the UK as an attempt to instil a sense of responsibility into fathers and mothers to improve their co-parenting. She describes this as a 'triumph of hope over experience', arguing that these changes in legal formalities do not seem to affect 'the complex problems of entrenched conflict families' (Newnham, 2011, p 148).

Denmark and Iceland have rejected the possibility of agreed or court-ordered joint residence. If parents decide on joint parental responsibility or it is ordered by the courts, the law requires a decision on formal residence with one of the parents (Christensen, 2009; Friðriksdóttir, 2011).

Contact

Contact as a legal concept is defined as the actual time a child spends with a non-resident parent and any other form of communication between them. Norway, Denmark and Iceland distinguish between formal residence and contact, as shown in Table 3.2, thus differentiating clearly between joint formal residence and equal contact (or 50/50 contact). The difference between alternating residence and extended contact is not quite as clear in Sweden (Singer, 2008; Sjösten, 2009). All of the Nordic countries recognise contact as a fundamental right for the child based on the notion of the significance for child well-being of maintaining a relationship with both parents (Danielsen, 2003). In practice, contact issues are paramount to non-resident fathers and their relationships with their children.

—

Legal regulation of contact, especially equal contact (50/50 contact), and the enforcement of contact has been debated in the Nordic countries. As with parental responsibility and formal residence, the debate has in part centred around the issue of presumed choices for children in law and practice (Harris-Short, 2010). Norway, Denmark and Iceland have explicitly rejected equal contact as the preferred choice. Gilmore (2006, p 360) convincingly argues that policymakers who have rejected recent calls for statutory presumptions of contact or of presumptive equal division of a child's time between parents 'appear to have acted appropriately' in the light of research. For example, research has shown that the extent of direct father–child interaction is not of primary importance, as favourable conditions on multiple, reciprocally interacting levels must exist if increased paternal involvement is to be possible and beneficial for a child (Lamb and Tamis-Lemonda, 2004).

Child maintenance

All of the Nordic countries have a long history of requiring non-resident fathers to provide financial support for their children. The parents can agree on child maintenance or the matter can be adjudicated in accordance with rules laid out in law and administrative regulations (Agell and Singer, 2003).

With the exception of Iceland, the Nordic child maintenance systems have undergone major reforms over the last decade (Eydal and Friðriksdóttir, 2012). One of the common objectives of law reform has been to develop just, simple and transparent regulations that reflect increased contact in practice between non-resident fathers and children (Backer, 2008; Skinner and Davidson, 2009; Lund-Andersen and Nørgaard, 2012).

Levels of discretion operating within child maintenance systems vary considerably. Norway, Sweden and Finland use cost indexes or statistical information, but Denmark and Iceland rely on standardised amounts to determine the base threshold for child maintenance. All of the Nordic countries take account of the non-resident parent's income levels, but there are considerable variations as to how other financial obligations are treated. In Norway, Sweden and Finland, the maintenance costs are shared between the parents according to both their incomes, and contact is then taken into account using different thresholds. Denmark has a more discretionary system in this respect, but Iceland disregards contact arrangements. The Nordic countries all have some agencies involved in the collection and forwarding of child maintenance which differ in terms of scope (Eydal and Friðriksdóttir, 2010). Agell and Singer (2003) note the complexities of child maintenance in family law and the added dimension of the interaction with public resource transfers in each country (see also Chapter Four, this volume).

Fathers who have not lived with their children

The sections above have outlined in broad terms the legal status of fathers living with their children and fathers post-separation. The legal status of fathers who have never lived with their children is in some ways the most precarious.

In numerous ways, Nordic family law reforms have generally strengthened the legal links between children and their fathers. All fathers have the option of negotiating joint parental responsibility with the mother, and they can demand sole or joint parental responsibilities in court according to the regimes in each country. All fathers also have contact rights and obligations and the right and duty to pay child maintenance. The main difference is in the automatic or presumed status of the father. There have been debates about whether all fathers should automatically share parental responsibilities with mothers after legal paternity has been established, irrespective of the relationship between the parents. However, such ideas have recently been expressly rejected in Denmark, Norway and Iceland, underlining the functions of shared parenting and acknowledging the different realities of children born under different circumstances (Betænkning 1475, 2006; Ot prp 104, 2008/09; Alþingi, 2011-12, A: 328).

Conclusion

As Collier and Sheldon (2008, p 236) point out, family law operates as a 'significant symbolic discourse that offers a state-sanctioned account of who is, and who is not, worthy of recognition as a father, in what form and to what extent.'

There are some discernible common trends in the development of family law in the Nordic countries that have been instrumental in the constructing and redefining of fatherhoods. Law reforms have consistently been based on similar abstract principles of justice, first and foremost on gender equality and gender neutrality and the priority of the best interests of children, with its embedded ideas that children benefit from the common responsibilities of parents to protect and care for them. But law is not just abstract principles; it also requires a much more detailed realisation of actual rights and responsibilities.

The foundation for the emerging trends in family law reforms in the Nordic countries can be traced back to the changes in marriage laws at the beginning of the 20th century, highlighting gender equality and joint responsibilities. Law reforms have since consistently revealed the inherent division of obligations that in many ways continue to be gender-related. In response, policy and law reform have worked to influence actual father involvement with some measure of success. The recognition of changes in social family structures and complex family transitions is also evident in Nordic family law. The emphasis on the role of the father as carer thus transcended the traditional family, and the focus shifted from the family form to the relationships, rights and responsibilities of fathers towards their children in general. Relying on the best interest principle, the idea of shared parenting has become a presumed social good for children (Kurki-Suonio, 2000).

This appears to be a narrative of holistic progression or a consistent construction of new fatherhoods in society and law (Andersen and Ravn, 2009). However, law reforms tend to be context-specific – different aims are pursued in different areas – and it is in the further detailed execution that inconsistencies and tensions are revealed. As Sverdrup (2012, p 312) points out, 'child law has become a battlefield for gender policy'.

Some inconsistencies in the Nordic family law reforms are obvious, such as the often-conflicting biological, contractual and/or social ideologies underpinning the right to become and be a legal father. The same can be said about juxtaposing marriage and cohabitation when it comes to legal fatherhood and parental responsibilities. It has also been very difficult to rationalise the dichotomy of the 'father versus mother' image in relation to same-sex parenting.

Post-separation fatherhoods warrant special attention. There is a difference between policies aimed at refiguring and subtly modifying parental involvement in two-parent families as opposed to the politicised one-dimensional ideology of shared parenting and construction of fathers as carers post-separation (and fathers as carers regardless of family ties with the mother). In actual reality, this may sometimes demand a confused and complex reshuffling and restructuring of parental roles that may ignore the existing division of care and obligations. This begs the question of whether legal optimism and cultural pressures can run counter to 'emotionally experienced' realities. Even more important questions are how, when, to what extent and in what form shared/equal parenting post-separation is consistent with the best interests of a child. It is clear from the major legislative Nordic policy documents and law reforms that, guided by the child perspective, Norway, Sweden, Denmark and Iceland have been trying in recent decades to balance positive symbolic ideologies with a claim for the institution of a legal presumption of shared equal parenting or equal contact.

In analysing Nordic family law reforms, it becomes evident that tension surrounding post-separation parenting has resulted in a growing number of legal provisions with the aim of guiding, clarifying and regulating various problematic issues. Ottesen and Stage (2011) underline that the law can only provide a certain framework, and that fathers and mothers have the ultimate responsibility of translating the regulations into practice. They question the extent to which fathers and mothers have each in their own way been able to fulfil the ambitious aims of the law reforms. There are clear indications that Nordic family law is adapting in this area by taking certain steps back from presumptive legal solutions and focusing more on actual care and the welfare of each child to protect its harmonious development. It remains to be seen how these latest reforms will affect the status of fathers and resonate with their realities. Maybe it is inevitable – and even rational – that modern complex family (law) chaos in reality constructs different and even conflicting notions of fatherhood. A challenge for the future will be to further develop and accept multifaceted fatherhoods while focusing on creating holistic childhoods.

Note

[1] Some countries, such as the US, use the concepts of joint legal custody (pertaining to legal authority to make decisions) and joint physical or residential custody (specifying that the child will alternate residence with each parent) (Amato and Dorius, 2010).

References

Agell, A. and Brattstöm, M. (2011) *Äktenskap, samboende, partnerskap* [*Marriage, cohabitation, partnership*] (5th edn), Uppsala: Iustus Förlag.

Agell, A. and Singer, A. (2003) 'Underhåll till barn' ['Child maintenance'], in P. Lørdrup, A. Agell and A. Singer (eds) *Nordisk børneret I: Farskap, morskap og underhåll till barn. Et sammenlignende studie af dansk, finsk, islandsk, norsk og svensk ret med drøftelser af harmoniseringsmuligheder og reformbehov* [*Nordic child law I: Paternity, maternity and child maintenance. A comparative study of Danish, Finnish, Icelandic, Norwegian and Swedish laws with a focus on harmonising and change*], Nord 2003:4, Copenhagen: Nordisk Ministerråd, pp 235-430.

Alþingi 2011-12 [Icelandic Parliament, A: 1529 *Lög um breytingar á barnalögum* [Parliamentary report in Iceland: *Amendments to law in respect of children*].

Alþingi 2011-12, A: 328 *Frumvarp til breytinga á barnalögum* [Parliamentary report in Iceland: *Bill for amendments to law in respect of children*].

Andersen, C. and Ravn, A.-B. (2009) 'From powerful to powerless fathers: gender equality in Danish family policies on parenthood', in K. Melby, A.-B. Ravn and C.C. Wetterberg (eds) *Gender equality and welfare politics in Scandinavia*, Bristol: Policy Press, pp 135-47.

Annfelt, T. (2009) 'The "new father": gender equality as discursive resource for family policies', in K. Melby, A.-B. Ravn and C.C. Wetterberg (eds) *Gender equality and welfare politics in Scandinavia*, Bristol: Policy Press, pp 119-33.

Backer, I.L. (2008) *Barneloven* [*Children's law*] (2nd edn), Oslo: Universitetsforlaget.

Barnalög nr 76/2003 með síðari breytingum [*Law in respect of children with later amendments*].

Bergman, H. and Hobson, B. (2002) 'Compulsory fatherhood: the coding of fatherhood in the Swedish politics of fatherhood', in B. Hobson (eds) *Making men into fathers: Men, masculinities and the social politics of fatherhood*, Cambridge: Cambridge University Press, pp 99-124.

Bernitz, U. (2007) 'What is Scandinavian Law?', *Scandinavian Studies in Law*, vol 50, no 1, pp 13-30.

Betænkning 1475 (2006) *Barnets perspektiv: Forældremyndighed, barnets bopæl, samvær og tvangsfuldbyrdelse* [Danish Government report 1475: *Child perspective: Parental responsibility, residence, contact and enforcement*].

Bradley, D. (2000) 'Family laws and welfare states', in K. Melby, A. Pylkkänen, B. Rosenbeck and C.C. Wetterberg (eds) *The Nordic model of marriage and the welfare state,* Nord 2000:27, Copenhagen: Nordic Council of Ministers, pp 37-67.

Bridgeman, J., Keating, H. and Lind, C. (2011) *Regulating family responsibilities,* Farnham: Ashgate.

Christensen, S.K. (2009) *Forældreansvarsloven* [*Law on parental responsibility*], Copenhagen: Thomson Reuters.

Collier, R. (2010) 'Fatherhood, law and fathers' rights: rethinking the relationship between gender and welfare', in J. Wallbank, S. Choudry and J. Herring (eds) *Rights, gender and family law*, Abingdon: Routledge, pp 119-43.

Collier, R. and Sheldon, S. (2006) 'Fathers' rights, fatherhood and law reform: international perspectives', in R. Collier and S. Sheldon (eds) *Fathers' rights activism and law reform in comparative perspective*, Oxford and Portland, OR: Hart Publishing, pp 1-26.

Collier, R. and Sheldon, S. (2008) *Fragmenting fatherhood: A socio-legal study*, Oxford and Portland, OR: Hart Publishing.

Danielsen, S. (2003) *Nordisk børneret II. Forældreansvar: Et sammenlignende studie af dansk, finsk, islandsk, norsk og svensk ret med drøftelser af harmoniseringsmuligheder og reformbehov* [*Nordic Child Law II. Parental responsibility: A comparative study of Danish, Finnish, Icelandic, Norwegian and Swedish law with a focus on harmonising and change*], Nord 2003:4, Copenhagen: Nordisk Ministerråd.

Dey, I. and Wasoff, F. (2006) 'Mixed messages: parental responsibilities, public opinion and the reforms of family law', *International Journal of the Jurisprudence of the Family*, vol 20, no 2, p 225.

Dowd, N.E. (2000) *Redefining fatherhood*, New York: New York University Press.

Eekelaar, J. (2010) 'Evaluating legal regulation of family behaviour', *International Journal of the Jurisprudence of the Family*, vol 17, no 1, pp 17-34.

Eriksson, A. and Saldeen, Å. (1993) 'Parenthood and science: establishing and contesting parentage', in J. Eekelaar and P. Šarčević (eds) *Parenthood in modern society*, Dordrecht: Martinus Nijhoff, pp 75-92.

Eydal, G.B. and Friðriksdóttir, H. (2010) 'Framfærsluskyldur foreldra. Meðlagskerfi Norðurlanda ['Parental duties to provide: advanced maintenance in Nordic countries'], in H.S. Guðmundsson (ed) Þjóðarspegill: Rannsóknir í Félagsvísindum IX (http://skemman. is/item/view/1946/6708).

Eydal, G.B. and Friðriksdóttir, H. (2012) 'Child maintenance policies in Iceland: caring mothers and breadwinning fathers?', *European Journal of Social Security*, vol 14 pp 267-85.

Eydal, G.B. and Rostgaard, T. (2011) 'Towards a Nordic childcare policy – the political processes and agendas', in G.B. Eydal and I. Gíslason (eds) *Parental leave, childcare and gender equality in the Nordic countries*, Copenhagen: Nordic Council of Ministers, pp 147-70.

Fineman, M. (1992) 'Legal stories, change and incentives: reinforcing the law of the father', *New York Law School Law Review*, vol 37, p 227.

Fineman, M. (1995) *The neutered mother: The sexual family and other twentieth century tragedies*, New York: Routledge.

Freeman, M. (2008) 'The right to responsible parents', in J. Bridgeman, H. Keating and C. Lind (eds) *Responsibility, law and the family*, Aldershot: Ashgate, pp 21-40.

Freud, A. and Solnit, A.J. (1979) *Beyond the best interests of the child* (2nd edn), New York: The Free Press.

Friðriksdóttir, H. (1996) 'The Nordic gay and lesbian "marriage": no children allowed', LLM thesis, Harvard Law School.

Friðriksdóttir, H. (2003) 'Leyfilegar og óleyfilegar fjölskyldur: Mannréttindi og lagaleg staða samkynhneigðra fjölskyldna' ['Right and wrong families: human rights and the legal status of gay and lesbian families'], in R. Traustadóttir and Þ. Kristinsson (eds) *Samkynhneigðir og fjölskyldulíf* [*Homosexuals and family life*], Reykjavík: Háskólaútgáfan, pp 47-74.

Friðriksdóttir, H. (2010) 'Ein hjúskaparlög fyrir alla' ['Marriage laws for all'], in Þ. Líndal (ed) *Heiðursrit. Ármann Snævarr 1919-2010* [*In memorium Ármann Snævarr 1919-2010*], Reykjavík: Codex; Rannsóknarstofnun Ármanns Snævarr um fjölskyldumálefni, pp 233-58.

Friðriksdóttir, H. (2011) 'Heimild dómara til að dæma sameiginlega forsjá' ['Court-ordered joint parental responsibility'], *Tímarit lögfræðinga*, vol 61, no 3, pp 273-326.

Friðriksdóttir, H. (2012) 'Munur á hjúskap og sambúð' ['Difference between marriage and cohabitation'], *Úlfljótur*, vol 65, no 2, pp 149-90.

Gilmore, S. (2006) 'Contact/shared residence and child well-being: research evidence and its implications for legal decision-making', *International Journal of the Jurisprudence of the Family*, vol 20, no 3, p 344.

Harris-Short, S. (2010) 'Resisting the march towards 50/50 shared residence: rights, welfare and equality in post-separation families', *Journal of Social Welfare and Family Law*, vol 32, no 3, pp 257-74.

Haugli, T. (2008) 'Er barnet i fokus?' ['Is the child in focus?'], *Tidsskrift for Familieret, arverett og barnevernrettslige spørsmål (FAB)*, vol 6, no 3, pp 156-72.

Herring, J. (2009) *Family law* (4th edn), Harlow: Pearson.

Hodgkin, R. and Newell, P. (2007) *Implementation handbook for the Convention on the Rights of the Child*, Geneva: UNICEF.

Kangas, U. (2010) 'Réttarreglur um sambúð í Finnlandi' ['Cohabitation law in Finland'], in Þ. Líndal (ed) *Heiðursrit: Ármann Snævarr 1919–2010* [*In memorium Ármann Snævarr 1919-2010*], Reykjavík: Codex, Rannsóknarstofnun Ármanns Snævarr um fjölskyldumálefni, pp 259-79.

Kurki-Suonio, K. (2000) 'Joint custody as an interpretation of the best interests of the child in critical and comparative perspective', *International Journal of the Jurisprudence of the Family*, vol 14, no 3, pp 183-205.

Lamb, M.E. (2010) 'How do fathers influence children's development? Let me count the ways', in M.E. Lamb (ed) *The role of the father in child development* (5th edn), Hoboken, NJ: John Wiley, pp 1-26.

Lamb, M.E. and Tamis-Lemonda, C.S. (2004) 'The role of the father', in M. Lamb (ed) *The role of the father in child development* (4th edn), Hoboken, NJ: John Wiley, pp 1-31.

Law, S. (1998) 'Homosexuality and the social meaning of gender', *Wisconsin Law Review*, p 187.

Lind, C. and Hewitt, T. (2009) 'Law and the complexities of parenting: parental status and parental function', *Journal of Social Welfare and Family Law*, vol 31 no 4, pp 391-406.

Lørdrup, P. (2003) 'Farskap og morskap' ['Paternity and maternity'], in P. Lørdrup, A. Agell and A. Singer (eds) *Nordisk børneret I: Farskap, morskap og underhåll till barn. Et sammenlignende studie af dansk, finsk, islandsk, norsk og svensk ret med drøftelser af harmoniseringsmuligheder og reformbehov* [*Nordic Child Law I: Paternity, maternity and child maintenance. A comparative study of Danish, Finnish, Icelandic, Norwegian and Swedish law with a focus on harmonising and change*], Nord 2003:4, Copenhagen: Nordisk Ministerråd, pp 21-210.

Lørdrup, P. and Asland, J. (2012) *Arverett* [*Inheritance law*], Oslo: Gyldendal.

Lovforslag 157, 2011/1 *Forslag til lov om ændring af forældreansvarsloven m v, 2011/1 LF 157* [*Danish Bill for amendment to law on parental responsibility*].

Ludvigsen, S. (2005) 'Åpning av seminaret ved Nordisk samarbeidsminister' ['Opening of a Nordic seminar'], TemaNord 2005:581, Nordisk seminar om barnerett [Nordic seminar on child law], Copenhagen.

Lund-Andersen, I. (2003) 'The Danish Registered Partnership Act', in K. Boele-Woelki and A. Fuchs (eds) *Legal recognition of same-sex couples in Europe*, Antwerp, Oxford and New York: Intersentia, pp 13-23.

Lund-Andersen, I. and Nørgaard, I. (2012) *Familieret* [*Family law*], Copenhagen: DJØF Publishing.

Masardo, A. (2011) 'Negotiating shared residence: the experience of separated fathers in Britain and France', in J. Bridgeman, H. Keating and C. Lind (eds) *Regulating family responsibilities*, Farnham: Ashgate, pp 119-36.

Newnham, A. (2011) 'Law's gendered understandings of parents' responsibilities in relation to shared residence', in J. Bridgeman, H. Keating and C. Lind (eds) *Regulating family responsibilities*, Farnham: Ashgate, pp 137-52.

NOU (Norges Offentlige Utredninger [Norwegian Official Report]) (2008:9) *Med barnet i fokus – En gjennomgang av barnelovens regler om foreldreansvar, bosted og samvær* [*The child in focus – An overview of the Act in respect of children regarding rules on parental responsibility, residency and visiting rights*], Oslo: Barne- og likestillingsdepartementet.

NOU (2009:5) *Farskap og annen morskap* [*Paternity and maternity*], Oslo: Barne- og likestillingsdepartementet.

NOU (2014:1) *Ny arvelov* [*New law on inheritance*], Oslo: Justis- and beredskapsdepartementet.

Ot prp (Odelsetingsproposisjon) 103, 2004/2005, *Om lov om endringer i barnelova m v.* [*Norwegian bill for amendments to the Child Act*].

Ot prp 104, 2008/09, *Om lov om endringer i barnelova m v.* [*Norwegian bill for amendments to the Child Act*].

Ottesen, M.H. and Stage, S. (2011) *Dom til fælles forældremyndighed: En evaluering af forældreansvarsloven* [*Court-ordered joint parental responsibility: Evaluation of the new law*], Copenhagen: The Danish National Centre for Social Research.

Proposition 2005/06:99, *Nya vårdnadsregler* [Swedish Bill, *New rules on custody*].

Rehof, L.A. (1993) *Guide to the Travaux Préparatoires of the United Nations Convention on the Elimination of All Forms of Discrimination against Women*, Dordrecht: Martinus Nijhoff.

Scherpe, J.M. (2007) 'The Nordic countries in the vanguard of European family law', *Scandinavian Studies in Law*, vol 50, no 1, pp 265-88.

Schiratzki, J. (2007) 'Gender in court – in the best interests of the child?', *Scandinavian Studies in Law*, vol 50, no 2, pp 477-94.

Schwenzer, I. (2007) 'Tensions between legal, biological and social conceptions of parentage', *Electronic Journal of Comparative Law*, vol 11, no 1, p 3 (www.ejcl.org).

Singer, A. (2008) 'Active parenting or Solomon's justice? Alternating residence in Sweden for children with separated parents', *Utrecht Law Review*, vol 4 no 2, pp 35-47.

Sjösten, M. (2009) *Vårdnad, boende och omgänge* (3rd edn) [*Parental responsibility, residence and contact*], Stockholm: Norstedts Juridik.

Skinner, C. and Davidson, J. (2009) 'Recent trends in child maintenance schemes in 14 countries', *International Journal of Law, Policy and the Family*, vol 23, no 1, pp 25-52.

Snævarr, Á. (2008) *Hjúskapar- og sambúðarréttur* [*Marriage and cohabitation law*], Reykjavík: Bókaútgáfan Codex.

Svenson, E. and Pylkkänen, A. (2004) 'Contemporary challenges in Nordic feminist legal studies', in E.-M. Svenson and A. Pu (eds) *Nordic equality at a crossroads: Feminist legal studies coping with difference*, Aldershot: Ashgate, pp 17-46.

Sverdrup, T. (2012) 'Norway: equal rights at any cost?', in E.E. Sutherland (ed) *Future of child and family law: International predictions*, Cambridge: Cambridge University Press, pp 296-329.

Therborn, G. (1993) 'The politics of childhood: the rights of children in modern times', in F.G. Castles (eds) *Families and nations: Patterns of public policy in Western democracies*, Aldershot: Dartmouth, pp 241-91.

Twine, F.W. (2011) *Outsourcing the womb: Race, class and gestational surrogacy in a global market*, New York: Routledge.

Wallbank, J. (2010) '(En)gendering the fusion of rights and responsibilities in the law of contact', in J. Wallbank, S. Choudrey and J. Herring (eds) *Rights, gender and family law*, Abingdon: Routledge, pp 93-118.

Wetterberg, C.C. and Melby, K. (2009) 'The claim of economic citizenship: the concept of equality in a historical context', in K. Melby, A.-B. Ravn and C.C. Wetterberg (eds) *Gender equality and welfare politics in Scandinavia*, Bristol: Policy Press, pp 43-62.

FOUR

Fathers' rights to family cash benefits in Nordic countries

*Mia Hakovirta, Anita Haataja, Guðný Björk Eydal
and Tine Rostgaard*

Introduction

All five Nordic countries have developed from a 'male breadwinner' model of the welfare state, in which the idea of the family celebrates marriage and a strict division of labour between father and mother, towards an 'individual' model whereby each spouse is individually responsible for their own maintenance, and fathers and mothers share the burden of financially supporting and caring for their children (Millar and Warman, 1996; Sainsbury, 1996). In the literature, the Nordic version of the individual model is often referred to as the dual earner/dual carer model (Mahon, 2002; Leira, 2006), and thus at the end of the continuum of models of gendered division of labour, described by Crompton (1999), running from a traditional male breadwinner/female carer to an idealised dual earner/dual carer society. In the dual earner/dual carer model, the explicit policy goal is to promote gender equality, the equal sharing of the responsibility of care for children and paid work among men and women. Thus, the contemporary Nordic welfare systems have developed policies to enable mothers to work and fathers to care and, for the most part, have abolished entitlements to breadwinner supplements in the form of cash benefits and tax deductions, emphasising individual entitlements (Jepsen et al, 1997).

Despite the fact that the development from the male breadwinner model towards the dual earner/dual carer model has been well accounted for in the welfare literature, few studies have focused on the development of fiscal and cash family benefits available for fathers, and how the welfare state has contributed to the shaping of fatherhood in that respect (for exceptions, see Hobson, 2002; Oláh et al, 2002; Haataja and Nyberg, 2006). This chapter thus examines the rights of fathers in Nordic countries to welfare cash transfers, including child benefit, child maintenance, paid parental leave and tax benefits for parents, here referred to overall as 'family benefits'. The chapter examines if the rights of fathers to these family benefits are in accordance with the dual earner/dual carer model, whether or not both parents have the same rights, and if not, if rights are associated with parental gender. The chapter studies the rights of fathers residing with their children and their spouse/partner as well as fathers who do not reside with their children. Sainsbury's (1996) analytical models of breadwinner versus individual are applied, shedding light on the extent to which the family benefit schemes in all five Nordic countries reflect the individual model of policy formation for fathers. Questions are raised as to whether fathers in general are regarded as individuals with the same entitlements as mothers, or if their rights are subject to conditions – for example, that they must share residency or custody with the mother in order to be entitled to benefits.

This chapter hence provides a picture of how policies on family benefits contribute to the construction of fatherhood in the Nordic region. There is a focus on the general cash transfers and fiscal welfare for parents, meaning that benefit schemes for families that have either social or health problems are excluded. The chapter opens with a discussion of joint and separate taxation before proceeding to address a father's rights to child benefits, paid parental leave and cash transfers for separated fathers. The policy analysis is based on secondary literature, primary data (policy documents, law texts and protocols) and national statistics. Furthermore, in order to compare family benefits between countries, model family calculations are carried out using simple fictive family types to describe how payments to fathers and mothers compare in each country and between the countries in two different situations: when parents live together and when they live apart. The calculations provide the opportunity to compare how sensitive the systems are to acknowledge the rights of both parents. The results show that only in Sweden, and to some extent in Norway, do the policies on cash family benefits provide the same rights for both parents independently of their family type. In the other Nordic countries – Denmark, Finland and Iceland – the policies support residential parents to a greater degree.

Fatherhood and family policies

Family policies, defined as family law, social services and systems of economic transfers (Wennemo, 1994) in the Nordic region, are based on the dual earner/dual carer model that challenges gendered parental practices and presumes an egalitarian partnership between mothers and fathers (Leira, 2006). The growing interest in fathers as their children's caregivers and the initiatives supporting this trend can be seen in a number of different ways. There is growing individualisation, where society's support is doled out to individuals instead of families. Historically, by the 1920s, Nordic family law was already emphasising the equal rights and duties of both parents as individuals; thus both parents should be able to provide and care for their children (Therborn, 1993; see also Chapter Three, this volume). Despite this clear emphasis on the individual model in family law, both parental practices and other family policies in the Nordic region remained more in line with the breadwinner model until the 1960-70s, when the policies were gradually changed in order to enable parents to share in both caring and providing for their children. In particular, recent changes in family law have affected the legal duties of parents after separation (see Chapter Three, this volume), and joint legal custody has become the most common arrangement in the case of divorce or separation in all of the Nordic countries (Eydal and Kröger, 2010). Furthermore, all of the Nordic countries have introduced reforms to parental leave, including the allocation of some parental leave to the father and increasing the flexibility of the schemes whereby parents can take parental leave and share it between them (Duvander and Lammi-Taskula, 2011). Clear effort has been made towards strengthening fathers' rights and responsibilities as regards care for children, and to encourage fathers to invest more time together with their children. The importance of this legislation for fathers is discussed at length in Chapters Six, Seven, Thirteen, Fourteen, Fifteen and Sixteen (all in this volume).

The sphere in which fathers' individual rights acquire very concrete meaning is family benefits. A recent study by Hakovirta and Rantalaiho (2011) on parental responsibilities for supporting a child when parents do not live together reveals the variations in the logic of the respective Nordic family policies. In Norway and Sweden, it is possible for parents to share benefits in a manner that supports the child to be able to live in the homes of both parents. According to the study in Finland, however, the situation of parents living apart but sharing in the daily care for their child has received insufficient attention. Thus, these results indicate that there are differences regarding how the Nordic countries support fathers, and point out the importance of the further investigation of the rights of fathers to family benefits. The extent to which policies on family benefits have followed the developments in family and gender equality law towards a dual earner/dual carer model is discussed further in the next section.

Breadwinners, taxation and child benefits

Tax systems were among the first public instruments used to support families with dependent children (O'Donoghue and Sutherland, 1998; Montanari, 2000). Earlier systems of joint taxation – where family members were counted as a single tax unit, and all income was taxed as the husband's income – supported the single breadwinner family policy – the father was assumed to be the breadwinner. The tax systems included characteristics such as 'marriage subsidies' and tax deductions for dependent children (Montanari, 2000). Separate taxation gradually became justified on the grounds that mothers had already entered or were encouraged to enter the labour market. Thus, the breadwinner model was gradually replaced in the Nordic region by the individual model, as shown in Table 4.1, where mothers and fathers were taxed as individuals and child benefit systems generally replaced the tax deductions for children (Lindencrona and Zimmer, 1988; Sainsbury, 1996; Eydal, 2005).[1] In this sense, the family policies have gradually come to reflect that the father is no longer the sole breadwinner in the family, whereas universal child benefits confirm that the state has assumed some of the responsibility for providing for children, which also entails some measure of relief for the dual breadwinners.

Table 4.1: Year of individual taxation, tax deductions for children and child benefits in Nordic countries, 1943–93

Country	Individual taxation	Child-related tax deductions	Child benefits
Denmark	1970 (earned income) 1983	Until 1987	1972* 1964 (universal, paid directly to mother) 1961 (universal, as tax deduction) 1951 (to low income families only)
Finland	1935–43 (earned income) 1976	Until 1993	1948
Iceland	1958* 1978	Until 1975	1946 Also means-tested benefits from 1984
Norway	1959 (optional)		1969
Sweden	1971	Until 1947	1947

Note: *Only individual taxation in theory; in practice, most couples choose joint taxation due to the 50% tax deduction for all income of married/cohabiting women.

Source: Wennemo, 1994; Eydal, 2005; Ravn, 2008; MISSOC database 2012.

Despite this departure from the breadwinner model, traces can still be observed when examining the allocation of child benefits, as illustrated in Table 4.2. Originally, child benefits were only paid to mothers (Wennemo, 1994). This historical legacy from the earlier breadwinner model is still apparent in both Denmark and Sweden in the case of parents sharing residency, since the benefits are still paid out to the mother (although it is possible to request payments to be made to either parent). In Finland and Norway, parents must decide who should receive the payments. Iceland is the only country that splits the amount equally between the parents, except in the case of a lone parent when the residential parent receives the full amount. Thus, Iceland is the only country that allocates the benefits in accordance with the individual model, assuming both parents are sharing the breadwinner role.

In Finland, Denmark and Iceland, if parents do not share a household, the child must have their legal residence with one of their parents, and child benefit is paid to the residential parent. In most cases, children have legal residence with their mother after divorce or separation (Hiilamo, 2009; Eydal and Kröger, 2010), meaning that fathers are not paid child benefit regardless of how much time the child spends living with them. Norway and Sweden have adopted different strategies. In Sweden, the Social Insurance Agency is able to split the child benefit into two and pay both parents. In order to do this, the parents must have joint custody, the child must spend equal time with both parents, and the parents must agree to share the child benefit (Swedish Social Insurance Agency, 2009). In Norway, it is also possible to split the child benefit. The preconditions for doing so are that the parents have an official joint custody agreement and can prove that they share equally in the care of their child, that is, that the

Table 4.2: Allocation of the child benefits to mother and father in different family situations, Nordic countries, 2012

Country	Recipient of child benefit if parents live in same household	Recipient of child benefit if parents do not live in the same household
Denmark	Mother, if not a special request to pay to both parents (1987)	Paid to the parent with whom the child has legal residency
Finland	Mother or father (since 1991)	Paid to the parent with whom the child has legal residency
Iceland	Divided equally between parents (50/50) (since 1978)	Paid to the parent with whom the child has legal residency
Norway	Mother or father	Parents can ask for allocation to both parents.
Sweden	Mother, if not a special request to pay to both parents	Parents can ask for allocation to both parents

Source: MISSOC database 2012; Hakovirta and Rantalaiho, 2011.

child spends at least 40 per cent of the time with the other parent. A child benefit increase for lone parents applies to parents practising shared residence arrangements. Both parents then have a right to half of the full lone parent allowance. The conditions for receiving the allowance are controlled separately for each parent, that is, depending on the household status of the parent, and one of the parents can receive half of the full allowance, while the other parent can be left without (NOU, 2008:9, p 93). It seems as though there are clear differences between the Nordic countries in this respect. Both Norway and Sweden have recognised the rights of fathers in the child benefit system and in the case of shared residence, while Denmark, Finland and Iceland do not consider non-residential parents – usually the father – as candidates for family benefits, regardless of how much time the child might spend with the parent in question. This demonstrates how the breadwinner model ideal continues to dominate the policies in these countries; as already outlined, the fathers are enabled to care for their child through changes in both family law and paid parental law, but at the same time, they are assumed to provide financially for their children without the same state support that the residential parent (usually the mother) enjoys.

Fathers' rights to paid paternity and parental leave

As the literature has established, all of the Nordic countries offer relatively long and substantially compensated parental leave schemes that support parental care of the child (Duvander and Lammi-Taskula, 2011). Fathers have the right to paid paternity leave after the birth of their child in all of the Nordic countries except Iceland, where they are entitled to a three-month father's quota, and following this, also to parental leave. In four of the five countries, they are also entitled to a father's quota, an individual entitlement to a number of weeks of parental leave, which cannot in principle be transferred to the mother and is based on a 'use-it-or-lose-it' principle (see also Chapters Six, Thirteen, Fourteen, Fifteen and Sixteen, this volume). As Table 4.3 shows, however, fathers only have the right to the same quota of parental leave as mothers in Iceland, Norway and Sweden, whereas married and cohabiting fathers are entitled to fewer weeks of paid parental leave than mothers in Denmark and Finland (Rostgaard, 2002: Duvander and Lammi-Taskula, 2011).

Table 4.3: Paid leave in Nordic countries, weeks of entitlements, 1 July 2013

	Denmark	Finland	Iceland	Norway	Sweden
Total weeks	50–64	44	39	47–57	69
– only mother (maternity leave)	18	18	13	14	8
– father with mother (paternity leave after child birth)	2	(3)*	0	2	2
– only father (father's quota in parental leave)	0	9	13	14	8
– father or mother, fully shareable parental leave	32	24	13	36	60

Note: * Fathers can opt to take three of the nine total weeks after the birth of their child.
Source: Nordic Statistical Yearbook, 2011; KELA, 2013; NAV, 2013.

In some of the countries, the father's right to paternity leave and the father's quota depends on who holds custody of the child and/or living arrangements. In most cases, this excludes non-resident fathers from taking paid parental leave, as seen in Table 4.4 (Duvander and

Table 4.4: Eligibility of Nordic fathers for paid parental leave

	Denmark	Finland	Iceland	Norway	Sweden
Paternity leave	Must share residency with child	Must be married or co-habiting with the mother and share residency with child	NA	Custodial fathers	Custodial fathers
Fathers quota	NA	Must be married/ cohabiting with the mother and share residency with the child	All fathers entitled – non-transferable rights Fathers need to be in an agreement with mother/other parent about the time spent with the child (visiting rights)	Custodial fathers (transferable to lone mothers)	Custodial fathers (transferable to lone mothers)
Parental leave	Must share residency with the child	Must be married/ cohabiting with the mother and share residency with the child	All fathers entitled	Custodial fathers	Custodial fathers

Sources: Duvander and Lammi-Taskula, 2011; *Lög um fæðingar- og foreldraorlof* [Act on paid and unpaid parental leave], no. 95/2000; NAV, nd).

Lammi-Taskula, 2011; Hakovirta and Rantalaiho, 2011). In Iceland, however, all fathers – regardless of their family and living situation – are entitled to paid parental leave, but parents who do not hold custody must reach agreement with the custodial parent in order to spend their leave with the child (*Lög um fæðingar- og foreldraorlof* [Act on paid and unpaid parental leave] no 95/2000). In the other countries, entitlements are aimed at fathers who hold custody alone or who share residency with the child.

The Finnish and Danish parental leave systems only give rights to parents who are living in the same household with the child. In Norway and Sweden, all parents who share the custody of the child can share the rights, and custodial fathers also have rights to paternity leave and the father's quota, but the quota can, in this case, be transferred to mothers. In these latter countries, the determinant is not whether the parents live together, but that they share the custody of the child. Parental leave schemes in Norway and Sweden therefore support shared parenting to some extent, even when parents do not live together as a couple. In Iceland, all fathers, regardless of custody or residential arrangement, are entitled to paid parental leave; thus, the Icelandic legislation best ensures the child's right to care from both of their parents as well as the equal opportunities of both parents to care for the child. Hence, the Nordic countries provide very different opportunities for lone fathers to care for their young children.

Fathers and child maintenance

In the Nordic context, social transfer programmes targeting lone mothers were developed during the 1940s and 1950s when divorce proceedings usually granted the sole legal custody of children to mothers, and lone fathers were legally obliged to pay child maintenance (Bergman and Hobson, 2002). Lone fathers were also gradually provided with the same legal entitlements to child maintenance as the lone mothers. After the legislative changes towards joint custody, it has become more common for the child to spend time with both parents (see also Chapters Three and Twelve, this volume). The joint custody arrangements, whereby parents do not live together but take an active part in the everyday life of their child and equal care for the needs of the child, create pressure for change in the organisation of child maintenance. Shared residence (or very broad visitation rights) raise the question of whether the parent with whom the child spends a lot of time should be obliged to pay child maintenance. In order to ensure the possibilities of both parents being able to care for the child, some of the Nordic countries have therefore recently made changes to policies regarding the maintenance duties of the non-residential parent. Sweden and Norway have thus reorganised their child maintenance systems in order to emphasise that 'fathers should not be socially excluded from families because of high child maintenance payments' (Bergman and Hobson, 2002, p 119). One effect of such policies is that a parent's maintenance payments can be reduced on account of visitation with the child in all Nordic countries, except Iceland.

Table 4.5 provides an overview of the legal rights to child maintenance, that is, if one parent has to pay maintenance to the other, if a lone parent is eligible for a special tax credit/allowance due to the child maintenance payments, and finally, if there is an advanced child maintenance scheme whereby the state guarantees the payment of the child maintenance.

Either parent, with whom the child is not living permanently, can be ordered to pay child maintenance, but this would be the father in most cases, since it is still only one or two of every 10 children living with lone parents who share residency with their fathers (17.6 per cent in Denmark, 13.5 per cent in Finland, 8.6 per cent in Iceland, 19.2 per cent in Norway and 22.4 per cent in Sweden) (NOSOSCO, 2012). In Denmark, Finland, Norway and Sweden, the capacity of the parents to pay child maintenance depends on the income(s) of the liable parent. Moreover, the time the child spends with the non-resident parent is also taken into account when determining the amount of child maintenance (Skinner et al, 2007, 2012; Skinner and Davidson, 2009; Hakovirta and Hiilamo, 2012). In the case of Iceland, however, there is a minimum child maintenance that all non-resident parents must pay, regardless of their child's situation (Eydal and Friðriksdóttir, 2010, 2012). In all of the compared countries, with the exception of Iceland, parents can agree between themselves on the amount of child maintenance provided, but none of them allow a parent to withdraw from their obligation to provide maintenance. The authorities are responsible for ensuring that the sum is not exorbitant, and that in cases of dispute, the judicial authority can confirm this amount.

In Finland, broad visitation rights do not necessarily result in the waiving of child maintenance. A parent's obligation to pay can be based on the fact that the other parent incurs constant daycare expenses, which are unrelated to the extent of visitation rights (Gottberg, 1997, p 58). Legal rulings also vary. In one case, the Finnish Supreme Court ruled that when a child spends half of their time with one parent, who pays the child's daily living costs, there is no requirement to pay child maintenance. In other cases, financial maintenance has been ordered

Table 4.5: Child maintenance and advanced child maintenance in Nordic countries, 2012

	Child maintenance-requirements	Tax credit/allowance for the parent that pays child maintenance	Child maintenance (Advanced maintenance)
Finland	Capacity of the parents to pay depends on the income(s) of the liable parent. Dual residence/wide visitation rights do not necessarily result in a situation in which a parent is not ordered to pay child maintenance; legal practices vary	Tax credit for parent who pays child maintenance	Paid to residential parent
Norway	Emphasis on residence arrangement and each parents' finances; dual residence/wide visitation rights do not automatically result in a situation where a parent is not ordered to pay child maintenance	NA	Means-tested; can be shared and paid to both parents
Sweden	Capacity of the parents to pay depends on the income(s) of the liable parent. Child maintenance not required from other parent under dual residence	NA	Means-tested; can be shared and paid to both parents
Denmark	Capacity of the parents to pay depends on the income(s) of the liable parent. Child maintenance not required from other parent under dual residence	Child maintenance payments can be deducted totally from payers' taxable income (non-taxable income to the recipient to certain limit)	Special Child Allowance (if there is no maintenance from one of the parents)
Iceland	The parent that does not share legal residency with the child is legally obligated to pay a minimum child maintenance, regardless of the number of days of visitation and other circumstances	NA	A flat rate benefit, same amount as child pension paid to pensioners, all parents that wish can receive advanced maintenance from the Social Security

Sources: Skinner et al, 2007; Eydal and Friðriksdóttir, 2010; Hakovirta and Rantalaiho, 2011; Eydal and Friðriksdóttir, 2012; Hakovirta and Hiilamo, 2012; Hakovirta et al, 2013.

even where the visitation rights are so broad that a child has spent almost half of the time with the other parent (Litmala, 2002, pp 190-1). However, parents who pay child maintenance are rewarded with a modest tax credit.

In Iceland, the parent who does not share legal residency with the child, usually the father, must pay child maintenance. The parents must sign a contract about the child maintenance, which must be ratified by the district magistrate. There is a minimum maintenance amount. If the parents fail to reach an agreement about the maintenance payments, the residential parent can request a verdict on an additional maintenance payment from the non-residential parent from the district magistrate. The district magistrate is supposed to evaluate the circumstances of both parents, but usually it is first and foremost the income of the non-residential parent (usually the father) that is taken into consideration (Eydal and Friðriksdóttir, 2010, 2012).

In Norway, the child's need for maintenance and the maintenance capacity of both parents determines the level of child maintenance. The amount of time the child spends with each parent is also taken into account when determining the maintenance responsibility of the parents. In Norway, the shared residence agreement does not therefore automatically lead to a situation in which a parent is exempt from child maintenance; if they are better paid, however, child maintenance may be required (Hakovirta et al, 2013).

In Denmark, if the children have a dual residence, for example, one week with each parent, and if the parents have joint custody, each parent is considered to be doing their part and no maintenance obligation will be set for either (Skinner et al, 2007; Hakovirta et al, 2013). Furthermore, Denmark is the only country in which child maintenance payments can be deducted entirely from taxable income. In Sweden, child maintenance payment is not required if the child spends equal time with both parents (Hiilamo, 2009).

All of the countries also have an advanced maintenance system in place through which the state guarantees that a lone parent receives minimum financial maintenance for their child when: (1) the parent obliged to pay child maintenance neglects to pay it; (2) the maintenance payment is too low because of the capacity to pay on the part of the liable parent; or (3) no one is liable for the provision of maintenance (Skinner and Davidson, 2009). The advanced maintenance system also varies on other issues, and the most substantive difference relates to the fact that, in both Sweden and Norway, advanced maintenance can be paid in certain situations to both parents when a shared residence arrangement is in place, whereas Finland, Denmark and Iceland have no corresponding arrangement (Eydal and Friðriksdóttir, 2010; Hakovirta et al, 2013).

In Norway and Sweden, the child maintenance system is designed to support parents to reach the optimal solution for their child's care and housing. The reason given has been that the system should not lead parents to make an agreement in which the child lives almost exclusively with one parent. The other Nordic countries do not pay the same attention to the rights of the non-resident parents and shared parenthood and shared residence as a solution that should be given particular consideration in regards to child support. Thus, the child maintenance policies in Denmark, Finland and Iceland are still based on the breadwinner ideology – the non-residential parent is first and foremost regarded as the parent who is providing (the breadwinner) despite that fact that changes to family law have paved the way for lone fathers sharing in the care for their children. This indicates that the child maintenance systems have not developed towards the dual earner/dual carer ideology at the same speed as family law.

Model families and family benefits to fathers and mothers

This chapter has outlined the policies of family benefits and how the Nordic countries have taken somewhat different paths, which has resulted in the very different design of entitlements of fathers to cash family benefits. In order to test the outcomes of the family benefit systems of the five countries, model family calculations were carried out. According to Bradshaw (2006, pp 69-70), 'the model family method is an attempt to compare social policies on systematic basis. The procedure is to identify a specific range of model families and to calculate what cash benefits, tax benefits and subsidies they would obtain given the rules in force at a particular time.' The models are based on two different family situations: (1) when the parents live together and (2) when the parents have separated or never been married or lived together. The model family method represents an attempt at making comparison of the tax/benefit package controlling the variation, and is based on a set of matrices, informed by authors and national informants.[2] The calculations are based on fictive family types consisting of an employed mother and father who earn the average wage in the respective country (both parents having the same wage) and having two children aged two and seven (see the Appendix at the end of this chapter). The family benefits, wage levels and taxation are based on the policies in place as of 31 December 2011. Housing costs are set at 20 per cent of average earnings.[3] The exercise aims to provide us with the opportunity to compare the sensitivity of the systems in acknowledging the rights of both parents. Average gross wages are first presented in the national currency. These wages are then transformed so that all gross wages have equal a fictive value = '1,000'. Other incomes, taxes and housing costs are then adjusted relative to this same value. The results thus demonstrate the relative values of other incomes, taxes and housing costs. These fictive incomes provide a comparative view into each relative income step of the parents between the countries, but no comparable information about the income levels or how representative average model family types are.

The calculations demonstrate that Sweden is the only country in which the level of the family benefits does not depend on family type. The results indicate equal incomes after paid taxes and family benefits for fathers and mothers when living together and after separation, if having joint custody and the children are living 50/50 with their parents. When living in separate households with lower earnings, parents might both receive a public maintenance allowance.

The situation in Norway resembles Sweden. According to the calculations, family benefits seem to provide more support for separated parents than parents living together, supporting lone parents via child benefits and tax deductions. In these cases, the father's total income does not change according to the living situation. However, it is possible for the parents to split the child benefit if living in separate households. In the model family, the lone mother is not entitled to a maintenance allowance, because it is means-tested and the incomes are too high. The calculations also assume that parents share the care of children equally, and that non-resident fathers do not need to pay child maintenance.

In the other Nordic countries – Finland, Denmark and Iceland – the mother's income after taxes and benefits increases when parents separate because mothers receive child maintenance paid by the father when the child and mother share the same address. Consequently, the father's income decreases. This is different from Sweden and Norway, where fathers are not required to pay maintenance if parents have shared care. In Finland and Denmark, fathers receive a tax deduction if they pay child maintenance. In Finland, it is a maximum of €80 per child deducted from taxes, whereas child maintenance payments can be deducted from the payer's taxable income in Denmark. Iceland has no tax deduction for non-resident fathers. Furthermore, lone mothers in Iceland are entitled to a tax-free child benefit, which is not the case when parents live together because the family income is too high. There is also a special taxable benefit for lone parents, called a mother/father wage, paid only to the residential parent, which makes the difference between the divorced parents even bigger.

In summary, the outcomes in terms of the amount of the cash family benefits differ, as do the policies. In Sweden, separation does not change the treatment of parents with average earnings. Fathers have the same right to family benefits regardless of whether they live together with the other parent or as a non-resident parent. In principle, the situation is the same in Norway, but child benefit is normally paid to either of the parents. The three other countries, Demark, Finland and Iceland, have a more traditional way of providing support for the residential parents, in this case, the lone mothers, even when parents share the custody and care of children. The result for these countries stands in clear contrast to the dual earner/dual carer model, and has obvious implications for the father's opportunities to provide for and care for his children. Providing a detailed examination of both the family benefit policies and the outcomes across different countries is important, as it helps expose the challenges faced by welfare states when dealing with widespread social changes in partnership formation and parenting practices.[4]

Conclusion

The aim of this chapter was to investigate fathers' rights to family benefits in the Nordic region as well as the outcomes of the various family policies, and if the rights of fathers are in accordance with the dual earner/dual carer model, which Nordic countries so often are described to represent. In these five countries, child benefit, child maintenance and paid parental leave resemble each other in their basic principles and structures, but fathers' rights and entitlements follow different logics across the countries.

All of the Nordic countries have more or less abandoned tax deductions for dependent children, and child benefits have become an important element in Nordic family policy in order to subsidise parents for the costs of having children. In this process, both Norway and Sweden have recognised the rights of fathers in the child benefit system, and parents can split the child benefit when parents live together and after separation. In Iceland, child benefits can be shared when both parents live together with the child; after divorce, however, the benefit is paid to the parent with whom the child has legal residency. In Finland and Denmark, each of the parents can receive child benefits if the parents agree and live together with their child.

After separation, child benefits are paid to the parent living with the child (usually the mother). This means that the child benefit systems are still more in line with the breadwinner model, that is, the mother automatically receives all of the child benefits.

All of the Nordic countries have made important changes to family law as well as legislation on paid parental leave in order to support the participation of fathers in care. However, fathers' entitlements to paid parental leave are very different among the Nordic countries. Equal rights for mothers and fathers only exist in Sweden and Iceland. Iceland is the only country that ensures the legal rights of all fathers to paid parental leave, regardless of their living/family arrangement. Furthermore, Sweden and Norway also offer these rights under certain conditions to fathers who do not share residency with their children. In Denmark and Finland, both parents must live in the same household in order for the fathers to be entitled to paid parental leave.

By applying model families, the family benefit system was put to the test, and the results show that, in the case of parents who are not living together, both Sweden and Norway have adapted the benefit systems to meet the special needs of families sharing care responsibilities, thus supporting caring fathers. This is not the case in Finland, Denmark or Iceland. In Sweden and Norway, it is increasingly the rule that parents can share child benefits, and the policies on child maintenance in these two countries also signal that the welfare state supports shared parenting as a normal family life model and the continued involvement of parents in their children's lives after separation or divorce. In summary, then, it would seem as though the family policies in Denmark, Finland and Iceland are supporting the residential parent more after separation, and family policies are generally less flexible than in the other Nordic countries, which is interesting in light of the fact that Iceland in particular has provided extensive rights for all fathers to paid parental leave. Thus, the results show that, in summary, Sweden provides the most convincing support for fathers by giving mothers and fathers equal rights to family benefit and paid parental leave, and applying a system of child maintenance that takes into account shared parenthood. There is no difference in financial compensation between parents who share residency and those who do not. Thus, the Swedish family policies seem to be most in line with the individual model supporting both parents to share care work and providing financially for their children. In the other Nordic countries, fathers do not have the same rights to family benefit support as mothers, because benefits are usually paid to the parent with whom the child resides. Thus, the policies are more in line with the breadwinner model. Here, it can be said that family policy does not (yet) support or promote shared parenting after separation or divorce. The model that has received the most support has been one parent, usually the mother, being responsible for the everyday care of the child or children on her own. Where they have featured in family policy, fathers have been seen as providers. Thus, despite the extensive policy changes in family law and paid parental leave in order to promote and support caring fathers, the results of this chapter indicate that policies regarding family benefits can still be improved in order to provide fathers with the same opportunities as mothers to care for their children.

Notes

[1] Here, the concept of 'child benefit' is used, but these benefits are sometimes referred to as 'family benefits'.

[2] We want to thank our national informants: Klas Lindström from Statistics Sweden, Tom Kornstad from Statistics Norway and Benedikte Salling Marstrand, from Aalborg University, Denmark.

[3] Bradshaw and Finch (2002) adopted the OECD method of taking rent as 20 per cent of average earnings. Thus, gross rent does not vary with the size of the dwelling or income, but is a consistent proportion of earnings in each country (for example, a couple with children, lone parent and single person have same amount of housing costs).

[4] See, for example, the Special Issue of the *European Journal of Social Security*, which focuses on child maintenance policies in five countries (Iceland, Finland, the Netherlands, the UK and the US). The results show that child maintenance schemes are diverse, and policy principles can contradict themselves within as well as between countries (Skinner et al, 2012).

References

Bergman, H. and Hobson, B. (2002) 'Compulsory fatherhood: the coding of fatherhood in the Swedish welfare state', in B. Hobson (ed) *Making men into fathers: Men, masculinities and the social politics of fatherhood*, Cambridge: Cambridge University Press, pp 92-124.

Bradshaw, J. and Finch, N. (2002) *A Comparison of Child Benefit Packages in 22 Countries*, Department for Work and Pensions Research Report, No 174, Corporate Document Services, Leeds.

Bradshaw, J. (2006) 'Child benefit package in 14 countries in 2004', in J. Lewis (ed) *Children, changing families and welfare states*, Cheltenham: Edward Elgar Publishing, pp 69-87.

Crompton, R. (1999) *Restructuring gender relations and employment: The decline of the male breadwinner*, Oxford: Oxford University Press.

Duvander, A. and Lammi-Taskula, J. (2011) 'Parental leave', in I. Gislason and G.B. Eydal (eds) *Parental leave, childcare and gender equality in the Nordic countries*, Copenhagen: Nordic Council of Ministers, pp 31-64.

Eydal, G.B. (2005) *Family policy in Iceland 1944-1984*, Gothenburg: Sociologiska Institutionen, Göteborgs University.

Eydal, G.B. and Friðriksdóttir, H. (2010) 'Framfærsluskyldur foreldra. Meðlagskerfi Norðurlanda' ['Parental duties to provide: Advanced maintenance in Nordic countries'], in H.S. Guðmundsson (ed) Þjóðarspegill- Rannsóknir í Félagsvísindum IX [*Social science research IX*], Reykjavík: Háskólaútgáfan (http://skemman.is/item/view/1946/6708).

Eydal, G.B. and Friðriksdóttir, H. (2012) 'Child maintenance policies in Iceland: caring mothers and breadwinning fathers', *European Journal of Social Security*, Special Issue on Child Maintenance, vol 14, no 4, pp 267-85.

Eydal, G.B. and Kröger, T. (2010) 'Nordic family policies: constructing contexts for social work with families', in H. Forsberg and T. Kröger (eds) *Social work and child welfare politics: Through Nordic lenses*, Bristol: Policy Press, pp 11-27.

Gottberg, E. (1997) *Perhe, elatus ja sosiaaliturva. Turun yliopiston oikeustieteellisen tiedekunnan julkaisuja* [*Family, maintenance and social security*], Turku: Turun yliopisto.

Haataja, A. and Nyberg, A. (2006) 'Diverging paths? The dual-earner/dual-career model in Finland and Sweden in the 1990s', in A. Leira and A.L. Ellingsæter (eds) *Politicising parenthood in Scandinavia: Gender relations in welfare states*, Bristol: Policy Press, pp 217-40.

Hakovirta, M. and Hiilamo, H. (2012) 'Children's rights and parents responsibilities: child maintenance policies in Finland', *European Journal of Social Security*, Special Issue on Child Maintenance, vol 14, no 4, pp 286-303.

Hakovirta, M. and Rantalaiho, M. (2011) 'Nordic family policy and shared parenthood', *European Journal of Social Security*, vol 13, no 2, pp 247-66.

Hakovirta, M., Kuivalainen, S. and Rantalaiho, M. (2013) 'Welfare state support of lone parents: Nordic approaches to a complex and ambiguous policy field', in R. Ulmestig and I. Harslof (eds) *Changing social risks and social policy adaptation in the Nordic welfare states*, Houndmills: Palgrave Macmillan, pp 50-73.

Hiilamo, H. (2009) 'Divergences in the Nordic model: economic consequences of partnership dissolution in Sweden and Finland', in H.J. Andress and D. Hummelsheim (eds) *When marriage ends: Economic and social economic consequences of partnership dissolution*, Cheltenham: Edward Elgar Publishing, pp 132-54.

Hobson, B. (2002) *Making men into fathers: Men, masculinities and the social politics of fatherhood*, Cambridge: Cambridge University Press.

Jepsen, M., Meulders, D., Plasman, O. and Vanhuynegem, P. (1997) *Individualisation of the social and fiscal rights and the equal opportunities between women and men*, ULB Institutional Repository, ULB – Universite Libre de Bruxelles (http://EconPapers.repec.org/RePEc:ulb:ulbeco:2013/8607).

KELA (2013) *Paternal leave* (www.kela.fi/web/en/paternal-leave).

Leira, A. (2006) 'Parenthood change and policy reform in Scandinavia, 1970s–2000s', in A.L. Ellingsæter and A. Leira (eds) *Politicising parenthood in Scandinavia: Gender relations in welfare states*, Bristol: Policy Press, pp 27-52.

Lindencrona, G. and Zimmer, F. (1988*) Nordisk Familie beskattning: Et komparativt studie [Taxation of families in Nordic countries: A comparative study]*, Stockholm: Forfatterne and Norsteds Förlag.

Litmala, M. (2002) *Lapsen asema erossa [Children and divorce]*, Helsinki: WSOY.

Mahon, R. (2002) 'Child care policy: toward what kind of "social Europe"?', *Social Politics,* vol 9, no 3, pp 343-79.

Millar, J. and Warman, A. (1996) *Family obligations in Europe*, London: Family Policy Studies Centre.

MISSOC (Mutual Information System on Social Protection) (2012) (http://ec.europa.eu/social/main.jsp?catId=815&langId=en).

Montanari, I. (2000) 'From family wage to marriage subsidy and child benefits: controversy and consensus in the development of family support', *Journal of European Social Policy*, vol 10, no 4, pp 307-33.

NAV (nd) *Bidragsforskudd [Advanced child maintenance]* (www.nav.no).

NAV (2013) *Parental leave on birth* (www.nav.no).

Nordic Statistical Yearbook 2011 (2011) Copenhagen: Nordic Council of Ministers (www.norden.org).

NOSOSCO Social tryhed I de nordicke lande 2010/11 [*Social security in the Nordic countries 2010/11*] (2012) Copenhagen: Nordic Council of Ministers.

NOU (Norges Offentlige Utredninger [Norwegian Official Report]) (2008:9) *Med barnet i fokus: En gjennomgang av barnelovens regler om foreldreansvar, bosted og samvær* [*The child in focus: An overview of the Act in respect of children regarding rules on parental responsibility, residency and visiting rights*], Oslo: Barne- og likestillingsdepartementet.

O'Donoghue, C. and Sutherland, H. (1998) *Accounting for the family: The treatment of marriage and children in European tax systems*, Occasional Papers, Economic and Policy Series EPS 65, UNICEF.

Oláh, L., Bernhardt, E. and Goldscheider, F. (2002) 'Co-residential parental roles in industrial countries: Sweden, Hungary and the United States', in B. Hobson (ed) *Making men into fathers: Men, masculinities and the social politics of fatherhood*, Cambridge: Cambridge University Press, pp 25-57.

Ravn, A.-B. (2008) 'Married women's right to pay taxes: debates on gender, economic citizenship and tax law reform in Denmark, 1945-83', in K. Melby, A.-B. Ravn and C.C. Wetterberg (eds) *Gender equality and welfare politics in Scandinavia: Limits of political ambition?*, Bristol: Policy Press, pp 63-83.

Rostgaard, T. (2002) 'Setting time aside for the father: father's leave in Scandinavia', *Community, Work and Family*, vol 5, no 3, pp 343-64.

Sainsbury, D. (1996) *Gender equality and welfare states*, Cambridge: Cambridge University Press.

Skinner, C. and Davidson, J. (2009) 'Recent trends in child maintenance schemes in 21 countries', *International Journal of Law, Policy and the Family*, vol 23, no 1, pp 25-52.

Skinner, C., Bradshaw, J. and Davidson, J. (2007) *Child support policy: An international perspective*, DWP Research Report No 405, Leeds: Corporate Document Services.

Skinner, C., Hakovirta, M. and Davidson, J. (2012) 'A comparative analysis of child maintenance schemes in five countries', *European Journal of Social Security*, Special Issue on Child Maintenance, vol 14, no 4, pp 330-47.

Swedish Social Insurance Agency (Försäkringskassan) (2009) *Barnbidrag och flerbarnstillägg* [*Child benefits*] (www.forsakringskassan.se).

Therborn, G. (1993) 'The politics of childhood: the rights of children in modern times', in F.G. Castles (ed) *Families and nations: Patterns of public policy in Western democracies*, Aldershot: Dartmouth, pp 241-92.

Wennemo, I. (1994) *Sharing the costs of children: Studies on the development of family support in the OECD countries*, Stockholm: Swedish Institute for Social Research, University of Stockholm.

Appendix: Model family calculations

	Denmark		Finland		Iceland		Norway		Sweden	
	Mother	Father	Mother	Father	Mother	Father	Mother	Father	Mother	Father
COUPLES WITH CHILDREN AT AGE 4 AND 7										
Average gross salary (national currency)	249,932	249,932	37,464	37,464	469,000	469,000	457,200	457,200	348,000	348,000
Average salary = 1,000	1,000	1,000	1,000	1,000	1,000	1,000	1,000	1,000	1,000	1,000
Taxes	−330	−332	−283	−283	−279	−279	−285	−285	−245	−245
Tax allowance due to children	2									
Net income	670	668	717	717	681	681	715	715	755	755
Total child benefits	110		69				51		78	
Housing costs 20% of gross taxable income	−200	−200	−200	−200	−200	−200	−200	−200	−200	−200
Housing allowance										
Disposable income after housing	581	468	586	517	481	481	566	515	632	555
Combined disposal parental income		1,049		1,103		962		1,081		1,187
JOINT CUSTODY, CHILDREN AT AGE 4 AND 7										
Average gross salary (national currency)	249,932	249,932	37,464	37,464	469,000	469,000	457,200	457,200	348,000	348,000
Average salary = 1,000	1,000	1,000	1,000	1,000	1,000	1,000	1,000	1,000	1,000	1,000
Other income due to children/family				4	13					
Taxes	−330	−231	−283	−279	−284	−279	−259	−285	−245	−245
Tax allowance due to children/maintenance	2	101								
Net income	670	769	717	721	689	681	741	715	755	755
Total child benefits	110		99		57		94		39	39
Child maintenance*	115	−115	92	−92	89	−89				
Housing costs 20% of gross taxable income	−200	−200	−200	−200	−200	−200	−200	−200	−200	−200

(continued)

	Denmark		Finland		Iceland		Norway		Sweden	
	Mother	Father	Mother	Father	Mother	Father	Mother	Father	Mother	Father
Housing allowance	6	6			13					
Disposable income after housing	701	461	707	430	660	392	635	515	594	594
Combined disposal parental income		1,162		1,137		1,052		1,150		1,188
SEPARATED PARENTS COMPARED WITH COUPLES:										
Mother/father	121	–7	122	–87	179	–89	69	0	–39	39
Combined income		113		34		90		69		0

* Minimum/basic maintenance allowance, which can also be means-tested as in Norway or in Sweden or not paid at all for wealthy parents sharing the custody, as in Sweden.

Finland: Local taxes are based on average tax rates.

Denmark taxation: Example is based on Copenhagen municipality regarding municipality taxes, which were 23.8% in 2011. The rest is based on countrywide conditions. The compensation for increased taxation (children) will only follow the father if he has full custody. Normally, the child benefit will follow the mother, unless the father has full custody. If the parents have joint custody and the children live 50/50, the parent with whom the child has their address registered will receive the child benefit. The child maintenance: If the parents have joint custody and the children live 50/50, the parent with whom the child has their address registered will receive the child maintenance.

Norway: Lone parents are entitled to child benefit for one more child than they actually live with (extended child benefit). There is also an infant supplement, which is extra child benefit for single parents with children aged three or under who receive the extended child benefit and full transitional benefit. The child's mother or father can receive the child benefit. If the child's parents have a dual domicile agreement for the child, the child benefit can be split equally between them. The calculations assume that the parents do not have an agreement. See www.nav. no/English/Stay+in+Norway/212728.cms

The Advance Maintenance Support Payment (ASP) is provided by NAV (NAV is the Norwegian Social Insurance Institution), and the support is means-tested. In this case, the threshold is lower than the actual income level of the mother, and the mother is not entitled to any ASP. See www.nav.no/Familie/Barnebidrag/Hovedregler/Fastsette+og+endre+bidrag; www.nav.no/English/ Stay+in+Norway/Advance+support+payment.805368912.cms

Sweden: Since the children are living together with the mother and father equal time, no maintenance allowance will be paid.

Sources for average wages:

Denmark: Average wage 2011: www.dst.dk/pukora/epub/Nyt/2012/NR246.pdf

Finland: www.stat.fi/til/ati/index_en.html; http://www.stat.fi/til/ati/2012/01/ati_2012_01_2012-05-31_en.pdf, appendix Table 12.

Iceland: Statistics Iceland (ND) Average income full time work 2011. http://hagstofa.is/?PageID=2594andsrc=/temp/Dialog/varval.asp?ma=VIN02010%26ti=Laun+fullvinnandi+launamanna+%E1+almennum+vinnumarka%F0i+eftir+starfsst%E9tt+og+kyni+1998%2D2011+%26path=../Database/vinnumarkadur/fulllaun/%26lang=3%26units=%DE%FAsundir%20kr%F3na

Norway: Based on average wage earnings per month for all employees (full-time equivalents) 3rd quarter 2011, see www.ssb.no/emner/06/05/lonnansatt/tab-2012-03-28-01.html

Sweden: Wages are for 2011. See www.scb.se/Pages/TableAndChart149087.aspx

Theme 2:
Fathers in everyday life
– culture, work and care

FIVE

Time use of Finnish fathers – do institutions matter?

Minna Ylikännö, Hannu Pääkkönen and Mia Hakovirta

Introduction

In this chapter, Finnish fatherhood is approached from the time use perspective. How individuals – and fathers – use their time reflects both the prevailing social norms and the impact of social policies (Sullivan et al, 2009). Paid and domestic work – and especially the time spent on childcare by Finnish fathers from the late 1980s until 2010 – is investigated. Within this time period, several policies attempting to promote gender equality in various aspects of work and family life have been implemented, such as the so-called father's quota and parental leave policies (see also Chapter Fourteen, this volume). Through such law reforms, fathers have been encouraged to take more responsibility for childcare (Haataja, 2009). At the same time, the idea of fatherhood has changed dramatically, and fathers are expected to be much more involved and to take more responsibility for the care work in the family than ever before.

In Finland, the tendency of strengthening fatherhood evolved as early as the 1970s, when the 'involved fathers' started participating in household chores, breaking the traditional paternal hegemonic (Huttunen, 1999). Since then, major changes have taken place in the labour markets as well as in the private sphere of family lives. The reasons for these changes are manifold. On the one hand, it can be argued that the family policies actively aiming to increase gender equality have played a central role. On the other hand, attitudinal changes which either precede or are a result of the policy changes should not be overlooked. According to Ylikännö (2009, p 127), instead of wishing for more time for fixing cars or doing other odd jobs around the house, as was still the case as recently as the late-1980s, Finnish fathers now prefer spending more time with their children instead.

Time use studies can indicate the effectiveness of family policies with regard to the daily lives of families and the division of labour between mothers and fathers. Previous comparative studies show that the Scandinavian approach to gender and family policy has been rather successful in terms of obtaining the gender equality objectives, as demonstrated by the more gender-equal division of time use than in countries representing other welfare regimes (Pacholok and Gauthier, 2004; Gornick and Meyers, 2005; Gálvez-Muños et al, 2011). Fathers are increasingly participating in household chores, and mothers' labour force participation rates are – perhaps as a related result – among the highest in the developed world (OECD, 2012). This has led to changes in how mothers and fathers understand their parenting roles, and how much time both genders allocate to paid employment, unpaid household work and childcare.

However, the gender gap remains visible in time use. As elsewhere, Finnish fathers still spend more time working outside the home and doing less household chores and childcare than Finnish mothers (Finch, 2006; Pääkkönen, 2009; Ylikännö, 2009). The existing empirical literature provides some insight into the predictors of how Finnish fathers use their time (see Ylikännö, 2009). Until now, however, the changes over time in the Finnish fathers' time use have not been assessed in detail. The aim of this chapter, therefore, is to provide a comprehensive analysis of how Finnish fathers use their time: how much time do the fathers allocate to paid and unpaid work? How does their time use differ from that of mothers? How has their time use changed over time? And how do changes in time use reflect the family policy changes mentioned above?

The attempt is not, however, to provide any direct causal relationship between changes in family policies and paternal time use. It should be kept in mind that other policies and general societal changes also affect time use (see Sullivan et al, 2009). In this chapter, the main focus is therefore on time use, and the family policy affecting the time use is only a secondary focus.

The chapter proceeds as follows. First, the basic principles of and changes in family policies in Finland are outlined, and how these changes might affect how fathers use their time. Second, the data and methods used in the analysis are introduced. In the empirical section, results from the analysis are presented followed by conclusions. The main result of the analysis shows that Finnish fathers spend significantly more time attending to childcare and other unpaid work and spend less time on paid work than two decades ago. With regard to childcare time, the change is more than half an hour per day, and the changes are statistically significant. The results indicate that the shifts in attitudes associated with family values have accompanied changes in the time use of fathers towards a more involved fatherhood.

Fatherhood in the Finnish family policy context

When considering the time use structures and the actual time use among fathers, family policies play a central role by providing opportunities for parents to share their earning and caring responsibilities. Nordic countries have been pioneers in introducing and promoting the parental rights of fathers, both with respect to the child's birth and in taking responsibility for childcare when the mother returns to employment. The individual father's right to take leave - paternity leave and parental leave - has been justified in order to promote both early father–child relationships and gender equality in the family and labour market (Haataja, 2009). Thus, the Home Care Allowance scheme (cash for care) has been criticised for counteracting these goals, since it is almost exclusively used by mothers, and very few fathers take long-term leave from work to care for children after having taken their parental leave (Rantalaiho, 2009).

Finland is often considered a member of the Nordic family policy model (Hiilamo, 2002; Bradshaw and Hatland, 2006), partly for having implemented the dual earner/dual carer model (Korpi, 2000). As a characteristic of this, in 2011, in 70 per cent of dual carer families with children, both the father and mother were gainfully employed. During infancy (child less than age three), however, the father usually works and the mother stays at home to care for the child, often while receiving the Home Care Allowance. As the child grows older, mothers typically return to full-time employment, and the so-called dual earner/dual carer model becomes the most typical arrangement. In 76 per cent of the two-parent families in which the youngest child is three to six years old, both parents are employed. The corresponding figure for families with school-aged children is as high as 83 per cent (Statistics Finland, 2011).

Family policies encourage mothers' labour market participation through the universal provision of social services and employee rights, extensive maternity and parental leave systems and daycare services (Forssén et al, 2008). In addition to public daycare services, the aforementioned Home Care Allowance scheme is available for parents of children younger than age three. Combined with the right to take leave, this opportunity to take leave until the child is three years provides for the longest possible leave period with a benefit in the

Nordic countries (Repo, 2010; Eydal and Rostgaard, 2011). Hence, Finnish family policy is characterised by individual social rights and relatively comprehensive income transfers and services to families with children. Another characteristic is the low degree of child poverty (Ferrarini, 2006; Forssén et al, 2008). The participation of fathers in care has also been promoted by different changes in family law, such as joint custody after divorce (see Chapter Three, this volume).

In Finland, 12 week days of paternity leave were introduced in 1978, which was increased to 18 week days in 1991. At the time, it could be taken while the mother was at home with the newborn child. In 2003, following a law reform, fathers were also entitled to a bonus leave: if the father used the last 12 days of the parental leave instead of the mother, he received 12 days extra paternal leave. This was lengthened to 12 + 24 days in 2010. Since the beginning of 2013, Finnish fathers have been entitled to 54 days of paternal leave, all of which be taken following the parental leave. Although fathers have been the focus of the Finnish family policies in recent decades, the rights of fathers and the leave take-up rates have remained modest compared to the other Nordic countries, with the exception of Denmark (see, for example, Haataja, 2009; see also Chapter Fourteen, this volume).

Family policy: potential for changing time use

One main goal of family policies has been to change the gendered division of labour in families. While the aim is to influence the decisions made regarding the earning and caring responsibilities in the family, the prevailing time use structures are also at stake. Should the family decide that the father is to take half of the parental leave, allowing the mother to return to work, there are direct effects both on the division of paid labour and presumably also on the division of unpaid work. However, indirect effects can also be expected. Changing attitudes towards a more participatory fatherhood, which are either the output of or input for legislative changes, may result in changes to the prevailing time use structures in families.

In a comparative study including Denmark, Australia, Italy and France, Craig and Mullan (2010) found that the Nordic discourse of paternal involvement is so pervasive that even in those Danish families where the mother was currently on maternity leave or outside of the workforce, fathers did more routine housework than in the other three countries. Based on their results, Craig and Mullan (2010) further suggest that the culturally dominant attitudes about masculinity may outweigh individual- and household-level characteristics, which consequently place emphasis on the centrality of family policies in changing the underlying social values and attitudes. The extent to which it is possible to change public opinion with legislative changes is questionable, however (Page and Shapiro, 1983; Crompton et al, 2005).

In his comparative study of Australia and Finland, Bittman (1999, p 40) found that family policies make a difference when aiming to reduce some of the pernicious effects of gender inequality. The entitlements to parental leave, high quality and affordable childcare, and family-friendly hours of paid work, were necessary components of an equitable solution to the difficulties of combining work and family, and hence directly affect the time use decisions made by families. Bittman's results support the notion that time use should be studied whenever there is interest in the family policy implications for families and their everyday lives.

Finch (2006) also examined the time use of mothers and fathers in eight countries using the Multinational Time Use Study (MTUS). According to her results, the breadwinner family model has grown weaker in all countries (Finland, Denmark, Norway, Sweden, Germany, the Netherlands, UK and Italy), but in Finland it has not weakened for families with young children. Finch (2006) also found that in Finland (and also in Norway), the difference in the time mothers spent on childcare compared to fathers changed very little when families transitioned from parental leave into employment, suggesting that although Finland is generally considered very gender-equal, deeply rooted gender roles remain visible in families with children.

Although it would be tempting to expect that the family policies implemented in Finland would be evident and directly result in positive changes in the time fathers spend on childcare and other unpaid work, these policies may fall on stony ground if different aspects of social, economic, and employer policies pull against each other, causing a 'stalling' of changes in the division of domestic tasks (see Crompton et al, 2005). Fathers may find it difficult to combine the expectations set by the labour markets and those deriving from gender-equality policy measures.

According to Finch's (2006) results, this may hold true for at least some Finnish fathers. More explicit explanation for the 'stalling' of changes could be the occupational gender segregation: according to the European Commission (2009), Finland belongs to the four high-gender segregation countries, together with Estonia, Slovakia and Latvia. The results of Bygren and Duvander (2006) for Sweden and Takala (2005) for Finland show that in male-dominated workplaces, fathers are less likely to use parental leave. For fathers working in the male-dominated industry, it may therefore be difficult to put family ahead of work, possibly due to the masculine work environment which still understates the importance of family.

Hence, even if fathers were interested in spending more time with their children, external factors might make it complicated for them to make this happen. Even in the Nordic countries, the ideals concerning gender equality in the division of work at home seem to be more prevalent than the actual practice (Bernhardt et al, 2008, p 286). According to the Finnish Equality Barometer from 2008, mothers in 44 per cent of the families with children felt that they were 'sometimes or often' responsible for too much of the unpaid work at home. The corresponding figure for men was seemingly less, only 5 per cent. At the same time, roughly 90 per cent of Finnish women and men thought that fathers should take more responsibility for childcare (Nieminen, 2008). The results for Sweden and Norway, two other representatives of the Scandinavian welfare model, are similar. Egalitarian views were held by 76 per cent of Swedish couples and 62 per cent of Norwegian couples, but a seemingly smaller proportion of the couples felt that the housework was shared equally in the family (50 per cent in Sweden and 49 per cent in Norway).

When considering shifts in time use patterns among fathers, it must be kept in mind that there is a limited number of hours to allocate to various activities, especially in families with small children, where feelings of busyness and a lack of time are all too familiar (Pääkkönen and Hanifi, 2012, pp 33-4; see also Bittman and Wajcman, 2000; Harvey and Mukhopadhyay, 2007). According to Ylikännö (2009), the amount of time fathers had all to themselves decreased during the 1990s, meaning that having a sense of not having enough time was becoming more common. However, fathers no longer wanted more time for their own leisure activities or for odd jobs around the house; above all, what they wanted was more time together with their family.

Data and methods

In this chapter, national time use surveys from Finland are used. The data of the study derive from the diaries and interviews of respondents to Statistics Finland's time use surveys in 1987–88 ($n = 7,758$), 1999-2000 ($n = 5,332$) and 2009-10 ($n = 3,795$) (Table 5.1).[1]

All men and women who reported they were married or cohabiting and had at least one child younger than age seven in their households were included in the analysis. The age limit is based on the typically

Table 5.1: Time use surveys examined

Fieldwork period	Sample age	Sample size (persons)	Fathers	Mothers	Number of days
Year					
1987–88	10+	7,758	577	574	Two days
1999–2000	10+	5,322	322	350	Two days
2009–10	10+	3,795	200	221	Two days

Source: Statistics Finland (nd)

used division of children into pre-schoolers (small children) and children already attending school. Finnish children begin attending school from the age of seven. The respondents to the time use survey described their time use in the special time use diaries for two whole days. It is possible to record two simultaneous activities in the diary – which of the two simultaneous activities was the main activity and which was the secondary activity depends on the respondent's own assessment. Gainful employment, however, was always treated as a main activity.

The main activities studied are time used in paid work, childcare and domestic work. Paid work time includes time in the main and any secondary job, employment-related activities and daily commuting. Unpaid work time is divided into childcare time and other domestic work time. Childcare time includes physical care and the supervision of a child, reading and playing with a child, and accompanying a child to hobbies, appointments and so on. Domestic work includes housekeeping, maintenance, shopping, helping adult household members and neighbours, and transport related to domestic work.

This analysis only includes main activities. As housework activities and childcare are often conducted while doing something else, the results most likely underestimate the time used in these activities to some degree (Pääkkönen and Hanifi, 2012, p 29). This chapter is based on descriptive analysis only, such as averages, their standard errors and two-sided 95 per cent confidence limits, which were calculated for the time use variables. If the 95 per cent confidence limits for the mean time of the individual activities and in different time points did not cross, it was assumed that the change in the time use was significant.[2]

Time used for work and care

In Finland, the fathers of small children (under the age of seven) have been strongly encouraged to participate in childcare through family policies. As seen in Table 5.2, Finnish fathers significantly increased their childcare time during the period in question. In 1987–88 Finnish fathers spent 46 minutes on childcare, 10 years later 60 minutes, and as much as 81 minutes per day in 2009–10 – an increase of over half an hour per day. At the same time, Finnish fathers of small children have cut their time spent on paid work by on average 29 minutes.

It must be noted that unemployed fathers are included here. While the unemployment rates were higher in 2010 than at the end of 1980s, the lower figure may also result from fewer fathers working than two decades earlier. As the change in paid work time is not significant in statistical terms, no further conclusions concerning the possible trend of Finnish fathers' paid work time can be made. With regard to unpaid work, Finnish fathers spend 19 minutes more on it than two decades earlier, and even though the 95 per cent confidence limits cross by only three minutes, the change can be considered statistically significant.

When narrowly studying changes in how fathers use time over time, the increase in the time devoted to childcare suggests that Finnish family policies have enabled or even encouraged the change. When also considering mothers' time use, however, the picture gets more complicated. Finnish mothers of small children have also increased the time they spend on childcare by half an hour per day over the 20-year period. This is consistent with the changes in childcare time use in other European countries: more time resources are invested in children than previously (see, for example, Gimenez-Nadal and Sevilla, 2012). In other words, fathers are more involved than before, at least time-wise, but the division of childcare time among the Finnish mothers

Table 5.2: Paid work, childcare and other domestic work time use of Finnish fathers and mothers of children under age 7 in 1987–88, 1999–2000 and 2009–10. Minutes per day (95% CL in parentheses)

	Fathers			Mothers		
	Paid work	Childcare	Other domestic work	Paid work	Childcare	Other domestic work
1987–88	348 (330, 365)	46 (41, 50)	128 (120, 136)	164 (150, 178)	134 (127, 142)	245 (237, 253)
1999–2000	337 (312, 362)	60 (53, 66)	130 (119, 141)	147 (136, 158)	147 (136, 158)	237 (226, 248)
2009–10	319 (286, 353)	81 (71, 90)	147 (133, 162)	152 (127, 178)	164 (149, 179)	211 (197, 225)
Change	−29	35	19	−12	30	−34
Significant	no	yes	no	no	yes	yes

Source: Statistics Finland (nd), own calculations

and fathers remains very unequal. Where we can see a more equal division labour is in the work around the house – where mothers have significantly reduced their time spent on domestic work, fathers have increased it (although the change for fathers is not significant).

While keeping in mind that factors other than family policy measures have an impact on time use decisions, it could be argued that such a significant change in how Finnish fathers spend their time would not have been possible without relevant changes in the institutional settings. The similar change in how Finnish mothers spend their time, however, indicates that rather than fathers spending more time alone with their children and taking away some childcare 'burden' from mothers, families are spending more time together. This may not be a negative trend at all, but it is worth discussing from the gender equality viewpoint.

While the interest of this book lies in fatherhood, childcare and the time spent on childcare are obviously central issues. On an aggregate level, we see a significant increase in the time Finnish fathers have spent on childcare over the past two decades. Childcare consists of different kinds of activities, however, including physical care and the supervision of a child as well as playing with a child or transporting the child to childcare. Even if parents spend an equal amount of time with the child, the other parent may be unequally responsible for the more scheduled care, and when it comes to physical care, also more demanding care (Craig, 2006).

As seen in Table 5.3, the most significant increase in the time Finnish fathers spend on childcare has been in the category of actual physical care and supervision of the child. Compared to the 21 minutes per day that fathers spent on physical care and the supervision of a child less than seven years of age at the end of the 1980s, the 18-minute increase over 20 years represents an almost doubling over that time. There has also been a significant increase of 13 minutes per day in the time fathers use for teaching, reading and talking with their children. Finnish fathers also spend significantly more time than before in accompanying the child to hobbies, appointments and so on.

Again, the results for fathers appear encouraging when considering the gender equality objectives of Finnish family policies. And again, when examining the corresponding figures for mothers, the picture grows more complicated. Although mothers have not increased the time spent on the physical care and supervision of their children to the same extent as fathers, they have also not reduced it. The same 'trend' appears regarding teaching, reading and talking to their child. It seems as though the more fathers spend time in childcare – whether it

Table 5.3: Time used in various childcare activities by Finnish fathers and mothers of children under age 7 in 1987–88, 1999–2000 and 2009–10. Minutes per day (95% CL in parentheses)

	Fathers			Mothers		
	Physical care, super-vision of child	Teaching, reading, talking with child	Transport-ing a child	Physical care, super-vision of child	Teaching, reading, talking with child	Transport-ing a child
1987–88	21 (19, 24)	26 (23, 29)	1 (0,1)	92 (86, 99)	47 (43, 50)	3 (2, 4)
1999–2000	28 (24, 32)	32 (28, 36)	2 (1, 4)	92 (84, 100)	55 (50, 60)	7 (4, 10)
2009–10	39 (33, 45)	39 (33, 45)	5 (3, 7)	102 (91, 114)	59 (51, 66)	8 (6, 11)
Change	18	13	4	10	12	5
Significant	Yes	yes	yes	no	yes	yes

Source: Statistics Finland (nd), own calculations

be physical care or another kind of childcare activity – the more time mothers also spend on childcare.

So far, the results have shown an increasing trend in how Finnish fathers spend time on childcare. Hence, it could be argued that the family policies encouraging fathers to be more involved in childcare have been at least somewhat successful. When considering the realisation of gender equality in the families, however, it is interesting to look at whether fathers are more involved than previously in all families regardless of the age of the children or only during the infancy, when the societal pressure (partly through family policies) is at its highest for fathers to spend time with their children. Table 5.4 presents the time used attending to various childcare activities by Finnish fathers and mothers with small children according to the age of the youngest child in the family.

In the families where the youngest child is under three years of age, fathers have significantly increased the time they spend on physical care and supervision of their child. In 2009–10, Finnish fathers with children under the age of three spent 55 minutes per day caring and supervising the child compared to 34 minutes two decades earlier. Compared to the mothers of small children, however, the gender difference in time use remains large. When the child is very young, mothers spend more than two-and-a-half hours daily physically caring for and supervising the child compared to the little less than one hour that the fathers spend on the same activities.

Table 5.4: Time used attending to various childcare activities by Finnish fathers and mothers, by age of youngest child in family

Child's age		Physical care, supervision of child	Teaching, reading, talking with child	Transporting a child	Physical care, supervision of child	Teaching, reading, talking with child	Transporting a child
0–2	1987–88	34	31	0	144	56	3
		(29, 38)	(26, 35)	(0, 1)	(135, 154)	(51, 61)	(2, 4)
	1999–2000	41	43	1	145	72	6
		(34, 48)	(36, 50)	(0, 1)	(137, 156)	(64, 80)	(1, 10)
	2009–10	55	42	3	156	76	6
		(45, 65)	(34, 50)	(1, 6)	(140, 172)	(66, 87)	(3, 9)
	Change	21	11	3	12	20	3
	Significant	Yes	no	yes	no	yes	no
3–6	1987–88	10	22	1	35	36	3
		(9, 12)	(18, 25)	(0, 2)	(32, 39)	(32, 41)	(2, 4)
	1999–2000	14	20	4	33	36	9
		(10, 17)	(16, 25)	(1, 7)	(30, 37)	(30, 41)	(6, 12)
	2009–10	16	34	7	32	36	10
		(12, 20)	(26, 42)	(3, 12)	(25, 38)	(27, 44)	(6, 15)
	Change	6	12	6	-3	0	7
	Significant	Yes	yes	yes	no	no	yes

Source: Statistics Finland (nd), own calculations

When the youngest child in the family is older (three to six years), the gender gap in childcare time use gets smaller. At age three, most Finnish children attend publicly or privately organised childcare while their mothers and fathers are working full time. Hence, there is less time available to spend with children for both parents. While the mother has usually been at home with the infant, however, moving into employment accordingly affects her time use more than that of the father. The childcare time use gender gap has also narrowed over time: in 1987–88, the fathers of children aged three to six spent on average 33 minutes per day on the given childcare activities compared to the 74 minutes for the mother. The 31 minute/day difference fell to 21 minutes in 2009–10. Although mothers still spend more time with their children in the family than the fathers – also in the case of older children – the trend is towards a more gender-equal division of childcare time.

Finnish fathers with small children have significantly increased the time they spend caring for their children and on domestic work; hence, they follow the overall trend of fathers assuming more responsibility for childcare and other unpaid work (see, for example, Jacobs and Gerson, 2001; Sayer, 2005; Craig and Mullan, 2010). However, it remains the case in the 2000s that the time use of families with children seems to fit with the traditional model of division of labour, whereby the father is the main earner and the mother the main carer. According to the results, Finnish fathers still spend more time working outside the home and less time on unpaid work than mothers.

Although the changes in how fathers spend their time seem rather gradual, there is still change, indicating that the active family policies have had an impact on the time use of Finnish fathers of small children, and have thus been somewhat successful. While very little can be said about the causality, however, the changing attitudes and opinions about fatherhood may ultimately affect the policymaking (see Page and Shapiro, 1983; Crompton et al, 2005). Hence, in order to elaborate more closely on the relationship between legislative changes and time use changes, more comprehensive data with both time use data and information about policy measures is required.

Conclusion: times are changing – slowly

In this chapter, Finnish fatherhood was studied in the context of time use. More precisely, the focus was on the time use of Finnish fathers with small children (under the age of seven) during two decades, from 1987 to 2010. The main interest was in the paid work, unpaid work and especially in the childcare time use of fathers. In order to obtain a more comprehensive picture of Finnish fathers' time use, however, comparisons were made to the time use of mothers with small children. The results were also compared against the institutional settings. When considering the time use of fathers in the Nordic countries, neither the impact of family policy measures nor the changing attitudes towards fatherhood can be overlooked.

If father-friendly policies were to have an impact on paternal behaviour with regard to parental leave take-up, a change in how fathers use their time ought to be evident. The starting point for this chapter was therefore that when the time use, and especially the shifts in time use, were examined, an increase in the time Finnish fathers spend on childcare and other unpaid work would be observed. The analysis is purely descriptive, and institutional settings are taken into account only as background information and something the time use changes are reflected against. Making a more detailed analysis of the actual effects of the law reforms and other changes in the institutional settings on the time use would require comprehensive combined data with time use variables and national level institutional variables. This kind of data would be very beneficial and could open new perspectives in both the planning and implementation of family policy reforms.

The results from the analysis show that fathers spent significantly more time in childcare in 2009–10 than in the two previous decades. The increase was from 46 minutes in 1987–88 to 81 minutes in 2009–10: an increase of 35 minutes. Thus, the time fathers spend caring and otherwise being together with their children has almost doubled in two decades. In the same time period, however, the time mothers spend on childcare has also increased by 30 minutes. Hence, it could be argued that gender equality goals have been met to some degree, if only considering childcare time use among Finnish fathers. But when the change in childcare time use among Finnish fathers and mothers is compared, the picture becomes more complicated. Both the fathers and mothers of small children have significantly increased the time they spend with their children, which could be considered a positive trend from the child's perspective. The results indicate, however, that the gender gap in childcare responsibilities is almost as wide as two decades ago when using the time use perspective.

Scrutinising childcare activities more closely, the results show that fathers have increased the time spent on the physical care and supervision of children more than mothers. Finnish fathers have thus assumed more responsibility in the actual care for their children, which has traditionally fallen to mothers in the family. Hence, even if the gender gap in childcare time use on the more general level has narrowed by only a few minutes, in qualitative terms there seems to be a trend towards a more equal division of care responsibilities in Finnish families.

Finnish fathers have also increased the time spent on other unpaid work, and spend less time on paid work. It can therefore be concluded that Finnish fathers are slowly but steadily moving towards a new, more involved fatherhood. With regard to gender equality, the interesting question becomes how mothers respond to the changes in time use among fathers. The time use decisions made in the families and their impact also present a question worth addressing in future research.

The results are in line with the expectations that Finnish fathers are now more involved than two decades ago. The assumption was that as Finnish family policies have actively encouraged fathers to take more responsibility with respect to childcare, this would be reflected in the time fathers spend on childcare. As statistical analysis cannot verify the actual impact of family policies on the time use of Finnish fathers, the results are merely indicative.

The significant increase in the time spent on childcare by Finnish fathers indicates that the strong emphasis on gender equality in the Nordic model has been somewhat successful. It also indicates that attitudes towards fatherhood have changed: the Finnish father is no longer the distant provider, instead assuming the role of the participatory father and a more equal parent to the child. It can be speculated whether the attitudes shape the policies or vice versa. Both are most likely required in order to further increase the time fathers spend on childcare and other unpaid household chores.

The usage of various forms of paternal and parental leave by the Finnish fathers is studied on a regular basis. While the take-up rates of parental leave days among Finnish fathers has remained rather low – although these rates have indeed been increasing – reforms have been made to the parental leave system. For example, the length of the paternal leave was increased in 2013. Even though the aim of the law reforms is rarely to change the prevailing time use structures, as with regard to family leave policies, the change in time use structures of families is inevitable when successful.

This highlights the value of time use within families. Only by investigating the everyday lives of families can we achieve sufficient understanding of the realms of gendered practices in families. The Nordic model – and in this case Finland as a representative of this model – may appear very gender-equal when considering statistics alone. When investigating the division of labour within families more closely, however, deeply rooted gender roles become visible. Rome was not built in a day, and neither are the changes in the ideas or practices pertaining to fatherhood. Finnish fathers are gradually taking their place as equal parents, but it will still take some time before equality is achieved.

Notes

[1] The Finnish data for 1999–2000 and 2009–10 are household-based, meaning that all family members over the age of 10 are included in the study. This means that the diary data for all family members is for the same dates. For 1987-88, the time use data is individual-based but considered comparable to the more recent household-based data.

[2] When calculating the standard errors and confidence limits of the means, the survey means procedure applicable in the SAS statistical software was used, which takes into account the intra-class correlation in the household data for the years 1999–2000 and 2009–10.

References

Bernhardt, E., Noack, T. and Lyngstad, T.H. (2008) 'Shared housework in Norway and Sweden: advancing the gender revolution', *Journal of European Social Policy*, vol 18, no 3, pp 275-88.

Bittman, M. (1999) 'Parenthood without penalty: time use and public policy in Australia and Finland', *Feminist Economics*, vol 5, no 3, pp 27-42.

Bittman, M. and Wajcman, J. (2000) 'The rush hour: the character of leisure time and gender equity', *Social Forces*, vol 79, no 1, pp 165-89.

Bradshaw, J. and Hatland, A. (2006) 'Introduction', in J. Bradshaw and A. Hatland (eds) *Social policy, employment and family change in comparative perspective*, Cheltenham: Edward Elgar Publishing, pp 1-12.

Bygren, M. and Duvander, A. (2006) 'Parents' workplace situation and fathers' parental leave use', *Journal of Marriage and Family*, vol 68, no 2, pp 363-72.

Craig, L. (2006) 'Does father care mean fathers share? A comparison of how mothers and fathers in intact families spend time with children', *Gender & Society*, vol 20, no 2, pp 259-81.

Craig, L. and Mullan, K. (2010) 'Parenthood, gender and work-family time in the United States, Australia, Italy, France, and Denmark', *Journal of Marriage and Family*, vol 72, no 5, pp 1344-61.

Crompton, R., Brockmann, M. and Lyonette, C. (2005) 'Attitudes, women's employment and the domestic division of labour', *Work, Employment & Society*, vol 19, no 2, pp 213-33.

European Commission (2009) *Gender segregation in the labour market*, Luxembourg: Publications Office of the European Union.

Eydal, G.B. and Rostgaard, T. (2011) 'Gender equality re-visited: changes in Nordic childcare policies in the 2000s', *Social Policy & Administration*, Regional Issue, vol 45, no 2, pp 161-79.

Ferrarini, T. (2006) *Families, states and labour markets: Institutions, causes and consequences of family policy in post-war welfare states*, Cheltenham: Edward Elgar Publishing.

Finch, N. (2006) 'Gender equity and time use: how do mothers and fathers spend their time?', in J. Bradshaw and A. Hatland (eds) *Social policy, employment and family change in comparative perspective*, Cheltenham: Edward Elgar Publishing, pp 255-82.

Forssén, K., Jaakkola, A.M. and Ritakallio, V.-M. (2008) 'Family policies in Finland', in I. Ostner and C. Schmidt (eds) *Family policies in the context of family change*, Wiesbaden: Verlag für Sozialwissenschaften, pp 75-88.

Gálvez-Muñoz, L., Rodríguez-Modroño, P. and Domínguez-Serrano, M. (2011) 'Work and time use by gender: a new clustering of European welfare systems', *Feminist Economics*, vol 17, no 4, pp 125-57.

Gimenez-Nadal, J.I. and Sevilla, A. (2012) 'Trends in time allocation: a cross-country analysis', *European Economic Review*, vol 56, no 6, pp 1338-59.

Gornick, J.C. and Meyers, M.K. (2005) 'Supporting a dual-earner/dual-carer society', in J. Heymann and C. Beem (eds) *Unfinished work: Building equality and democracy in an era of working families*, New York: The New Press, pp 371-408.

Haataja, A. (2009) *Fathers' use of paternity and parental leave in the Nordic countries*, Online Working Paper 2/2009, Helsinki: Social Insurance Institution.

Harvey, A.S. and Mukhopadhyay, A. K. (2007) 'When twenty-four hours is not enough: time poverty of working parents', *Social Indicators Research*, vol 82, no 1, pp 57-77.

Hiilamo, H. (2002) *The rise and fall of Nordic family policy? Historical development and changes during the 1990s in Sweden and Finland*, Research Report 125, Helsinki: Stakes.

Huttunen, J. (1999) 'Muuttunut ja muuttuva isyys' ['Changed and changing fatherhood'], in A. Jokinen (ed) *Mies ja muutos, kriittisen miestutkimuksen teemoja* [*Man and change, themes of the critical men's studies*], Tampere: Tampere University Press, pp 169-93.

Jacobs, J.A. and Gerson, K. (2001) 'Overworked individuals or overworked families? Explaining trends in work, leisure, and family time', *Work and Occupations,* vol 28, no 1, pp 40-63.

Korpi, W. (2000) 'Faces of inequality: gender, class, and patterns of inequalities in different types of welfare states', *Social Politics*, vol 7, no 2, pp 127-91.

Nieminen, T. (2008) *Tasa-arvobarometri 2008* [*The equality barometer 2008*], Helsinki: Ministry of Social Affairs and Health.

OECD (Organisation for Economic Co-operation and Development) (2012) *Labour force statistics* (www.oecd.org).

Pääkkönen, H. (2009) 'Total work allocation in four European countries', *Social Indicators Research*, vol 93, no 1, pp 203-7.

Pääkkönen, H. and Hanifi, R. (2012) *Time use changes in Finland through the 2000s*, Helsinki: Statistics Finland.

Pacholok, S. and Gauthier, A.H. (2004) 'A tale of dual-earner families in four countries', in N. Folbre and M. Bittman (eds) *Family time: The social organization of care*, London: Psychology Press, pp 197-223.

Page, I.P. and Shapiro, R.Y. (1983) 'Effects of public opinion on policy', *The American Political Science Review*, vol 77, no 1, pp 175-90.

Rantalaiho, M. (2009) *Kvoter, valgfrihet, fleksibilitet. Indre spenninger i den nordiske familliepolitikken* [*Quotas, choice, flexibility. Inner tensions in the Nordic family policy*], Copenhagen: NIKK.

Repo, K. (2010) 'Families, work and homecare: assessing the Finnish child homecare allowance', *Barn*, vol 28, no 1, pp 43-63.

Sayer, L.C. (2005) 'Gender, time and inequality: trends in women's and men's paid work, unpaid work and free time', *Social forces*, vol 84, no 1, pp 285-303.

Statistics Finland *Time use surveys 1987–88, 1999–2000 and 2009–10*, Helsinki: Statistics Finland

Statistics Finland (2011) *Labour Force Survey 2011. Families and work In 2011: Both parents of families with children are usually employed*, Helsinki: Statistics Finland (http://tilastokeskus.fi).

Sullivan, O., Coltrane, S., McAnnally, L. and Altintas, E. (2009) 'Father-friendly policies and time-use data in a cross-national context: potential and prospects for future research', *The Annals of the American Academy of Political and Social Science*, vol 624, no 1, pp 234-54.

Takala, P. (2005) 'Use of family leave by fathers: The case of Finland', Paper presented at the Childhoods 2005 Conference 'Children and Youth in Emerging and Transforming Societies', 29 June-3 July, Oslo.

Ylikännö, M. (2009) 'Uuden isyyden hidas esiinmarssi' ['The slow emergence of new fatherhood'], *Yhteiskuntapolitiikka* [*Public Policy*], vol 74, no 2, pp 121-31.

SIX

Parental leave and classed fathering practices in Norway

Berit Brandth and Elin Kvande

Introduction

This chapter deals with fathers' care practices in relation to parental leave. From an international perspective, Norway and the other Nordic countries offer extensive parental leave schemes to families in order for them to be able to practice parenting in more gender-equal ways. Subsequently, many Nordic studies have provided evidence indicating a shift towards the increased involvement of fathers in everyday life with children (Bekkengen, 2002; Brandth and Kvande, 2003a; Lammi-Taskula, 2007; Aarseth, 2008, 2011; Eydal, 2008; Forsberg, 2010; Klinth and Johansson, 2010).

An important question when assessing the benefits of parental leave for fathers is how they actually spend their time when on such leave. Previous research has focused on differences in how fathers use parental leave depending on their working conditions, family life and parental leave length (Brandth and Kvande, 2002, 2003a, 2003b). As O'Brien (2009) has pointed out, however, more knowledge on this question is still required, particularly concerning what fathers actually do when on leave. In recent decades, the concept of the 'new father' has gained cultural status in the Nordic countries, indicating that traditionally gendered parental roles have changed notably and created more dual earner/dual carer families. This dominant fathering discourse has been found to represent a middle-class conception of 'good parenting' and how parental leave should be used (Stefansen and Farstad, 2008). It has been argued that middle-class economic, cultural and social capital is often projected as a standard example for parents to follow (Gillies, 2005, p 850). Conversely, studying the class dimension of Norwegian childcare policies, Ellingsæter (2012) shows that these policies have reduced class differences over time. Most fathers use their individual leave rights; only the length of the leave shows class-related variations in the statistics.

This chapter addresses variations in fathers' leave use. Earlier research has shown how various time cultures in working life explain variations in how parental leave is used (Brandth and Kvande, 2003a, 2005). Here, class and gender are brought into the unpacking of fathers' care practices. The analysis contains two parts. First, class differences in parental leave take-up are explored. The second part concerns what fathers do when home on parental leave. Are there class-related differences? Findings show that the gender-egalitarian values mediated through the father's quota seem to change practices with both working- and middle-classes.

Classed and gendered father practices

'Practices' is a well-established sociological concept (see Faber, 2010). This chapter draws on David Morgan's (1996, 2011) idea of 'family practices'. According to Morgan, family practices are 'those relationships and activities that are constructed as being to do with family matters' (1996, p 192). His concept of 'practices' is applied in the analysis of how fathers practise care for their children. Consequently, men's care practices are not understood as abilities or personality traits that make them either more or less adept at exercising care. Rather, the focus is on the active process, asking what they do as opposed to how they are as people.

Regarding fathering as practice implies that it can be learned and developed if and when the situation invites or demands it. It is a potential that may be formed in different ways depending on the situated and interpersonal context of the individual father. Such a perspective enables us to study how mothers and children influence fathering practices. It allows for recognition that fathering is created and reproduced through interactions with family members as well as the wider society. On the one side, the perspective includes the regular, everyday practices of the involved actors, requiring micro-level examination. On the other, the 'significance of these practices derives from their location in wider systems of meaning' (Morgan, 1996, p 190), including the processes of history that shape the practices and meanings of fathering (Morgan, 1996, p 192). The immediate is interlinked with the historical and social. Consequently, fathering may appear ambiguous and varied. Variations and changes occur not only in how fathering is constructed individually and practically, but also when it comes to its meanings or moral significance.

Morgan emphasises that the term 'practice' also communicates a sense of fluidity (1996, p 190), entailing an overlap between social practices, so that any set of practices can be described in several ways. Accordingly, father practices may also be family, business, gender or class practices. Choosing to describe a certain practice in one particular way does not prevent it from being understood as another type of practice. In this chapter, the aim is to understand the intersection of father practices with class and gender practices (see also Chapter Seven, this volume, for an application of practice).

In focusing on how class gets done when it comes to fathering, literature that understands class as a dynamic process that runs over time and is part of people's life projects offers a source of inspiration (Stefansen and Farstad, 2008; Stefansen and Skogen, 2010). A cultural focus (that is, variations in values, meanings and practices) is valuable, as it provides a micro-level demonstration of the meaning of parental practices as purposeful rather than mere reflections of their structural positions (Stefansen and Skogen, 2010). Cultural models of care are often not articulated as class in everyday life, as they are taken for granted.

Norwegian and international research document how parenting practices are differ according to social class. In their study of 60 Norwegian families, Stefansen and Farstad (2008) identified two distinctly different care models that were clearly related to class. Middle-class parents were found to have a very 'tidy trajectory' of care that followed the track laid out by the welfare state. Working-class parents, on the other hand, emphasised the child's need for home-based care and their parental responsibility to provide a 'sheltered space' for their children. Thus, the father staying home to care for children while the mother returns to work is seen as irrelevant. Their study illustrates how classed care practices are also gendered.

Linking parenting to a cultural understanding of children's needs and parents' obligations, Stefansen and Farstad (2008) and Lareau (2003) see father practices as constructed by how the two classes use parental leave differently. Lareau (2003) conceptualises different cultural logics for parental care in middle- and working-class families, and shows how this produces different childhoods. How parents understand children and their own responsibilities as parents leads to everyday childcare practices with very different rhythms and contents. Her two concepts – 'concerted cultivation' in the middle classes and 'accomplishment of natural growth' as a working-class practice – have formed the basis of many other studies in the field.

The practice approach corresponds to the development within gender research whereby gender is understood as an active constructing process, as doing gender (West and Zimmerman, 1987; Kvande, 2007). When gender is seen as constructed through practices, it is easier to avoid understanding it as dichotomous. Variations in practices appear instead. Gender research has been marked by a trend towards adopting more open-ended concepts and perspectives allowing for plurality and variations. One development in the field concerns the intersection of gender, class and ethnicity.

De Los Reyes and Mulinari (2004) criticise what they see as the hegemonic way of understanding gender equality in Scandinavian countries, namely, a type of equality that can be measured, assessed and acted on. One of the consequences of this is that the subsequent focus on women's representation in politics and working life and men's involvement in family matters obscures issues relating to the unequal life conditions between women and between men. The Nordic countries are marked by a strong focus on affirmative action to achieve equality. This easily becomes a general narrative of progress that obscures the situation and circumstances of less privileged groups of women and men in the Nordic countries.

Even if agreeing that race, class and gender should be understood and analysed as interlocking elements, the question of how best to understand this intersection is a key issue for discussion (West and Fenstermaker, 1995; Fenstermaker and West, 2002). Joan Acker (2006) has pointed out that class is not theorised within gender studies, but new norms for constituting men and women as equal show class-related differences. For instance, there are other terms and conditions for gender equality when both parents are highly educated, gainfully employed and have excellent career prospects than is the case with working-class families in which the parents cannot decide their working life conditions to the same degree. Gender equality conditions vary – materially and ideologically – between groups of parents (Kvande and Rasmussen, 2007). The arrangements in working and family life therefore depend on both gender and class.

Data and methods

This chapter builds on an interview study conducted during the years 1997–2001 in Norway. Thirty white, heterosexual parents, 60 people in total, were interviewed. The respective mothers and fathers were usually interviewed separately. The interviews were carried out when the leave period was over and the children were in their second year.

The study was conducted when the father's quota was relatively new. Thus, it may provide recognisable patterns of usage in countries that are now in the process of introducing similar policies.

Studying practices, one must keep in mind that interviews generate data in terms of 'told practices'. Interviews may therefore not be the best method for gathering data on classed practices, particularly as middle-class fathers may be better at explaining their practices (Faber, 2010). However, the benefit of long, qualitative interviews is the opportunity they represent to gain insight into how meaning is produced.

In line with Stefansen and Farstad (2008) and international research in this field (Lareau, 2003; Gillies, 2005), the chapter adopts a pragmatist approach to the definition of class based on educational level and occupation. On this basis, eight of the couples are defined as working class, that is, none of the parents in these families had any post-secondary education. The fathers held jobs such as shop assistants, mail carriers, drivers, industrial workers and warehouse workers. These eight families are part of a working-class segment in which people manage to cope (Vincent et al, 2008; Stefansen and Skogen, 2010); that is, they have a steady but often limited income.

Sixteen of the couples are categorised as middle class. They held a college or university degree, the fathers working as engineers, teachers, consultants or researchers. Lastly, six of the couples are lower middle class and/or have a mixed class composition. In order to limit the problems involved in identifying classes, these composite families were not included in the analysis. We are aware of the dangers of dichotomised categories and the difficulties with reading off what values they hold from their type of occupations (Vincent et al, 2004). What happens to father practices in mixed-class composition couples is interesting, and would perhaps have shown greater variation and more changes. For the purpose of this analysis, however, working- and middle-class fathers are compared and contrasted, and effort is made to avoid neglecting the variations within these two categories.

The parental leave system and class variations in how fathers use leave

In Norway, mothers-only parental leave had already been phased out in 1978 when, with the exception of the first six weeks after birth, fathers and mothers were allowed to share the paid parental leave period. However, being able to share parental leave did not lead to more fathers taking leave. As a consequence of this failed policy, four weeks of the leave period were reserved for fathers in 1993 (and at the time of the interviews), a so-called 'father's quota', an entitlement to individualised, non-transferable parental leave for fathers, based on a 'use-it-or-lose-it' principle. In a short time, this resulted in the wide use of parental leave by fathers (from 4 to 45 per cent of fathers in one year). In 2014, the father's quota is currently 10 weeks, and quotas that mildly force parental leave on fathers have evolved in several countries and encouraged fathers to take a greater share of childcare obligations (Eydal and Gíslason, 2011). Nearly all of the eligible fathers in Norway make use of the quota, and 96 per cent took the whole quota in 2006 (Grambo and Myklebø, 2009). As the quota has been extended, greater variation in take-up has become more common among fathers (Fougner, 2012) (see also Chapters Thirteen, Fourteen, Fifteen and Sixteen, this volume, for father's quota policies in the other Nordic countries).

When fathers use the father's quota, the law allows mothers to remain home together with the father and child. This was not the original intention. The initial intention was for the father to care for the child while the mother returned to work. Due to strong protests from parents, the law was changed regarding this point. Grambo and Myklebø (2009) conducted a survey that found that 46 per cent of the mothers returned to full-time employment or education when the fathers took their quotas, a figure that has proved stable over the last decade. Furthermore, 24 per cent of the mothers are partly at home because of part-time work, and 30 per cent are home on vacation or leave on a full-time basis while the fathers make use of their quota (Grambo and Myklebø, 2009).

In Norway, greater gender equality and father–child contact have been the aims of parental leave for fathers from the very start. The original idea was that giving fathers an individual right, which was forfeited if not used, was the best policy to encourage fathers to share in childcare more equally. Gradually, greater flexibility and choice have made their mark on the quota. The leave period can be divided, taken in various chunks over three years, and as part-time leave combined with part-time work. An increasing number of parents avail themselves of flexible use (Fougner, 2012). This means that the one measure aims at two very different ideas: a quota intending to ensure gender equality by means of 'mild coercion' on the one side, and choice on the other.

Leave practices among working-class fathers

Among the couples with limited education and jobs in industry, transport, cleaning and retail, fewer fathers than among the middle-class fathers in our sample have fully exercised the right to various forms of leave to which they are entitled. Some have taken a few days off in connection with the birth of their child (so-called paternity leave). Some of the fathers in this group would possibly suffer financial losses if they took parental leave because their partners work part time. Until 2010, the parental benefit was curtailed according to mothers' working hours. If mothers worked part time, fathers were only entitled to a 'part-time father's quota'. Moreover, some of these fathers may not see the point in taking leave because they are at home so much anyway due to shift or rota work.

A common practice in all eight of the working-class families in our sample is for the mother to remain home while the father takes his leave. Mothers might possibly return to work on a part-time basis or remain home on a full-time basis using various arrangements such as prolonged unpaid leave, a vacation, voluntarily opting out of work temporarily or becoming unemployed.

One example of a working-class practice is Halvor and his wife Hanne. Hanne does cleaning work and returned to work half-time after her leave was over. Halvor works in a paper mill on a full shift basis that implies afternoon, night and weekend work, but also every fourth week off. They have two children (ages two and four). Halvor did not take any parts of the parental leave, not even the father's quota. When asked why, he explains:

> "We received the information, which we found to be very complicated. We didn't understand much of it. I thought it was, you know, very stupid to ask the authorities. So we decided … we discussed it a bit, and then we chose … because I have shift work, we found out that we would go for that. I work for a private company, and it is hard for an employer to choose to give a man leave, so…. Quite simply, it had to do with the brochures and stuff. I feel that they are not made for the common man in the street. I understand very little of it."

The parental leave system consists of several parts with different terminology and eligibility rules. Hanne and Halvor were particularly uncertain about the financial consequences of Halvor taking leave, and what his shifts and her part-time work would mean. Not knowing the rules, Halvor relied on what he had 'heard'. This was, among other things, that using the father's quota meant reduced income, that he would be paid according to his wife's level of income. They were very nervous about this, as they had bought a house two years earlier and depended on Halvor's income. In his explanation, Halvor positions himself as a 'common man in the street', struggling to understand the parental leave system and to apply it to their situation.

The quote from Halvor above also provides a second reason for him not taking leave. His reluctance to bring up the issue at his workplace possibly has to do with the masculine working culture at the mill. He could have requested more information and approached the personnel department. But taking childcare leave may have endangered his reputation as a good worker. Staying home to care for a baby when part of a male environment in which everyone depends on each other might not be considered appropriate working-class, masculine behaviour. This aspect marks his practice as both gendered and classed.

Halvor ended up taking three weeks of vacation and his regular week off work when the youngest child was one month old; thus, he stayed home with the mother and his children for one month. He took leave of the same length as the quota at the time, and was thus able to spend time with his family in an early period in his child's life when his presence was much needed. Halvor did not, however, assume full responsibility for the child's care when his wife returned to work.

Another couple, Fred and Frida, have two boys (ages two-and-a-half and one). Neither of them has any secondary or higher education. Frida has worked in a café for 12 years and is tired of her job. Before the children were born, she worked full time and alternated between day and evening shifts. She only returned to work half-time after her first leave, and quit her job after the second. Mothering is important to her. "I'm home because I want to", she explains.

Frida's husband is a production worker in a printing office and has just advanced to a middle manager position. They have not negotiated who should take the sharable parental leave – it was taken for granted that Frida would do so. "It was automatic. It was me", she says, and continues:

> "I think it has always been like the mother who is closest to the children, since she does the breastfeeding and stuff. And therefore she should be the one to stay at home, I think.... Everyone I know, who has had kids, it's the mother who is at home. And then it became like this for us as well. No,

we didn't start talking about Fred staying home and me going to work."

The compulsory father's quota has been somewhat troublesome for them. The first time, Fred split it up and took a day off now and then during his wife's leave. The second time, he took half of the leave, two weeks in a row. Both times, Frida was home at the same time. Since she was home, they thought it was unnecessary for him to take the father's quota. Besides, he would rather work. As Fred says:

> "There was a lot to do at work, and we [he and Frida] talked about it. So, I was home while she was home since she had resigned her job. The leave did not matter, really. It became more like a vacation, something we did not object to, but I could have been useful at work. So, since we were not allowed to move the leave over to her.... I'm so stubborn that I want my rights."

His reason for taking leave was not so much an interest in staying home to care for the child, but rather that he thought it was important to use it because he had a right to paid leave. In his mind, the father's quota was a worker's right. He was also doubtful that the father's quota would benefit fathering, but he thought it good for mothers who would get some help with everyday care work.

Both couples above have a complementary division of work, which is mirrored in how they use the parental leave system. Care work holds a central place in the lives of the mothers, employment for the fathers. Sharing the parental leave is not of interest, and gender equality is remote as a practice. In both cases, the mother is home with the father. Halvor is home when the baby is very young and the mother needs a bit of care herself and assistance with the children. Fred defines his leave as a legitimate holiday, thinking that it is the mother who is in control at home. Although Fred takes leave and not Halvor, Halvor's practice is more open to change towards the 'new father' model, and he would have liked to have more leave/time off together with his children. Fred's practice is more sedentary. He does not use his leave as an opportunity to become more active in childcare. Their complementary gender relationship is not set in any motion. He turns his leave into a holiday, whereas Halvor turns his holiday into childcare leave.

Parental leave practices among middle-class fathers

Middle-class fathers take the father's quota and also tend to take a longer period of leave than the quota, as many share part of the leave time with the mothers (Brandth and Kvande, 2003a). Moreover, they take their leave after the mother has had hers, and most of them take care responsibility alone during the day, as the mothers return to working full time after their leave is over (Brandth and Kvande, 2003b).

Among this group of fathers, Aksel represents an example in relation to the intention of the law. Aksel is 30 years old, a computer engineer and cohabiting with Anja, who is also an engineer. They have a two-year-old daughter. They shared the parental leave so that they had a total of six months of leave each, including the father's quota. When Aksel started his leave, Anja returned to her full-time job. Anja and Aksel regard themselves as an equal couple. Anja says the following about their choice of leave:

> "We discussed it before she [the daughter] was born.... I wanted to go back to work and not be away from it for too long, and Aksel had his arguments for staying home. We found that sharing 50–50 is pretty fair, as we have very similar wages."

Their similar jobs and wages are one reason they give for sharing the leave. As Aksel explains: "We agreed, and I think she was pleased that I wanted to stay home. I saw it as natural – why shouldn't I be home as much as she?" The opportunity to spend time with his daughter is his distinct motive. This matches what they think is good for the child – for her to receive care from both parents. Many other fathers in this category express the same: "there is always this ... that we are concerned with how the kids should be close to both parents".

Moreover, working in the knowledge economy, Aksel and Anja know their worth. When deciding how to organise the sharing of the leave, they chose 'full leave' instead of flexible leave. They did so for the child, he says, "... as working two days a week, and then be home three or something, was not desirable. From experience, you know that you still get one hundred per cent work anyway." The employer wanted him to organise his leave part time, but he was very determined that the leave time belonged to his child.

Anja and Aksel embody the values advocated by the welfare state's policy intentions: they share equally and use parental leave to mark boundaries against working life so that they are concentrating on the child.

Many of the other middle-class fathers in our sample also shared the leave (in addition to the father's quota), but not as much. "It was obvious that we both should take leave", Gunnar said. "I wanted as much as possible, and she wanted as much as possible." He ended up with two-and-a-half months and was fairly satisfied. Gunnhild, Gunnar's wife, was home six-and-a-half months after the birth. Gunnar and Gunnhild are both highly educated with university degrees. He is a teacher, she a researcher. They have one son. Gunnhild returned to work full time when Gunnar took his leave. In retrospect, she thinks she returned too early, because it became very tiresome, as she was still breastfeeding. Nevertheless, they are careful to dissociate themselves from seeing the parental leave as a mother's privilege.

A third case in this group is Anders, an engineer with a PhD, who manages a research institute. He is married to a social worker, Anne. They have two girls, and their third child is on the way. After their first child, he was basically home on leave, but he was only home together with his wife for a few days after the birth because he had to give a lecture abroad. This pattern is repeated when he uses the father's quota. He describes how:

> "Both of us agreed that I would use the quota, but in actual practice I found it hard, even if my intentions were clear. It was difficult because of my job, my obligations.... It was difficult to use 100 per cent of the leave. I took some days off, and then some days I just couldn't take off. In fact, this happened with both my children."

He is not at all opposed to taking leave in principle, but is subjected to what he feels are conflicting interests. Even if nearly all middle-class fathers use their quota, Anders' example shows how it was more good intention than good practice. There were other fathers in our sample who similarly reported difficulties in cutting out work completely.

Common for these fathers is that they intend to share and have an agreement with their partner that the father should take leave and be involved early in childcare. They see it as important that the father avails himself of the leave in order to be a close care person for the child. The examples presented here show that some may succeed, others struggle to share, and some do not manage to take the quota quite as intended.

In comparison, the working-class fathers in our sample draw different aspects out of the parental leave system than the middle-class fathers. Similar to the findings of Stefansen and Farstad (2008), the fathers in this study do not follow the sequenced trajectory, instead assembling their respective leave packages differently. Working-class fathers also explain their practice differently.

The classing of care practices

Comparing the leave practices of fathers in the two classes, the next question becomes what fathers do when home on leave.

Children's needs define father practices

How do middle-class fathers who have stayed home alone use their time? Aksel, who enjoyed staying home for six months, explains:

> "We had a very good time together when I was home those six months, and I have so many nice memories from that period.... One of the good memories is those lazy mornings.... We would take a little walk, and she was sleeping in the carriage, and I had an hour or two for myself, which I used either for some household chores, or I'd go on the internet a bit."

These fathers feel that time acquires another meaning when care work is their primary responsibility; they gain an understanding that care means devoting their time to the child. The fathers' descriptions of how their day-to-day lives were spent while on leave help us understand this. So what was a typical day during the leave period like? One of the fathers describes the following:

> "It was to get up early. The children wake up quite early, and that's more or less OK. They wake up around seven, and they rise and shine, so like in the weekends, they can loaf around in their pyjamas and avoid the stress of getting changed. There's breakfast, then getting dressed, and then outside if the weather's nice. And then we would be outdoors at the playground or in the forest, maybe go to the store for some shopping, and then home to start dinner, and then mummy would be home, and then dinner and children's TV and then good night. Typical day."

He describes a day that is not filled with major events – basically, there are very few things on the agenda. The child's required sleeping and eating times regulate the day. There is no impression here of a busy everyday life; rather, the day is dictated by the slow rhythm of childcare. The children get him up in the morning and control his time. Their activities give him a perception of 'slow time' (Eriksen, 2001; Brandth and Kvande, 2003a, 2003b). The fathers who are not home on a full-time basis experience time as more fragmented.

One father who is shouldering the full childcare responsibility during the day explains how care work possibly represents a learning situation:

> "Sure, I believe the fact that you have so much time with your kids – you virtually learn how to read how they tell you stuff, which you might have lost if you didn't have so much time. Because if you go to work and come home in the evening, the kids may be in a phase where they're tired and grumpy and the father is also tired and grouchy, and then you don't want to do anything with them. I think there's something there. But if you spend a whole day with them you see the overall picture of their days and understand why they are cross and crabby."

Ivar points out the advantages of having this responsibility. It is a learning experience, as he points out, that he is learning to "read" his children, or that it makes them "be logged on to the same tune" in the words of another father. By spending a great deal of time together with them, the day-to-day affairs of their children make it easier for fathers to understand why they might be in a particular mood (see also Chapter Nine, this volume, for fathers learning caring practices).

Fathers who have been 'home alone' develop a need-oriented care practice for the very reason that they spend much and continuous time together with their child. Using time in this manner appears to be essential for their potential to develop a direct and practical sensitivity for the shifting states and needs of their small children.

The working-class fathers, who have been at home together with the mother of their child during their leave, are also able to see that spending much time with their children is important. For example, they understand that the mother's extended period of leave is important for her contact with the children. Magnar, a transport worker who took his father's quota on a part-time basis, makes a major point of the fact that the children are more closely tied to their mother;

they communicate better with her, and she knows their signals better because she is home with them all day. He says:

> "It's easier for her to 'read' them because they spend so much time with her.... She has had time to become thoroughly familiar with them, for better or worse. Needless to say, I know their good and bad sides too, but not in the same way, really. She's able to understand the children way before I can. I need more information to determine what.... Of course she has been with them in the day, and.... This is what it's about; I think this is the cause."

Magnar compares himself to his wife, who will be on leave for the second year running. "She'll say to me, 'Can't you see he's thirsty?' But I can't see, because I'm not with him 24 hours a day." The children are more easily drawn to those they spend the most time with, he believes. Nevertheless, Magnar feels that his son got to know him better during the quota period, even if it was only part time. Others point to the same conclusion – that the father's quota constitutes a break from the everyday grind, thus allowing the child to get to know their father better. The fact that the mother is home at the same time is seen as less important when the quota means he can avoid coming home from work too tired to give the child the attention needed from a good father. In this way, the leave represents a break with previous practice, but not as much as if it had been longer and more continuous.

Fathers as supporting players

The children in all of the families have had their mothers as their primary care person during her leave, and when the father's quota is due in most cases towards the end of their first year of life, the mother has had the primary responsibility for almost a year. The child and mother have developed a close, physical relationship through nursing, they have established daily routines together, and they have got to know each other well by being together on a full-time basis. The middle-class fathers seem prepared to take over, and they tell of finding their own style of childcare.

When the working-class father starts his leave, he enters the picture as a 'virtual visitor', since the mother is still present. One of the fathers describes this situation: "Because she was home and had been home and knew everything and had the routines, I just continued the same routines. I did a bit more with the kids, but basically, it was all on her terms." Halvor comments: "If the father is home while the mother is still breastfeeding, obviously it's going to become like that."

The implications of the mother having stayed home on leave and remaining home when the father is taking his father's quota emerges clearly when these fathers describe what they did while at home. They describe it as being like a weekend. They do more of the daily chores than if they had not taken leave, but they are unable to assume full primary responsibility and unable to 'test their mettle' alone with the child. Thus, they may not develop the confident caring for the baby that they would have come by had they borne the primary caring responsibility alone. Caring for a child involves a lot of routine work, and these fathers see their task as playing a supporting role for the mothers.

The fathers in our sample who are working in transport and manufacturing do shift work. This means that they are often home during the day and have many days off. Halvor offers an example of how shift work provides him with extra time to be together with his children while his wife, Hanne, is at work: "Even if I didn't take the father's quota, I still got to spend much time with them," he says. Another couple 'parenting in shifts' is Tore and Grete. Grete works in a convenience store and Tore is a driver. "Every Wednesday and every other weekend I have them all to myself", he says. "Yes, and evenings – a lot of evenings! It works really well." Similar to Stefansen and Farstad's (2008) findings, homecare as long as possible before the children start kindergarten is an important aspect of the working-class 'parenting project'. Tore continues:

> "To the question of who is to care for the children when you're at work … we managed to arrange it so that one of us is always at home with them – that is, after the leave. It's important to us to be with the kids as much as possible."

They think it is very important that mothers extend their leave and that the best arrangement is for the mother to stay home when the children are small. The mother is regarded as the primary care person for the first year of the baby's life. Grete characterises her husband in the following manner:

> "He's the kind of father who feels more at ease with slightly older children. As long as they're infants, it's more like: 'no, you do it, because you know best', right? I noticed that he's

a bit distant … and yes, then there's the breast, you know.
It's a bit difficult for fathers as long as babies are nursing."

The fact that the mother has the dominant position in the care arena during the first year has led fathers to shift their fatherhood project a little further along the time scale. It is when they start speaking about their children and their expectations for when they are older that they get excited, feeling they can master it and cope better. "It's more challenging and that sort of thing when they're older. It's more enjoyable and more important", one of the fathers explains. Obviously, the working-class fathers in our study feel more confident when it comes to fathering slightly older children. When the children are able to start kicking a ball around or do other 'fun things', fathering acquires more meaning for them. Similarly, the working-class fathers who were home at the same time as the mothers often assume a special responsibility for the older siblings. This becomes visible when Tore tells about the first and second time he took his father's quota:

> "The first child leave meant staying home from work, relaxing. It was almost like a holiday…. With the second, I thought the same: 'Oh, it will be nice to be home and have a holiday', right? But it wasn't. I was totally wrong! It was a real toil and moil, so I longed to be back at work."

This means that what they do when on leave largely depends on whether it is the first or second child, as the mother is home at the same time. Gudmund, who had two weeks of paternity leave after the birth of his two youngest children, says: "I got up in the morning and had breakfast with all of the kids, and then I followed the eldest to kindergarten…." Similarly, Halvor, who had two sons only one-and-a-half years apart, points out that when he was home he took special care of the eldest.

Because they emphasise their father practice in relation to slightly older children, 'playing father' has a prominent place in their narratives about how they perform their care. Children prefer their fathers for rough types of play, they say, and fathers feel that they gain importance through this. Magnar says: "We'll throw some snowballs and stuff, see? We'll balance on the rail and jump down and do a somersault, right?" The activities many of these fathers describe enjoying together with their children take place outdoors. Thus, father and son can be found in the sandbox and on the football pitch. Being outside is an aspect of the 'daddy role' where they get positive feedback. "But I really enjoy being outside, like. I like doing small things and keeping my children happy, pushing them when they're sitting on the swing, you know – things like that."

Playing, taking short hikes and other outdoor activities have been considered a type of care that typically concerns doing something side-by-side. Nevertheless, Gudmund, a mailman and one of the fathers who is keenest to hike in the woods with his children, describes how:

> "It's really important for me to tell them that I love them and ... be nice to them and hug them, too. Physical contact is important to me. Yes, I think it's very important for the kids to feel that they have somebody who loves them and that they feel they can rely on you."

"A real man", according to Halvor, "has a firm grasp on things, and this also involves taking good care of his children." As these quotes illustrate, even if they are not letting go of what they find to be important father practices, which is to do things together, outdoors, they add enjoying each other's company and letting the children know how much they love them. As Haavind (2006) has pointed out, when fathers indicate 'emotional involvement with their children' to be a reason for more participation, this implies an extension to the meaning of masculinity. Thus, working-class fathers expressing this motivation are also contributing to a change in the very meaning of masculinity.

Conclusion

This chapter has been concerned with the classed underpinnings of parenting, with a focus on fathering. As is known from statistical data on the uptake of parental leave, our interview material provides insights into the practices and preferences of fathers from different class backgrounds.

As mentioned, the parental leave policies have been claimed to mediate middle-class values at the family level. What has been found, however, is that working-class fathers (and mothers) seek to incorporate leave rights for fathers into their care projects. The father's quota is (re)defined to fit with working-class values and practices. Thus, what has sometimes been understood as a 'middle-class' model seems to be given working-class meaning. The fathers rationalise their parenting styles by adapting them to their cultural conceptions about who should care and what characterises 'good care'. Less use of the quota is not interpreted as any indication of bad fathering. Parental leave use is thus more than a question of practicalities with respect to reconciling work and childcare; it becomes a classed social morality in relation to partners and children. Thus, the father's quota and parental leave use are embedded in the type of care project practised in the different groups. Among other things, this concerns part-time work for mothers that, to a great degree, is part of working-class mothers' care project and strongly contributes to set its mark on paternal involvement.

The fathers in both classes use the opening which the father's quota represents to transform their gendered and classed father practices. Although mothers remain the primary parent, the gender-egalitarian values mediated through the father's quota seem to change practices within both classes. Class practices are not static. The middle-class parents see the father as a parent who can more or less serve as a substitute for the mother and who is just as competent as the mother, that is, a dual earner/dual carer model. The father is just waiting on the sidelines to step in at the end of the mother's leave period. Working-class fathers use their leave to be supporters – and some of the respondents describe how this opened up new horizons. They are important supporters in the first year with a new baby, and assume a more independent fathering practice when the child is older. By staying home on a more flexible basis, with the mother present, concentrating on older siblings and children, other aspects are emphasised that are different from the middle-class fathering practices.

Men's greater responsibility for childcare has contributed to a change in the understanding of masculinity – the transformation of what it means to be a man. Parental leave for fathers has been influencing men's practice and also the norms of what a good father should do. Care is reconciled with norms of masculinity in both classes. It may, however, proceed at different speeds and along rather varied roads.

References

Aarseth, H. (2008) 'Samstemt selvskaping. Nye fedre i ny økonomi' ['Coordinated self-construction. New fathers in a new economy'], *Tidsskrift for kjønnsforskning*, vol 32, pp 4–21.

Aarseth, H. (2011) *Moderne familieliv* [*Modern family life*], Oslo: Cappelen Damm Akademisk.

Acker, J. (2006) *Class questions: Feminist answers*, Oxford: Rowman & Littlefield.

Bekkengen, L. (2002) *Man får välja – om föräldraskap och föräldraledighet i arbetsliv och familjeliv* [*One has to choose – parenthood and parental leave in work and family life*], Malmö: Liber.

Brandth, B. and Kvande, E. (2002) 'Reflexive fathers: negotiating parental leave and working life', *Gender, Work and Organization*, vol 9, no 2, pp 186-203.

Brandth, B. and Kvande, E. (2003a) *Fleksible fedre* [*Flexible fathers*], Oslo: Universitetsforlaget.

Brandth, B. and Kvande, E. (2003b) 'Father presence in childcare', in A.M. Jensen and L. McKee (eds) *Children and the changing family: Between transformation and negotiation*, London: Routledge Falmer, pp 61-75.

Brandth, B. and Kvande, E. (2005) 'Fedres valgfrihet og arbeidslivets tidskulturer' ['Fathers' freedom of choice and the time cultures of working life'], *Tidsskrift for samfunnsforskning*, vol 46, no 1, pp 35-54.

de Los Reyes, P. and Mulinari, D. (2004) *Intersektionalitet. Kritiska reflektioner over (o)jämnlikhetens landskap* [*Intersectionality. Critical reflections on unequality*], Malmö: Liber.

Ellingsæter, A.L. (2012) 'Familiepolitikk i klassesamfunnet' ['Family policy in class society'], in A.L. Ellingsæter and K. Widerberg (eds) *Velferdsstatens familier* [*Families of the welfare state*], Oslo: Gyldendal Akademisk, pp 99-121.

Eriksen, T.H. (2001) Øyeblikkets tyranni: rask og langsom tid i informasjonssamfunnet [*Tyranny of the moment: Fast and slow time in the information society*], Oslo: Aschehoug.

Eydal, G.B. (2008) 'Policies promoting care from both parents: the case of Iceland', in G.B. Eydal and I.V. Gíslason (eds) *Equal rights to earn and care*, Reykjavik: Félagsvisindastofnun Háskóla Íslands, pp 111-48.

Eydal, G.B. and Gíslasson, I. (2011) *Parental leave, childcare and gender equality in the Nordic countries*, Copenhagen: Nordic Council of Ministers.

Faber, S.T. (2010) 'Den subjective oplevelse af klasse' ['The subjective experience of class'], *Dansk Sociologi*, vol 21, no 1, pp 75-89.

Fenstermaker, S. and West, B. (2002) *Doing gender, doing difference: Inequality, power and institutional change*, London: Routledge.

Forsberg, L. (2010) 'Engagerat föräldraskap som norm och praktikk' ['Engaged parenting as norm and practice'], *Sosiologi i dag*, vol 40, no 1-2, pp 78-98.

Fougner, E. (2012) 'Fedre tar ut hele fedrekvoten – også etter at den ble utvidet til ti uker' ['Fathers take the whole quota: also after the extension to ten weeks'], *Arbeid og velferd*, no 2, pp 71-7.

Gillies, V. (2005) 'Raising the "meritocracy": parenting and the individualization of social class', *Sociology*, vol 39, pp 835-53.

Grambo, A.-C. and Myklebø, S. (2009) *Moderne familier – tradisjonelle valg. En studie av mors og fars uttak av foreldrepermisjon* [*Modern families – traditional choices. A study of mothers' and fathers' use of parental leave*], NAQ rapport nr 2, Oslo: Arbeids- og velferdsdirektoratet.

Haavind, H. (2006) 'Midt i tredje akt? Fedres deltakelse i det omsorgsfulle foreldreskap' ['In the midst of the third act? Fathers' participation in caring parenting'], *Tidsskrift for norsk psykologforening*, vol 43, pp 683-93.

Klinth, R. and Johansson, T. (2010) *Nya svenska fäder* [*New Swedish fathers*], Umeå: Boréa.

Kvande, E. (2007) *Doing gender in flexible organizations*, Bergen: Fagbokforlaget.

Kvande, E. and Rasmussen, B. (eds) (2007) *Arbeidslivets klemmer* [*Time binds in working life*], Bergen: Fagbokforlaget.

Lammi-Taskula, J. (2007) *Parental leave for fathers? Gendered conceptions and practices in families with young children in Finland*, Research Report 166, Helsinki: Stakes.

Lareau, A. (2003) *Unequal childhoods: Class, race and family life*, Berkeley, CA: University of California Press.

Morgan, D.H.J. (1996) *Family connections*, Cambridge: Polity Press.

Morgan, D.H.J. (2011) *Rethinking family practice*, Houndmills: Palgrave Macmillan.

O'Brien, M. (1999) 'Fathers, parental leave policies, and infant quality of life: international perspectives and policy impact', *The Annals of the American Academy of Political and Social Science*, vol 624, pp 190-213.

Stefansen, K. and Farstad, G. (2008) 'Småbarnsforeldres omsorgsprosjekter. Betydningen av klasse' ['Care projects of parents of small children. The meaning of class'], *Tidsskrift for samfunnsforskning*, vol 49, no 3, pp 343-74.

Stefansen, K. and Skogen, K. (2010) 'Selective identification, quiet distancing: understanding the working-class response to the Nordic daycare model', *The Sociological Review*, vol 58, no 4, pp 587-603.

Vincent, C., Ball, S.J. and Braun, A., (2008) '"It's like saying 'coloured'": understanding and analysing the urban working classes', *The Sociological Review*, vol 56, pp 61-77.

Vincent, C., Ball, S.J. and Kemp, S. (2004) 'The social geography of childcare: making up a middle-class child', *British Journal of Sociology of Education*, vol 25, no 2, pp 229-44.

West, C. and Fenstermaker, S. (1995) 'Doing difference', *Gender and Society*, vol 9, no 1, pp 8-38.

West, C. and Zimmerman, D.H. (1987) 'Doing gender', *Gender and Society*, vol 1, no 2, pp 125-51.

SEVEN

Negotiating leave in the workplace: leave practices and masculinity constructions among Danish fathers

Lotte Bloksgaard

Introduction

Studies on time use show that Danish fathers are increasingly spending time with and caring for their small children (Bonke, 2009), indicating that childcare has become a central part of contemporary fatherhood in Denmark today. However, the extent to which Danish fathers convert these fatherhood practices into leave use is limited. Danish fathers are among those in the Nordic countries taking the least leave (*Nordic Statistical Yearbook*, 2012). According to figures from 2010 and 2011, Danish fathers took on average 26 days of leave, whereas mothers took on average 276 days, fathers taking only 7.7 per cent of the total parental leave (Statistics Denmark, 2012).

One explanation may be that the Danish legislation on leave differs from most of the other Nordic countries in terms of encouraging fathers to use parental leave: not having a 'father's quota', an entitlement to individualised, non-transferable parental leave for fathers (Haas and Rostgaard, 2011, Bloksgaard, 2013, see also Chapter Thirteen, this volume). Research has established that a legislated father's quota increases leave use among fathers, as such entitlement helps set limits for work–life (Brandth and Kvande, 2002, 2005; Haas and Rostgaard, 2011). In Denmark, however, leave entitlement is not only regulated by law but is also part of the various collective agreements established in the respective occupational sectors and at the local workplace level. Consequently, Danish fathers have very different leave entitlements, depending on the sector, branch and workplace in which they are employed (Bloksgaard, 2013). Moreover, contrary to mothers, Danish fathers must negotiate their leave individually with their immediate superior (Olsen, 2005; Bloksgaard, 2009, 2011). Danish and Nordic research has documented that the workplace is a central arena for the development of father practices, being the arena where the modern, flexible and 'greedy' work–life is unfolded (Brandth and Kvande, 2002, 2003; Haas et al, 2002; Olsen, 2005; Bygren and Duvander, 2006; Lammi-Taskula, 2007). Nevertheless, relatively few Nordic studies of leave have focused on the entitlement and negotiations at the workplace level, and how these influence fathers' leave practices. Hence, this chapter focuses on leave negotiations among Danish fathers within three specific workplace arenas: investigating how Danish fathers construct leave practices – and individual male identities – in the workplace, and how leave practices are influenced by the fact that fathers must negotiate leave individually with their superior in the workplace – which demands flexibility and presence from employees, especially from men, as masculinity ideals are often closely connected to work (Morgan, 1992; Connell, 1995; Brandth and Kvande, 2002). This chapter explores these issues, applying perspectives on fatherhood practices and work organisations as arenas of continuous negotiations and power struggles.

The chapter begins with a description of present leave entitlements in Denmark, then outlines the theoretical perspectives on how fathers' leave negotiations can be seen as constructions of fatherhood practices and male identity. Following this, it is shown how in Danish workplaces, masculinity is closely linked to work, leaving limited space for the construction of fatherhood practices in the form of a long leave. Finally, the fact that fathers must negotiate leave individually in the workplace, without the support that a legislative father's quota may provide, is discussed as an important explanation for the limited use of leave among Danish fathers.

The Danish leave context

As mentioned, the Danish legislation on leave does not provide fathers with the right to a father's quota such as that enjoyed by fathers in most of the other Nordic countries (see also Chapter Thirteen, this volume). In 2012, a commission was set up by the Danish government to investigate the issue of a father's quota in Denmark, but it did not result in any new policy. There is a prevailing discourse concerning 'freedom of choice' for mothers and fathers in Denmark regarding the division of parental leave, and the current Danish legislation on leave (in effect since 2002) is based on the idea of gender neutrality (Rostgaard, 2002; Borchorst, 2006). It provides for 52 weeks of leave in total, with 100 per cent of the basic social security benefit: 18 weeks of maternity leave for the mother – four weeks before the birth, *graviditetsorlov*, and 14 weeks following the birth, *barselsorlov*, of which the two first weeks are obligatory, two weeks of paternity leave for the father, *fædreorlov*, to be taken during the first 14 weeks after the birth, and 32 weeks of parental leave, *forældreorlov*. Each parent is entitled to 32 weeks of parental leave, but only 32 weeks of the total 64 parental leave weeks are compensated. The parental leave has some built-in flexibility – for example, returning to work part time is an option (with reduced benefits; such an extension is subject to agreement with the employer) (Krarup and Andersen, 2004).

As already mentioned, in addition to national legislation, leave is also regulated in Denmark via collective agreements and agreements in the workplace, where individual employees may be offered a supplementary leave entitlement. This is a result of the Danish labour market model, whereby labour conditions are primarily determined by collective and local agreements. Collective agreements and corporate-level agreements determine the pay during leave (Due and Madsen, 2006). Furthermore, many collective agreements and corporate policies are more progressive than the legislation in terms of encouraging fathers to take part of the parental leave: in 2007, the industrial sector gave families the right to nine weeks of pay during parental leave, with three weeks earmarked for the father, three weeks earmarked for the mother and three weeks for the parents to share. In 2008, the public sector also introduced a 'father's quota'. These earmarked periods have been extended in later collective agreements (Bloksgaard and Rostgaard, 2014). Not all employees in the Danish labour market are covered by collective agreements –approximately 25 per cent of the labour force is employed outside of the collective agreement system (Ibsen, 2011). In addition, many workplaces have not implemented family-friendly policies and leave entitlements. For example, the public sector, which has a large proportion of female employees, is known for having family-friendly policies and benefits, whereas the private sector has been commonly regarded as the 'less family-friendly' sector (Skyt Nielsen et al, 2004). Thus, as a consequence of the Danish labour market model, different groups of employees in the labour market enjoy very different leave entitlements, meaning that Danish fathers have very different opportunities to take leave from work (Bloksgaard, 2013; see also Chapter Thirteen, this volume).

Moreover, workplace studies have found that unlike mothers, Danish fathers must negotiate leave individually in their workplace (Olsen, 2005; Bloksgaard, 2009, 2011). A female leave-taker will typically just announce how long she plans to be away from work, often in writing. However, male leave-takers are present in the workplace when they need to announce that they want to take parental leave, and it has to be agreed or negotiated with their immediate superior 'how long' and ''when' they can take the leave (Bloksgaard, 2009, 2011). Thus, this chapter focuses on fathers' negotiations of leave in the workplace and their constructions of leave practices and masculinity.

Theoretical perspectives: leave practices and workplace negotiations

The analysis is inspired by Brandth and Kvande's (2002, 2003) conceptualisation of 'fatherhood practices', which they developed from Morgan's 'family practices' concept (see also Chapter Six, this volume). When applying a 'practice' perspective on fathers and leave, focusing on what fathers *do* becomes central, on how they construct their masculine identity, including fatherhood, in their daily interactions with others, for example, in the workplace. The practice approach is compatible with the well-known 'doing gender' perspective (West and Zimmerman, 1987; Kvande, 2007), where masculinity and femininity are not understood as something we 'are'; instead these are seen as being continuously constructed in interaction. Thus, individual women and men can construct different gender identities among several possibilities, as depicted in Connell's famous concept 'multiple masculinities' (Connell, 1995, 2000). Yet gender cannot be 'done' freely. Brandth and Kvande (2002, 2003) understand fatherhood practices as always being constructed or negotiated in relation to different structures in society and organisations: fatherhood ideals, work–life demands and existing leave entitlement. Fatherhood practices are seen as the outcome of the various negotiation processes within these different structures (Brandth and Kvande, 2002).

One structure shaping fatherhood practices is the ideals of fatherhood in society. As Morgan (2002, p 280) explains, 'despite the apparent range of ways of "doing masculinity", there remain deeply embedded and subtly coercive notions of what it really means to be a man.' Men (and women) are held responsible for acting according to the cultural ideals of masculinity (and femininity), that they are behaving in 'gender-appropriate' ways (West and Zimmerman, 1987). Morgan (1992, pp 96-7) argues that the cultural ideals of masculinity are further developed locally at the workplace level, where they 'set limits for the range of masculinities that might be legitimately developed'. Following these thoughts, it becomes vital to study how fathers' constructions of fatherhood practices, and in this chapter leave practices in particular, are influenced by existing cultural ideals of masculinity and fatherhood in society and in the workplace (Brandth and Kvande, 2002, 2003).

Work–life is also seen as an important structural context for the construction of fatherhood practices. Modern work–life is characterised by demands regarding flexibility and presence or availability (Sennett, 1999; Beck, 2000; Kvande and Rasmussen, 2007; Bloksgaard, 2009). Researchers point out how the construction of masculinity in particular is connected to the demands of modern organisations (Acker, 1990; Morgan, 1992, 2002), and that the cultural ideal for men to work and be successful in working life has very deep roots (Connell, 2000). This can make it extra difficult for fathers to prioritise childcare – especially fathers employed as managers, as they are expected to be especially devoted to work–life (Collinson and Hearn, 1994, 1996; Morgan, 2002). The last point emphasises the importance of understanding gender/masculinity as a social category intersecting with other social categories; here, educational background or work life position (Christensen and Jensen, 2014; see also Chapter Six, this volume, for a discussion of the relationship between class and leave practices among fathers).

Morgan (2002) argues that the ideal connecting masculinity and work has varying strength depending on the competing ideals at play within a certain context. For example, he argues that how Scandinavian fathers construct work/career and fatherhood will be more conflicting as a result of the development of a strong discourse regarding 'the present father' and leave entitlement for fathers in the Scandinavian countries (Morgan, 2002). It is important, however, to remember that the Scandinavian (and Nordic) countries represent very different contexts. In Denmark, the public discourse concerning the importance of fathers' involvement in the care for small children and parental leave for fathers has not been as extensive as in the neighbouring Scandinavian countries (Rostgaard, 2002; Borchorst, 2006). This might influence Danish fathers' constructions of masculinity and leave practices – as mentioned earlier, Danish fathers only convert fatherhood practices into leave use to a limited degree.

This must be seen in relation to the current Danish leave legislation. Leave practices among fathers are also constructed in relation to existing legislative leave entitlement to fathers, Brandth and Kvande (2002, 2003) emphasise, as this constitutes strong normative guidelines on the conduct of fathers and has a strong impact on their leave practices. Norwegian, Swedish and Icelandic research documents that the legislative father's quota in these countries helps limit work–life demands, and supports fathers in taking leave from work (Haas et al, 2002; Brandth and Kvande, 2002, 2003; Gíslason, 2007).

Workplaces as arenas for negotiations and power

The 'negotiation' concept stands central in this chapter. In the perspective presented above, fathers' constructions of leave practices and male identity are understood as the result of continuous negotiations with different structures in everyday (work) life. Strauss (1978) uses the term 'negotiated order' to illustrate how all organisational processes must be seen as the outcome of continuous negotiations, for which reason the negotiation concept must be linked to power. Power relations are part of all interactions and workplace cultures, and influence the practices and identities constructed there, including our identity constructions in the workplace as men and women, respectively. Thus, power 'includes what men and women are allowed to do, how they are allowed to behave and how men and women are to be ranked and valued' (Kvande, 2007, p 51). In a study focusing on fathers' negotiations of leave, however, it also becomes relevant to draw on more classic understandings of power as linked to formal authority, which is practised downward in the organisation, being connected to hierarchy and positions (Hatch, 2006). In modern organisations, the traditional hierarchy is often replaced by more 'de-layered' and flexible structures. Managerial power is still being exercised, however, even if this is often done in more subtle and blurred ways (Foucault, 1988; Rose, 1999). In negotiations about leave from the workplace, managerial power becomes central, as the management has the power to reward or punish certain forms of behaviour among the employees – for example, with pay and/or promotion. The hierarchical power relation between the father and his immediate superior in leave negotiations possibly has an impact on this negotiation process and the outcome hereof: fathers' leave practices and potential leave use.

Data and methods

The empirical data analysed in this chapter originate from a research project on leave negotiations conducted in three private workplaces in Denmark employing mainly lower-ranking white-collar and blue-collar workers (Bloksgaard, 2009). Extensive field work focusing on leave negotiations was conducted in the three workplaces; interviews, observations and document analysis were the primary methods applied. This chapter is based on 12 fathers and their leave negotiations, and analyses the actual sequences of the negotiation process between these fathers and their immediate superiors. The leave negotiations analysed were recent or ongoing. This research strategy allows for exploring fathers' *actual* choices and practices regarding leave, and not just speculation over what they might have done in some contrived situation or did in a previous situation. This is important, as research shows that there is often a discrepancy between ideals and practice in relation to fathers and leave (O'Brien et al, 2007; Bloksgaard, 2009, 2012).

The cases of the 12 leave negotiations were selected on the basis of a wish for variation in the fathers' position (seven employees and five middle managers) and leave use. Interviews with both the fathers – several times during the negotiation process in a few cases – and their immediate superiors are analysed, as are interviews with Human Resources (HR) and management representatives and colleagues. The leave use among all of the fathers employed in the three participating workplaces is also included in the analysis for the purpose of drawing comparisons between the workplaces in relation to the leave entitlement offered and fathers' leave practices.

Three Danish workplaces

The three workplaces are all in the private sector, as this is where most Danish men are employed (Emerek and Holt, 2008). Moreover, research has indicated that fathers employed in the private sector face more barriers in relation to obtaining leave than those employed in the public sector, which is renowned for being more 'family-friendly' (Olsen, 2000). The three participating workplaces were IKEA (an international furniture and interior concern), Telia (a Nordic telecommunications company) and 'The Shop' (pseudonym) (a national chain of retail shops). Both IKEA and Telia are characterised by a nearly equal gender distribution, whereas The Shop is a female-dominated workplace in which approximately 70 per cent of the employees are women.

The workplaces are either covered by the collective agreement reached by the industrial sector (Telia) or the collective agreement reached by the union 'HK', organising commercial and clerical employees (IKEA and 'The Shop'). The workplaces were chosen as they were characterised to varying degrees by 'family friendliness', including leave entitlement for parents. At the time of the study the entitlement was as follows:

IKEA: Family friendliness (and diversity) is a central element in IKEA's image; various entitlement types for different employee groups are developed as part of the company's employment policy (such as senior benefits and part-time positions). IKEA DK supplements the six weeks paid parental leave in the collective agreement reached by HK with four additional weeks of paid parental leave, and offers four extra weeks of paid paternity leave to fathers.

Telia: Telia's employment policy is not a central part of its image, and family friendliness is not an explicit part of its employment policy – for example, it is not generally possible to opt for part-time employment. However, Telia offers parents good leave entitlement, supplementing the six weeks paid parental leave in the collective agreement with four additional weeks full pay.

'The Shop': In 'The Shop', the company policy offers entitlement for senior staff and parents (for example, 'family-friendly working hours', 7am–3pm). 'The Shop' does not offer extra leave entitlement above what is offered in the HK collective agreement.

Table 7.1 illustrates the leave entitlement for fathers employed in the three workplaces.

Fathers' leave practices in the three workplaces

Beginning with the fathers' leave practices in the three workplaces, considerable differences are found among the fathers, depending on which workplace they are employed in and, to some extent, the leave entitlement they are offered there.

In IKEA, the leave take-up (for the period 2003-07) in the local workplace shows that all employees becoming fathers here in the period ($n = 21$) have taken the six weeks of paid paternity leave offered. None of the fathers in this workplace have exercised their right to paid parental leave as secured in the legislation and collective agreement. IKEA's head office explained that this is common practice among fathers throughout IKEA DK Corporation during the period studied, where almost all fathers had taken the six weeks of paid paternity leave, whereas only 3 per cent had taken only part of the paid parental leave (Bloksgaard, 2009). The interviews with the HR representative, the fathers and their superiors all indicate that it is common practice in

Table 7.1: Leave entitlement for fathers in the three workplaces – law-given, via collective agreement and at the workplace level, 2007

	Danish legislation*	Collective agreements**	IKEA***	Telia***	'The Shop'
Paternity leave (*fædreorlov*)	2 weeks	2 weeks with wages	4 weeks extra with wages (6 weeks with wages in total)	– (2 weeks with wages in total)	– (2 weeks with wages in total)
Parental leave (*forældreorlov*)	32 weeks to each of the parents	6 weeks with wages	4 weeks extra with wages (10 weeks with wages in total)	4 weeks extra with wages (10 weeks with wages in total)	– (6 weeks with wages in total)

* With low unemployment benefit

** HK's agreement and the Industry agreement, both from 2004. Pay is contingent on the leave taker having been employed in the company for at least nine months. Pay during parental leave is contingent on leave being held in continuation of the maternity leave, that is, 15 weeks after the child's birth (to ensure that the companies can receive the low benefit refund from the municipality).

*** Also with regard to the local leave entitlement, pay is contingent on the leave taker having been employed in the company for at least nine months. And pay during parental leave is contingent on leave being held in continuation of the maternity leave, that is, 15 weeks after the child's birth.

IKEA for fathers to split the six weeks of paternity leave into three two-week periods. In this way, the interviewees explain, the leave becomes flexible and easily adjusted to work–life needs. This might be one of the reasons why all of the fathers in IKEA, including the managers, are using this leave entitlement. However, the use of the six weeks paternity leave – which is explicitly labelled 'for fathers' – possibly makes fathers in IKEA refrain from taking part of the parental leave.[1]

The leave take-up (for the period 2005–07) in Telia indicates a breakthrough in fathers' leave practices. All fathers ($n = 37$) but one have taken the two-week paternity leave. Most of the fathers (31) have taken some parental leave – and more than half (21) have taken all 10 weeks, with pay offered as a combination of collective agreements and workplace entitlement. In Telia, a (female) HR manager has decided to disregard a clause in the collective agreement, determining that pay during parental leave is contingent on leave being taken immediately after the maternity leave, that is, from the 15th week after birth.[2] Two thirds of the fathers taking parental leave in Telia have taken leave at a later date. Leave use among fathers in Telia suggests that paid parental leave, combined with flexible usage and the fact that other fathers are taking leave from the workplace, has contributed to the fathers employed there taking part of the parental leave.

In 'The Shop', it is normal practice for fathers to take the two-week paternity leave and no parental leave. As one HR representative explains: "No man has ever taken some of the parental leave. We have simply never had a man, who wanted to take some of that...". This shows that paid parental leave entitlement in the collective agreement does not necessarily mean that fathers use this entitlement to take time off from work to prioritise childcare – an entitlement here does not necessarily result in changed leave practices among fathers in all workplaces. Research shows that fathers appear to be influenced by the leave practices of other fathers in the workplace – fathers employed in workplaces where other fathers have never taken leave are therefore also less likely to take leave (Olsen, 2005; Bygren and Duvander, 2006; Bloksgaard, 2011). The absence of role models – other fathers who have taken parental leave – in 'The Shop' offers one possible explanation as to why the fathers employed here do not use the parental leave to which they are entitled.

Fathers negotiating leave in the workplace

But what influences fathers' negotiations of leave in the workplace and determines if leave is taken? Examining how two fathers negotiated their parental leave in Telia and 'The Shop' – being entitled to 10 and six weeks paid parental leave, respectively – this section explores this question further.

Janus is a Telia employee. He has successfully negotiated a flexible leave agreement with reduced hours, something that the Danish legislation opens up for but must ultimately be agreed to with the employer. As mentioned earlier, all of Telia's employees are normally employed full time, and the leave agreement has only been possible in Janus' situation because his immediate superior has accepted it. However, the manager to whom Janus' own superior refers has been opposed to the agreement. Janus recounts: "Kim, my superior's superior, said 'No!'... But then the HR manager said that I should send him up to talk to her. She got angry about his 'we're-not-even-going-to-talk-about-this' attitude." Janus' case demonstrates how superiors can play an important role for fathers' constructing leave practices, both negatively as well as positively. Guerreiro and colleagues (2004) use the term 'the management lottery' to illustrate the variable and discretionary power that managers hold in relation to ensure – or hinder – employees' access to and use of family-friendly entitlements in the workplace. For fathers, taking parental leave requires approaching their immediate superior with a request to prioritise family life over work–life for some period. This is possibly difficult in a work–life characterised by demands for both flexibility and presence. Facing costs at the workplace as a consequence of taking leave might get fathers to limit leave use, as Bygren and Duvander find in their study of Swedish workplaces (2006). The interviews carried out in three Danish workplaces, a study among Danish fathers in different branches and sectors (Bloksgaard, 2011), and a recent Danish survey (DJØF, 2011) all indicate that this may also be the case in Denmark.

Janus' case shows that Telia fathers do not stand entirely alone when negotiating leave with their superiors; they enjoy the support of a female HR manager (who is a mother herself and states openly that she is favourably disposed towards fathers on leave). Together with the aforementioned bending of rules concerning the placement of parental leave – implemented by the same HR manager – this is a possible explanation for the considerable leave take-up among fathers in Telia. At the same time, there is a large group of younger employees and managers in Telia with young children, who must balance their work and family lives and who are positive towards family-friendly work conditions and entitlements; other Danish workplace studies emphasise the importance hereof for fathers' leave use (Holt, 1994; Olsen, 2005).

Ulrik, a manager in 'The Shop', is another father whose negotiation of parental leave was studied. Ulrik was interviewed three times over a one-year period. In the first interview, approximately a month before becoming a father, Ulrik explains that he wants to take the two weeks of paternity leave as well as one or two months of parental leave towards the end of the parental leave period so that his wife, who is also in a managerial position, can return to work. Ulrik is thus the first male employee in 'The Shop' to request parental leave, and he explains that "I have told them about my intentions about taking parental leave. In HR they said, 'We'll have to figure out how we do that…'. I'm not sure how willing the company is in relation to this…. But I think they'll accept it." As the earlier quote from the HR representative in 'The Shop' also illustrated, however, no other fathers employed in 'The Shop' have ever taken parental leave, meaning that procedures for 'fathers' leave' will have to be invented.

The second interview with Ulrik is one month after he became a father and he has already used his two weeks of paternity leave. In this interview, he expresses very strong feelings for his little daughter, and an ideal of 'the present father', which he relates to lengthy leave:

"Even if there would be fire and brimstone [at the workplace], I would take leave – I had already decided that when my wife got pregnant. It was so important to me. Cause I will not be the kind of father about whom people say 'that guy – he's always working'. Damn it, I want to be there! It might sound like an old romantic speech or an ideal that will not turn out – but hell, I mean it!"

Ulrik earned a promotion at work at around the same time he became a father. When asked about the one or two months of parental leave that he indicated he would take in the first interview, he responds that he would still like to take a month of parental leave but that he is not sure whether it is possible in his new position. The third time Ulrik is interviewed, his daughter is almost one year old. He explains that because of personal reasons in the family and his new position at work, he has ended up not taking any parental leave at all. Thus, Ulrik explains the lack of using his leave entitlement as "the unintended results of everyday life incidences". However, looking at several cases, Haavind (1987) emphasises that it often becomes evident that parents' divisions of parental tasks are not individual but must be seen in relation to structural factors. The negotiations Ulrik started in his workplace about parental leave therefore never came to be, as Ulrik ultimately never lived up to his fatherhood ideals about taking longer leave. The next section discusses how the limited leave use among Danish fathers may be understood as a result of conflicting ideals of work and fatherhood within masculinity constructions.

Work or leave: conflicting ideals in fathers' identity constructions?

Ulrik's case illustrates that resistance from superiors in the leave negotiations or fear of leave having negative consequences in the workplace for one's career might not be the only barriers for fathers' leave use. Thus, ideals regarding work and family, respectively, can be competing when individual fathers negotiate *with themselves* about leave. In their construction of masculinity – and leave practices – fathers are influenced by existing ideals regarding masculinity, work and fatherhood and the practices of others in the workplace (Acker, 1990; Morgan, 1992; Brandth and Kvande, 2002, 2003). As described earlier, Morgan (2002, p 281) argues how Scandinavian fathers' constructions of masculinity may be conflicting, as the ideal combining masculinity and work is challenged by strong fatherhood ideals and leave entitlements encouraging fathers to take leave in these countries. The interviews with the Danish fathers, however, indicate that the ideal combining masculinity and work is rarely challenged in Danish workplaces – at least when it comes to taking leave, putting fatherhood ideals into practice.

Among the fathers who are *managers*, an ideal of the present father is most often expressed – and some of these fathers link this ideal to taking parental leave; look back at the quote from Ulrik above. However, a strong work/career ideal can also be observed among these fathers. Martin, a manager in Telia, explains his considerations in relation to taking leave:

> "I took two weeks, and then another two weeks a month later. Because this was the most practical at home.... And by doing it like that, I could also better handle being away from work. As a man, I think that's important. And as a manager ... well, it's not common practice for managers to do something like that.... My new boss, I think that he would react reasonably if I came and told him that I'd take 10 weeks leave. But I don't think that I would do it myself – there's just a lot to take care of at work. So – actually, I think the barrier in relation to work is more psychological than real ...?"

The quote from Martin indicates that even in Telia, with many fathers taking parental leave, it is not 'common practice' for (male) managers to take the 10 weeks' paid parental leave available to them (whereas it is normal practice, expected and seen as unproblematic that female managers take leave for an entire year; the interviewees in all three workplaces mention this without commenting on the obvious contradiction). The quote reflects how individuals themselves are contributing to the (re)production of certain working life and masculinity ideals. Holgersson and colleagues (2004) argue that management ideals are usually more a culture reproduced by managers than actual demands from the companies. In all three workplaces, management is associated with long hours and presence (see also Hochschild, 1997; Rutherford, 2001; Kvande and Rasmussen, 2007). When a young male employee without children in 'The Shop' is asked if he thinks that his male superior, who will soon be a father, would be taking three to four months' parental leave, he replies: "No, I definitely don't think so! [Laughing]. Mark's a very serious man! He's very involved and ... no, really, I don't think he'd be the type to leave his job for so long." Perceptions like this are expressed in all three workplaces, showing that fathers who are managers or who aspire to become managers may be met with scepticism if they make a request for a lengthy period of leave (see also Nordberg, 2007).

The analysis indicates that such ideas regarding masculinity, management and leave produced by colleagues, superiors and the fathers themselves possibly influence fathers' constructions of leave practices. In Martin's case, the work/career ideal determines his construction of leave practice. Those interviewed fathers who are managers all prioritise work over a longer period of parental leave. And the managers who express fatherhood ideals linked to a lengthy parental leave, such as Ulrik, express no ambivalence when this is not transformed into actual parental leave use, indicating that career ideals are more powerful than ideals of fatherhood in the form of long parental leave among these fathers (Collinson and Hearn, 1996).

An ideal of the present father is also expressed by some of the interviewed fathers who are *employees*: Brian, from IKEA, has taken the six weeks of paid paternity leave offered over three two-week periods, which is common practice for fathers employed at IKEA. He explains: "I've participated at home on equal terms with my wife.... I'd like to prove, with my three kids, that fathers can be just as closely attached to their children as their mother." However, none of these fathers link their ideals of 'the present father' to taking parental leave. Alex, an employee in 'The Shop', is married to a stewardess and therefore spends a lot of time caring for his children alone. But despite constructing a fatherhood practice, being often the primary parent responsible for caring for his children in the family, he has not taken any parental leave. He explains: "I didn't know that I could share some of it with my wife. Even if you receive the papers, you're thinking 'leave – that's for the mother'. You're not even thinking that it might be relevant for yourself." And Rolf, a Telia employee who has taken 10 weeks of parental leave, comments on sharing leave between him and his girlfriend:

> "My girlfriend has 'full leave' – except for the 10 weeks that I have stolen from her.... I took parental leave because she would also like to get back to her normal life and job.... We found the leave entitlement rules very confusing. So when we found out that Telia offers 10 weeks with pay – well, then that was how we did it."

The quotes clearly show that parental leave is perceived as 'for mothers' and therefore must be 'stolen' if fathers want part of it; this perception is widespread in the interviews in all three workplaces. Despite the gender-neutral intentions in the parental leave in the Danish legislation, this entitlement is automatically linked to motherhood and not fatherhood. The highly gendered expectations of work and leave in the workplace mean that fathers taking parental leave are defying expectations, which might not be regarded as 'gender-appropriate behaviour' (West and Zimmerman, 1987). When Bryan, an IKEA employee, is asked if it would be acceptable for a male IKEA employee to take a long period of parental leave, he answers: "It's hard to imagine.... Because that's to be expected of a woman. But if a man does it.... I think it would be frowned on." The analysed negotiations show that such gendered expectations regarding work and leave at the workplace level can influence fathers' constructions of leave practices and their actual leave use (see also Haas and Hwang, 1995).

All of the fathers who are IKEA employees and who have taken paternity leave, and most of the fathers who are Telia employees and who have taken a lengthy period of parental leave, have divided this leave into shorter periods, as doing so can be better combined with work–life, they explain. The quote from Rolf above illustrates one more thing in common for the majority of fathers who are employees and take leave: an ideal pertaining to sharing parenthood responsibilities and equal opportunities for women in the labour market – rather than an ideal of the present father – is often given as the reason for fathers taking parental leave. The analysis indicates that, in Denmark, the ideal combining work and masculinity largely goes unchallenged. The (perceived) hindrances in work–life seem to legitimise fully that Danish fathers do not take parental leave. This result is culturally framed by the Danish context, where, as earlier mentioned, there is neither a father's quota in the legislation to constitute normative guidelines for the practices of fathers nor any strong ideal according to which fathers ought to become involved in childcare by taking leave – and thereby a long time off from work. Despite the fact that ideals of the present father and childcaring fatherhood practices are identified among the interviewed Danish fathers, the analysis suggests that these fatherhood ideals are not challenging the work/career ideal – at least not in a way that leads to lengthy parental leave use.

Conclusion

This chapter clearly illustrates that the workplace level is important when attempting to understand Danish fathers' limited leave use compared to fathers in most of the other Nordic countries. The analysis shows that the fact that fathers must negotiate leave individually in the workplace – without support from a legislated father's quota – can affect fathers' leave practices. Paid leave entitlement for parents (or fathers specifically) given in collective agreements and at the workplace level can contribute to making longer leave a possibility for fathers – in some workplaces. However, the existence of such an entitlement is no guarantee that fathers actually use it, as shown in the analysis in the three studied workplaces. Instead, workplace norms, including masculinity ideals and 'what other fathers do' in relation to leave in the workplace, seems to be significant for masculinity constructs and leave practices among fathers. As fathers must negotiate their leave with their immediate superior, the question of taking leave or not can depend on the superiors and their goodwill and individual attitudes towards 'fathers and leave-taking'. The managerial power present in the leave negotiations and fathers' fear of leave having negative consequences in work–life may limit whether or not they take leave – and their willingness to bring leave-taking up for negotiation in the workplace. The analysis indicates that support from the HR department in the leave negotiations with the superiors is important for fathers' leave use, as it may counteract the power of the superiors in these negotiations.

This chapter has shown that highly gendered expectations for women and men as parents/leave-takers and workers/providers, respectively, exist in the three workplaces studied. These findings confirm earlier Danish workplace studies (see, for example, Holt et al, 2006). Furthermore, the sharable and assumed gender-neutral Danish parental leave is perceived as being 'for mothers'. This finding supports research in the other Nordic countries showing that the mother usually takes all of the sharable leave entitlement and the father only the elements earmarked specifically for fathers (Duvander and Lammi-Taskula, 2011). When considering the construction of masculinity observed among the Danish fathers in this study, work ideals seem to be more important than ideals of 'the present father' as one who takes a long period of leave. If a longer parental leave (or extended paternity leave) is taken, it is typically divided into shorter periods, which makes it more adaptable to work–life demands. These findings must be seen in relation to the fact that, in Denmark, there is neither a strong cultural ideal of 'the present father' as one who takes leave nor a legislative father's quota setting limits for fathers' work–life and legitimising leave as 'appropriate behaviour' for fathers in the workplace.

The findings emphasise the importance of minimising the element of individual negotiations at the workplace level in relation to encouraging more Danish fathers to put their fatherhood ideals and practices into leave use. The fact that fathers must negotiate leave individually in the workplace, where the ideal connecting masculinity and work is strong and without the support that a legislative father's quota may provide, must be seen as an important explanation for the limited leave use among Danish fathers.

Notes

[1] Correspondingly, Holter (2007) argues that the Norwegian father's quota has – unintentionally – been instrumental in cementing the traditional perception that parental leave (in general) is 'leave for the mother'.

[2] This clause has been changed in the collective agreement in the industrial sector from 2012, allowing parents to take the parental leave within a year form the birth of the child.

References

Acker, J. (1990) 'Hierarchies, jobs, bodies: a theory of gendered organizations', *Gender and Society*, vol 4, no 2, pp 139-58.

Beck, U. (2000) *The brave new world of work*, Cambridge: Polity Press.

Bloksgaard, L. (2009) 'Arbejdsliv, forældreskab og køn: Forhandlinger af løn og barsel i tre moderne virksomheder' ['Work life, parenthood and gender: Negotiations of wage and parental leave in three modern work organisations'], Unpublished PhD thesis, Aalborg University.

Bloksgaard, L. (2011) *Mænd, barselsrettigheder og brug af barsel* [*Men, leave entitlement and leave use*], Copenhagen: 3F.

Bloksgaard, L. (2012) '"No, gender doesn't make a difference…?" Studying negotiations and gender in organizations', *Qualitative Studies*, vol 3, no 2, pp 150-62.

Bloksgaard, L. (2013) 'Uten fedrekvote i lovgivningen: Danske fedres forhandlinger om permisjon fra arbeidet' ['Without a father's quota in the legislation: Danish fathers negotiating leave from work'], in B. Brandth and E. Kvande (eds) *Fedrekvoten og den farsvennlige velferdsstaten* [*The father's quota and the father friendly welfare state*]. Oslo: Oslo Universitetsforlag, pp 194-210.

Bloksgaard, L. and Rostgaard, T. (2014) 'Denmark country note', in: P. Moss (ed) *International Review of Leave Policies and Research 2014*. Available at: www.leavenetwork.org/fileadmin/Leavenetwork/ Country_notes/2014/Denmark.pdf

Bonke, J. (2009) 'Forældre bruger stadig mere tid på deres børn' ['Parents are using still more time with their children'], in *Nyt fra Rockwollfondens forskningsenhed* [*The Rockwool Foundation Research Unit Newsletter*], October.

Borchorst, A. (2006) 'The public-private split rearticulated: abolishment of the Danish daddy leave', in A.L. Ellingsæter and A. Leira (eds) *Politicising parenthood: Gender relations in a Scandinavian welfare state design*, Cambridge: Polity Press, pp 101-20.

Brandth, B. and Kvande, E. (2002) 'Reflexive fathers: negotiating parental leave and working life', *Gender, Work and Organization*, vol 9, no 2, pp 186-203.

Brandth, B, and Kvande, E. (2003) *Fleksible fedre* [*Flexible fathers*], Oslo: Universitetsforlaget.

Brandth, B. and Kvande E. (2005) 'Valgfri eller øremerket permisjon for fedre?' ['Leave for fathers: optional or earmarked?'], in B. Brandth, B. Bungum and E. Kvande (eds) *Valgfrihetens tid. Omsorgspolitikk for barn møter det fleksible arbeidsliv* [*The freedom of choice. The politics of care in the flexible working life*], Oslo: Gyldendals Akademisk, pp 44-62.

Bygren, M. and Duvander, A. (2006) 'Parents' workplace situation and fathers' parental leave use', *Journal of Marriage and Family*, vol 68, pp 363-72.

Christensen, A.-D. and Jensen, S.Q. (2014) 'Combining hegemonic masculinity and intersectionality', *NORMA: International Journal for Masculinity Studies*, vol 9, no 1, pp 60-75.

Collinson, D. and Hearn, J. (1994) 'Naming men as men: implications for work, organization and management', *Gender, Work and Organization*, vol 1, no 1, pp 2-22.

Collinson, D. and Hearn, J. (1996) '"Men" at "work": multiple masculinities/multiple workplaces', in M. Mac an Ghaill (ed) *Understanding masculinities*, Buckingham: Open University Press, pp 61-76.

Connell, R.W. (1995) *Masculinities*, Cambridge: Polity Press.

Connell, R.W. (2000) *The men and the boys*, Cambridge: Polity Press.

DJØF (2011) *Danskernes holdninger til barselsorlov* [*Attitudes towards parental leave among the Danes*], Copenhagen: DJØF Publishing.

Due, J. and Madsen, J. S. (2006) *Fra storkonflikt til barselsfond: Den danske model under afvikling eller fornyelse?* [*From conflict to maternity fund: The Danish model – phasing out or renewal?*], Copenhagen: DJØF Publishing.

Duvander, A. and Lammi-Taskula, J. (2011) 'Parental leave', In I.V. Gislason and G.B. Eydal (eds) *Parental leave childcare and gender equality in the Nordic countries*, Copenhagen: Nordic Council of Ministers, pp 31-61.

Emerek, R. and Holt, H. (eds) (2008) *Lige muligheder, frie valg? Om det kønsopdelte arbejdsmarked gennem et årti* [*Equal rights, free choices? The gender-segregated Danish labour market*], Copenhagen: The Danish National Centre for Social Research.

Foucault, M. (1988) 'Technologies of the self', in H. Luther, M.H. Gutman and P.H. Hutton (eds) *Technologies of the self: A seminar with Michel Foucault*, Amherst, MA: University of Massachusetts Press, pp 24-39.

Gíslason, I.V. (2007) *Parental leave in Iceland. Bringing the fathers in. Developments in the wake of new legislation in 2000*, Helsinki: Centre for Gender Equality, Ministry of Social Affairs.

Guerreiro, D.D.D., Abrantes, P. and Pereira, I. (2004) *Consolidated case study report for the EU Framework 5 funded study: Gender, parenthood and the changing European workplace*, Manchester: Research Institute for Health and Social Change.

Hatch, M.J. (2006) *Organization theory: Modern, symbolic and postmodern perspectives*, Oxford: Oxford University Press.

Haas, L. and Hwang, P. (1995) 'Company culture and men's usage of family leave benefits in Sweden', *Family Relations*, vol 44, pp 28-36.

Haas, L. and Rostgaard, T. (2011) 'Father's rights to paid parental leave in the Nordic countries: consequences for the gendered division of leave', *Community, Work and Family*, vol 14, no 2, pp 177-95.

Haas, L., Allard, K. and Hwang, P. (2002) 'The impact of organizational culture on men's use of parental leave in Sweden', *Community, Work and Family*, vol 5, no 3, pp 320-42.

Haavind, H. (1987) *Liten og stor: Mødres omsorg og barns utviklingsmuligheter* [*Little and big: Caring mothers and children's opportunity of development*], Oslo: Universitetsforlaget.

Hochschild, A. (1997) *The time bind – When work becomes home and home becomes work*, New York: Henry Holt & Co.

Holgersson, C., Hook, S.L. and Wahl, A. (2004) *Det ordner sig: Teorier om organisation og køn* [*Things will work out: Theories of organisation and gender*], Lund: Samfundslitteratur.

Holt, H. (1994) *Forældre på arbejdspladsen: En analyse af tilpasningsmulighederne mellem arbejdsliv og familieliv i kvinde- og mandefag* [*Parents in the workplace: An analysis of the possibility of combining work life and family life in female and male professions*], Copenhagen: The Danish National Centre for Social Research.

Holt, H., Geerdsen, L.P., Christensen, G., Klitgaard, C. and Lind, M.L. (2006) *Det kønsopdelte arbejdsmarked: En kvantitativ og kvalitativ belysning* [*The gender-divided labour market*], Copenhagen: The Danish National Centre for Social Research.

Holter, Ø.G. (2007) 'Kjønn som innovasjon og det nye pappasporet' ['Gender as innovation and the new "daddy track"'], in E. Kvande and B. Rasmussen (eds) *Arbeidslivets klemmer* [*Tangled up in work life*], Trondheim: Fakbokforlaget, pp 249-79.

Ibsen, F. (2011) *Kollektiv handling: Faglig organisering og skift af fagforening* [*Collective action*], Copenhagen: Nyt fra Samfundsvidenskaberne.

Krarup, M. and Andersen, A. (2004) *Barselsregler: Fleksibilitet, fravær og dagpenge* [*Leave entitlement: Flexibility, absence and benefits*], Copenhagen: Forlaget Thomsen.

Kvande, E. (2007) *Doing gender in flexible organizations*, Bergen: Fakbokforlaget.

Kvande, E. and Rasmussen, B. (2007) 'Indledning' ['Introduction'], in E. Kvande and B. Rasmussen (eds) *Arbeidslivets klemmer: Paradokser i det nye arbeidsliv* [*Tangled up in work life*], Trondheim: Fakbokforlaget, pp 13-28.

Lammi-Taskula, J. (2007) 'Faderskap på arbetsplatsen – att komma ut ur skapet' ['Fathering at the workplace – getting out of the closet'], in Ø.G. Holter (ed) *Män i rörelse. Jämstalldhet, förändring och social innovation i Norden* [*Men in movement. Gender equality, change and social innovation in the Nordic region*], Riga: Gidlunds Förlag, pp 62-74.

Morgan, D. (1992) *Discovering men*, London: Routledge.

Morgan, D. (2002) 'Epilogue', in B. Hobsen (ed) *Making men into fathers: Men, masculinities and the social politics of fatherhood*, Cambridge: Cambridge University Press, pp 1-4.

Nordberg, M. (2007) 'En "riktig man" gör karriär… Diskursbrott, ambivalenser och mäns längtan' ['"Real" men have careers… Discourse violations, ambivalences, and men's longing], in Ø.G. Holter (ed) *Män i rörelse. Jämstalldhet, förändring och social innovation i Norden* [*Men in movement. Gender equality, change and social innovation in the Nordic region*], Riga: Gidlunds Förlag, pp 312-59.

Nordic Statistical Yearbook (2012) Nordic Council of Ministers, Copenhagen.

O'Brien, M., Brandth, B. and Kvande, E. (2007) 'Fathers, work and family life: global perspectives and new insights', *Community, Work and Family*, vol 10, no 4, pp 375-86.

Olsen, B.M. (2000) *Nye fædre på orlov* [*New fathers taking leave*], Copenhagen: Department of Sociology, University of Copenhagen.

Olsen, B.M. (2005) *Mænd, orlov og arbejdspladskultur* [*Men, leave and workplace culture*], Copenhagen: The Danish National Centre for Social Research.

Rose, N. (1999) *Governing the soul: Of the private self*, London: Free Association Books by Chase Publishing.

Rostgaard, T. (2002) 'Setting time aside for the father: father's leave in Scandinavia', *Community, Work and Family*, vol 5, no 3, pp 343-70.

Rutherford, S. (2001) 'Are you going home already?', *Time and Society*, vol 10, no 2-3, pp 259-76.

Sennett, R. (1999) *Det fleksible menneske – eller arbejdets forvandling og personlighedens Nedsmeltning* [*The corrosion of character*], Højbjerg: Forlaget Hovedbjerg.

Statistics Denmark (2012) *Statistiske efterretninger: Dagpenge ved graviditet, fødsel og adoption 2011* [*Statistical news on social security benefits in relation to pregnancy, birth and adoption*], Copenhagen: Statistics Denmark.

Skyt Nielsen, H., Simonsen, M. and Verner, M. (2004) 'Does the gap in family-friendly policies drive the family gap?', *Scandinavian Journal of Economics*, vol 106, no 4, pp 721-44.

Strauss, A. (1978) *Negotiations: Varieties, contexts, processes and social order*, San Francisco, CA: Jossey-Bass.

West, C. and Zimmerman, D.H. (1987) 'Doing gender', *Gender and Society*, vol 1, no 2, pp 125-51.

EIGHT

Gender regime, attitudes towards childcare and actual involvement in childcare among fathers

Mikael Nordenmark

Introduction

Going beyond the approach taken in the other chapters in this book, which focus specifically on the Nordic countries, and in order to better illustrate the 'Nordicness' of fatherhood, this chapter compares the attitudes and behaviour among fathers in the Nordic and Southern European regions. The reason for comparing these two regions is that they represent two very different gender policy regimes: the Nordic countries (in this chapter represented by Denmark, Finland, Iceland, Norway and Sweden) are often considered to represent a typical dual earner/dual carer regime, whereas the Southern European countries (in this chapter represented by Greece, Portugal and Spain) are often considered to represent a typical male breadwinner regime. The question then becomes whether the gender policies fit the attitudes: does the lack of policy development in the direction of more active fatherhood policies in the Southern European region correspond to the general perceptions among fathers in this region about gender equality in household work and caring for children? And do the Nordic fathers stand out in their perceptions about such matters? Another question is if the fathers' attitudes correspond to their practices.

The analysis is based on an extensive cross-country data set collected within the framework of the European Social Survey (ESS) 2004. Results show that the dual earner/dual carer regime fathers are more involved in both housework and childcare than the male breadwinner regime fathers. There is a correspondence between statements about which role fathers should play and how they actually become involved in family life, and fathers' attitudes towards family responsibilities explain some of the differences between gender policy regimes regarding the actual involvement of fathers in housework and childcare.

The chapter is structured as follows. First, there is a presentation of the general goals within the European Union (EU) to strengthen policies for equal opportunities and responsibilities for mothers and fathers and what has been introduced. This part also discusses differences in this respect between different parts of Europe, and explains why the Nordic countries and countries in Southern Europe can be considered as opposites regarding types of gender policy regimes, and that this fact may have a varying influence on fathers' attitudes and behaviour. It ends with a formulation of some specific research questions to analyse. The next part presents the data and variables used in the study. This is followed by a presentation of the results from descriptive and multivariate analyses of the research questions. The chapter ends with a presentation of the conclusions and discussion of the results.

Background

How do the policies aimed at strengthening equal opportunities for fathers and mothers in work and family life vary across Western Europe? When considering Europe and the EU as a whole, one of the main political goals is to strengthen the policies aimed at providing equal opportunities and responsibilities for men and women. Special attention has been paid in the EU to policies aimed at stimulating employment among mothers, childcare responsibility among fathers and the reconciliation of work and family life, followed up in some member states more than others. This should largely be brought about by providing abundant and high-quality childcare services, encouraging fathers and mothers to share family and professional responsibilities, and facilitating the return of parents to work after parental leave. Policies should facilitate career breaks, parental leave and part-time work for both fathers and mothers. It is particularly important that member states provide adequate childcare, thereby removing one of the barriers to female labour force participation in order to support the entry and continued participation of women in the labour market. On a more concrete level, the Barcelona European Council agreed in 2003 that member states should be providing childcare by 2010 for at least 90 per cent of all pre-school children ages three and older, and at least 33 per cent of all children under age three (Council Directive 2003/578/EC).

There are, however, crucial differences in how far various countries have come in the process of creating policy measures aimed at stimulating an equal sharing of work and family responsibilities among mothers and fathers. The Nordic countries are outliers in this area.

In research related to organisation and the characteristics of different types of social policy contexts and welfare states, the Nordic states are normally classified as representing an extensive and comprehensive policy context. Characteristics include encouragement for independence, mainly through paid labour, combined with universal social policy schemes. The goal is to maximise individual autonomy and minimise family dependence. Family policy encourages female labour market participation, emphasises gender equality and women's independence from men, and aims at enabling the combination of paid work and parenthood among both mothers and fathers (Lewis, 1992; Walby, 1994; Duncan, 1996; Korpi and Palme, 1998; Esping-Andersen, 1999, 2009; Bradshaw and Hatland, 2006; Ellingsæter and Leira, 2006; Lewis et al, 2008; Gíslason and Eydal, 2011).

Overall, the policies are directed towards providing conditions that facilitate increased gender equality and making social citizenship more gender-neutral. While somewhat different from country to country, the Nordic countries all have relatively long and flexible parental leave schemes with relatively high compensation levels. There are also publicly subsidised, full-time childcare facilities, which enable women and men to continue to work after taking leave. To stimulate the involvement of fathers in childcare, all of these countries, except Denmark, have introduced a father's quota, meaning that some of the months of parental leave cannot be transferred to the other parent (see also Chapters Six, Thirteen, Fifteen and Sixteen, this volume). Although there are differences between the Nordic countries, the evident similarities imply that these countries can be classified as representing a typical gender policy regime: the dual earner/dual carer regime (Lewis, 1992; Sainsbury, 1999; Ellingsæter and Leira, 2006; Lewis et al, 2008; Backhans et al, 2011; Eydal and Rostgaard, 2011).

When considering the countries in Southern Europe, there is greater heterogeneity regarding the types of policies and welfare state arrangements. Cross-country variations are significant. There have also been several shifts in the parental leave schemes in most of these countries in recent years towards more generous and lengthier benefit levels (Morgan, 2009). For example, Spain now has one of the longest total parental leave plans in Western Europe (although the number of 'paid' weeks is relatively low) (Ray et al, 2009).

Despite this diversity among the countries in Southern Europe and the development towards similarities with the Nordic model, these countries are generally characterised by more passive, less comprehensive family policies than the Nordic countries. Although family policies have become more similar to the family policies in the Nordic countries, the Southern European policies still primarily consist of support from the state for the male breadwinner family, that is, families consisting of a full-time employed man and a woman shouldering the primary responsibility for the housework and childcare. There are fewer policy measures aimed at breaking up the traditional division of labour and the strengthening of women's independence from men. The Catholic Church has played a central role in promoting traditional, family-oriented values, resulting in a family-centred ideology wherein the family plays a central role in the organisation of welfare. This means that the policy largely supports the preservation of traditional family ties and norms contributing to the maintenance of a family-centred welfare state type (Lewis, 1992; Walby, 1994; Duncan, 1996; Korpi and Palme, 1998; Esping-Andersen, 1999, 2009; Lewis et al, 2008). Consequently, these countries have been classified as belonging to a specific welfare state model, often referred to as the Latin Rim, Mediterranean model or Southern European model (Leibfried, 1992; Ferrera, 2007; Esping-Andersen, 2009; Tavora, 2012). The Southern European states are therefore classified as representing a typical gender policy regime: the male breadwinner regime (Lewis, 1992; Sainsbury, 1999; Backhans et al, 2011).

Corresponding to the type of gender policy in the Nordic countries, the Nordic countries subscribe to a relatively egalitarian gender ideology, meaning that most people hold attitudes that are largely in line with the policy. An attitude may be defined as an individual's evaluation of people, objects, activities or ideas (Allport, 1935). Comparative studies have shown that most of the people in these countries support the notion of gender equality (Sundström, 2003; Nordenmark, 2004a, 2004b; Strandh and Nordenmark, 2006). Correspondingly, Southern Europeans generally also hold attitudes that are more in line with the gender policy in these states. Comparative studies have thus indicated that Southern European women and men are more likely to express a more traditional gender ideology than those living in the Nordic countries, meaning that they are more inclined to support the idea that women should bear the main responsibility for the household while men should be the main breadwinners. (Nordenmark, 2004a, 2004b; Telpt, 2008; Tavora, 2012). Telpt (2008) shows that the residents of Southern Europe – along with populations in Eastern Europe – generally have the most traditional gender values in Europe.

There is also some support for the type of gender policy regime and gender ideology possibly influencing the behaviour of women and men. The employment rates for women in the Nordic countries are high in relation to the employment rates for Southern European women, with the exception of Portugal, where female employment rates are similar to the Nordic countries (Lewis et al, 2008). The average number of working hours per week shows that although many Nordic women work part time, they work more hours in relation to the countries in Southern Europe (Nordenmark, 2004a, 2004b; Strandh and Nordenmark, 2006; Lewis et al, 2008; OECD, 2010). Moreover, research indicates that there is a more equal division of household labour in the Nordic countries, as Nordic men do more housework than Southern European men, including Portuguese men (Gershuny and Sullivan, 2003; Nordenmark, 2004a, 2004b; Ellingsæter and Leira, 2006; Strandh and Nordenmark, 2006; Lewis et al, 2008; Craig and Mullan, 2010; OECD 2010).

With this background, it becomes possible to draw some general conclusions regarding the connections between gender policy contexts, attitudes and actual practice in working and family life in the countries of Western Europe. Although the EU has a general political goal aimed at strengthening the policies contributing to equal opportunities and responsibilities for women and men, differences remain in terms of how far the respective countries have come in the process of creating these policy measures. Despite the fact that there are significant variations between single states, it is possible to discern two regions representing rather opposing gender policy regimes.

At one end of the continuum is the Nordic model, where considerable resources are invested in extensive and ambitious family policies aimed at facilitating the combination of work and family responsibilities among mothers and fathers alike, not to mention gender equality in general. Furthermore, existing research indicates that this policy is reflected somewhat in popular attitudes to gender and female and male behaviour. The gender policy in the Nordic states can therefore be classified as a typical dual earner/dual carer regime. At the other end of the continuum are the Southern Europe states, which have less comprehensive and more passive family policies, consisting mainly of state support for the male breadwinner model. These policies support the preservation of traditional attitudes and gender roles. The gender policy regime in this region can be classified as a typical male breadwinner regime.

Most of the above studies regarding attitudes and behaviour in different gender policy regimes have been based on samples from the whole population of various countries. This study further analyses the relationships between gender policy regime, attitudes and behaviour by focusing on *fathers*, contrasting fathers living in dual earner/dual carer and male breadwinner regimes, respectively. The main interest in this chapter is to study if the level of paternal involvement in family life is somewhat in line with the attitudes towards family responsibilities and the type of gender policy regime surrounding the fathers.

In light of the discussion above, one hypothesis is that the type of gender policy regime that has been implemented in a country will influence the attitudes of fathers towards family responsibilities, and that these attitudes will in turn influence their involvement in family life. The type of gender policy regime will possibly also have a direct influence on behaviour. However, significant relationships between policy, attitudes and behaviour can also be interpreted as an opposite causal direction; namely, that behaviour influences attitudes, which in turn will form policy (the question about causality is discussed further in the next section regarding data and measures). A final hypothesis is that the possible differences in attitudes between fathers living in dual earner/dual carer versus male breadwinner regimes will reduce some of the differences in the level of involvement in family life possibly existing between the fathers living in the two different gender policy regime types. This leads to the following aim and research questions.

The aim is to study the relationships between gender policy regime, attitude towards family responsibilities and actual involvement in family life among fathers by analysing the following research questions:

- First, is there a relationship between the type of gender policy regime and actual involvement in housework and childcare among fathers?
- Second, is there a relationship between the attitude towards family responsibilities and actual involvement in housework and childcare among fathers?
- And last, can attitudes towards family responsibilities reduce some of the differences between gender policy regimes regarding the actual involvement of fathers in housework and childcare?

Data and methods

The data stem from the European Social Survey (ESS) 2004 (ESS, 2012a). Conducted since 2002, the ESS is a comparative study that now includes more than 30 European countries. It includes thematic sections that appear cyclically across the investigation occasions. The 2004 investigation contains the in-depth theme 'Family, work and well-being' in 25 countries. This section focuses on the relationships between work, family and well-being. There is a 2010 version of the ESS with the same theme, but that data set does not include all of the questions used in this study and excludes Iceland. The investigation includes questions about gender role attitudes and actual levels of involvement in working and family life. The ESS represents a further development of the International Social Survey (ISSP) in two respects: (1) data are collected via interviews, resulting in a higher response frequency and better quality data; and (2) background variables have been standardised. This study only includes cohabiting/married fathers living with children.

Different gender policy regime types are identified by categorising states representing a typical dual earner/dual carer regime in one category and states representing a typical male breadwinner regime in another. In the light of the discussion in the introduction to this chapter, the Nordic countries are defined as representing a dual earner/dual carer regime, whereas the states of Southern Europe represent a male breadwinner regime. The ESS includes the Nordic countries Denmark, Finland, Iceland, Norway and Sweden, which together form a typical dual earner/dual carer regime. The Southern European countries included in the ESS are Greece, Portugal and Spain, which together form a typical male breadwinner regime.

The individual's attitude towards family responsibility is measured in terms of the survey statement: 'Men should take as much responsibility as women for the home and children'. Responses vary in five steps from 'disagree strongly' to 'agree strongly'. Actual involvement in housework is measured by a question asking how much of the total time the respondents spend on housework (defined as things done around the home: cooking, washing, cleaning, care of clothes, shopping and property maintenance). Responses vary in six steps from 'none or almost none of the time' to 'all or nearly all of the time'. Very few fathers do most or even half of the housework, so the variable is therefore dichotomised to does 'more than a quarter' and 'less than a quarter' of the housework.

There is no question in the ESS focusing entirely on childcare responsibility, but there is a question formulated as 'Apart from housework, do you look after others in your household, such as small children or someone ill, disabled or elderly?' (Yes or No). Here, it is acknowledged that there is no indication of how much time needs to be invested before one can fully claim that one is looking after others in the household, which makes the question imprecise. Furthermore, the question is very broad and general, which can make comparing the responses from different parts of Europe problematic. Ho the analysis of the question shows that only 10 per cent of those who are *not* living with children have answered 'Yes' to this question. This indicates that the question mainly measures childcare, which legitimises the use of the question as a broad indication of the level of childcare responsibility.

The multivariate analyses control for background characteristics that can be assumed to be of relevance for the attitudes to family responsibility and actual involvement in family life among fathers. 'Stage in life' is indicated by the respondent's age. Qualification level is measured using the respondent's and partner's highest level of education (primary, secondary, tertiary education). Labour market status is indicated by questions asking if the respondent and the partner are gainfully employed or not (Yes or No).

Obviously, establishing the causal directions between policy, attitude and behaviour is difficult, especially in cross-sectional studies such as this, and it is reasonable to assume that these factors influence each other in complicated ways. However, although many of the family policies are recent, one can at least argue that some policies exist before the individual is born, implying that at least some part of a relationship between policy and attitudes can be interpreted as an influence of policy on attitudes. Similarly, one might argue that many of the individuals' attitudes are formed during the childhood and teen years, which is normally before the individual meets a partner and becomes a parent. This makes it even more reasonable to consider the relationship between attitude and behaviour in terms of the former having an influence on the latter (Nordenmark, 2004b).

Finally, analysing statistics generated from comparative statistics is not entirely unproblematic. The results should therefore be interpreted with some caution. There are at least two main limitations that are important to bear in mind when analysing the material. First, the framing of questions and attitudes is context-dependent, meaning that certain questions may be understood and interpreted differently in different cultural and national contexts. For instance, different societal traditions and cultures might possibly influence how the individual will report attitudes and behaviour, entailing a risk that the answers will reflect differences in how people respond to surveys rather than indicating genuine differences in attitudes and behaviour (Harzing, 2006). This is possibly most problematic regarding the behaviour. When analysing the attitudes, one aim is in fact to study if societal differences in the form of policies will in some sense structure the attitudes of the individuals. Second, there are some differences between the studied countries regarding sampling, representativeness and response rates. However, the respondents are weighted according to the principles described on the web page for ESS 2004 (ESS, 2012b) in order to assure that the samples correspond to comparable sources of statistics in each country. This means that the samples should be fairly nationally representative.

Gender policy regime shaping fathers' attitudes and involvement in family life

This section analyses the general aim of this chapter, which is to study if a father's level of family life involvement is in line with his attitudes towards family responsibilities and the type of gender policy regime surrounding them, and to try to answer the research questions formulated in the end of the 'Background' section.

Table 8.1 provides a descriptive picture among all of the countries included of the percentage of fathers doing more than a quarter of the total housework in the home, who are looking after children and who state that men and women should share the responsibility for the home and children equally. Table 8.1 thus displays the differences *within* gender policy regime models as well as *between* models before proceeding to analyse the differences between models.

As the results in Table 8.1 illustrate, there are numerous similarities in attitudes and involvement between the countries that are defined as representing male breadwinner and dual earner/dual carer regimes respectively, but there are also some interesting differences within each cluster of states. The results regarding the variable indicating the level of involvement in housework show that fathers in countries representing a dual earner/dual carer regime report that they do more housework than fathers in male breadwinner regime states. Swedish fathers are self-reportedly the most involved in housework, whereas Greek and Portuguese fathers report being the least involved among the studied countries.

The results regarding paternal involvement in childcare show some intra- as well as inter-regime differences. Portugal in particular differs from the other states in the male breadwinner regime, and Portuguese fathers are even more involved than the fathers in some of the states in the dual earner/dual carer category. Danish fathers are self-reportedly less involved in childcare than the fathers in the other Nordic countries. Attitudes to family responsibilities seem to be structured by the type of gender policy regime, with the exception of Norway, where the percentage is on the same level as the countries representing a male breadwinner regime. Despite the fact that there

Table 8.1: Involvement in housework, involvement in childcare and attitude towards family responsibilities among cohabiting/married fathers in all countries included (%)

	Do >25% of the total housework	Are looking after children	Men should have as much responsibility as women for home and children (agree strongly)	N
Male breadwinner regime				
Spain	28	34	23	324
Greece	15	33	21	449
Portugal	15	49	22	318
N				1092
Dual earner/dual carer regime				
Denmark	58	29	40	219
Finland	62	59	35	313
Iceland	60	44	33	127
Norway	56	55	23	322
Sweden	70	55	32	285
N				1266

are some intra-regime differences, overall the countries seem to follow a common pattern. The next part of this chapter therefore focuses on gender policy regime differences. This makes it possible to develop a perspective on the 'Nordic/Southern fatherhoods'.

This section describes proportions and correlations regarding the actual involvement in housework and childcare, attitudes towards family responsibilities and background variables among fathers living in male breadwinner and dual earner/dual carer regimes, respectively.

Table 8.2 compares values on the independent variables between the male breadwinner and dual earner/dual carer regimes. The results indicate that it is more common for fathers living in a dual earner/dual carer regime to state that they are involved in housework and childcare to a considerable degree. Twenty-four per cent of those living in the male breadwinner regime and 63 per cent in the dual earner/dual carer regime state that they do more than a quarter of the housework; 36 per cent in the male breadwinner regime and 50 per cent in the dual earner/dual carer regime respond that they look after their children relatively often; 22 per cent of the fathers living in the male breadwinner regime and 33 per cent of those in the dual earner/dual carer regime say that they agree *strongly* with the statement that men should take as much responsibility as women for the home and children.

Table 8.2: Cohabiting/married fathers living in a male breadwinner regime and a dual earner/dual carer regime, by attitude towards family responsibilities, actual involvement in housework, actual involvement in childcare and background variables (%)

	Male breadwinner regime	Dual earner/dual carer regime
Do >25% of total housework	24	63
Looking after children	36	50
Men and women equal responsibility	22	33
Age (mean)	49	43
Education		
Primary	41	7
Secondary	42	57
Tertiary	18	36
Education partner		
Primary	39	5
Secondary	45	56
Tertiary	17	39
Gainfully employed	78	92
Gainfully employed partner	42	78
N (weighted)	1019	311

The mean age indicates that dual earner/dual carer regime fathers are on average six years younger than male breadwinner regime fathers. It is much more common for fathers and their partners in the dual earner/dual carer regime to have an education above primary level. Only a small percentage of the respondents and their partners have an education less than tertiary education in the dual earner/dual carer regime, whereas the same figure is around 40 per cent for the male breadwinner regime. Table 8.2 shows that almost all of the dual earner/dual carer regime fathers are gainfully employed, as compared to 78 per cent of the male breadwinner regime fathers. As many as 78 per cent of the partners in the dual earner/dual carer regimes are gainfully employed, which is a substantially higher proportion than the proportion of working partners in the male breadwinner regime. This is important to bear in mind when analysing the results.

Table 8.3 illustrates how the variables measuring involvement in housework and childcare, attitude to family responsibilities, age, respondent and partner's education, and respondent and partner's labour market status are correlated to each other in the male breadwinner regime (in plain text) and dual earner/dual carer regime (in bold), respectively.

Table 8.3: Correlation between the variables included within the different gender policy regimes. Male breadwinner regime in plain text, dual earner/dual carer regime in bold (Pearson)

	>25%	Looking after children	Men as much responsibility	Age	Education	Education partner	Gainfully employed	Partner gainfully employed
>25%		0.143**	0.198**	-0.124**	0.199**	0.320**	-0.035	0.363**
Looking after children	0.100		0.192**	-0.399**	0.183**	0.240**	0.144**	0.206**
Men as much responsibility	0.230**	0.041		-0.108**	0.126**	0.176**	0.075**	0.204**
Age	-0.069	-0.461**	-0.002		-0.236**	-0.349**	-0.615**	-0.301**
Education	0.105	0.056	0.052	-0.056		0.552**	0.203**	0.195**
Education partner	0.143*	0.129*	0.091	-0.109	0.441**		0.285**	0.370**
Gainfully employed	-0.055	0.073	-0.040	-0.256**	0.133*	0.163**		0.218**
Gainfully employed partner	0.206**	0.011	0.084	-0.008	0.093	0.198**	0.201**	

**p < 0.01, *p < 0.05

Generally speaking, there are more significant correlations within the male breadwinner regime than the dual earner/dual carer regime. Fathers doing more than a quarter of the housework look after their children significantly more often in the male breadwinner regime, but this correlation is not significant in the dual earner/dual carer regime. Fathers' attitudes towards family responsibility are in general in both models positively correlated to actual involvement in housework and childcare, meaning that those arguing that men should take as much responsibility as women for the home and children also do so more often. However, the correlation between attitude and childcare responsibility is non-significant in the dual earner/dual carer regime.

In the male breadwinner regime, age is significantly negatively correlated to actual involvement in housework and childcare; the older the respondent, the lower their involvement in family responsibilities. However, the correlation between age and involvement in housework is non-significant in the dual earner/dual carer regime. The education levels of the respondent and partner are positively correlated to the variables measuring actual involvement in family life, but the correlation between respondent's education and level of involvement in housework is non-significant in the dual earner/dual carer regime. The male breadwinner regime fathers who are gainfully employed look after the children more than fathers who are not active in the labour market, and the fact that the partner is gainfully employed is positively correlated to actual involvement in family responsibilities. The only significant correlation between labour market involvement and involvement in family responsibilities among the dual earner/dual carer regime fathers is the correlation indicating that fathers living together with an employed partner do more housework.

The results thus far indicate that the dual earner/dual carer regime fathers are more inclined to agree that men should assume an equal responsibility for family life, and they are also more involved in housework and childcare. This attitude is positively correlated with the actual involvement in both housework and childcare, but the correlation between the attitude and childcare is non-significant in the dual earner/dual carer regime. These results generally support the notion that attitudes towards family responsibility possibly influence the actual involvement in family life, and that they may explain some of the differences in the actual involvement between fathers in the respective gender policy regimes.

Furthermore, the dual earner/dual carer regime fathers are generally younger and better educated. They are more likely to live together with a well-educated, gainfully employed partner. In general, age is negatively – and own and partner's education positively – correlated with the attitude and actual involvement in housework and childcare; this is especially true among the male breadwinner regime fathers. This implies that age and education level can also be factors that possibly explain some of the differences between dual earner/dual carer regime fathers versus male breadwinner regime fathers.

These relationships are analysed further using logistic regressions in Tables 8.4 and 8.5. The first regression analysis focuses on the relationships between the dependent variables – actual involvement in housework and childcare – and the independent variable 'attitude to family responsibilities' together with the background variables in the male breadwinner and individual earner-carer contexts, respectively. The second regression analysis examines the relationships between the dependent variables, indicating the actual involvement in family life, and the independent variable gender policy regime when controlling for attitude towards family responsibilities and background characteristics.

Table 8.4 shows how the actual involvement in housework and in childcare are associated with attitudes towards family responsibilities when controlling for the background variables in the respective gender policy regimes. The multivariate results confirm to some extent the general picture in Table 8.3, which illustrated that the relationships among fathers living in the male breadwinner regime are more significant. Models 1, 3, 5 and 7 illustrate the bivariate relationships between the attitude that men should take as much responsibility as women for family life and actual involvement in housework and childcare. Results show that this attitude is strongly related to housework involvement in both gender policy contexts. However, the relationship between the attitude and actual involvement in childcare is only significant in the male breadwinner regime.

When controlling for the background variables in models 2, 4, 6 and 8, the relationships between the attitude and actual involvement in housework and childcare are close to unaffected. Age is significantly negatively related to actual involvement in housework and childcare in all of the models, with the exception of model 4; in other words, the older the respondent, the less time spent on such chores. The only significant relationship between education and involvement in family responsibilities is the relationship in the dual earner/dual carer regime showing that fathers living together with a highly educated partner are more involved in housework than those with a partner with little education (model 2). Gainfully employed fathers are significantly less involved in housework and childcare, but this relationship is non-

Table 8.4: Logistic regression. Actual involvement in housework and actual involvement in childcare, by attitude towards family responsibilities and background variables among cohabiting/married fathers in different gender policy regimes (b-coefficients)

	Do >25% of total housework				Looking after children			
	Male breadwinner		Individual earner-carer		Male breadwinner		Individual earner-carer	
	Model 1	Model 2	Model 3	Model 4	Model 5	Model 6	Model 7	Model 8
Men as much responsibility	0.578***	0.434***	0.691***	0.650***	0.460***	0.417***	0.115	0.107
Age		-0.029**		-0.027		-0.096***		-0.133***
Education								
Primary		-0.452		0.028		-0.363		0.046
Secondary		-0.427		-0.406		-0.017		-0.009
Tertiary ref								
Education partner								
Primary		-1.539***		-0.653		-0.452		-0.648
Secondary		-0.921***		-0.266		-0.298		-0.480
Tertiary ref								
Gainfully employed		-1.670***		-1.234*		-1.076***		-0.224
Gainfully employed partner		1.524***		1.078**		0.255		0.151
Constant	-3.436	0.218	-2.359	-0.302	-2.355	3.484	-0.470	5.571
R² (Nagelkerke)	0.064	0.319	0.071	0.166	0.052	0.296	0.002	0.309
N (weighted)	1007	996	308	305	1010	998	310	308

***p < 0.001 **p < 0.01 *p < 0.05

significant in model 8. Fathers living together with a working partner are more involved in housework, and this is true for both types of gender policy regimes.

The final logistic regressions in Table 8.5 illustrate the degree to which attitudes towards family responsibilities and background variables can explain the differences between fathers living in the dual earner/dual carer and male breadwinner regimes regarding their actual involvement in housework and childcare. Models 1 and 4 support the results from Table 8.2 illustrating that dual earner/dual carer regime fathers are more involved in housework and childcare than male breadwinner regime fathers. When the attitude that 'men should be as involved as women in family responsibilities' is introduced in models 2 and 5, the coefficient for the dual earner/dual carer regime fathers decreases slightly, thus indicating that the attitude explains some of

Table 8.5: Logistic regression. Actual involvement in housework and actual involvement in childcare, by gender policy regime, attitudes towards family responsibilities and background variables among cohabiting/married fathers (b-coefficients)

	Do >25% of total housework			Looking after children		
	Model 1	Model 2	Model 3	Model 4	Model 5	Model 6
Dual earner/dual carer regime	1.667***	1.543***	1.053***	0.587***	0.451**	–0.130
Men as much responsibility		0.603***	0.486***		0.398***	0.362***
Age			–0.029***			–0.101***
Education						
Primary			–0.401			–0.323
Secondary			–0.412*			–0.002
Tertiary ref						
Education partner						
Primary			–1.344***			–0.493*
Secondary			–0.687***			–0.360*
Tertiary ref						
Gainfully employed			–1.593***			–1.020***
Gainfully employed partner			1.413***			0.216
Constant	–1.153	–3.538	–0.137	–0.573	–2.108	3.963
R^2 (Nagelkerke)	0.151	0.206	0.384	0.020	0.056	0.304
N (weighted)	1320	1315	1301	1325	1320	1305

***$p < 0.001$ **$p < 0.01$ *$p < 0.05$

the difference in involvement between the respective gender policy regimes.

Models 3 and 6 also control for the background variables. The influence of the attitude that men and women should share equal responsibility for the home and children remains at a similar level. However, the coefficient for the fathers in the dual earner/dual carer regime falls off even more and becomes non-significant regarding the level of responsibility for children. This means that the background variables explain some of the difference between the gender policy regimes regarding the involvement in housework and all of the still-existent differences regarding childcare involvement.

Specific analyses of the importance of the background variables in models 3 and 6 (not shown) indicate that partner's education explains most of the difference, but age also offers some explanation. This means that the dual earner/dual carer regime fathers are more involved in childcare, because they generally have a more 'egalitarian' attitude, are younger and live together with a well-educated partner more often than the male breadwinner regime fathers. This is also somewhat true for the level of involvement in housework, although the gender policy difference remains significant after controlling for the background variables.

Conclusion

The aim of this study was to analyse the relationships between gender policy regimes, attitudes towards family responsibilities and actual involvement in family life among fathers by analysing three research questions.

The first question was whether there is a relationship between gender policy regime and actual involvement in housework and childcare among fathers, which the results confirm. The dual earner/dual carer regime fathers are more involved in both housework and childcare than the male breadwinner regime fathers. However, the relationship seems stronger between gender policy regime and level of involvement in housework than with childcare involvement. In other words, the equal sharing of unpaid work is more pronounced with regards to daily household chores than childcare. This difference is important, as it structures the availability of men and women for gainful employment. Childcare responsibilities are often less flexible and require immediate, on-the-spot attention, whereas household chores can be planned ahead.

The second question was whether there is an overall relationship between the attitudes towards family responsibilities and the actual involvement in housework and childcare among fathers, regardless of policy regime model. The results reveal a correspondence between statements about which role fathers should play and how they actually become involved in family life. The fathers who agree with the statement that men should share equal responsibility with women for the home and children are more involved in housework and childcare than those who disagree. This could be interpreted as fathers who believe that men and women should share family responsibilities also live out their beliefs to a greater extent than fathers who do not share this idea or, vice versa, that the fathers who are involved in family life also believe that this is how it should be.

The third question was whether fathers' attitudes towards family responsibilities reduce some of the differences between gender policy regimes regarding the actual paternal involvement in housework and childcare. The results show that fathers' attitudes towards family responsibilities explain some of the differences between gender policy regimes regarding the actual involvement of fathers in housework and childcare. The differences in housework and childcare between fathers in the two regime types become smaller when controlling for their attitudes.

Besides the fact that the fathers' attitudes towards family responsibilities explain some of the relationship between gender policy regime and family life involvement, much of the remaining difference between the fathers in the two regimes regarding the level of involvement in childcare and housework is explained by the background characteristics of the fathers. The relationship between gender policy regime and housework involvement is weakened considerably, and the relationship between gender policy regime and level of involvement in childcare is wiped out when controlling for attitude, age, education level and labour market status. Separate analyses (not shown) indicate that much of the explanation power comes from age and partners' level of education, meaning that the partner's education level appears to be of greater importance than the father's own level of education. This is possibly due to highly educated women placing more pressure on their partners to share in the family responsibilities, and that men feel that they must contribute more to family life when their partner is highly educated and has a demanding job.

It is somewhat surprising that the direct relationship between gender policy regime and housework involvement is stronger than the relationship between gender policy regime and childcare, especially in light of the fact that most Nordic countries have introduced policies that are aimed at stimulating the father's involvement in childcare. One explanation might be that the question concerning childcare involvement is rather imprecise and general. Fathers from different parts of Europe might interpret the question differently, which can make comparing the responses from different parts of Europe problematic. This means that the results based on this question should be interpreted with caution.

How should these results be interpreted in relation to the overall aim of this study, which was to analyse the relationships between gender policy regime, attitudes towards family responsibilities and actual involvement in family life among fathers? The fact that age and partner's level of education play a major role can be interpreted in terms of the role of gender policy regime being of minor importance in this case. Conversely, one might argue that a main goal in the dual earner/dual carer regime is to promote egalitarian values, labour market activity among women and women's independence of men. This means that more egalitarian attitudes among fathers and higher education levels among their partners in the dual earner/dual carer regime may result from the policy implemented in this type of gender policy regime. If true, at least some of the explanatory power found in the father's attitudes towards family responsibilities and the partner's level of education can be interpreted as an indirect influence of gender policy regime.

These results imply that some of the differences in the level of involvement in family responsibilities that can be found between the fathers living in the two regime types can be explained by the type of gender policy regime they are living in, and factors strongly connected to the type of gender policy regime, including attitudes towards gender relations and the qualifications and position of women in the labour market. This means that if it is a political goal to equalise the level of involvement in working and family life for men and women in the male breadwinner regime, egalitarian gender attitudes and education – especially among women – should be promoted.

The results from this study generally support earlier research on welfare state types and fatherhood. In line with earlier research, this study illustrates the notable variations between single countries in Europe regarding the type of gender policy regime, attitudes and behaviour among fathers. On the other hand, there are also similarities that render it possible to define a cluster of countries that can be classified as a typical male breadwinner regime (the Southern European countries) and a typical dual earner/dual carer regime (the Nordic countries). For instance, all of the Nordic countries, except Denmark, have introduced some level of father's quota (Eydal and Rostgaard, 2011; see also Chapters Six, Thirteen, Fifteen and Sixteen, this volume) to stimulate paternal involvement in childcare. This probably offers one explanation for the more positive attitudes to father's involvement in family life and the higher levels of actual family involvement found among Nordic fathers in this study.

References

Allport, G. (1935) 'Attitudes', in C. Murchison (ed) *A handbook of social psychology*, Worcester, MA: Clark University Press, pp 789-844.

Backhans, M.C., Burström, B. and Marklund, S. (2011) 'Gender policy developments and policy regimes in 22 OECD countries, 1979-2008', *Gender Policy and Politics*, vol 41, no 4, pp 595-623.

Bradshaw, J. and Hatland, A. (2006) *Social policy, employment and family change in comparative perspective*, Cheltenham: Edward Elgar Publishing.

Council Directive (2003) 578 EC 22/07/2003.

Craig, L. and Mullan, K. (2010) 'Parenthood, gender and work-family time in the United States, Australia, Italy, France, and Denmark', *Journal of Marriage and Family*, vol 72, no 5, pp 1344-61.

Duncan, S. (1996) 'The diverse worlds of European patriarchy', in M.D. Garcia-Ramon and J. Monks (eds) *Women of the European Union: The politics of work and daily life*, London: Routledge, pp 74-110.

Ellingsæter, A.L. and Leira, A. (eds) (2006) *Politicising parenthood in Scandinavia: Gender relations in welfare states*, Bristol: Policy Press.

Esping-Andersen, G. (1999) *Social foundations of postindustrial economies*, Oxford: Oxford University Press.

Esping-Andersen, G. (2009) *The incomplete revolution*, Cambridge: Polity Press.

ESS (European Social Survey) (2012a) (www.europeansocialsurvey. org).

ESS (2012b) (http://ess.nsd.uib.no/ess/round2).

Eydal, G.B. and Rostgaard, T. (2011) 'Gender equality revisited: changes in Nordic childcare policies in the 2000s', *Social Policy & Administration*, vol 45, no 2, pp 161-79.

Ferrera, M. (2007) 'Democratisation and social policy in Southern Europe: from expansion to "recalibration"', in Y. Bangura (ed) *Democracy and social policy*, New York: Palgrave Macmillan, pp 90-113.

Gershuny, J. and Sullivan, O. (2003) 'Time use, gender, and public policy regimes', *Social Politics: International Studies in Gender, State and Society*, vol 10, no 2, pp 205-28.

Gíslason, I.V. and Eydal, G.B. (eds) (2011) *Parental leave, childcare and gender equality in the Nordic countries*, Copenhagen: Nordic Council of Ministers.

Harzing, A.W. (2006) 'Response styles in cross-national survey research. A 26-country study', *Cross Culture Management*, vol 6, no 2, pp 243-66.

Korpi, W. and Palme, J. (1998) 'The paradox of redistribution and strategies of equality: welfare state institutions, inequality and poverty in the Western countries', *American Sociological Review*, no 63, pp 661-87.

Leibfried, S. (1992) 'Towards a European welfare state? On integrating poverty regimes into the European Community', in Z. Ferge and J.E. Kolberg (eds) *Social policy in a changing Europe*, Boulder, CO: Westview, pp 120-43.

Lewis, J. (1992) 'Gender and the development of welfare regimes', *Journal of European Social Policy*, no 2, pp 159-73.

Lewis, J., Campbell, M. and Huerta, C. (2008) 'Patterns of paid and unpaid work in Western Europe: gender, commodification, preferences and the implications for policy', *Journal of European Social Policy*, vol 18, no 1, pp 21-37.

Morgan, K.J. (2009) 'Caring time policies in Western Europe: trends and implications', *Comparative European Politics*, vol 7, no 1, pp 37-55.

Nordenmark, M. (2004a) *Arbetsliv, familjeliv och kön* [*Working life, family life and gender*], Boréa: Umeå.

Nordenmark, M. (2004b) 'Does gender ideology explains differences between countries regarding the involvement of women and men in paid and unpaid work?', *International Journal of Social Welfare*, vol 13, pp 233-43.

OECD (Organisation for Economic Co-operation and Development) (2010) *OECD factbook 2010: Economic, environmental and social statistics*, Paris: OECD Publishing.

Ray, R., Gornich, J.C. and Schmitt, J. (2009) *Parental leave policies in 21 countries: Assessing generosity and gender equality*, Washington, DC: Center for Economic and Policy Research (www.lisdatacenter.org).

Sainsbury, D. (ed) (1999) *Gender and welfare state regimes*, Oxford: Oxford University Press.

Strandh, M. and Nordenmark, M. (2006) 'The interference of paid work with household demands in different social policy contexts: perceived work–household conflict in Sweden, the UK, the Netherlands, Hungary and the Czech Republic', *British Journal of Sociology*, vol 57, no 4, pp 597-617.

Sundström, E. (2003) 'Gender regimes, family policies and attitudes to female employment: A comparison of Germany, Italy and Sweden', PhD thesis, Umeå: Umeå University.

Tavora, I. (2012) 'The Southern European social model: familialism and the high rates of female employment in Portugal', *Journal of European Social Policy*, vol 22, no 1, pp 63–76.

Telpt, E. (2008) 'Attitudes and behaviour concerning reconciliation of paid work and housework: comparison of European countries', in M. Ainsaar and D. Kutsar (eds) *Estonia in European comparison*, Tallinn: Ministry of Social Affairs, Republic of Estonia, pp 67–82.

Walby, S. (1994) 'Methodological and theoretical issues in the comparative analysis of gender relations in Western Europe', *Environment and Planning*, no 26, pp 1339–54.

Theme 3:
Constructing fatherhood in different family settings

NINE

Fathering as a learning process: breaking new ground in familiar territory

Steen Baagøe Nielsen and Allan Westerling

Introduction

This chapter explores the learning processes of fathers engaging in everyday caregiving practices in family life based on a cross-Nordic qualitative study. The fathers were selected because they were seen as 'pioneers' in having made unconventional commitments regarding childcare. They had chosen to take longer paternity leave than normal, reduced their working hours or altered their career path so as to be actively involved in the everyday caring for their children. From a historical perspective, their commitments could be seen as avant-garde, and they are possibly the frontrunners of a broad social development.

The notion of 'modern' family life is itself an ambiguous term. This chapter departs from an understanding of Western societies as marked by ongoing modernisation and individualisation processes, meaning that contemporary family life unfolds in a context of continual social change (Beck and Beck-Gernsheim, 1995; Dencik et al, 2008; Westerling, 2008). Gillis' renowned distinction between 'families we live by' and 'families we live with' (Gillis, 1997, p xv) is also central to the understanding of family and family life that informs the analysis in this chapter. Ideologies and practices are seen as related and connected but cannot be reduced to one or the other; both must be considered, and their relationship cannot be understood in simple or linear terms.

Informed by understandings of social learning and the modernity of critical theory, Olesen (2003) argues that a common disintegration of 'the normal biography' is occurring in modernity, requiring new types of social participation and practices – and possibilities for learning. Accordingly, it is possible to understand the involvement of fathers in childcare not merely as 'chosen', but also as 'necessary', that is, related to the unavoidable, practical arrangements and demands of everyday life.

In this sense, we see these fathers as 'pioneers' at the cutting edge of the social change in family life (Roseneil and Budgeon, 2004), challenging traditional, general and conventional forms of fatherhood and constructions of masculinity. In the analytical perspective adopted in this chapter, the fathers emerge as particular men with specific stories about practices and modes of orientation towards care and intimacy in everyday family life. This is not to say that social background, educational biographies or economic resources do not matter for the culture and conduct of the fathering in focus. Since this chapter explores the shifting practices and understandings of a few of these fathers in contemporary Nordic societies, however, the analysis explores the challenges and possibilities for contemporary fatherhood and family life with a focus on the particular learning processes of the 'fathering' pioneers.

The analysis focuses on men who find the space, time and support necessary to become caring fathers. Their narratives comprise different ways of participating and different learning processes, but they all illustrate how fathers may contribute with 'practical solutions' in the context of everyday family life. These stories are concrete responses to specific challenges in everyday life; as such, they are particular expressions of general challenges facing the family in a context of ongoing social change.

The starting point for this analysis is that the learning processes experienced by these fathers unfold in relation to practical challenges in everyday family life. The analysis focuses on these challenges and how cultural resources, such as narratives of work–life, hegemonic discourses of masculinity and personal biographies, are invoked in the interview situation in order for the fathers to arrive at intelligible and legitimate subject positions from where their stories can be told.

The chapter focuses specifically on three dimensions in these learning processes, asking three intrinsically linked questions:

- Relationships between caring competence and fatherhood: how do fathers engage and become acknowledged as competent caregivers?
- Relationships and reconfigurations between fatherhood and masculinity: to what extent and by which means is it possible for fathers to draw on conventional configurations of masculinity while caring for their children?
- Relationships between the care of fathers and children's needs: how do fathers become legitimate interpreters of children's needs?

Across these themes runs an overall theme regarding the motherhood–family connection in the light of the ongoing social change. We argue that the pioneering involvement of fathers is often followed by ambiguity and ambivalence – and a need to deal with and learn from the extraordinary and challenged situation. Their extraordinary paternal involvement challenges the previous organisation of their everyday lives as well as challenging hegemonic constructions of masculinity and traditional family ideologies. Their practices thus represent responses to the challenges emerging in everyday family life while at the same time themselves posing challenges to conventional understandings and practices of masculinity and to the organisation of care and intimacy in family life. At the same time, the caring and practical involvement of fathers in the everyday life of their children constitutes a key element in the negotiation of good motherhood, which in turn contributes to breaking new ground for modern family life.

Data and methods

This chapter reports from a Nordic research project entitled 'Welfare, Masculinity and Social Innovation' (initial findings reported in Holter, 2007). The project functioned as an umbrella for six very different national empirical studies (one in each major Nordic country, two in Norway). Together, these projects covered around 50 qualitative, semi-structured, in-depth interviews. For this chapter, a number of fathers who had taken extra time off with the explicit intention of establishing caring relationships with their infant and/or pre-school children were chosen in order to explore variations and different local perspectives on pioneering fatherhood. These fathers saw themselves as living in well-functioning – albeit often also stressful – heterosexual relationships. Like Ari and Matti, most of the men presented in this chapter were in their thirties or forties, had pre-school children and had recently taken time off. Other fathers, like Eirik, had taken extensive leave 10-15 years earlier. The longitudinal design of two of the six studies allowed follow-up on these fathers. These fathers were generally somewhat older – in their forties and fifties. Some, like Eirik, were divorced and had new partners – and often with more children added in the years between.

The fathers in the studies were all recruited using different strategies. The fathers from the longitudinal studies had been participants in previous studies focusing on the handling of extended paternal leave periods, but most were simply found through snowballing, researchers asking their peers for fathers who had taken extraordinary measures. For instance, these measures were: extended paternity leave; reduced working hours; the alteration of career paths to adapt to children's needs during a change in the family's situation; voluntary unemployment to devote time to care taking, and so on. Snowball sampling allowed the researchers to find new interviewees by asking the initial fathers if they knew of other men in similar family situations.

The fathers represent diverse backgrounds, although most of them come from urban settings, have university degrees and could be said to be from middle-class backgrounds. Clearly, there is a higher representation of men in professional positions in the studies, more with academic degrees and more who are employed in the public sector than found among men and fathers in general. Although some could be said to be in a privileged economic position, they have all made some investment in their positions and practices as fathers, privileging time with their families over reduced or even no work income at all for a period of time (Holter, 2007).

In an interview-based study, it is a challenge to specify the conditions between the narratives in the interview room and the everyday practices that the interview is about (Alvesson and Sköldberg, 2000; Olsen, 2004). One common problem facing fatherhood studies is that fathers' narratives must take place within the framework of the hegemonic discourses in the given historical situation (Bekkingen, 2002), which constitute the interpretative reservoir by which the problematic and inconsistent aspects of the everyday practices and life experiences can be articulated. To remedy this, the interviews were carried out using a method constructing two or more 'narrative spaces', which investigated the experiences of becoming a father, paying very close attention to the actual involvement of the fathers in (changed) everyday practices. This was done using a detailed investigation of narratives of daily practices with the child(ren) setting the scene and asking questions such as: 'Please describe your practices "going through an ordinary day": what would you normally do in the morning?' (Olsen, 2004, p 167).

Furthermore, the analysis paid particular attention to challenges encountered in everyday situations, where the fathers strive to achieve legitimacy and recognition of their engagement in their respective relationships to their children. The analytical attention was directed towards the men's narratives and scripts (Oftung, 2009) as they deal with ambivalence, when they attempt to legitimise and justify their practices and relations – or when the interview setting poses a challenge for their attempt to provide a clear description of their experiences and practices.

As with all qualitative research, the validity of the statements in these analyses is not tied to their representative character. Instead, the validity of the analysis is first and foremost found in the recognition of the consistency and exemplary character of the statements and the analyses; in other words, the intelligibility or credibility of the narratives and the analytical perspectives used in order to cast light on these stories in a thematic manner (Alvesson and Sköldberg, 2000).

Social change of fathering as a challenge to motherhood ideologies

In light of the negotiations of parenthood and the increasingly democratic state of the modern family, constructions of hegemonic masculinity pose a significant challenge to fathers. The gravity of change in practices against the forces of traditionalism must therefore now be considered.

Research shows that men's caring and intimate involvement with children becomes part of negotiations of masculinity, family identities and the organisation of parenting practices (Brandth and Kvande, 2003; Haavind, 2006; Aarseth, 2007). Following Connell (2005), it may be argued that the attempts to construct new paternal identities and practices may be understood as relatively harmless challenges to the gender order and 'complicit' to the established configurations of hegemonic masculinities, 'which embodies the currently accepted answer to the problem of legitimacy of patriarchy, guaranteeing (or taken to guarantee) the dominant position of men and the subordination of women' (Connell, 2005, p 77f). However, there still seems to be a dominant assumption linked with the hegemonic understandings of masculinity that caring is basically 'women's business' and that women should carry the main responsibility and organise the caring as well as its homely context, in the Nordic countries as well (Holter and Aarseth, 1993; Plantin, 2001). The ideology of maternal care has developed and thrived for generations and, along with the construction of 'the home' and 'homeliness', has been imbued with strong and naturalised, feminine connotations, which has been thriving and strongly promoted by the middle class since the 19th century. Mother-centred understandings of care have thus also been shaped in regard to the (unpaid) work and reproductive functions, which take place in the home and family – at a certain distance from the instrumental, utility-maximising logics of the market (Ambjörnsson, 1981; Nielsen, 2005).

This historical and ideological background underlines the importance of understanding masculinity – and men's caring practices – as fragile, social and subjective constructions. Fathers are expected to negotiate the meaning of their participation and practices in the family in relation to their partners and among colleagues, friends and peers to become intelligible as 'masculine' as well as fathers (Plantin, 2001; Olsen, 2005; Aarseth, 2007; see also Chapter Seven, this volume).

Nordic research has focused on the challenging link between transitions of family practices and the changes of motherhood ideologies. Danish family historian Løkke (1993) argues that although caring for children remains very closely ideologically tied to traditional ideas of motherhood and romanticised understandings of mother's care in the family home, dramatic change is going on at the practical level: 'Fathers move closer to their children, both emotionally and in their care for their children. In short, it would appear as though "Mother" is being toned down while the significance of the [professional] "care-worker" and "father" are turned up' (Løkke, 1993, p 8). While several researchers argue that involved and intimate care for children has become a common 'project' for parents, where men and women alike actively participate in childcare, this transition can be highly challenging for both, since it is still a common expectation that women have caring dispositions; partly because of this, they are also expected to have a privileged position in the decision making around and organisation of family practices (Holter and Aarseth, 1993; Plantin, 2001; Olsen, 2005; Aarseth, 2007). Thus, a central step in the transformation of fatherhood is the shift away from the mythological and sentimental understandings of motherhood as naturally or essentially imbued with particular caring competencies. The Nordic countries are undoubtedly witnessing ongoing transitions towards egalitarian and democratic participation in caring and intimate practices, but motherhood ideologies continue to put pressure on mothers (Haavind, 2006). This curbs the full participation of fathers, in the family (Holter and Aarseth, 1993), and mother-centred views may exclude fathers from full participation in parent-related public services, such as health and infant care (Madsen, 2003).

Understanding fathering as a learning process

Becoming a father and – as in the case of the fathers in this chapter – choosing unconventional commitments and extended involvement in childcare may cause encounters with a number of familiar and unfamiliar situations. The individual father will often experience previous practices and taken-for-granted understandings as insufficient. According to theories of social learning, such new situations will often comprise contradictions and paradoxes, which cannot be settled once and for all. Instead, they stir up ambivalence or lead to new adequate practices to deal with the changed social situation (Weber, 1995).

Learning is far from always the outcome of the experience of ambivalence, but ambivalence and frustration will often be a prerequisite of active engagement in transformation and learning processes. Learning takes place through a break with past experiences and/or practices. Although not always consciously, the individual will draw on past experiences to engage in – and possibly break away from – the current contradictory situations and the ambivalence they cause (Weber 1995). Thus, transformative learning requires and entails not only reflexivity but also a reconfiguration of experiences that may lead to an introduction of new perspectives and practices on everyday life, which might – or might not – challenge hegemonic or shared 'truth' and conventional practices.

Perspectives on learning and learning experiences are the focus of this chapter, because these phenomena are seen as prerequisites of broader social change, and indications of necessary learning processes among these 'pioneering' men, as investigated below in the analysis, may point to some of the common obstacles facing fathers-to-be and the possibility of and obstacles to a broader break with hegemonic constructions of masculinity among fathers.

Negotiations of competent care

The first narrative of such a pioneering man belongs to Ari and is based on his experiences with making space for his involvement and being acknowledged as a competent father. Ari is from Iceland, around 40 years old, and has an academic education. He has taken the extraordinary decision to quit his busy job as a self-employed consultant, sold his company, and is presently 'unemployed' and living off of the profits from the sale, the sole reason being that he wants to spend time with his infant daughter and family.

Ari's narrative is particularly interesting because it is an illustration of a major shift in practical orientation and perspective – giving up the life of a well-earning private consultant in favour of a life with his child and family. The birth of the child is an opportunity to make profound new priorities followed by concrete practices. Not only does

Ari participate equally in the preparation for and birth of the child, he illustrates how this change of practice creates the backdrop for both an empathetic and reflexive assessment of the opportunities and possibilities available to him and his partner in relation to the overall needs of the child, the partner/mother and family as a whole. Ari's participatory and reflexive approach to his new position (as a father) appears to give him the right to engage himself in competent fathering in a manner that is mirrored in many of the other interviews.

While Ari certainly seems dedicated to his new life, his account often seems to be one of conflict and a striving to handle the reorganisation of his everyday life with the family. The legitimacy of him being near the child and participating on an equal basis with his partner in the caring for their daughter – and his competence to do so – is a major issue. One of the first 'arenas' in which Ari claims the right to be met as a fully engaged and equal parent is in his and his partner's meeting with institutionalised perceptions of motherly care in the social and health care sectors.

Ari initially gives an account of the communal participation in the parenting classes with his partner prior to the birth, which Ari felt had provided him and his partner with knowledge and a common engagement in the possible and optimal ways of breastfeeding. After the birth, they are then confronted with a midwife who Ari feels to be old-fashioned. He explains how he and his partner were 'not very happy with' the midwife, as "she was a little, I think ... instead of being an adviser, she was a little ... a little commanding". Ari refers to a conflict between him and the midwife regarding some difficulties with breastfeeding. This came up during talks with the midwife, who then told the mother (Ari's partner) in no uncertain terms that it would be better if she supplemented breastfeeding with formula:

> "I'd imagine – that for a woman who is home alone in such a situation ... and if a person like that [the midwife] comes along and says ... in a slightly demanding tone: 'She [the baby] needs something extra. You aren't doing so well. You aren't able to support your child', I'm totally convinced that she has complete power over a woman like that. But we ... because we were together, because we confronted her as a team and protested and argued.... Before she left, she said, 'I ... if it was me, I'd do it [supplement breastfeeding with formula].' After that episode, we just looked for advice from other sources and made a choice ... and then ... chose which way we wanted to go ... you know, we bought a

supplemental nursing system[1] so that she [the baby] got a little extra, but in the most natural way possible. And we found out that of course there are 30 different kinds of advice for these situations.... But I think that it was really good to be two to handle the problem, and that I wasn't at work and had a lot to do. We could tackle the problem together. I think that it had been really difficult if she had to stand through it all on her own."

Here, Ari shares how he found it challenging to negotiate with professional authorities, such as midwives and public health nurses, and the equal participation of fathers in parental care resonates in several interviews. Many men – and women – seem to experience that the authorities support motherhood as the primary form of childcare. Madsen (2003) documents a consistent understanding of infant childcare among health professionals as typical 'women's issues', which renders the equal participation of fathers difficult.

Ari's account of the midwife's authoritarian approach serves as the subtext for the interpretation of the next section of the interview. Ari's particular interest in this episode enlightens his experience of being (expected to be) peripheral in the decision making around breastfeeding. He highlights how they do not receive legitimate professional advice, and how the midwife's statements and judgements are not merely excluding him, but also potentially misleading. He underlines this experience by a making clear distance of him (and his wife), from the dramatic exit and appeal of the midwife's explicitly personalised address to the mother of the child: "I ... if it was me, I would do it."

Instead of accepting his peripheral position, Ari expresses the need to stand by his partner against pressure from the midwife, a pressure which aims at making his partner accept a traditional and personalised perspective on the needs of the child, directed towards the mother only, implicitly accusing her of not being able to meet the needs of her child – and promoting the highly authoritative understandings of 'good mothering': "You aren't able to support your child" (the midwife repeatedly using the pronoun 'you', which in the Icelandic language is distinctly singular, and thus indicates a personal address).

Ari and his partner do not accept such arguments; on the contrary, Ari seems particularly distressed by the direct, personalised address: "I ... if it was me, I would do it", implicitly referring to experiences shared 'among women' about the necessary actions of the mother with respect to the needs of the child. In this sense, Ari's account is quite common for the men in the study, who must distance themselves from what we term 'mother-centred' approaches and understandings of care.

The central designation of the need for cooperation between partners regarding their parental practices is worth noting here, that is, building on shared understandings and responsibilities for the new child, negotiating through participatory discourses and differently informed decisions and understandings of proper practices to meet the needs of the child. In Ari's narrative, his commitment is clearly marked by his recurrent use of the pronoun 'we', thus indicating a common voice and understanding of both partners in the family.

When Ari steps up as the mouthpiece for the family, he changes from speaking about himself and 'she' in the singular (or the midwife's 'you' and 'your own') to predominantly referring to the two of them 'together', as a 'we': "… because we were together at the time, we only protested and argued with her". Through Ari's use of this 'we', he maintains an active part in this common experience and the construction of opposition to traditional, mother-oriented family practices of caring. At the same time, he is both part of and protecting the family and its interests, which he feels are 'under attack'.

This confirms Ari's position in the caring project, and underlines Ari and his partner's competence and their rightful scepticism towards the mother-centred perspective. Ari emphasises this dimension in his personal account, which illustrates how the traditional division of labour places pressure on younger women, who can hardly resist this pressure alone. Against this, he emphasises the couple's communal and reflexive way of dealing with the conflict. In this narrative, there is an intelligible position for Ari, which is framed by the fact that it is not possible to refer to unquestionable guidelines for how to provide childcare and do family life. Surely there are guidelines ('30 different kinds of advice'), but their authority and relevance must be assessed and evaluated. Here, Ari appears to place emphasis on a combination of intimacy and common, process-oriented and reflexive competencies, which he relates to common practices and demands in his (former) job as manager of a consulting business, demanding of him both the flexibility of situational advice and considerable self-awareness.

In light of this development, it is interesting how Ari's narrative constructs 'family' through his seemingly well-informed intervention as opposed to the midwife's mother-centred project. In this passage, taking care of his own interests and those of his partner and child are all interwoven as part of adding substance and meaning to his profound shift of orientation and perspective. Ari insists that their choice of practice is better informed – and not least shared – and that he contributes to a better decision by insisting on his right to participate. Ari's narrative also invokes another narrative, which is not explicitly addressed, but which serves as the backdrop for their struggle: motherhood as the primary model for care is an obstacle for Ari's efforts and legitimacy to assume a position as a competent caregiver. Conversely, Ari finds that he is able to bring something extra to the table via support, information and reflexivity. The experience has apparently been significant but also seems to confirm a more general challenge of legitimacy, which Ari faces in his position as a father. Claiming equal authority over the interpretation and necessary actions to meet the needs of the child along with his partner is, in fact, a task that challenges not only the mother-centred view of authorities; it also potentially undermines very well established gender roles – hereby threatening dominant or hegemonic constructions of masculinity as well as femininity (and the extended agency of his partner). Throughout the interview, these types of negotiations regarding legitimate participation in childcare seem to add emotional energy to Ari's decision to make his significant 'career' change. Ari's account tells a significant and recognisable story of frustration as a prerequisite of his new engagement and the transformation linked to his new orientations towards a social intelligible position as 'competent carer'. While breaking with his past practices, he also seems to draw on experiences from his previous work as a consultant to help deal with the contradictory nature of his engaged fathering – and to engage and deal with the challenges in his everyday life with his family.

Work performance and the reconfiguration of masculinity

Ari's account of a pathway into an intelligible position as 'caregiver' involves reference to a type of behaviour most commonly associated with public and professional fields such as debating, researching and confronting professional authorities. The analysis in this section sharpens its focus on the learning processes that cut across professional and private identities: the modes of orientation linking professional experiences from work–life with private and intimate challenges of competent childcare. The insight in the analysis is drawn from the narratives of Ari from Iceland and Eirik from Norway.

Ari tells of the widespread scepticism he met among his colleagues, friends and family regarding his decision to quit his job, sell his business and devote his time to being a father. The interview with Ari reflects a particularly common experience among care- and family-oriented men: they are challenging the conventional understandings of masculinity. Ari talks about his experience with friends and peers seeing him as being 'lost' and how they encourage him – directly or indirectly – to seek more conventional paths and to return to his work. According to Ari, he must actively demonstrate to his peers that he is 'okay' and that nothing is wrong. Similar to men pursuing education or employment within traditional female occupations and professions (Nielsen, 2003), Ari attempts to establish narratives and practices that maintain and emphasise his conventional 'masculinity', hetero-normative affiliations (see also Nordberg, 2005) and normalcy in the eyes of the world around him (see also Olsen, 2000). At the same time, men in positions similar to Ari's often experience a considerable and persistent need to explain themselves.

Here, Ari describes how his decision to quit his job and become a full-time caregiver challenges his friends. He feels he must constantly defend himself and account for his priorities:

> "One of my friends in particular always asked 'anything new?', and I'm like 'just fine', 'Well, nothing special' or you know. Something like that.... Finally, I said: 'What do you mean by "anything new"'?"

Ari accounts for his elaborate response in this exchange:

> "I'm here at home with my daughter, and it takes a lot of time. I feel I belong to a privileged group – that I'm able to do so.... Many [men] just can't [quit their job] – they have to place their child somewhere and go to work to pay their mortgage. So it's a privilege [for me] to be able to live this way, and so ... so really, there's nothing 'new', and I don't think that there will be 'anything new'."

Here, Ari talks about how he must point out, first, that the care he provides as a father is 'enough'. It is hard work – and he appears uninterested in returning to work before his child starts in school and he has sufficient savings. Instead, he emphasises that it is a privilege to be a stay-at-home-dad. Ari refers to the professional and financial success he has had, which enables him to sell his company and actively choose to become a stay-at-home-dad. In other words, Ari refers to his well-established status in a conventionally masculine-connotated field – work and business – in his efforts to avoid marginalisation and to legitimise his way of fathering. As such, he reaffirms his position as 'a proper man' and reconstructs his position as intelligible within the discourses and practices of hegemonic masculinity. He never really leaves it untold that he has already performed to the full as a traditional breadwinner, providing for his family – underpinning his own status as a 'proper' man (Morgan, 1997).

For Eirik from Norway, referring to his professional success seems similarly important. Eirik is in his fifties from Oslo, separated and remarried – and recently fathered his fourth child. Besides being a devoted father and the primary cook in the household, he is also – like his present partner – a dedicated architect, both of them striving to balance and combine their professional passions with their domestic duties. In doing so, they give extra priority to 'family time', with 'engaging conversations' and time spent around the kitchen table. In legitimising his extended participation in the family, he uses a similar narrative strategy to Ari's: he invokes practices of hegemonic masculinity and positions his work performances well within the boundaries of this configuration of masculinity. Moreover, Eirik's account of his orientation and caring practices is argued to be a personal choice, yet another feature of hegemonic masculinity. Eirik refers directly to the connection between working life and family life as being important – also for his fathering. He emphasises his professional identity when describing himself, and gives examples of how his professional competences serve as a platform for social relationships and his orientation in life. This also has an impact on his relationship with his two children. In the interview, the topic becomes his divorce from his first wife, and he brings up his relationship to work without any prompting from the interviewer:

> "... in relation to the divorce, [I felt] how incredibly important my job was.... I had a very stable job, because I was a partner in the firm and was able to work a little less for a period of time, so it wasn't a problematic situation. Work became very important, became very meaningful. And you want to be able to have both – whether it's a job, a hobby or whatever."

Eirik elaborates on how his work is also in many ways his hobby, and that it facilitates a connection to his current spouse. Architecture is an "all-embracing profession that ... is about politics, care, aesthetics, art and engineering." By underlining the 'hobby-like' status of his job, Eirik implicitly claims that his work experience is in fact relevant to his current situation as a father – and as a reflexive and mature adult man – while avoiding the stigma of the traditional 'workaholic' breadwinner.

This part of the interview is from a point where the interviewer tries to nudge the conversation towards a question about love and childcare. Note here how Erik draws parallels and shifts from the child orientation to professional perspectives and considerations – and back again.

In the interview, the conversation concerns Eirik's relationship with his son from a former marriage. The son alternates between the two families, living with each family alternate weeks. He started playing football in early primary school, and Eirik felt inclined to take an interest in it. Eirik talks about making an effort to support his son's new interest. This is not without complications and some sacrifice, however, as the boy's interest in football seems to stem from the enthusiasm and active involvement of Eirik's ex-wife's new husband (the boy's step-father), who is actually coaching Eirik's son. Eirik himself is not really interested in football.

Eirik is still occupied with creating a special relationship with his son and wants to participate in his hobbies, even though he simultaneously expresses some ambivalence about his son's interest in football, as this hobby will obviously 'occupy some of the time' Eirik would have preferred to use to build their relationship – Eirik talks about time as a scarce commodity and conveys a sense of missing his son and longing for his companionship. At the same time, Eirik tells of how the experience of keeping up with his son's football helps maintain a good relationship between the two of them. Through this, he is reassured of his own ability to meet the boy's needs.

> "Indeed, I learn a lot from being in my child's life – and not only my son, but also his friends and their parents. I get insight into new aspects of life and a different network of contacts. I get to know other functions in society. I get a whole new relationship to many things, such as football. I have never been particularly interested in football before, but upon becoming involved in it, I find it incredibly fascinating … which is kind of a new world…."

Eirik first and foremost emphasises how the time together with his son – and insight into his interests – has turned out to be, in his words, "incredibly fascinating". He explains how their time together gives his life quality and meaning ("a new little world"), which provides him with new forms of insight guided by the interests of the child.

While his narrative makes clear that his understanding of football is not very extensive and his interest limited, it is also evident that he will go to pains to adapt to and support that which is obviously the boy's (current) wishes. Identifying with the boy's needs – and gaining access to intimacy and identification with his activities and interests – would thus appear to be a central factor that renders Eirik's care orientation quite clear, and provides meaning and justifies the paternal interest, from Eirik's perspective. Eirik translates this in terms of a course of learning ("I learn to become familiar with ..."), and this also appears to develop new forms of actual practice in terms of how Eirik is fathering when he participates in his son's hobbies and interests.

Eirik experiences a blurred boundary between his professional and private life. He provides an extensive account of how his working life and profession provide a sense of perspective. This is a source of meaning, which can be accessed when Eirik refers to his time together with his son as something that has expanded his horizons. In this sense, his account of parental relationship building is formed in the same fashion as he talks about his professional interests. Yet this is no impersonal account of a father–son relationship. On the contrary, Eirik describes his time with his son as being interwoven with his own personal development and orientation to his own life. The next section illustrates these kinds of learning processes more clearly with the case of Matti from Finland.

Children's needs and intimate fathering

Matti from Finland talks about how he has felt his relationships with his children as being a basic need, something he must have, cannot do without, something necessary and desirable. He is in his late thirties, with two pre-school children and a wife with a career, which has allowed him to take significant time off from work (or between jobs) to be with his children. He prefers working as a stage actor, but in fact has a very diversified career, supplementing his acting work with puppeteering in a theatre. He has also worked as a certified masseur and a social worker, providing care for older people, as well as in a children's home. In other words, he has had a number of different jobs, some of which are traditionally carried out by women and associated with the conventional feminine domain. In order to make ends meet financially as well as on a personal level, Matti draws on his improvisational talents and caring skills – and refers to these caring and practical competencies as being significant for his family life. He reflects on his unique orientation as being something that breaks with the common and hegemonic understandings of masculinity.

> MATTI: "… even if people say it's wonderful to stay at home with children, I still feel that many people don't really understand. Especially men! They see it as a woman's job. They don't get it, that someone stays at home for a whole year with the children; they don't have a clue [why]."
>
> INTERVIEWER: "It's quite unusual to do so. How can you know if you never try?"
>
> MATTI: "It's funny – yesterday I visited this French guy. He's a dancer, and we're in a similar situation – he also has two little ones. So somehow I belong to a weird crowd of people. This guy is a dancer and a clown, and he does puppet theatre too, I have done puppet theatre too. We are like aliens. How many men would play with puppets or stay at home with children, really?"

When describing his children, Matti draws on some of the skills and talents he has acquired and developed at work; he interprets the needs of his children and cares for them, describing this as a considerable source of satisfaction. He orients himself in relation to his experience that his children need his intimacy, being close to him, but also in relation to his own interest in and considerable talents with respect to this intimacy:

> "For me, the 'baby time' was nice. There have been more problems after that. I used to do baby massage, put on some lovely music and she loved it. I gave her massage several times a week for about seven months and she liked it a lot. She was in the front pack for long periods at a time and I went on long walks with her. It was just wonderful when I went to do Hebraic folk dance and she was bouncing there as we danced. She heard the music. We also went for baby swimming and everything. It was the same with my son, but he did not like the massage as much. Both of the children have been swimming since they were three months old – water is kind of my element, we have been at the swimming pool hundreds of times. My daughter is five and she can swim. It has been both play and closeness. I believe it has been important for them…. Being close in the water, and the massage has also created intimacy."

Matti's narrative focuses on physical closeness and a playful, empathetic and holistic approach to the children, which reflects that his relationships to his wife and children are influenced by a new-age inspired, feeling-based approach. In other parts of the interview, he further emphasises the intuitive elements of his relationship to his children as well as a certain measure of self-consciousness, which he directly relates to the learning he has acquired via extensive work with himself, including therapy. Although Matti emphasises the significance of the mother–child connection when nursing, he also sees it as necessary or desirable to 'compensate' so that he can also achieve considerable intimacy with his children.

This does not appear to cause him any great difficulty. But this closeness and continuous contact obviously also involves some measure of sacrifice – it drains Matti and eats away at his capacity to work. This becomes apparent in the interview, when he clearly states that he does not want any more children, since he wants to spend more time on theatre work. Matti describes how his social orientations are filled with innovative practices, which also present trials and challenges, demanding his attention – but he also describes how these challenges lead to new perspectives in his life.

His unusual working life and his priorities in family life both lead to learning processes – and very innovative orientations with respect to his fathering practices – coupled with a somewhat 'acrobatic' lifestyle and orientation. Interestingly, these very individual orientations also reflect a needs-oriented practice in relation to himself and the needs of the child. Here, it would appear as though Matti's broad competencies and rich experiences provide him with an excellent point of departure for both innovative fathering and reconfiguring practices, which challenge hegemonic understandings of masculinity.

Conclusion

The analysis of the interview excerpts with Nordic men shed light on the challenges that pioneering men encounter while making extraordinary personal and emotional investments as fathers, caring for and developing intimate relations with their children. Fathers are breaking new ground in family life and the territory of care, a territory that has previously been (and still seems to be experienced as) a 'woman's world', predominantly constituted through discourses and practices of traditional motherhood.

The fathers in the study often describe their competence and ability to interpret the needs of their children in relation to practical experiences with care and intimacy with their children. The account of these experiences reflects learning processes that transgress traditional family practises and divisions of labour. These transgressions leave a vacuum in which the caring fathers shift from the periphery of the family into its centre and attempt to create legitimate space for the greater provision of care and intimacy. The analysis has discussed how this shift often appears to result in the recognition of the men's fathering competencies by themselves, their partners and others. In turn, this recognition may sustain new common fathering practices. Because motherhood and the mother–child relationship continue to dominate the conventional understandings of 'the needs of the child', men often experience how the traditional understanding of motherhood – ideologically, practically or institutionally – gets in the way and curbs their efforts to become centrally involved in care.

The analyses illustrate how the fathers are primarily preoccupied with the concrete and practical challenges of everyday family life. These involve, on the one hand, finding an intelligible position in relation to hegemonic discourses of masculinity – and 'man as the main economic provider' and protector. On the other hand, they are helped along by a new horizon of opportunities for the family in general, and men's relation to children in particular. They thereby contribute to a demystification and de-traditionalisation of motherhood. These fathers become involved through new paths to children and family, which they explore in the context of everyday life. These paths are marked by the gender-equal practices, supported by equal opportunity discourses on fatherhood, as well as by the rationales found in negotiating, democratic families (for example, shared leave arrangements). The fact that these fathers build their engagement on practical changes (rather than ideology) does not imply that they are successful in their orientation – neither personally, nor for the family – but it does indicate a practical break with the mythology of motherhood as the only way to perform childcare.

The fathers in this study not only present themselves as competent carers, but they are also able to provide elaborate accounts of their experiences of possessing childcare skills. These men learn to develop personal, relationship-oriented competences that contribute to intimacy with their children. At the same time, the learning processes involved comprise an orientation towards the children as a personal turning point that helps them thematise their previous experiences in new ways, invoking new practices and changing their perspectives on their relationship, to the home and the children in particular. They pose challenges, raise fundamental questions and invoke contradictory life and work experiences, which the fathers draw on when searching for solutions to new (and old) problems. These learning processes can be very ambiguous but seem to constitute a path to the territory of family care.

On the one hand, the fathers are engaged in a struggle for recognition as competent caregivers and are therefore confronting a traditionally favoured and protected relationship between mother and child. On the other hand, they will all be more or less explicitly challenged by dominant discourses and practices which have hitherto given them certain privileges as men.

The fathers' considerations, negotiations and actions cannot be labelled as merely 'complicit' to a 'hegemonic masculine' legitimisation of patriarchal power (Connell, 2005). On the contrary, they and their actions seem to support a break with fundamental divisions of labour around caregiving, which have been a basis for male dominance.

The fathers in the study seem to develop 'tools' in this situation (in cooperation with their partners) for dealing with the challenges and changes of everyday life. They display considerable reflexivity and a fundamental motivation for developing their relationships with their children, in particular the opportunities that have emerged in relation to the conflicts included in a life closer with their children. They are confronted by professional discourses addressing the needs of the child. Some of these discourses will be traditional in their orientation and thus challenge the new orientations and reorganisations of father's care, while others – partly supported professional, gender-neutral understandings of the needs of the child – may help to support fathers in their attempts to legitimise competence and sustain fathers' orientations towards intimacy with their children. Men venturing into the field of intimate fathering open up for a split and separation of the dyadic mother–child relationship (and 'good mothering' and 'children's needs') – within the framing of the nuclear family and 'home'. New discourses allow for discussions about the practices of fathers and mothers – and the needs of the child – as separate entities, which may, in turn, possibly open up new understandings of care, parenthood and the potentials and joys of fathering.

The active involvement of fathers in childcare and their participation in everyday family life can be understood as a practical orientation towards the family with whom they live. This involves new ways of 'doing' family, new rationales and forms of practice that not only challenge the traditionally gendered forms of practice but actually contribute to establishing common grounds in family life and to negotiating the normative guidelines found in the cultural ideals of the family we live by.

Note

[1] The Icelandic term that Ari uses is directly translated as 'help breast' or 'assisting breast'. The device is also sometimes known as a feeding tube and may have other brand names, depending on the producer. It is not particularly straightforward to use, and the products often come with instruction manuals and illustrations explaining how to use them. Basically, the straws are attached to the nipple and a bottle, aiding the baby's ability to suck and sustaining the production of breast milk. In relation to Ari's narrative, it is important to note that this is a device which aids the breastfeeding strategy preferred by Ari and his partner, and that contradicts the midwife's advice.

References

Aarseth, H. (2007) 'Nye fedre 1990–2005: Fra fascination og romanticering til kjønnsnøytrale livsstilsprojekter i familien' ['New fathers 1990-2005: from fascination and romanticisation to gender-neutral lifestyle projects in the family'], in Ø. Holter (ed) *Menn i rörelse – Jämställdhet, förändring och social innovation i Norden* [*Men in movement – Gender equality, change and social innovation in the Nordic region*], Gothenburg: Gidlunds Forlag, pp 118-45.

Alvesson, M. and Sköldberg, K. (2009) *Reflexive methodology: New vistas for qualitative research*, Thousand Oaks, CA, London, New Delhi and Singapore: Sage.

Ambjørnsson, R. (1981) 'Barnets fødsel' ['The birth of the child'], in C. Clausen (ed) *Barndommens historie: En antologi* [*The history of childhood: An anthology*], Copenhagen: Tiderne Skifter, pp 9-46.

Beck, U. and Beck-Gernsheim, E. (1995) *The normal chaos of love*, Cambridge: Polity Press.

Bekkengen, L. (2002) *Man får välja – om föräldraskap och föräldraledighet i arbetsliv och familjeliv* [*One has to choose – parenthood and parental leave in work and family life*], Malmö: Liber.

Brandth, B. and Kvande, E. (2003) *Fleksible fedre* [*Flexible fathers*], Oslo: Universitetsforlaget.

Connell, R.W. (2005) *Masculinities* (2nd edn), Berkeley and Los Angeles, CA: University of California Press.

Dencik, L., Jørgensen, P.S. and Sommer, D. (2008) *Familie og børn i en opbrudstid* [*Family and children in a time of change*], Copenhagen: Hans Reitzels Forlag.

Gillis, J.R. (1997) *A world of their own making: Myth, ritual, and the quest for family values*, Harvard: Harvard University Press.

Haavind, H. (2006) 'Midt i tredje akt? Fedres deltakelse i det omsorgsfulle foreldreskap' ['In the middle of the third act? Fathers' participation in the caring parenthood'], *Tidsskrift for Norsk Psykologiforening*, vol 43 no 7, pp 683-93.

Holter, Ø. (ed) (2007) *Menn i rörelse – Jämställdhet, förändring och social innovation i Norden* [*Men in movement – Gender equality, change and social innovation in the Nordic region*], Gothenburg: Gidlunds Forlag.

Holter, Ø. and Aarseth, H. (1993) *Menns Livssammenheng* [*Men's life context*], Oslo: Ad Notam, Gyldendal.

Løkke, A. (1993) 'Forældrebilleder – skitser til moderskabets og faderskabets historie' ['Images of parenthood: outlines for a history of motherhood and fatherhood'], *Social Kritik*, no 25-26, pp 7-21.

Madsen, S.A. (2003) 'Svangreomsorgen og barnets far' ['Prenatal care and the child's father'], *Ugeskrift for Læger*, vol 165, no 46, pp 4423-5.

Morgan, D.H.J. (1997) 'Socialisation and the family: change and diversity', in B. Cosin and M. Hales (eds) *Families, education and social difference*, London: Open University/Routledge, pp 4-29.

Nielsen, S.B. (2003) 'Vi trænger til nye kræfter, sagde lederen, og ansatte en mand – Om barrierer for mænds omsorg i daginstitutioner' ['We need new blood, said the manager, and hired a man: On barriers regarding male care in daycare institutions'], in K. Hjort and S.B. Nielsen (eds) *Mænd og omsorg* [*Men and care*], Copenhagen: Hans Reitzels, pp 136-63.

Nielsen, S.B. (2005) 'Mænd og daginstitutionernes modernisering' ['Men and the modernisation of daycare institutions'], PhD dissertation, Roskilde: Graduate School in Lifelong Learning, Roskilde University.

Nordberg, M. (2005) *Jämställdhetens spjutspets?* [*The gender-equality spearhead*], Gothenburg: Arkipelag.

Oftung, K. (2009) *Skilte fedre: Omsorg, mestring og livskvalitet* [*Divorced fathers: Care, coping and quality of life*], Oslo: Universitetet i Oslo.

Olesen, H.S. (2003) 'Individualisering – fast food eller fælles buffet. Behovet for en ny uddannelsestænkning' ['Individualisation – fast food or common buffet. The need for new thought on education'], in A.S. Andersen and F. Sommer (eds) *Uddannelsesreformer og levende mennesker* [*Education reforms and living people*], Frederiksberg: Roskilde University, pp 81-103.

Olsen, B.M. (2000) 'Nye fædre på orlov – en analyse af de kønsmæssige aspekter ved forældreorlovsordningen' ['New fathers on leave – an analysis of the gender-related aspects of the parent leave scheme'], PhD dissertation, Copenhagen: University of Copenhagen.

Olsen, B.M. (2004) 'Fædres fortællerum' ['Fathers' narrative space'], in S. Reuterstrand (ed) *Konferens. Nationellt seminarium om mansforskning 11-12 mars 2003. Nationella sekretariatet för genusforskning*, nr 1/04. Gothenburg, pp 165-72.

Olsen, B.M. (2005) *Mænd, orlov og arbejdspladskultur. Fire danske virksomheder [Men, leave and workplace culture: Four Danish companies]*, Copenhagen: SFI – The Danish National Center for Social Research.

Plantin, L. (2001) *Män, familjeliv och föräldraskap [Men, family life and parenthood]*, Umeå: Boreá Bokförlag.

Roseneil, S. and Budgeon, S. (2004) 'Cultures of intimacy and care beyond "the family": personal life and social change in the early 21st century', *Current Sociology*, vol 52, no 2, pp 135-59.

Weber, K. (1995) *Ambivalens og erfaring [Ambivalence and experience]*, Roskilde: Erhvervs- og voksenuddannelsesgruppen, Roskilde University.

Westerling, A. (2008) 'Individualisering, familieliv og fællesskab: en socialpsykologisk analyse af hverdagslivets sociale netværk i en refleksiv modernitet' ['Individualisation, family life and community: A social-psychological analysis of social networks in everyday life in a reflexive modernity'], PhD dissertation, Roskilde: Roskilde University.

TEN

Minority ethnic men and fatherhood in a Danish context

Anika Liversage

Introduction

Most of the Nordic research on fatherhood focuses on the norms and practices among the majority population. Due to migration, however, Nordic populations have become increasingly multicultural over the past four decades, rendering investigations of fatherhood practices among minority ethnic groups relevant. In a country such as Denmark, immigrants and their descendants now make up about 10 per cent of the population, with non-Western immigrants and their descendants making up around 6 per cent (Statistics Denmark, 2011).

These non-Western minority ethnic groups are very diverse, and a wide range of different fatherhood practices can be found among them. This chapter provides insights into some of these practices and focuses on the potential challenges of being a father under the circumstances of migration and variations between how different minority ethnic men practise fatherhood. The focus is predominantly on non-Western men from Muslim countries. Empirically, the chapter is primarily based on 24 interviews, 16 of which stem from an investigation of minority ethnic men and masculinity (Jensen and Liversage, 2007), the remaining eight being with divorced Turkish men drawn from a larger interview material of Turkish divorcees in Denmark (Liversage, 2012a, 2012b; Charsley and Liversage, 2013).

The chapter begins with a discussion of the interrelated themes of masculinity, ethnicity and migration, and how migration may bring different models for family life into contact as well as challenge immigrant fathers' positions in their new country. Second, the chapter discusses fatherhood in cases in which minority ethnic marriages have broken up. Third, it compares the narratives of two men, both raised in Denmark, whose family lives and fathering styles are very different. The main points of this chapter are that minority ethnic fatherhood practices are often circumscribed by challenges of migration and/or their minority ethnic position, which commonly correlates with a low class position. Such low positions may undermine the father's position as breadwinner, which is a central aspect of the complementary gender roles often found in their countries of origin. While some fathers struggle to cope with their life circumstances – and possibly lose contact with their children after a divorce – others are better able to practise fatherhood. They might do so more or less aligned with the relatively egalitarian parental practices characteristic of the Nordic country in which they live.

Gender relations: complementarity versus equality

Practices of fatherhood among minority ethnic men must take into account both norms and practices in countries of origin and changes and challenges occurring in the post-migration context (Ochocka and Janzen, 2008). Regarding their country of origin, understandings of fatherhood are intimately entangled with notions of being a man. Contemporary research documents the wide range of international variations in how masculinity is interpreted (Kimmel et al, 2005; Whitehead, 2006), and the very different ways fatherhood is practised around the globe (Miller and Maiter, 2008). Immigrants in Denmark predominantly originate from Middle Eastern countries, parts of Asia and North Africa – the part of the world labelled 'the patriarchal belt' (Caldwell, 1978). Briefly sketched, a patriarchal family structure entails a hierarchy wherein men generally hold more power than women, and authority generally increases with age (Kandiyoti, 1995; Moghadam, 2004). Furthermore, there is a marked division between the male/ public and female/private spheres (Peristiany, 1974; Abadan-Unat, 1986). This division matches an understanding of gender roles whereby men and women are seen as having different duties. While significant variations possibly exist depending on factors such as levels of education and family history, many families tend to conceptualise men and women as being complementary rather than equal (Predelli, 2004): the male breadwinner and the female homemaker. The 'patriarchal belt' countries are also marked by large differences between male and female engagement in paid labour, thereby generally rendering women financially dependent on men.

In Denmark, the main non-Western immigration countries are Turkey, Iraq, Iran, Lebanon and Pakistan (Statistics Denmark, 2011). As these countries are all part of the patriarchal belt and less economically developed than Denmark (with, for example, lower levels of education), there are marked contrasts between how family life is generally organised in these countries of origin and in the country of destination.

This occurs as Denmark, like the other Scandinavian countries, has gradually shifted over the last century towards an ever more equal conceptualisation of the family and gender roles (see also Chapter Three, this volume). Thus, a traditional gendered division of work between the male breadwinner and female homemaker has gradually given way to a model wherein men and women share in both paid work and domestic life: with families needing two incomes to make ends meet, the employment rate among women in Denmark is only a few percentage points below that of men (OECD, 2011), and both parents participate in housework and childrearing, albeit in different measures (Bonke, 2009; see also Chapter Eight, this volume).

Unsurprisingly, male immigrants and descendants from patriarchal cultures may experience life in a Nordic country as a marked change – if not an outright challenge – as family dependency and the importance of the husband as breadwinner is generally much lower than in their (parents') countries of origin. Thus, the economically well-developed Nordic states have overtaken many of the functions that formerly belonged to the family, including care for children and older people as well as financial support for people with a disability, those who are unemployed and others. Although Danish majority women still often do more domestic work than Danish majority men (Bonke, 2009; OECD, 2011), and are more inclined to work part time (Holt et al, 2006; Deding and Holt, 2010), the development of the welfare state structures has been central for women's positions and possibilities inside and outside the Scandinavian labour market (Hernes, 1987; Ellingsæter, 1999). This has strengthened women in relation to men, as compared to the situation in many of the minority ethnic groups' countries of origin (Müftüler-bac, 1999). Such female independence may be perceived as undermining the position and authority of men, which is deemed so central in patriarchal societies.

This chapter begins by sketching the challenges to fatherhood arising from migration. Next, it draws on interviews with minority ethnic men to discuss practices of fatherhood, both in intact families and in cases of divorce, before comparing two minority ethnic men, both raised in Denmark, to bring out significant variations in ways of being fathers. In conclusion, the chapter demonstrates both how the migrant condition possibly undermines the ability of some minority ethnic men to be good fathers to their children and that different individuals may choose different paths as they negotiate the variable understandings of gender roles and fatherhood in their countries of origin and destination.

Challenges to fatherhood arising from migration

Besides gender roles in Scandinavia providing a contrast to the situation in the countries of origin of many immigrant men, migration itself can also produce changes and challenges. Thus, not only the context prior to, but also very much the post-migration context is important for understanding practices of, and challenges to, immigrant fathers (Gonzalez-Lopez, 2004; Ochocka and Janzen, 2008). Here, we return to the central value attributed to male breadwinning. In Denmark, for example, the employment rate among non-Western immigrants and refugees falls well below that of the majority (Statistics Denmark, 2011), and both unemployment and underemployment are main stressors for immigrant fathers (Shimoni et al, 2003; Roer-Strier et al, 2005). Explanations for this phenomenon include the lower levels of education among immigrants, their sometimes limited language skills and discrimination in the labour market (Tranæs and Zimmermann, 2004). While the employment level of minority ethnic men in Denmark increases from the first to the second generation, it remains below the level of the majority. In sum, minority ethnic groups are overrepresented in the lower echelons of Danish society, and some first-generation men in particular may struggle to find a foothold in the Danish labour market, where a high minimum wage demands correspondingly high (locally assessed) qualifications. Besides unemployment, this situation may also lead to precarious employment or a need for these men to work long days and/or outside of normal working hours (Schmidt, 2002) – all either challenging their positions as breadwinners and their roles as fathers, or more generally challenging their lives. Such labour market experiences may thus undermine the ability of immigrant men to be the fathers they desire to be.

Regarding the gendered division of work in minority ethnic families, research shows that this is often more 'traditional' than in the majority, with a breadwinner/homemaker model being more widespread. A Danish survey among first-generation immigrants from Turkey, Iran and Pakistan shows both this general point as well as documenting the existence of wide varieties depending on factors such as the country of origin and educational levels. Thus, Pakistani immigrants have a far more gendered division of work than Iranian immigrants, who share many traits with the pattern found in the Danish majority (Jakobsen and Deding, 2006). The survey also shows that minority ethnic men spend about the same amount of time on household tasks as Danish majority men. The more strongly gendered pattern in immigrant families thus arises from Danish majority women doing less housework than minority women than from the differences between different groups of men.

Specifically regarding fatherhood, this survey also shows that while only 6 per cent of Danish majority men and women disagree with the statement that 'Fathers are as good as mothers to take care of children', 20 per cent of Iranian men believe mothers to be better childcare providers than fathers, and a full 43 per cent of the Pakistani women (and 29 per cent of the Pakistan men) hold this view (Jakobsen and Deding, 2006). These survey results document that understandings of gender roles and of fatherhood may be rather different in many minority ethnic families as compared to the majority among whom they live.

Data and methods

This chapter builds on interviews with 24 non-Western men who were either immigrants or descendants of immigrants. Sixteen of the interviews were made for an investigation of minority ethnic men and masculinity in 2007 (Jensen and Liversage, 2007). The remaining eight interviews are drawn from a larger base of 31 interviews with male and female Turkish immigrants in Denmark, all of whom had divorced. All 24 men were recruited through channels such as as personal networks, language schools and non-government organisations (NGOs). Of the 24 interviewed men, 16 had children of their own, but all had views on fatherhood. The respondents had roots in non-Western countries such as Turkey, Pakistan, Afghanistan, Iraq, Lebanon and Sri Lanka. They were 20-44 years old, most in their late twenties or in their thirties. While some had an education and a good job, others were unskilled and some were unemployed. Interviews were carried out in Danish, English or Turkish in the case of recently arrived immigrants from Turkey (spoken by the author).

All interviews were made combining a life-story approach supplemented with specific questions regarding family and private lives. The interviews were tape-recorded and transcribed, and all quotes have been anonymised.

Immigrant fathers facing difficulties

Migration can change individuals' lives in many ways and may result in gender, class and ethnic relations being transformed over time (Pels, 2000; Abraham, 2005; Pels and de Haan, 2007). The reasons for migration (whether for work or marriage or due to fleeing persecution or war) may centrally shape immigrants' subsequent lives in Denmark. Also important, of course, are the resources immigrants bring with them to their new context.

The interviewed first-generation men (18 of the 24 respondents) who had arrived in Denmark as adults came from both lower-class backgrounds and (mostly in the case of refugees) the middle class. Most of these first-generation men told of having been raised in families where their fathers had worked, whereas their mothers had typically been homemakers (sometimes also caring for the family farm). In such family constellations, the father holds the primary financial responsibility – a position demanding respect. Khalid offers an example of a man from such a family. With a wife and two children, he fled to Denmark in 2000. He tells the following about his background:

> "[In my home country] you must show great respect for your parents – that's normal. Why? It's about money. When there are financial problems, the family helps. The father always works, while the rest of the family eats, drinks and has a good time. That's why they show the father respect and listen more to dad than to mum, even though she works harder than dad. The wife listens more to her husband than here. It's because her husband goes out and works, makes money, and is the one to decide.... If the wife doesn't work, she must always listen to her husband." (Khalid, 41, Afghanistan)

Khalid's description of the family structure in his native country can be read like a classic tale of patriarchal power, explicitly tied here to the husband's economic position. Khalid's interjection that the mother possibly works even harder than the father may be interpreted as being due in part to the interviewer being a majority Danish female researcher. Khalid's story, which is rather typical for first-generation men, reveals that the central, pre-migration experiences with gender roles could differ substantially from the dominant pattern found in Denmark.

This gendered division of work from the country of origin may, however, be difficult to recreate in Denmark. This could be due partly to the migration itself, often undermining the ability of immigrant men to become the breadwinners. First, as previously discussed, finding satisfying employment – or employment at all – can prove difficult. Second, their wives may be encouraged to get an education and/or work in Denmark, sometimes leading to a sharing of the breadwinning in line with the Nordic norm. In other cases (even though it is not the dominant picture), wives may gain better labour market positions than their husbands. The assistance offered by the welfare state, including help to single mothers and young people, can also be felt as pulling the carpet out from under the formerly powerful male heads of households (Kleist, 2010; Liversage, 2012a, 2012b).

Such a post-migratory loss of authority is a recurring theme in the literature on migrant men (Mortensen, 1996; Prieur, 1999). Besides their limited labour market opportunities, such a loss of authority may also spring from some men's limited language skills and lack of understanding of the societal structures in the new country, all factors impeding their opportunities to be the fathers they aspire to be.

Regarding the interviewed men with more education and high-level jobs in their countries of origin, they had generally (as also seen in other countries) been unable to regain their former status in the Danish labour market (Brandi, 2001; Bauder, 2003). Fathers in such situations did not narrate this life situation as providing a rare opportunity to spend more time with their families. Instead, it challenged their ability to live up to masculine expectations, which could have a negative affect on their respective relationships with their children.

Non-working immigrant men with limited Danish skills and limited access to resources in Denmark could feel poorly equipped for supporting their children and guiding them regarding their future here. One respondent, Ali, expressed as much. Because of torture-inflicted leg injuries, he had been without work since fleeing to Denmark in 1990. His wife was Danish-born but of immigrant descent. Not only was she employed, she was also further improving her education. Ali felt less competent than his wife regarding life in Denmark. When talking about their nine-year-old daughter, he went so far as to comment, "I think she already knows everything better than I do. Because she lives here, she's born here" (Ali, 44, Iraq).

Ali felt unable to be a good, strong father for his child. On the contrary, he feared coming to depend on his daughter's support. However, not all first-generation fathers indicated that their lack of knowledge regarding life in Denmark necessarily undermined their paternal authority. In this regard, Khalid commented that even though his children knew more than he did about some things, they should still listen to their father:

> "I tell them: 'My dear son, you speak the Danish language better than I do. But there are some things I know better than you right now. I explain it to you in our language, but then it's up to you to find out what it means in Danish. You must also help me, so I can learn Danish'. In that way, very kindly." (Khalid, 41, Afghanistan)

Khalid is asserting that he instructs his son 'very kindly' – not in a harsh, authoritarian manner. Nevertheless, it can be difficult to get family members to listen to you when lacking basic skills in Danish society. Here, for many fathers, that they would be shown 'respect' – that their children would listen to and obey them – often became both a central and challenging ambition. This need for respect could be culturally related, with reference to the importance held by the father in patriarchal societies, but it might also spring from feelings of inferiority due to their difficulties with respect to maintaining their role as breadwinner, and due to the men generally finding themselves on the lower rungs of their new society.

From the other end of the relationship – from the viewpoint of the second-generation sons – it might be difficult to respect a father weakened by migration and struggling to fill the man-of-the-house role adequately. This occurred for Roshan, who fled to Denmark together with his parents when he was a child. On his father's arrival to Denmark, Roshan tells of how:

> "... Suddenly, he was nothing. He earned nothing.... He was bad at speaking [Danish], so he depended a lot on my mother and us.... I lost respect for him, and I think my younger brother did too, because somehow he was just a figure for us. He didn't hold the authority you expected a father to hold. A few times, he told my mother that she didn't respect him. And that us kids didn't respect him.... I think they both had a lot of pain – also because things didn't turn out like they expected." (Roshan, 34, Sri Lankan background)

Thus – as expressed by Roshan – immigrant fathers may feel their positions in the family undermined in Denmark. This may stem both from their own challenged position, from women's increased participation in work, and from the existence of welfare state support measures (see Kleist, 2010, regarding Somali men in Denmark). Such changes can make it difficult for fathers to live up to their own expectations of being good – authoritative – fathers, while sons can struggle to be good – respectful – sons. This may lead to a perceived loss of masculinity for the fathers, and challenge their status as role models for their children. While very prominent in the lives of several immigrant fathers, such challenges to masculinity in a modern, ever-changing world are hardly unique to minority ethnic men; they are a risk confronting men in general (Ekenstam, 2005).

Migrant men, fatherhood and divorce

In some cases, the migration-related changes and shifts in power structures subsequent to arrival in Denmark are implicated in the break-up of minority ethnic families – a rather understudied topic. From Sweden, we know that Iranian marriages often break up (Darvishpour, 1999). An underlying dynamic is that, among Iranian refugee couples, the wives often adapt better to the new life circumstances than their husbands. Combined with the presence of welfare state measures, this may lead to marital conflict and divorce (Darvishpour, 1999). In Denmark, studies among Turkish immigrants and their descendants (the largest minority ethnic group in Denmark and Europe in general) have found the frequency of divorce in this group to be steadily increasing over the last three decades (Liversage, 2012a). Different factors can contribute to these divorces, which can occur at the initiative of the husband or wife (Liversage, 2013), but one common underlying dynamic seems to be shifts in gendered power structures, resulting in both changes in expectations of marriage and giving women in particular easier access to divorce (Liversage, 2012b).

Even though divorce is more accessible to men than to women according to Muslim religious understandings (Pearl and Menski, 1998; Shah-Kazemi, 2001; Khir, 2006), the great importance of marriage is reflected in the social stigma attached to divorce – stigma that often also reflects on men (Foblets, 2008). Furthermore, divorce sometimes leaves immigrant fathers in very difficult positions, challenging their opportunity to maintain good contact with their children (Ahmad, 2008).

Regarding the opportunity for divorced minority ethnic men to practise fatherhood, studies indicate that the norms against breaking up families may result in marriages often being quite dysfunctional before actually ending in divorce among minority ethnic groups. As post-divorce parental cooperation is often more difficult when pre-divorce conflict levels have been high, some divorced minority ethnic parents might have difficulty bringing up their children in a collaborative manner (Ottosen et al, 2014). Already living precarious lives, some minority ethnic men may even end up homeless after a divorce (Järvinen, 2003).

These findings can be put in perspective through comparison with the post-divorce contact between majority Danish fathers and their children. Here, one important factor is the paternal involvement in parenting practices: fathers who are more involved in parenting before a divorce generally enjoy closer post-divorce ties with their children. Another important factor is class: while one third of divorced majority fathers from the top echelons of society have extensive contact with their children, also when the children are teenagers, and only few lose contact with their offspring entirely, the opposite pattern is true for the Danish majority fathers who are excluded from the labour market (see also Chapter Twelve, this volume).

A recent register data analysis shows that minority ethnic children in Denmark increasingly experience parental divorce: this occurs for every fourth child with a minority ethnic background as compared to for every third majority Danish child. However, while only around 20 per cent of majority children after a divorce have no contact at all with one of their parents (usually the father), this situation is twice as frequent (around 40 per cent) for minority ethnic children (Ottosen et al, 2014).[1] This difference must also be understood in relation to the lower class position of minority ethnic fathers in Denmark as compared to the majority.

Similarly, while half of all divorced children from the Danish majority live with one parent but regularly visit the other, this is only the case for one third of minority ethnic children. Finally, while 12 per cent of majority children share their time roughly equally between their parents, this is rarely (3 per cent) the case for minority ethnic children. While these figures are based on a limited survey sample and should be treated with caution, the numbers nevertheless indicate that minority ethnic fathers are less present in their children's lives after a divorce as compared to the situation for the majority (see also Chapter Twelve, this volume). The survey material also shows that divorced minority ethnic women with children begin living with a new partner less often than majority women. This difference can at least partially be explained as arising from the importance nevertheless attributed to paternity in many Muslim immigrant families: while women are generally responsible for childcare, the children fundamentally belong to the father (Mehdi, 2007; de Carli, 2008). A divorced mother who finds a new partner may be felt to upset this pattern, for which reason divorced immigrant mothers may remain single. There have been isolated cases in which fathers from countries such as Lebanon, Morocco, Syria and Egypt have abducted their children, in some cases spurred on by their ex-wives finding new partners (Udvalget for børnebortførelser [Committee on Child Abduction], 2004; Liversage and Jensen, 2011; Liversage, 2012c).

Halil: a divorced marriage migrant father

The complexities and challenges of being both a divorced father and a recent immigrant become apparent in the interview with Halil, a Turkish marriage migrant. He arrived in Denmark in 2001 after an arranged marriage with a Turkish woman raised in Denmark.[2] The marriage was troubled and the couple – who had a young son – after four years separated in an acrimonious divorce. As the Danish probationary period – the time necessary for marriage migrants to gain a permanent residence permit – was seven years, Halil did not meet this requirement when he divorced. When interviewed in 2006, Halil had irregular contact with his son, who lived with his former wife, and he was unsure of whether he would be able to remain in Denmark.

As Halil felt that his former wife was an unfit mother (alleging that she beat their child), he hoped to gain custody. As a man, however, his sister questioned whether he would be able to shoulder the responsibilities of single parenthood. As Halil explained:

> "[My sister asked] 'If you got the child, how would you care for him? You'd have to work.' Then I say: 'Imagine, if I hadn't been divorced and my wife had died in a traffic accident. Then I'd have been able to care for the child, right?' Divorce or death, that's similar – you can do it, because you have to." (Halil, 25, Turkey)

This reflects how the notion of a man assuming full responsibility for a young child is unusual. Responding to his sister's question, Halil's further considerations about how to care for his son as a single father also includes different females, as if the thought of unassisted male parenthood is indeed strange:

> "My sister says [caring for a child] would be hard. Yes, I know that – very hard. But it's my responsibility. And then there's this possibility: my mother is old, so she and my father could come visit for 3-5-12 months. And then she could care for the child. They could easily get a permit. Or else, there's this new law about women from Russia who can come as nannies. I'd be able to arrange that, to have someone to look after my child, even if it would cost half my salary. Or I could take [son] to Turkey, if that was allowed. Then I could live with my mother for the first 3-4 years, so he could grow a bit older before we would return to Denmark." (Halil, 25, Turkey)

Here, Halil mentions three ways he could practise single fatherhood: by bringing his mother to Denmark, by taking his son to his mother in Turkey, or by fetching a nanny from Russia in keeping with the au pair arrangement possible in Denmark (Liversage et al, 2013). In all three scenarios, Halil would be able to shift much of the daily childcare responsibility on to a woman (while public provisions for childcare are fully absent). It is also worth adding that even if Halil acquired a residence permit in Denmark, despite having been divorced within the probationary period, all three of these constructions would most likely not be possible under Danish law.

Halil's difficult situation shows, first, that residency status, including the risk of being expelled from Denmark after divorce, may seriously shape the options of some immigrant men for practising fatherhood. Second, Halil's considerations about how to handle the challenges if he did indeed become a single parent show how seeing childcare as a female task may be deeply ingrained.

Another example of a Turkish marriage migrant divorcing in Denmark is Can. Having lived in Denmark longer than Halil, Can had no problem remaining in Denmark after divorcing. Here, he agreed with his ex-wife that their two children should live mostly with their mother but see their father regularly; however, the visitation model was different from that usually practised among divorced Danes:

> "I can see my children when I want to, and they come to my place every other Saturday. I pick them up around nine in the morning, and they're here until around nine in the

evening. Then I take them back to their mother. After all,
I also work, and I live alone." (Can, 36, Turkey)

While this visitation scheme could be considered limited from a
majority Danish perspective, this should not be linked to a lack of
importance attributed to being a father, and Can indicated that he
felt very close to his two children. But his arrangement – seeing his
children every second weekend and only in the daytime – made for
fewer care demands on a single father.

Fathers of the second generation

While so far this chapter has presented some of the challenges facing
first-generation immigrant fathers, the last section compares and
contrasts the family practices of two minority ethnic fathers, who
were both born and raised in Denmark. The two men, Tarek and
Jakup, have been chosen for the very different ways they structured
their family lives.

The first respondent, Tarek, had a Pakistani background, was
31 years old, and held a degree in engineering. He worked full time
as a school administrator and drove a cab for his father's taxi company
in the evening. He had entered into an arranged marriage with a
Pakistani woman who had come to Denmark as a marriage migrant.
She was educating herself to become a childcare worker, and they
had two young children together. The second respondent, Jakup, had
a Turkish background and was 36 years old. He had dropped out of
university and was a self-employed retailer. After a short-lived marriage
to a marriage migrant from Turkey, he was cohabiting with a Danish
majority woman with whom he had two children.

There are pronounced differences in how these two men live and
practise fatherhood. Thus, their two narratives exemplify different ways
of understanding and practising masculinity and fatherhood among
minority ethnic men, illustrating some of the broad differences found
within this group.

Tarek: complementary gender roles

Tarek's parents came to Denmark as labour migrants decades ago.
Tarek had been raised in Denmark in a family modelled according to
principles of gender complementarity. As he explained, "my mother
was in charge at home and my father worked". Today, Tarek and his
wife live according to similar principles. Regarding his wife, Tarek

told of how "she has the main responsibility – you may say that she's the queen in the home. She decides where to put the sofa."

For his own part, Tarek was often away from home, combining his full-time job with driving a taxi. He considered this breadwinner/homemaker division of work as based on the fundamental biological differences between men and women:

> "I think that a man is a man for natural reasons – and a woman, she's a woman. I don't think it can be changed – that's just the order of things. I think that every man has the instinct of a provider, and I think – regardless of whether he's an immigrant or a Dane or whatever – he has to work. And someone should be in the home, to take care of things.... I think you have to be careful about talking too much about this equality thing, because you may have equality, but you just can't be equal in every way.... I don't think humans are made in that way. I think everything would collapse. Men are better at some things and women at others – that's just how it is. The man should be the strong one. He should be the one saying 'Stop' and marking some boundaries, whereas women, they're more ... now I'm talking based on my own experiences – they're more giddy, more emotional.... It takes a man to go and say 'That's how it should be – I've decided it like that'."
> (Tarek, 31, Pakistani background)

Here, Tarek expresses a traditional understanding of the gendered division of work between him and his wife, a division aligning with the patriarchal family model prevailing in his parents' country of origin. As a father, he should be both the figure of authority for the whole family and also the economic provider. But as two incomes are generally necessary in Denmark to make ends meet, practising this gendered division of work depended on Tarek taking two jobs (as a school administrator and taxi driver) – something which kept him away from the family home. Complementing this role, his wife provided care for their young children, even when Tarek was present:

> "She's the one who takes the pram and picks up the child if it cries. People might think that this man just doesn't care, but they haven't understood how it works.... They don't know that maybe I was out driving a taxi for 12 hours that night and I'm tired. But my wife knows that.... And then

she makes even more sure that I can just relax and don't have to take care of what the children do." (Tarek, 31, Pakistani background)

The interview with Tarek does not indicate that the family's gendered division of work is contested, which may partly be due to Tarek's wife having arrived through marriage migration, and Tarek tells of how – in his view – he and his wife have a fine, harmonious family life.

Jakup: more egalitarian parental practices

Jakup's parents also came as labour migrants, arriving from Turkey. After a short-lived marriage to a marriage migrant, Jakup began dating a Danish majority woman. At the time of the interview, he was living with her and their two common children. In line with many other cohabitating couples in Denmark, they were unmarried (Ottosen, 2011). In the beginning of their relationship, Jakup expected his Danish girlfriend to shoulder the main responsibilities in their home, but his girlfriend contested this:

> "It has been a bit difficult for me to be Turkish – and a Turkish man. I've been raised with children and breastfeeding and all that being female issues.... So we've had some arguments where I've said: 'Listen, you're the mother, so it's natural that you breastfeed – and then it's okay that I go to a birthday party'. But then she has felt like: 'No, it's not okay. You should show solidarity and stay at home' and 'it will be boring'. And we've had some small fights. In the long run, maybe I can see that what she says is right. Maybe it would be comforting, if I was there too.... So in that way, I think it has been quite hard for me to become a father – to get used to it, mentally." (Jakup, 36, Turkish background)

Jakup underscores that he has changed, and that he now shares in the care for his children with his partner. But the quote above shows that this is not merely something he has 'chosen' to do – his active participation has developed out of family negotiations. When this couple became parents, they had rather different understandings of how life with an infant should be, and how a 'good father' and 'good partner' should behave. For Jakup, developing his present-day fathering style, as compared with how he had originally envisioned fatherhood, has involved negotiations as well as struggles. Tarek, on the other hand, has not faced such demands for change. He could thus be a father and provider in largely the same way he himself was raised.

Their different constructions of family life also rendered Jakup less of a (sole) breadwinner than Tarek. In fact, while Tarek placed great emphasis on how much money he made in his two jobs, Jakup – whose wife also worked – explicitly distanced himself from being too material. Instead, Jakup underscored that he would rather spend time with his family than make lots of money. He shared the following about him and his partner:

> "We aren't people who will put ourselves into debt for 30 years, buy a car and pay into a pension fund. And many people think we're weird because we don't. But that's not how it is for my partner and me.... You shouldn't take work too seriously, because then you can only take your children half seriously, and that causes stress...." (Jakup, 36, Turkish background)

The different levels of importance which Tarek and Jakup place on having a high income echoes with similar differences found among men from the majority (Connell, 1993). At the time of the interview, Jakup, his partner and their children were in fact about to move to Turkey, where they hoped to escape materialism and the 'rat race' for a more holistic family life and be able to be more in touch with nature. They were planning to settle on the Mediterranean coast and start a 'hippie Bed and Breakfast':

> "Like 'don't touch nature' ... maybe build some wooden houses or get some old caravans and paint them. And then have a big common kitchen and provide a different kind of vacation for friends and acquaintances.... Like – today we pick oranges with the children and make juice, sort of ... that's what we have in mind." (Jakup, 36, Turkish background)

With his focus on having close relations with his children rather than increasing his family's material standing, Jakup's priorities as a father clearly differ from Tarek's, illustrating some of the massive variation in how minority ethnic men practise fatherhood.

Conclusion

Overall, survey data and the interviews behind this chapter demonstrate that minority ethnic men on average practise fatherhood in ways that diverge somewhat from the fatherhood practices of the Danish majority. In line with the norms in their countries of origin (often in the 'patriarchal belt' of North Africa, the Middle East and parts of Asia), minority ethnic men are more inclined to understand the roles of men and women in the family as complementary rather than equal. Thus, they believe that fathers should be breadwinners and hold the central responsibility for the family, whereas mothers are more responsible for the home and children.

However, migration processes may pose various challenges to the ability of minority ethnic men to be successful providers. This is both due to the un-/underemployment of minority ethnic men, whose skills may be difficult to apply in the Danish labour market; through to the importance of the dual earner model in Denmark, according to which women are also expected to work; and through to the provision of various sorts of welfare state services and benefits. These combined factors – as well as exposure to a different way of life in the destination country – may, in some cases, be felt to undermine the position of minority ethnic fathers in the family. In other cases, they may lead to various forms of adaptation to life in new circumstances, including the practice of more egalitarian cooperation between parents. Thus, minority ethnic fathers 'do fatherhood' very differently.

Some minority ethnic fathers end up in particularly vulnerable positions. Men, already weakly positioned in the labour market, may thus experience that divorce leaves them without contact with their offspring, possibly even homeless in some cases (Järvinen, 2003; Ahmad, 2008; Liversage, 2012b). Such challenges, including the lack of established practices regarding post-divorce parental cooperation on bringing up children, partially explain why survey studies indicate that minority ethnic children see their fathers less (if at all) than Danish majority children with divorced parents.

In sum, fathers with minority ethnic backgrounds (from both the first and second generation) may thus – in their different ways – have to contend with the turmoil and challenges often resulting from migration. In negotiating complementary and egalitarian gender roles, minority ethnic fathers may find themselves challenged as their children head towards a future which is often very different from their own lives. While some of these men find it difficult to practise fatherhood in the ways to which they aspire, others are – in their own unique ways – able to do so successfully. With the passage of time, it is likely that men from minority ethnic groups in Denmark's increasingly multicultural population will develop further their own diverse ways of being fathers.

Notes

[1] These figures are based on two surveys: first, the Children and Youth in Denmark – a survey from 2009 with approximately 6,300 children from Denmark aged 3-19. Of the original sample (of 9,750 individuals), 9 per cent had a minority ethnic background. Second, from the Danish Longitudinal Survey of Children had an initial sample of approximately 6,000 majority Danish children born in 1995. A parallel survey with an initial sample of approximately 600 minority ethnic children was started the same year. In both surveys, the response rate among minority ethnic groups was substantially lower than among the Danish majority, limiting the conclusions which can be drawn (Deding and Olsson, 2009; see Ottosen et al, 2010; Ottosen, 2012).

[2] In the 1990s, about 80 per cent of the marital partners of young people of Turkish descent, raised in Denmark, came from Turkey as marriage migrants. This share has dropped since 2002, when major restrictions on marriage migration were introduced (Schmidt et al, 2009; Liversage and Rytter, 2014). For further details on Halil, see Liversage (2012b).

References

Abadan-Unat, N. (1986) *Women in the developing world: Evidence from Turkey*, University of Denver Monograph Series, Denver, CO: University of Denver.

Abraham, M. (2005) 'Domestic violence and the Indian diaspora in the United States', *Indian Journal of Gender Studies*, vol 12, no 2-3, pp 427-51.

Ahmad, A.N. (2008) 'Gender and generation in Pakistani migration: a critical study of masculinity', in L. Ryan and W. Webster (eds) *Gendering migration: Masculinity, femininity and ethnicity in post-war Britain*, Aldershot: Ashgate, pp 155-70.

Bauder, H. (2003) '"Brain abuse", or the devaluation of immigrant labour in Canada', *Antipode*, vol 35, no 4, pp 699-717.

Bonke, J. (2009) *Forældres brug af tid og penge på deres børn* [*Parents' use of time and money on their children*], Odense: University Press of Southern Denmark.

Brandi, C.M. (2001) 'Skilled immigrants in Rome', *International Migration*, vol 39, no 4, pp 101-31.

Caldwell, J.C. (1978) 'A theory of fertility: from high plateau to destabilization', *Population and Development Review*, vol 4, no 4, pp 553-77.

Charsley, K. and Liversage, A. (2013) 'Transforming polygamy: migration, transnationalism and multiple marriages among Muslim minorities', *Global Networks*, vol 13, no 1, pp 60-78.

Connell, R.W. (1993) 'The big picture: masculinities in recent world history', *Theory and Society*, vol 22, no 597, pp 597-623.

Darvishpour, M. (1999) 'Intensified gender conflicts within Iranian families in Sweden', *Nora: Nordic Journal of Women's Studies*, vol 7, no 1, pp 20-33.

de Carli, E.F. (2008) *Religion, juss og rettigheter: om skilsmisse, polygami og shari'a-råd* [*Religion, law and rights: on divorce, polygamy, and Shari'a councils*], Oslo: Institute for Social Research.

Deding, M. and Holt, H. (2010) *Hvorfor har vi lønforskelle mellem kvinder og mænd? En antologi om ligeløn i Danmark* [*Why do we have wage differences between men and women? An anthology about equal pay in Denmark*], Copenhagen: SFI – The Danish National Centre for Social Research.

Ekenstam, C. (2005) 'Rädslan att falla' ['Fear of falling'], *NIKK magasin*, vol 1, pp 5-8.

Ellingsæter, A.L. (1999) 'Patriarkatet. Teori og kritikk' ['Patriarchy. theory and criticism'], in F. Engelstad (ed) *Om makt – teori og kritikk* [*On power – theory and criticism*], Oslo: Ad Notam Gyldendal, pp 151-73.

Foblets, M.-C. (2008) 'Marriage and divorce in the new Moroccan family code: implications for Moroccans residing in Europe', in R. Mehdi, H. Petersen, E.R. Sand and G.R. Woodman (eds) *Law and religion in multicultural societies*, Copenhagen: DJØF Publishing, pp 145-76.

Gonzalez-Lopez, G. (2004) 'Fathering Latina sexualities: Mexican men and the virginity of their daughters', *Journal of Marriage and the Family*, vol 66, no 5, pp 1118-30.

Hernes, H. (1987) 'Women and the welfare state: the transition from private to public dependence', in A.S. Sassoon (ed) *Women and the state*, London: Hutchinson, pp 72-92.

Holt, H., Geerdsen, L.P., Christensen, G., Klitgaard, C. and Lind, M.L. (2006) *Det kønsopdelte arbejdsmarked* [*The gender-segregated labour market*], Copenhagen: SFI – The Danish National Centre for Social Research.

Jakobsen, V. and Deding, M. (2006) *Indvandreres arbejdsliv og familieliv* [*Work and family life of immigrants*], Copenhagen: SFI – The Danish National Centre for Social Research.

Järvinen, M. (2003) 'Negotiating strangerhood: interviews with homeless immigrants in Copenhagen', *Acta Sociologica*, vol 46, no 3, pp 215-30.

Jensen, T.G. and Liversage, A. (2007) *Fædre, sønner, ægtemænd – om maskulinitet og manderoller blandt etniske minoritetsmænd* [*Fathers, sons, husbands – on masculinity and the male role among ethnic minority men*], Copenhagen: SFI – The Danish National Centre for Social Research.

Kandiyoti, D. (1995) 'Patterns of patriarchy: notes for an analysis of male dominance in Turkish society', in S. Tekeli (eds) *Women in modern Turkish society: A reader*, London: Zed Books, pp 306-18.

Khir, B.M. (2006) 'The right of women to no-fault divorce in Islam and its application by British Muslims', *Islam and Christian-Muslim Relations*, vol 3, pp 295-306.

Kimmel, M., Hearn, J. and Connell, R.W. (2005) *Handbook of studies on men and masculinities*, London: Sage.

Kleist, N. (2010) 'Negotiating respectable masculinity: gender and recognition in the Somali diaspora', *African Diaspora*, vol 3, pp 185-206.

Liversage, A. (2013) 'Gendered struggles over residency rights when Turkish immigrant marriages break up', *Oñati Socio-Legal Series*, vol 3, pp 1070-90.

Liversage, A. (2012a) 'Divorce among Turkish immigrants in Denmark', in K. Charsley (ed) *Transnational marriage: New perspectives from Europe and beyond*, London: Routledge, pp 146-60.

Liversage, A. (2012b) 'Gender, conflict and subordination within the household: Turkish migrant marriage and divorce in Denmark', *Journal of Ethnic and Migration Studies*, vol 38, no 7, pp 1119-36.

Liversage, A. (2012c) 'Muslim divorces in Denmark: finds from an empirical investigation', in R. Mehdi, W. Menski and J.S. Nielsen (eds) *Interpreting divorce law in Islam*, Copenhagen: DJØF Publishing, pp 179-201.

Liversage, A. and Jensen, T.G. (2011) *Parallelle retsopfattelser i Danmark – et kvalitativt studie af privatretlige praksisser blandt etniske minoriteter* [*Parallel conceptions of law in Denmark – a qualitative study of civil law practices among ethnic minorities*], Copenhagen: SFI – The National Centre for Social Research.

Liversage, A. and Rytter, M. (eds) (2014) *Ægteskab og migration - konsekvenser af de danske familiesammenføringsregler 2002 - 2012 [Marriage and migration - consequences of the Danish rules on family migration 2002 - 2012]*, Aarhus: Aarhus University Press.

Liversage, A., Bille, R. and Jakobsen, V. (2013) *Den danske au pair-ordning – en kvalitativ og kvantitativ undersøgelse [The Danish au pair scheme – a qualitative and quantitative investigation]*, Copenhagen: SFI – The Danish National Centre for Social Research.

Mehdi, R. (2007) *Integration og retsudvikling [Integration and the development of the law]*, Copenhagen: DJØF Publishing.

Miller, W. and Maiter, S. (2008) 'Fatherhood and culture: moving beyond stereotypical understandings', *Journal of Ethnic and Cultural Diversity in Social Work*, vol 17, no 3, pp 1-28.

Moghadam, V.M. (2004) 'Patriarchy in transition: women and the changing family in the Middle East', *Journal of Comparative Family Studies*, vol 42, no 2, pp 137-62.

Mortensen, L.B. (1996) *Kortlægning af problemfeltet 'udstødte tyrkiske og kurdiske mænd' i det storkøbenhavnske område [Mapping of the problem area 'excluded Turkish and Kurdish men' in Greater Copenhagen]*, Copenhagen: Social Development Centre SUS.

Müftüler-bac, M. (1999) 'Turkish women's predicament', *Women's Studies International Forum*, vol 22, no 3, pp 303-15.

Ochocka, J. and Janzen, R. (2008) 'Immigrant parenting: a new framework of understanding', *Journal of Immigrant and Refugee Studies*, vol 6, pp 85-111.

OECD (Organisation for Economic Co-operation and Development) (2011) Better Life Index (www.oecdbetterlifeindex.org).

Ottosen, M.H. (2011) 'Familien' ['The family'], in H. Andersen (ed) *Sociologi – en introduktion [Sociology – An introduction]*, Copenhagen: Hans Reitzel, pp 181-96.

Ottosen, M.H. (2012) *15-åriges hverdagsliv og udfordringer [Everyday life and challenges of 15-year-olds]*, Copenhagen: SFI – The Danish National Centre for Social Research.

Ottosen, M.H., Andersen, D., Lausten, M., Nielsen, L.P. and Stage, S. (2010) *Børn og unge i Danmark – velfærd og trivsel, 2010 [Children and youth in Denmark – welfare and well-being, 2010]*, Copenhagen: SFI – The Danish National Centre for Social Research.

Ottosen, M.H., Liversage, A. and Olsen, R.F. (2014) *Skilsmissebørn med etnisk minoritetsbaggrund [Minority ethnic children with divorced parents]*, Copenhagen: SFI – The Danish National Centre for Social Research.

Pearl, D. and Menski, W. (1998) *Muslim family law*, London: Sweet & Maxwell.

Pels, T. (2000) 'Muslim families from Morocco in the Netherlands: gender dynamics and fathers' roles in a context of change', *Current Sociology*, vol 48, no 4, pp 75-93.

Pels, T. and de Haan, M. (2007) 'Socialization practices of Moroccan families after migration: a reconstruction in an "acculturative arena"', *Young*, vol 15, no 1, pp 71-89.

Peristiany, J.G. (1974) *Honour and shame: The values of Mediterranean society*, Chicago, IL: University of Chicago Press.

Predelli, L.N. (2004) 'Interpreting gender in Islam: a case study of immigrant Muslim women in Oslo', *Gender and Society*, vol 18, no 4, pp 473-93.

Prieur, A. (1999) 'Maskulinitet, kriminalitet og etnicitet' ['Masculinity, crime, and ethnicity'], *Social Kritik (Social Criticism)*, vol 65, pp 32-43.

Roer-Strier, D., Strier, R., Este, D., Shimoni, R. and Clarke, D. (2005) 'Fatherhood and immigration: challenging the deficit theory', *Child and Family Social Work*, vol 10, pp 315-29.

Schmidt, G. (2002) *Tidsanvendelse blandt pakistanere, tyrkere og somaliere – et integrationsperpektiv* [*The use of time among Pakistanis, Turks, and Somalis – an integration perspective*], Copenhagen: SFI – The Danish National Centre for Social Research.

Schmidt, G., Graversen, B.K., Jakobsen, V., Jensen, T.G. and Liversage, A. (2009) *Ændrede familiesammenføringsregler* [*Changed family reunification rules*], Copenhagen: SFI – The Danish National Centre for Social Research.

Shah-Kazemi, S.N. (2001) *Untying the knot: Muslim women, divorce and Shariah*, London: Signal Press.

Shimoni, R., Este, D. and Clarke, D. (2003) 'Paternal engagement in immigrant and refugee families', *Journal of Comparative Family Studies*, vol 34, no 4, pp 555-69.

Statistics Denmark (2011) *Indvandrere i Danmark 2011* [*Immigrants in Denmark 2011*], Copenhagen: Statistics Denmark.

Tranæs, T. and Zimmermann, K.F. (2004) *Migrants, work, and the welfare state*, Odense: University Press of Southern Denmark.

Udvalget for børnebortførelser [Committee on Child Abduction] (2004) *Redegørelse om børnebortførelser* [*Report on child abductions*], Copenhagen: Ministry of Justice.

Whitehead, S.M. (2006) *Men and masculinities, Volume V: Global masculinities*, London: Routledge.

ELEVEN

Making space for fatherhood in gay men's lives in Norway[1]

Arnfinn J. Andersen

Introduction

The chapters in this book provide evidence as to how the construction of fatherhood is undergoing changes as a result of closer and more independent relations between fathers and children. This also affects gay men and their prospects for and realisation of fatherhood. Norms pertaining to fatherhood (and parenthood) are changing along with the political struggle among gays and lesbians for greater acceptance and recognition, including parenthood. What insight can the experiences of homosexual men who choose to be fathers bring to the understanding of these changes in fatherhood norms, roles and relations? This chapter is based on a study of homosexual men from the Norwegian middle class who have had children with a lesbian friend. The central question for this study is how these fathers establish their fatherhood in light of the child being born outside of the traditional frame of a heterosexual couple in a shared home. The chapter applies an understanding of the importance of space to the analysis of fatherhood. By focusing on the spatial dimensions of home and parenthood, a theoretical perspective is established that differs from a tradition in family sociology where the focus is more on social interaction but not on how this interaction also contributes to the construction of space.

The central question is divided into two sub-questions. The first concerns the importance of the child for how the fathers construct a space for their fatherhood. The second concerns how the fathers establish a position of fatherhood in a situation where the child already has several parenting figures to relate to: a mother, a co-mother and often also a co-father. The study shows that the 'space' of parental collaboration takes the place that a shared parental home traditionally occupies. One important finding is that although the fathers choose to have children in an unconventional manner, the space of collaboration which they establish with the mothers serves to confirm conventional values and traditional family relations. In this manner, these fathers contribute to continuity in conceptions about family and home. The analysis of the spatial dimension of fatherhood is carried out in two stages: first, how fathers shape their own home into a space that includes their child; second, how the fathers collaborate with the mothers (and co-mothers) to create a common social space for the child in two separated homes.

Political and social contexts of fatherhood

The stories of the respective fathers in this chapter cannot be seen in isolation from significant changes that have taken place in how gender equality and individual sexual freedom have been viewed in Norway and the Nordic region over the last 30 years. In the wake of a political struggle for greater gender equality among heterosexuals, a political movement has also emerged among gays and lesbians for greater acceptance and recognition of gay and lesbian relationships (Rydström, 2008; Andersen, 2009). This movement has undergone two phases in the Nordic countries. Most of the Nordic countries introduced partnership legislation for gays and lesbians at the beginning of the 1990s (Denmark in 1989, Norway in 1992, Sweden in 1995, Iceland in 1996 and Finland in 2002; see also Chapter Three, this volume). This gave a homosexual person entering into a partnership access to the same legal protection as the marriage law provided to married couples, with the exception of church marriages and regulations involving children (adoption/assisted reproductive technology). The second phase came with the introduction of a gender-neutral marriage law applicable to all married couples – including same-gender couples. This law was introduced in Norway in 2008 (Sweden in 2009, Iceland in 2010 and Denmark in 2012), and in the Norwegian case, the law also gives gays and lesbians the right to adopt and lesbians to make use of assisted reproductive technology. These legal changes have led many lesbian couples to choose to have children through assisted reproductive technology instead of having children with a gay male friend, which was more common before this opportunity occurred through the legal changes. Gay men increasingly opt for a surrogate mother, usually from another country. However, this practice is not legal in any of the Nordic countries (Westlund, 2009). For the fathers in question in this study, however, fatherhood became possible via an arrangement with a lesbian friend, creating the need to negotiate the spatial construction of fatherhood in a different way than in a conventional partnership.

Spatial construction of fatherhood

The importance of the home as a spatial setting for the construction of gay fatherhood and how gay fathers raise their children is a central perspective in this chapter, as the home has been viewed as the primary base for the family in the 20th century. Until the 1970s, the home served as the place for establishing where the heterosexual nuclear family belonged (Gullestad, 1984, 1989; Beck and Beck-Gernsheim, 1995; Aarseth, 2008). Many would argue that the statement 'My home is my castle' is a hackneyed and outdated expression that no longer resonates as it once did in the past. This is not the case for the fathers who participated in this study. For them, the home was very important in terms of how they used it to create the content in their role as fathers, despite the fact that their children spent most of their time with their mothers and for the most part were growing up in another home.

A fatherhood established by becoming a father together with a friend does not follow traditional conventions. In our culture, the ideal fatherhood is built on a heterosexual relationship and life together with the child's mother in a common home. This coupling of heterosexuality, sexual relationship, shared home and child could be said to represent a hegemonic normative ideal of how fatherhood will and ought to be organised, which can be termed 'heteronormativity' (Ingraham, 1996). Although this ideal stands strong, many families are characterised by much more varied family practices. The increase in the share of broken relationships and remarriage contributes to many families not practising family life according to the normative ideals. The fathers who participated in this study have violated this heteronormative way of organising fatherhood in three alternative ways in relation to the conventional notions of family life: the parents do not build parenthood on a mutual sexual relationship; they are not − nor have they ever been − a couple; and they do not share a home together.

The investigation of gay and lesbian families and fatherhood has had a special focus on the significance of these breaks in the design of family and parenthood (Weston, 1991; Berkowitz and Marsiglio, 2007). In the Norwegian research context, the question of what significance having same-gendered parents has for a child and how this challenges the hegemony of heterosexuality as idea and norm figure prominently (Andersen, 2003; Folgerø, 2008). The present study positions itself in this tradition but differs from other studies in terms of its focus on social spatiality. The notion of 'space' as structuring human existence in conjunction with categories related to time and society are based on the theories of French philosopher Henri Lefebvre, and further developed by sociologist David Harvey. In this perspective, space – in line with time – represents an independent, structuring condition for human action. Individuals contribute to the creation of space, but space nevertheless represents a fundamental and structuring condition for individuals to be able to express their own existence. According to Harvey and Lefebvre, the space for the existence of the individual is created in combination between material, social and mental imagery and ideas (Harvey, 1990; Lefebvre, 1991). This means that the individual objectivises the space but actually becomes part of the space itself by doing so (Lysgård, 2001). It is within this dialectical interplay between individuals and their environment that space is constructed. In this sense, the home is a space in which the interior, architecture and decorations not only serve as practical items, but also provide signals about who lives here, and are used by the residents to express who they are (see also Gullestad's study, 1984, of working-class women in Bergen). The physical definition of the home in terms of the front door and who has the keys to the house contributes to the creation of a border between 'us' and 'them' – those who belong and those who do not have access to this space. But the home does not merely represent a distinction in the relationship to an external reality. The division of labour in the home between mother and father, children and teens having different bedtimes, shared meals, cleaning and so on constitutes the practical organisation of the home but creates different spaces for the life opportunities of the individuals. According to this perspective, space represents both physical space, a social spatial community, and not least a mental and abstract space based on a sense of belonging. The design of this space that the family and home are part of assumes shape via the construction of the material, social and mental ideas and beliefs in new ways in order to create space for the family.

Data and methods

From this perspective, the objective of this chapter is to cast light on the space gay fathers create in order to accommodate their position as fathers in relation to their children. The analysis therefore focuses on how these fathers understand time and space in relation to the child's upbringing, and how they use places to bring about a space for fatherhood. The study is based on qualitative interviews with seven gay men living as single men or in relationships who have chosen to have a child together with a lesbian mother, most of whom were living in a stable relationship. In most cases, the mother of the child was a long-time friend of the fathers. The fathers were between the ages of 36-46, the mothers slightly younger. Three of the children were between 0-5 years of age, seven of them were 5-7 years old, and one of the children was older than 7 at the time of the interview. In all of the cases studied, the regulation of the relationship between mother, father and the child was based on an agreement between the parties.[2] Most of the fathers – and mothers alike – were well educated and had good incomes. The sample is not assumed to be representative in terms of education and income compared with heterosexual parents with small children: three of the fathers had college educations and four had university degrees. Some of the man were or had been a part of the gay liberation movement in Norway.

The interviews were conducted in 1997 and 2000, using an interview guide including themes such as: own childhood, experiences related to coming out as gay, the experience of having children, cooperation together with the mothers, how they experienced becoming a father, and the organisation of their everyday life. The interviews were tape-recorded and later transcribed and analysed. In the analyses all of the informants were anonymous.

The analysis was carried out by focusing on the relationships emphasised by the informants as being important in relation to their position as a father, including their experiences from their own upbringing and childhood, how they felt their own fatherhood was unfolding, and their dreams and ideals about being a father. The analysis places special emphasis on the 'plots' in their narrative, which refers to the points that serve to bind the informants' narratives together in such a manner that the narratives become understandable on the background of the context they are a part of. These 'meaning-bearing plots' provided access to central elements in the fathers' respective constructions of social reality, and how their narratives gave life to their individual constructions.

New fathers, new family patterns

The fathers' decision to parent a child with a close friend appears to be an untraditional way of having children. As the interviews illustrate, however, when the child is a fact of life, the organisation and practical arrangement of parenthood through visitation arrangements[3] is actually quite similar to those chosen by divorced, heterosexual men (Arendell, 1995; Lyngstad, 2004). The fathers themselves often point this similarity out. But there is also a difference. The child is not the product of a couple, an intimate relationship between two people, justified instead by the fathers' own independent desire to have a child. To begin with, becoming a father is thus justified as an individual action, which initially points back to themselves as individuals and people. This is a break with the perception of the child as the result of a shared love between mother and father.

Both symbolically and practically, the fathers do not break entirely with the prevailing social and political ideals for fatherhood. The contemporary norms of fatherhood in Norway regarding gender equality are not fathers who appear as distanced main breadwinners and who develop their position as a father through alliance with the mother. In order to be a good father, the contemporary father is expected to develop an independent relationship with the child – independent of his relationship to the child's mother (Marsiglio, 1995; Brandth and Kvande, 2003; Holter et al, 2009). The increasingly independent position of the father breaks with the triad that parenthood was formerly based on, whereby men were responsible for providing for the family while the mother cared for the child. From the side of the state, the fathers have been attributed increased rights, both in relation to parental leave schemes and when divorce occurs, to safeguard fathers' independent custodial responsibility for their own child (Andersen, 2009). The objective for the state is not merely to create a framework for stable relationships but also, in the name of gender equality, to ensure the development of the independent position of the father as caregiver for their own children. As Beck and Beck-Gernsheim (1995) see it, the child's position in the family is thus not only a position to fill the couple with hope and romantic ideals in their upbringing of children, but also important for each individual parent. Individual parenthood, especially for the father, has come into focus in a new manner. New discourses of parenthood do not differentiate between parental genders, thus assuming that both mother and father are equally capable of parenting. This has contributed to the reconstitution of the family as a social arrangement with the father in a more responsible position for the upbringing of the child (Andersen, 2003). The forms of fatherhood that grow forth in light of these new discourses also give the informants in this study the opportunity to create their own space as fathers without breaking significantly with the contemporary notions and organisation of parenthood.

Creating space for the care of one's own child

The home is both a place and a space. In terms of a place, it represents a point of reference in everyday life. Living life and having a sense of belonging also provides a geographical position – an address. But the home is not only a physical place. Details in the interior design, choice of colours and domestic order and organisation also provide signals about who we are. At the same time, the home represents a small community, and the members of the family are in constant negotiations regarding the content of this community. The concrete formation of this community – who belongs where (for example, whether or not the child can sleep together with the parents) and at what times (for example, when is the child's bedtime?) – contributes to the creation of an order in the home, all of which has a position in the spatial landscape. As men and fathers, the fathers are very occupied by the question of how this space is formed when they are together with their own child. Even though the child does not live together with them every day of the week, they are also very aware of their home also being one of the child's two homes, as Anders illustrates:[4]

> "So I want to use time really well when we're together – to have her here and have her inside and have her kind of in our home. And to establish indoor routines and … and kind of create a sense of closeness and intimacy here in the home." (Anders, 39)

The fathers' attempts at providing the child with a sense of belonging in their own home is not merely about consideration to the child; it also bears witness to the fathers' work with giving parenthood content and an identity. For example, the fathers who had the room to be able to do so provided a separate bedroom for their child. Those who had less room made do with a corner in their own bedroom and used the space as a 'child's space' in which the child's toys, pictures, books and bed were placed. Pictures of the child enjoyed a central position in the living room. Depending on the age of the child, the flat was also furnished differently. Small children require measures allowing for small fingers that are interested in exploring the world, so doors and the kitchen oven were childproofed and breakable objects had been moved beyond the child's reach. For visitors, the flat was marked by clear signs of being a home with children.

Characteristics other than the physical design of the home and its organisation can be changed when a space is given different content subsequent to the creation of relations:

> "I'm very neat. And Solveig [the mother] was also very neat. And when she tells me – but she also means herself – that we must not be so damned neat that he … or that we don't make the same demands of him – that he always has to be tidying up. We somehow have to let him make a mess. I can't take mess. I can't take it when he comes home from childcare. I get annoyed when I have to take care of trousers and dirty clothing…. I know it's stupid, and I've worked on it. I actually tolerated this weekend that they ate and made a mess and cut things – sat and spread things around the living room here. I actually didn't say a thing…. I have a bit of a guilty conscience about all of my tidiness. He must be allowed to try things. Because I can see that he's so capable of doing things when he's allowed. Instead, I should be better at arranging the situation…. I should be laying a waterproof tablecloth on the table when he paints – rather than being afraid about what is going to happen to the table. I place limits on his ability to express himself. And – as I said about what happens when he's given more freedom – I can see that he actually grows – that he manages more and more." (Jan Kristoffer, 46)

In order to create space for the child in the home, the routines and activities in the home must be re-arranged when the child is born. When you have children, there is one more person at the breakfast and dinner table, more people to take responsibility for, and as the child grows older, more negotiations about food and what is to be on the table. Household chores must be gone about differently, new routines established – these are changes that at one and the same time create space for the child and a sense of identity for the men's actions as fathers. As Giddens (1991, p 36) claims, the individuals' conceptions of ontological security 'ties in closely to the tacit character of practical consciousness.' This implies that through daily routines, the fathers gain a more firm understanding of their identity as fathers in terms of ontological security. This awareness of practical considerations also includes a sense of intimacy, as Anders puts it in the introduction to this section. Having his daughter visiting and establishing routines helped – as he saw it – to create "closeness and intimacy" within the framework of his own home.

This is especially so with respect to establishing routines such as making meals, putting the child to bed in the evening and so on, where fathers indicate that they experience intimacy together with their child. In this manner, the fathers' ideas regarding fatherhood are tied together with the practical organisation of the household, everyday life and the home. The home as a spatial structure thus adds decisive conditions to the realisation of their ideas regarding fatherhood and the work that very tangibly confirms their identity as men and fathers.

Design of parenthood in time and space

Growing up in two homes provides these children with different beginnings than children who grow up with both of their parents in a single, shared home. Adding to this, their parents have never and will never desire to become up a couple, to live in a shared home. These fathers want to live separate lives, even though they have a child together with another person or couple. For their part, the mothers have their own family and home, which represents a physical basis in their own lives. Similarly, all of the fathers live alone or together with a partner in their own home. In the organisation of home and household, whether as a lone parent or couple, the home represents a key place for the anchoring of individual and relational concerns. The collaboration to have a child together must therefore be organised between two households. As the interviews indicate, the parents experience this to be a challenge, both because it presents challenges with respect to organisation and cooperation, but also with respect to agreements between the parents about which shared content the space for the child's upbringing is to have.

Even before the child is born, this room for the baby is in the course of taking shape. The parents draft a cooperation agreement as the basis for the collaboration aimed at having a baby. The most important detail in this agreement is the rules for visitation arrangements. To accommodate their respective, individual parenting, organising time well is of central importance. Without clear arrangements for when the child is to be where, there will be no space for the parents' individual parenthood. Several of the parents had used a proposed text for an agreement that can be found on the internet on a website for 'LGBT and children'. According to point 8:

'Ola's visitation arrangements with the child will, unless otherwise agreed, take place at home with 'Kari' and 'Ellen' until the child is one year old. In this time, 'Ola' is to be together with the child three times per week, one of these times being in the course of the weekend. When the child is one year old, the visitation arrangement can gradually shift to taking place in 'Ola's' home, such that he/she will end up being together with 'Ola' every Wednesday and every second weekend.' (Andersen, 2003)[5]

Not all of the parents in the study organise themselves according to the basis of this agreement, but most of the informants have a similar kind of visitation arrangement. For the child's first year, this means that these fathers cannot make use of the resource that their home represents when caring for their child. Their first experiences as a father therefore do not take place in their own home but in the mother's home.

"... I go over there on Wednesdays, and Tove has a little evening job, after which she has choir practice, so she's not at home ... There – I take her out with me, or we go out and visit someone ... It's all right that Tove isn't there, because that makes it easier to get in contact with Siri. If her mom is there, she just clings to her mother...." (Anders, 39)

When the meeting with the child could not be in their own home, the fathers also found that it could be difficult to create space for their own parenthood. According to the fathers, the relationship with the child often therefore became slightly distant. Which space could they, as fathers, occupy when caring for their child? When bottles, blankets, bedroom and living room – everything – belonged to someone else, which they, as fathers, did not have the right to decide over without first asking the mother's permission? The lack of opportunity to be together with the child in their own home in the beginning thus posed a clear limitation with respect to how they could create space for care and intimacy with their own child. In the mother's home, they crossed an invisible boundary into that which was someone else's home, others' relationships and others' parenting. They were visiting by virtue of being the child's biological father, but other than the biology and legal rights associated with being fathers, they found it difficult to find space for their own parenthood in the home. A kind of duality developed. They were fathers, but found it difficult to establish a sense of autonomy in relation to the child as long as the house in which the relationship was to play out in could not be used in the same manner as they used their own home. In order to win back their autonomy, they chose to 'escape' from the mother's home when together with the child. They spent much of the time going for walks, going to a café or playing with the child (in parks close to the mother's home. According to the fathers, these activities contributed to establishing an independent basis for their contact with their own child.

In order to create space for their own parenthood, the fathers, in addition to having the child alone without the mother, must become a partner in structuring the time for childcare. The organisation of time created space for their time together with the child, and at the same time, it contributed to creating content in the parental relationship. The regulation of time was about more than negotiating the time and date. Being late to pick up or deliver the child could put a number of different things in motion. As one of the informants, Erling, explains: "When we're supposed to pick up or deliver at 5 pm, that doesn't mean 5:05 pm."

To change the times because of their own needs or coming late to pick up or deliver the child created tension. Respecting the mother's time was a decisive expression of reciprocity and respect for one another as parents, but also in relation to one another's separate lives, with or without children, for that separate life to be realised successfully. The regulation of this time together with the child – or separately – for the parents therefore became important, as it ensured both a shared and separate space in relation to their responsibility for the child they had together. As such, the organisation of time became a very central factor in the formation of how they were parents together, which they built up around their care for the child they had together, with a fatherhood based on an agreed-on visitation agreement:

> "I had to return to Oslo with Torfinn [his son] at 3pm, and I was there at around 3.30–4.00 pm. She [mother] was totally pissed off. And then I got pretty upset. Because at the time I was doing all right together with Torfinn, and I thought it was pretty miserable to be confronted in that manner.... But then she said that her breasts had been swollen and painful while we had been gone. So we had a few 'conflicts' like that." (Jan Kristoffer, 46)

The child's movement in time and space therefore came to have structural significance for the mother and father alike, both individually as well as for their shared parenthood. They had to grant consideration to the other's position as parent. Whether this was about swollen breasts or something else, the needs and choices made by the other parents also had consequences for their own time together with the child. But it was not just the space in time that was significant – the content – how the fathers spent their time caring for the child – was also subject to discussion:

> "There was a lot of finger-pointing in the beginning. They had these sentences or things that they would start with on the phone, like: 'Hey you, we have something to talk about.' That would get my heart racing – I knew that I'd done something wrong." (Jan Kristoffer, 46)

According to the fathers, fingers were often being pointed, especially in the first period of time that they had the child alone with them in their own home, and the mothers were uncertain regarding the ability of the fathers to care for their own children. For their part, the fathers also experienced the first period of time alone with the child in their own home as a considerable challenge. Previously, when the child cried, the mothers were usually present, meaning that there were three people present to handle the situation. When they were in their own home, the fathers were alone with the tears, and had to deal with the situation on their own, calming the child and drying tears. At the same time, this was a learning process: "Since then, I've gone on the offensive. He's three years old now, and I have more experience" (Jan Kristoffer, 46).

It was important for Jan Kristoffer to "go on the offensive". As the fathers gained more independent experience with their child, there was also a greater basis for negotiations with the mothers. More experience with their own child – good and bad experiences alike – led to exchanges between the parents. The meetings and telephone conversations between the parents included discussions about how they could each solve the various everyday challenges in their respective time together with the child they had together. The conversations between the parents therefore also included negotiations about what the space for the child's upbringing should be like. The parents' exchange of experiences often led the fathers to take the mothers' advice when arranging the care for the child in their own home. They did not lock the mothers out, participating instead in an exchange of experiences that helped them cope with the care. The home the fathers created for their child therefore did not represent a closed sphere built on their own ideas regarding how their care for their child was to be practised. Instead, the discussions with the mothers about the child's needs provided content for how they should be good parents together. The incessant conversations with the mother and co-mother about the child's reactions, bedtimes, meals and all of the other everyday details provided content to their shared 'lifeworlds' as parents. As the fathers each gradually became more familiar and comfortable with their child as well as with their other parent(s) – not just as friends but also as mothers – this created, according to the fathers, a sense of mutual respect and trust between the parents.

Common space for family based on different homes

How can you create a family when key people with responsibility in relation to the child do not live together? The informants in this study are not alone with this challenge; it is something they share with many other parents, including parents who have chosen to separate after a divorce (Moxnes, 1990). But the parents in this study have never previously shared a home, and thus have never had the opportunity to coordinate their lifestyles and norms about family and household. The home as a physical place becomes synonymous with the space for what is one's family; the household functions as a norm and physical border for what belongs to the family. A study of children's drawings has shown how, after a divorce, children can express a sense of belonging to two homes by drawing themselves as part of both of them (Levin, 1994). How do the fathers understand the space for the child's upbringing when the child is growing up in two separate homes?

The fathers in this study are very conscious about this challenge – for where does the child really belong? They do not regard shared custody as a perfect solution and a good base for the child, which gives them a nagging, guilty conscience. In order to alleviate this guilty conscience and to create the best possible connection between the two homes, they try as much as possible – working together with the mothers – to agree to common guidelines for the care of the child regardless of where the child is. In order to create the best possible connection between the two homes, they do everything they can to reach agreement on how the care for the child is to be arranged, and that it is to be as similar as possible, regardless of where the child is. The cooperation between the parents on the child is not merely about their agreements about visitation and pick-up and delivery times; it is also about creating a common space for the child's upbringing, and developing common values and standards for the care of their child. The cooperation is based on the child, but it finds its concrete form when the parents use their own respective homes to arrange and provide this care. This is care that is established on many of the same standards as chosen by the other parent. An important requirement for this development is trust between the parents, trust which is supported by having happy children and regular contact via telephone whereby the events of the day in the child's life can be exchanged, as the conversation with Erling illustrates.

> INTERVIEWER: "How have you established trust to [mother]?"
> ERLING (35): "No, it's about everything.... You have trust.... I see that Renate [daughter] is doing well and that Greta is good with Renate. And I see that Renate is doing well here and that we figure things out together. The mother and I talk on the phone once a week and tell each other what we have done and what we are going to be doing. Once in a while we have conversations on the phone where we exchange experiences. So we experience much the same in relation to Renate – how she reacts to things. I feel that the mother and I are on the same wavelength with respect to parenting. It's not as though she has a permanent answer – she's open to parenting and siblings in relation to raising a child. So she asks me, 'What do you do when that happens?' I like the way that feels."

But their cooperation has not been entirely conflict-free. There were disagreements and agreements on this and that – big and little things alike – but they generally reached compromises. The conflicts could be about everything from the kind of food the child was supposed to eat, mealtimes, suitable television programmes, bedtimes, whether the lights should be on or off when the baby was sleeping, and so on. These kinds of negotiations came to fortify the relationship between the parents. The agreement they reached was about more than just practical questions regarding vital needs such as sleep and food. It was also about questions related to the child's social and cultural development (Fürst, 1994). Food is not just about nutritional needs, however – it is also about sociality and traditions, and questions about basic things such as food and sleep also touch on the emphasis of social and cultural values (Bourdieu, 1986). Parental cooperation was therefore not merely about the coordination of the child's time; it also created a space for collaboration, something for the parents to share in common, a space that expressed shared values in relation to what the parents viewed as being of value to the child. As Giddens has written: 'What makes a given response "appropriate" or "acceptable" necessitates a shared – but unproven and unprovable – framework of reality' (1991, p 36).

Over time and through their common experience as parents, they gain trust in each other and are able to refer to a common parenthood. But this shared framework of reality was fought for and negotiated. That which they have experienced in relation to the child represents a foundation that gave content to fatherhood and drove them as parents. Their shared framework of reality in relation to the child is both unverifiable and fragile, as it was neither fully shared nor fully equal. Overcoming this frailty is part of the parents' ability and will to continuously negotiate the space for the child's upbringing. These negotiations generally seek to make the two homes as similar as possible so that the child is able to grow up in 'one home' to the extent that this is possible. In this cooperation, it is also important to grant consideration to the parent who is not present in order to maintain their position in the child's awareness.

> "One of the things that I really commend Solveig for – which I think she does really well – is that she.... For example, now when it comes to Kjetil, who is so small [and who] and doesn't have any language or understanding, she prepares him with respect to daddy coming soon. And when I come, 'Oh, there's daddy!' That's all right. I mean, giving positive feedback. She believes it's important to provide positive feedback, even though Kjetil really doesn't show that he understands all that much, she still thinks he understands a lot. As she said yesterday ... when she said, 'here comes daddy and Ivar' [his eldest son, three years old], he really lit up." (Jan Kristoffer, 46)

The father's position as a parent was maintained by the child's mother through consideration for their common child. By making the child aware of him, the mother symbolically made him present in her home, even when he was not actually present. Several of the informants shared the same experience described by Jan Kristoffer here. At the same time, however, there was a sense of uncertainty as to who the informants perceived to be their family:

TROND, 42: "I have a rather traditional approach – and I don't really feel as though Anne, Eva and I are a family. I mean, we are two families, in a way.... Because I don't feel as though I am in a family together with Anne and Eva. But we have a child together.... We're married, in a sense. But we aren't really a family."

INTERVIEWER: "How do you understand 'family'?"

TROND: "No, I joke around about 'my wives' once in a while. But it's ... it's very wrong. It's just to be funny. No, I'm probably.... I'm a single father – a single weekend dad, but with a close relationship to the mothers. Closer than most single fathers, I think."

There is a certain sense of ambiguity in Trond's joke about the mothers also being his two wives. Even though they do not have a sexual relationship, his friendship with the mothers has been changed by becoming parents together with them. That which began as an ordinary friendship has, through the child they share together, also become close and intimate family ties. He shares a sense of familial community with the mothers through parenthood. This close cooperation regarding the child challenges the categories 'home' and 'family' when the fathers, in close cooperation together with the mothers, create a common space for the child's upbringing. When the ties get so tight between the respective homes in the care of the child, the categories pertaining to who we are in relation to others are challenged. For the fathers, the autonomy in one's own home and their own fatherhood is not an unambiguous point of reference for family and fatherhood when the emphasis on cooperation on the child they share is so strong. This contributes to challenging the social categories and what they cover. For the fathers, this contributes to reflection concerning the social categories and what they cover when 'community' can be established in new ways. When paternity builds on collaboration between different homes, traditional and conventional conceptions about fatherhood do not always provide safe and unambiguous clues when the togetherness related to parenthood is to be formed in new ways.

Conclusion

Gay liberation in Norway represents a struggle for the political and societal recognition of gay and lesbian cohabitation as well as a sexual liberation movement (Andersen, 2009). Several of the informants participating in this study had participated actively in the political movement for gay and lesbian liberation, a struggle against that which they called the 'hetero-state', in the sense of society's one-sided perception of family values and neglect of sexual freedom. The fathers therefore felt that the choice to have a child with a lesbian couple was a radical, socially transformative project; they were creating an alternative family model to that of the nuclear, heteronormative family. Yet once they had a child and started caring for him or her, they experienced a paradox. Although creating an alternative family model, they became involved in conventional homemaking immediately after having the child, one of the characteristic aspects of heteronormative family life that they had otherwise protested against.

These changes, created through everyday life's practical organisation in relation to children, home and family, make new normative structures and ideals available for the informants related to who they are as men after they have been fathers. According to these ideals, being a good father requires them to develop a unique relationship with their children regardless of the child's relationship with their mother (Marsiglio, 1995; Brandth and Kvande, 2003; Holter et al, 2009). Gender equality and the surrounding ideology of the independent caring role of the father in their relationship with their children is also something the fathers in this study used in order to emphasise the similarities between themselves and heterosexual fathers. They also point out the fact that many heterosexual fathers experience divorce, and that the two groups are therefore in a similar position as fathers in many respects. In this way, the model of the father as an independent caregiver is something the fathers in this study can relate to, because it supports aspects of their (single) fatherhood status as something positive.

In a Norwegian context, home and family are often synonymous entities (Gullestad, 1989). One of the consequences of the fathers in this study not sharing a home together with the mother of their child is a need for a space between the parents that replaces the non-existent shared home. This study reveals how the room for cooperation between parents takes over the position traditionally occupied by a shared home. This challenges the traditional demarcation between home and family. The ideas pertaining to the home as the family space, as Gullestad (1989) emphasises, cannot be fully utilised as long as the child's everyday life unfolds in – physically – separate homes. As a result, the institutional borders surrounding the family are in flux. The home – understood as the parents' individual homes – no longer represents the space that creates the external boundary of the family. Instead, it is the child and the parents working together with respect to the child's upbringing that comes to represent the space for parenthood. In this form of cooperation, the parents' separate homes provide them with tools for realising this shared space, which replaces the traditional, shared home.

The study of 'non-traditional' gay men and their family formations casts light on the space the informants create as fathers and the position they give their respective children in their own lives, and the study builds on recognisable notions of family, house and home. In order to realise these ideas, the fathers negotiate a space for the child's upbringing that structures these ideals and ideas. When a shared home is not accessible, it is created through cooperation between the parents regarding the creation of a shared space for the child that contributes to a substitute for the shared home.

Notes

[1] An earlier, longer, version of this chapter was originally published as an article in *Tidsskrift for Samfunnsforskning* [*Journal of Social Research*], 3/2010, Norwegian University Press, and can be accessed at www.idunn.no. The author thanks the Norwegian publisher for permission to republish this translation of the article.

[2] Based on the agreement, the parents decide on a structure for how they want to cooperate with respect to their child. The agreement includes the time the fathers have together with their own child. In addition to visitation, it also regulates where the child is to live primarily, who has custodial responsibility, and who has the right to make important decisions with a bearing for the child. The agreement also includes questions regarding baptism, the death of the parents and the child's contact with their respective relatives (Andersen, 2003, p 236). The agreement is negotiated prior to the birth of the child.

[3] The fathers chose to have regular interaction after the baby stopped breastfeeding, in most cases when the child turned one. 'Regular interaction' is defined as follows in the 'Law on children and parents' (The Children Act): 'If there is agreed regular visitation, this will give the legal right to be with the child one afternoon a week, every other weekend, 14 days in the summer holidays, Christmas and Easter'.

[4] In practice, the fathers usually have the child once in the course of the week and every third weekend, but this varies considerably. The visitation usually increases as the child grows older.

[5] See Andersen, 2003.

References

Aarseth, H. (2008) 'Homemaking as modern magic', PhD, Oslo: Department of Sociology and Human Geography, University of Oslo.

Andersen, A.J. (2003) 'Men create space for parenthood and family: Terms for fatherhood in a heteronormative culture', PhD, Trondheim: Department of Sociology and Political Science, Norwegian University of Science and Technology (NTNU).

Andersen, A.J. (2009) 'The Norwegian sexual citizenship', in W. Mühleisen and Å. Røthing (eds) *Norwegian sexualities*, Oslo: Cappelen Damm, pp 121-39.

Arendell, T. (1995) *Fathers and divorce*, London: Sage.

Beck, U. and Beck-Gernsheim, E. (1995) *The normal chaos of love*, London: Polity Press.

Berkowitz, D. and Marsiglio, W. (2007) 'Gay men: negotiating procreative, father, and family identities', *Journal of Marriage and Family*, vol 69, no 2, pp 366-81.

Bourdieu, P. (1986) *Cultural sociological texts. Selected by Donald Broady and Mikael Palme*, Stockholm: Salamander.

Brandth, B. and Kvande, E. (2003) *Fleksible fedre [Flexible fathers]*, Oslo: University Press.

Folgerø, T. (2008) 'Queer nuclear families? Reproducing and transgressing heteronormativity', *Journal of Homosexuality*, vol 54, no 1-2, pp 124-49.

Fürst, E.L. (1994) *Food – another language. A study of rationality, body and femininity illuminated by literary text*, Raport nr 7, Oslo: Department of Sociology and Human Geography, University of Oslo.

Giddens, A. (1991) *Modernity and self-identity: Self and society in the late modern age*, Cambridge: Polity Press.

Gullestad, M. (1984) *Kitchen-table society: A case study of the family and friendships of young working-class mothers in urban Norway*, Oslo: University Press.

Gullestad, M. (1989) *Culture and everyday life: In search of the modern Norway*, Oslo: Det Blå Bibliotek, Universitetsforlaget.

Harvey, D. (1990) *The condition of postmodernity: An enquiry into the origins of cultural change*, Oxford: Blackwell.

Holter, Ø.G., Svare, H. and Egeland, C. (2009) *Gender equality and quality of life*, Oslo: The Nordic Gender Institute (NIKK).

Ingraham, C. (1996) 'The heterosexual imaginary: feminist sociology and theories of gender', in S. Seidman (ed) *Queer theory/sociology*, Oxford: Blackwell, pp 168-93.

Lefebvre, H. (1991) *The production of space*, Oxford: Blackwell.

Levin, I. (1994) *Stepfamilies – Variations and diversity*, Oslo: Aventura Forlag.

Lyngstad, J. (2004) 'Non-resident parents' visitation with their children: more than actually agreed visitation', *Samfunnsspeilet* 2, Oslo: Statistisk sentralbyrå, pp 47–54.

Lysgård, H.K. (2001) 'Production of space and identity in transnational regions: an example of political cooperation in the Middle Nordic Countries', PhD, Trondheim: Department of Geography, Norwegian University of Science and Technology (NTNU).

Marsiglio, W. (1995) 'Fatherhood scholarship: an overview and agenda for the future', in W. Marsiglio (ed) *Fatherhood: Contemporary theory, research, and social policy*, London: Sage, pp 1–20.

Moxnes, K. (1990) *Core bursting of the family? Family changes by separation and the formation of new relationship*, Oslo: Universitetsforlaget.

Rydström, J. (2008) 'Legalizing love in a cold climate: the history, consequences and recent developments of registered partnership in Scandinavia', *Sexualities*, vol 11, no 1–2, pp 193–226.

Westlund, J (2009) 'Introduction', in J. Westerlund (ed) *Rainbow families and their positions in the Nordic countries: Politics, legal rights and conditions*, Oslo: Nordic Gender Institute, pp 7–14.

Weston, K. (1991) *Families we choose: Lesbians, gays, kinship*, New York: Columbia University Press.

TWELVE

The long-term impacts of early paternal involvement in childcare in Denmark: what happens after nuclear family dissolution

Mai Heide Ottosen

Introduction

While earlier theories assumed that a dual-earner family model would tend to destabilise the nuclear family institution (for example, resulting in fewer children) (Parsons and Bales, 1956; Becker, 1981), recent studies find a positive correlation between female labour market participation and the desire to have children in the Nordic countries. This is often said to be due to generous family policies providing women with the opportunity to combine motherhood with a career (Andersson et al, 2009; Esping-Andersen, 2009). One must also assume, however, that the success of such a family model depends on the internal division of labour in the individual household. Thus, studies suggest that approximate gender equality in the families and fathers taking paternity leave appear to be positively associated with continued childbearing (Oláh, 2003; Duvander and Andersson, 2006).

Trends towards equal parenting are among the key characteristics in the (late) modern family in the Nordic countries. As dual-earner families, both parents contribute to the state and household economy through labour force participation, and both share in the household tasks and childcare at home. Compared to other European fathers, Nordic fathers spend more time on childcare tasks, even if the Nordic mothers still provide most of the care in the home while the fathers are still spending more hours at work (Bonke, 2009). Scholars have observed the emergence of a father role characterised by increased presence, commitment to and involvement in childcare (see, for example, Plantin, 2001; see also Chapter Eight, this volume). Family policies allowing (or even encouraging) fathers to take leave for childbirth and childcare possibly support this development (see also Chapters Six, Thirteen, Fifteen and Sixteen, this volume).

Similarly, in another corner of welfare policy, Nordic family law has moved towards increased gender neutrality over the past 15-20 years by equalising the opportunities available to mothers and fathers to provide care (see also Chapter Three, this volume). Similar to the other Nordic countries, the Danish legislation pertaining to parental responsibility assumes joint legal custody to be the normal point of departure for separated parents, even if they do not agree. Moreover, family law enables the legal authorities to determine that a child is to reside for equal amounts of time in each of the parent's households (equal, shared residence). Time panel studies on custody and contact arrangements from Denmark (Ottosen, 2004) indicate that separated/divorced fathers now spend more time with their children than previously.

Little is known about how these trends towards equal parenting are interrelated: does the father taking the paternity, parental and childcare leave provided to him by the welfare state help stabilise the family institution, thus consolidating the social relations between fathers and their children? When fathers take leave for care for a brief period, are they then more inclined to become involved in everyday childcare in the long run? And is there any connection between how men manage their role as fathers before and after the break-up of the family?

As the following theoretical section outlines, this chapter focuses on the short-term and long-term impacts of paternal involvement in childcare, defined as taking leave and providing daily care during early childhood. As described in the section on methods, the chapter relies on data from the national representative and prospective Danish Longitudinal Study of the 1995 Cohort (DALSC). The first question to be examined is if fathers who are highly involved in childcare (that is, living in an 'equal parenting' regime) experience the same risk of family dissolution as fathers from families in which the parents tend towards a traditional gender order. The study hypothesises that an equal parenting regime works as a protective factor (that is, against families breaking up), because the equal distribution of the care burden would tend to reduce the interest of the mother in divorce. Moreover, intimate relationships between fathers and children (resulting from close paternal involvement) would tend to reduce the motives of fathers to leave the family. The second question to be examined is if an equal parenting regime (in intact families) leads to equal parenting arrangements and close father–child bonds after a family breaks up. The study hypothesises that fathers adapting to a role as a modern father from an early stage in their child's life are more likely to develop a close relationship to their child after the family breaks up, at least in the short term (Ottosen, 2001; Duvander and Jans, 2009). But would it also be possible to track long-term effects? Finally, the chapter examines what characterises the involved versus uninvolved post-separation/divorce fathers in their socio-demographic set-up. As becomes evident in this chapter, the study findings suggest that a lack of paternal involvement in early childhood is associated with a risk of the nuclear family breaking up, also in a long-term perspective. The analysis leaves a more mixed picture regarding the associations between fathering before and after a break-up. Moreover, it suggests that divorced men at the top of the occupational hierarchy are more likely to maintain contact with their child (and thus be socially included as fathers) than divorced men outside the labour market.

Conceptualising paternal involvement in the Danish context

Paternal involvement is not only interesting from a gender equality perspective; equally important is the question of the effects of the involvement of fathers on child development outcomes. Based on reviews of a number of longitudinal studies, Sarkadi et al (2007) find evidence supporting the positive influence of paternal involvement: active and regular involvement with the child predicts a range of positive outcomes, although no specific form of engagement has been shown to yield better outcomes than another. '... Fathers' engagement seems to have differential effects on desirable outcomes by reducing the frequency of behavioural problems in boys and psychological problems in young women, and enhancing cognitive development, while decreasing delinquency and economic disadvantage in low SES families' (Sarkadi et al, 2007, p 157). This review also finds evidence that cohabitation with the mother and her male partner is associated with fewer external behaviour problems.

Turning to research on post-divorce parenting, it is widely assumed that a child's adjustment to post-divorce life is eased when non-resident and residential parents are positively involved in their children's lives within the context of cooperative co-parental relationships (Amato et al, 2011). Moreover, children appear to benefit when they have close, supportive relationships with their non-resident parents (usually the father) (Amato and Gilbreth, 1999; King and Sobolewski, 2006). A certain level of contact appears necessary for non-resident fathers to maintain high-quality relationships with their children and to engage in responsive parenting (Amato et al, 2009).

The impact of family policy measures is only sporadically explored. From the Nordic context, however, Duvander and Jans (2009) find that fathers taking leave is positively associated with post-separation father–child contact. They suggest that parental leave strengthens father–child bonds, and that these bonds remain after the father returns to work or in the case of separation.

Defining paternal involvement in the intact family

This study operates with two dimensions of paternal involvement in the intact family: the first dimension refers to how parents exercise the rights provided by the welfare state, in this case concretised by whether or not fathers take leave for caring for children, as discussed later. The second dimension refers to how the family practises everyday life, that is, how mothers and fathers – as a possible outcome of bargaining or necessities – allocate their resources in childcare tasks. Such everyday activities are outside the scope of welfare state regulation.

With regard to this first dimension, the study examines if there are any observable short-term or long-term effects of fathers taking paternity leave (*fædreorlov*, immediately following the birth of the child), parental leave (*forældreorlov*, during the first year of the child's life) or childcare leave (*børnepasningsorlov*, after the first year[1]). Despite similarities in the family policy area in the Nordic countries, Denmark distinguishes itself from its Scandinavian neighbours by taking a withdrawn stance when it comes to the issue of a father's quota, that is, parental leave specifically earmarked for the father on a 'use-it-or-lose-it' basis (Duvander and Lammi-Taskula, 2011). Danish fathers do have an earmarked right to take two weeks of paternity leave immediately following the birth of their child, but it is up to the parents themselves to decide whether and when the father should take parental or childcare leave. This liberal policy position is in contrast with the schemes in Iceland, Norway and Sweden, which operate with more extensive 'use-it-or-lose-it' quotas for fathers (see Chapter Thirteen, this volume). Within the time horizon of this analysis (starting in 1995), most fathers exercised their right to two weeks' paternity leave immediately after the birth of the child, while a tiny proportion extended this period with parental leave, as discussed later. Very few fathers took childcare leave (which, at that time, was possible until the child was nine years old). Because few Danish fathers exercised these rights, one might expect the effects of this instrument to be modest. Nevertheless, it is interesting to map out whether these fathers are favoured in the long run by developing a close relationship with their child.

How families respond to specific family policy instruments is one question. Another is how parents, as social actors, organise their everyday family life around having a young child. Such behaviour patterns are not directly affected by family policy regulations, possibly deriving instead from broader normative expectations about how young families should organise parenthood. Additional indicators of paternal involvement in early childhood must therefore be included in the analysis. In relation to the infant period (the first six months of the child's life, when most mothers take maternity leave), it appears relevant to focus on the gendered division of childcare, as this period is said to be important for how children attach to significant others: do parents share the childcare tasks roughly equally (an egalitarian regime)? Or is the mother the primary (or exclusive) caregiver? Later, in early childhood, when most mothers have returned to work, it is relevant to examine how the families handle the basic childcare tasks that might interfere with the demands of working life.

Outcomes: operationalising separated/divorced fathers' relationships to their children

Turning to the outcome variables in the study, the access of separated/divorced fathers to their non-resident children involves legal, social and emotional factors. For analytical purposes, when illuminating the organisation of post-separation parenting, it appears relevant to follow the same procedure as above by distinguishing between aspects both inside and outside the realm of family law regulation.

By establishing norms and taking legal decisions, family law regulates the framework of parenthood, that is, legal custody, residence and contact, after family dissolution, by separation or divorce (see also Chapter Three, this volume). Regarding custody, the Danish development in the 1995-2007 period has been characterised by a gradual automation of joint legal custody, which has equalised the opportunities available to fathers and mothers to provide care. This development culminated in 2007, when the Act on Parental Responsibility gave the courts the authority to decide that parents could have joint legal custody against the will of one of the parents (*Familiestyrelsen* [Division of Family Affairs], 2011). Similarly, since 1995, the norms for contact frequency between children and their non-resident parent have shifted in an upward direction (Ottosen, 2004). According to the 2007 legislation, family law authorities can now decide that a child of separated/divorced parents should live the same amount of time with both parents. The prevalence of joint legal custody and extended contact arrangements can be viewed as indicators of the father's continued presence in relation to the child, and thus as a trend towards increased gender equality in parenthood. When it comes to the question of the residence of the divorced child, however, trends are less clear. Now, as then, most children come to share their home address with their mother after the family dissolves. Some studies[2] suggest that when divorced children come to reside with their father, these arrangements often rest on pragmatic or exceptional grounds (for example, the mother being ill or struggling with social problems) rather than being motivated by gender equality ideals (Christoffersen, 1998; Ottosen, 2000; Ottosen et al, 2011).

However, the constitution of co-parenting after family dissolution also includes more substantive aspects beyond state regulation. One of these concerns the quality of parental cooperation, that is, whether parents are able to cooperate in a constructive manner to protect the best interests of their child instead of carrying out a parallel-organised parenthood without any substantial communication or even an absence of dialogue. Despite the pedagogical intentions in family legislation to make divorced parents more cooperative, Danish research evidence suggests that the legislation has very little (if any) power to affect the quality of parental relationships (Ottosen and Stage, 2011). Another important aspect concerns the quality of the father–child relationship: to what degree do divorced fathers remain a significant person for their children following family dissolution?

Analytical framework

The considerations above lead to an analytical framework containing a pre-and post-perspective as well as distinguishing analytically between the dimensions of paternal involvement, which can be attributed to the family policy initiatives and social practices resulting from the interactions between family members, see Table 12.1.

Data and methods

The data stems from the DALSC, a nationally representative and prospective longitudinal study of 6,000 children born in 1995 to mothers with Danish citizenship.[3] Until now, the data has been collected five times, by visiting the families in their homes. The first wave was in 1996 (child aged 4–5 months), the second in 1999 (age 3½), the third in 2003 (age 7), the fourth in 2007 (age 11) and the fifth in 2011 (age 15). The mothers were primary respondents in waves 1–4.

Table 12.1: Analytical framework for illuminating paternal involvement

Dimensions	Prior to family breakup	After family breakup
Framework of parenthood, (subject of family policy regulation)	– Paternity leave (2 weeks following birth) – Parental leave (10 weeks before the child is 1 year old) – Childcare leave (26 weeks until the child is 9 years old)	– Legal custody (joint) – Contact (extended or equal shared)
Content of parenthood (the social practices of the families)	– Paternal involvement in infancy – Paternal involvement in childcare tasks during early childhood (3–7 years)	– Parental cooperation (extended) – Quality of father–child relationship

To ensure high data quality, they completed questionnaires through standardised, face-to-face interviews. In wave 5, the mothers filled out a self-completed questionnaire. Fathers (defined as the mother's live-in partner) filled out self-completed questionnaires in waves 1, 3 and 4. As participating respondents from 2007, the children filled out a self-completed questionnaire (CAPI with audio stimuli) and were interviewed face to face in 2011 (and thus regarded as primary respondents). DALSC has an overall high response rates from mothers and children, and missing information for individual variables is low (Ottosen, 2011). Central background variables (for example, income and socio-economic status) are register-based information.

Within the context of this analysis, one limitation of the dataset lies in the DALSC design strategy of selecting fathers for participating in the survey, as they are defined as the mother's husband (or live-in partner). In some cases, they are not identical with the biological father (that is, a step-parent). Another implication of this household-centred strategy is that the DALSC has very little (if any) information from the separated/divorced fathers themselves, unless they have become the resident parent following family break-up (that is, the parent with whom the child has their permanent address).

The present analysis is based on responses solely from mothers, except for a single item deriving from the 2011 child questionnaire. Due to the limited number of observations, all of the cases in which the fathers act as the primary respondent in the survey are omitted. This could happen if the mother did not participate for whatever reason, or if the child shared their father's address after the family has broken up. A few comments on the prevalence of family break-ups should be mentioned: by the first wave, 4 per cent of the infants did not live in a two-parent family. At age 3½ (wave 2), 11 per cent of the children had experienced family dissolution. This share rose to 19 per cent at age 7 (wave 3) and 29 per cent at age 11 (wave 4). When reaching wave 5, the sharp increase in the number of break-ups appeared to level off, as 31 per cent of the 15-year-olds now had divorced/separated parents. In this study, the terms 'dissolved families', 'children of divorce' and so on include formerly married parents who have been formally divorced as well as formerly cohabiting parents.

The variables used to measure early paternal involvement are:

- Two weeks of paternity leave immediately following childbirth. Seventy-four per cent of the fathers in the survey exercised this right. An additional 4 per cent of the fathers took the opportunity to take some of parental leave from the portion that may be taken by either the father or mother (up to 10 weeks at that time).
- The participation of fathers in childcare leave, which was a right for both biological parents (six months can be taken until the child is nine years old). When asked in 1999, 4 per cent of the fathers had taken childcare leave. When the parents were re-interviewed in 2003, 44 per cent of the mothers, 2 per cent of the fathers and 2 per cent of both parents had exercised this option. The survey data cannot cast light on the duration of the parental leave or childcare leave periods.
- Distribution of care for the infant in the first two weeks after birth: 77 per cent replied that it was primarily the mother, and 23 per cent that the parents shared the childcare tasks.
- Parents' childcare regime when the child was 4-5 months of age: egalitarian (both parents sharing the tasks) or traditional (primarily the mother). This instrument is an index formed by five individual items illuminating the division of responsibility in relation to playing, changing nappies, comforting, bathing and putting the baby to bed.
- The participation of fathers in childcare tasks for older children: care for a sick child; leaving the workplace to take the child to the doctor or dentist; taking time off to fetch a sick child from daycare/ school; and attending parents' meetings. These questions were asked in 1999 (age 3½) and 2003 (age 7).

Four variables are included to measure the post-separation father–child relationship:

- Do parents have joint legal custody after separation (1999, 2003, 2007, 2011)?

- Extension of father–child contact arrangement based on the number of overnights per month (1999, 2003, 2007, 2011).
- Extension of parental cooperation. This variable is an index based on four single items (parents talking about child's well-being; agreement in childrearing questions; how to support their child in case of problems; and talking about experiences from the child's everyday life (1999, 2003, 2007, 2011).
- The social significance of the father according to the child at age 15 (2011). This variable is an index formed by three items ('Your relationship to your father is important for you'; 'You trust your father'; 'Your father plays a rather significant role in your life'). According to the summarised index, the father has less importance for 33 per cent of the divorced children, great importance for 31 per cent and very great importance for 36 per cent of the children.

Early paternal involvement and the probability of nuclear family dissolution

The first analysis examines the relationship between the involvement of fathers in early childhood and the likelihood of the nuclear family remaining intact. Bivariate correlations are presented. The variables included for the earliest period (1996) are whether the father took paternity and parental leave for two weeks (or more) in the first year of the life of the child, and whether there was an egalitarian care regime at the time around the childbirth and when the child was 4–5 months old (at which time the mothers were still on maternity leave and most fathers had returned to work).

When dividing data according to the subsequent family type three years or later (in terms of who split up or remained together), the impact of parental social practices in the period immediately after childbirth is very limited (limited or no correlation). However, the analysis suggests that how fathers use paternity/parental leave and the family care practice when the child is 4-5 months old are correlated with the probability of later family dissolution. Compared to the families that remained intact in 1999 (child age 3½), fathers from dissolved families (in 1999) had taken paternity/parental leave less often and were less involved in childcare tasks when the child was 4–5 months of age (see Table 12.2). These relations remain significant in 2003, 2007 and 2011, although the differences between intact families and broken families tend to fade. This is probably due to the fact that the 'dissolved families' category is gradually supplemented

Table 12.2: Associations of paternal involvement in childcare in nuclear families that later dissolved or remained intact, 1999–2011

	Family type											
	Wave 2 (1999) (sample size = 4,487)			Wave 3 (2003) (sample size = 4,369)			Wave 4 (2007) (sample size = 3,955)			Wave 5 (2011) (sample size = 3,564)		
	Dissolved	Intact	P <	Dissolved	Intact	P <	Dissolved	Intact	p <	Dissolved	Intact	P <
	N = 466	N = 4021		N = 789	N = 3580		N = 1002	N = 2953		N = 1052	N = 2512	
WAVE 1: 1996												
Paternity/parental leave			***			***			***			***
None	46	23		36	21		32	22		28	21	
2 weeks	53	74		63	75		64	75		69	76	
>2 weeks	1	4		1	4		4	3		3	4	
Care for new born			*			*			ns			ns
Mainly mother	82	77		82	77		79	77		79	77	
Equal parenting	17	22		17	22		22	21		20	22	
Mainly father	2	1		2	1		1	1		1	1	
Care for infant (4–5 months)			***			***			***			***
Equal parenting	36	52		42	52		43	52		45	54	
Mainly mother	65	48		58	48		57	47		55	46	

(continued)

Table 12.2: Associations of paternal involvement in childcare in nuclear families that later dissolved or remained intact, 1999–2011 (continued)

	Family type											
	Wave 2 (1999) (sample size = 4,487)			Wave 3 (2003) (sample size = 4,369)			Wave 4 (2007) (sample size = 3,955)			Wave 5 (2011) (sample size = 3,564)		
	Dissolved	Intact	P <	Dissolved	Intact	P <	Dissolved	Intact	p <	Dissolved	Intact	P <
	N = 466	N = 4021		N = 789	N = 3580		N = 1002	N = 2953		N = 1052	N = 2512	
WAVE 2: 1999												
Paternal participation in childcare leave						ns			ns			*
None				97	96		97	96		97	96	
Leave				3	4		3	4		3	4	
Paternal involvement in childcare tasks						***			***			***
No involvement				48	24		45	26		37	26	
Involved in 1 task				23	27		22	26		26	26	
Involved in 2–4 tasks				29	49		33	48		37	49	
WAVE 3: 2003												
Paternal participation in childcare leave									**			**
None							98	96		98	96	
Leave							2	4		2	4	
Paternal involvement in childcare tasks									***			***
No involvement							45	13		35	13	
Involved in 1 task							30	38		33	39	
Involved in 2–4 tasks							25	49		32	49	

Note: * <0.05; ** <0.01; *** <0.001
Source: DALSC 1996–2011

with new generations of separated/divorced parents, where the factors contributing to the break-up of a family can vary.

In the second (1999, child age 3½) and third waves (2003, age 7), respondents (mothers) were asked whether the fathers: (1) had taken childcare leave; and (2) had participated in the various care tasks related to the present everyday life.

Whereas 44 per cent of the mothers had taken childcare leave, few fathers (4 per cent) had used this opportunity. Although statistically significant, there are only minor percentage differences between the families that subsequently remained intact versus those that broke up. In contrast, the social practices of everyday life appear not only to be statistically significant, but also more explanatory. Fathers from subsequently dissolved families had failed to help with childcare to a significantly higher extent (46 and 44 per cent, respectively) than the fathers who remained in intact families (24 and 13 per cent, respectively). These differences remain persistent, also at the subsequent points in time measured, despite the supply of newly separated/divorced parents.

The next step in the analysis tests these immediate associations between (lack of) paternal involvement and family status by using logistic regression. This step controls for a range of demographic, economic and interpersonal predictors of family breakdown (see, for example, Amato, 2010). To examine if there are any observable long-term impacts of early paternal involvement, the analysis focuses on the family status in 2011 (wave 5, child age 15). To get a more parsimonious model, the seven input variables are collapsed into four: (1) (none) paternity/parental leave (1996); (2) (none) paternal involvement in caring for the infant (1996); (3) the father has (not) taken childcare leave (1999 and 2003 and (4) father has (not) handled childcare tasks at ages 3½ and 7 (1999 and 2003). It is possible to include these four input variables simultaneously in the model, as a correlation analysis has shown that they are mutually weakly correlated.

The results indicate an impact of all four input variables (see Table 12.3): the father not taking up leave nor caring for the infant or young child increases the likelihood that the child, as a teenager, will experience the break-up of their family, even when controlling for the impact of a number of socio-demographic and interpersonal predictors. Thus, early paternal involvement in childcare appears to help protect the nuclear family model.

However, the analysis also indicates that other factors influence the risk of nuclear family dissolution by age 15. Children of young mothers and parents living in (non-married) consensual unions have

Table 12.3: Regression on factors associated with the probability of having experienced family dissolution at age 15

Variables	P <	OR point estimate	Confidence interval	
No paternity/parental leave during first 6 months, 1996* (ref. at least 2 weeks)	0.0289	1.236	1.022	1.495
(Dummy: missing for paternity/parental leave)	0.1005	1.693	0.903	3.176
Father not participating in early childcare (0–6 months), 1996 (ref. equal parenting)	0.0025	1.283	1.091	1.507
(Dummy: missing for childcare)	0.1024	0.131	0.011	1.502
Father took childcare leave (1999 or 2003)*	0.0002			
(Dummy: missing for childcare leave)	0.5442	0.788	0.365	1.702
Father not participating in childcare task (1999/3; 2003/7 years) (ref. involved)*	0.0179			
Mother <25 years at child's birth (=> 25 years)	<0.0001	1.678	1.345	2.093
Non-married consensual union in 1996 (ref. married)	<0.0001	4.953	4.042	6.070
Child was not planned 1996 (ref: planned)	0.1692	1.189	0.929	1.522
(Dummy: missing for unplanned child)	0.1003	7.560	0.677	84.413
Parents disagreed on labour division in home, 1996	<0.0001	2.336	1.543	3.536
Mother's education, 1996: vocational (ref. basic school)	0.0817	1.277	0.970	1.681
Mother's education, 1996: higher (ref. basic school)	0.0814	0.837	0.686	1.022
Father's education, 1996: vocational (ref. basic school)	0.0028	1.655	1.190	2.302
Father's education, 1996: higher (ref. basic school)	<0.0001	0.659	0.540	0.805
Mother: Cash benefit, 1996	0.2944	1.257	0.819	1.929
Father: Cash benefit, 1996	0.0293	2.042	1.074	3.880
No. of observations	3.628			

Notes: *The years mentioned refer to the point of the data collection; **no OR point estimate produced of technical reasons

Source: DALSC 2011

a higher risk of experiencing family breakdown. These observations, which are recognisable from other studies (Ottosen, 2001; Jensen and Clausen, 2003; Liefbroer and Dourleijn, 2006; Amato, 2010), reflect that increasing age (in terms of maturity) and an institutional framework for the family relationships appear to consolidate the nuclear family model.

The variable '(dis)agreement on division of labour at home (1996)' is included in the model as a modifying factor for the early parenting regime, but this variable proves to have a strong independent relationship with the risk of subsequent family dissolution. Finally, the analysis suggests that the socio-economic status of the father appears to be decisive (albeit partially reverse). While fathers with a vocational educational background have a higher risk of separation/divorce than those with only a basic school education, the analysis suggests that fathers depending on subsidised public income transfers in 1996 (for example, unemployment insurance, early retirement, social welfare payments), have an increased risk of separation/divorce, whereas the likelihood decreases for highly educated fathers. The latter casts light on a paradox regarding the role of the modern father: while being involved in an egalitarian caring regime (on the same terms as the mother) strengthens the position as a father, it also increases the probability of remaining a full-time father in the intact family if the father has 'breadwinner' potential.

Early paternal involvement and the relationship with the child after family break-up

This section examines if there is consistency between the organisation of fathering before and after family dissolution. This part of the analysis focuses on observable, short-term and long-term associations, beginning with the short-term findings.

'Short term' is defined as a 3-4 year interval between the two measurement points. At the first point, the father is still a caregiver in the intact family, and the same indicators as above are used to illuminate various caring practices. At the second measuring point, the father has become a separated/divorced father. His position to the child is illuminated by examining his legal position (joint legal custody), father–child contact frequency and the extent of parental cooperation with the mother. Thus, the family is dissolved between those two points. Three intervals are included in the analysis: 1996–99, 1999–2003 and 2003–07. Table 12.4 illustrates the findings as (significant) associations between the input and outcome variables at the bivariate level.[4]

The first time interval, 1996–99, includes the early separations/ divorces. The bivariate analysis produces a rather mixed pattern. As a whole, the findings do not support the assumption that egalitarian parenting during infancy should subsequently favour the divorced father in terms of access to his child. However, separated/divorced fathers with joint legal custody (child age 3½) had taken paternity/

parental leave early in the child's life (65 per cent) more frequently than those who did not become custody holders (55 per cent). Paternity/parental leave is also correlated with post-separation co-parenting: among the separated/divorced fathers who managed to collaborate extensively with the mother, 68 per cent had taken paternity/parental leave for at least two weeks, whereas the remaining 31 per cent did not take any leave at all. Among the separated/divorced fathers who never communicated with the mother, only 35 per cent took at least two weeks leave after the birth, whereas 65 per cent took no leave at all. Between these extremes are categories of divorced parents with moderate or limited cooperation (not shown).

One explanation of why no significant interactions are found between the organisations of fathering before and after family break-up during the first years of the child's life may depend on the fact that other, more compelling, reasons contribute to forming the post-separation family relationships. Thus, previously published analyses from the DALSC data set suggest (Ottosen, 2000, 2001) that early family break-ups are characterised by an excess incidence of young mothers, short cohabitations and a social gradient (lack of education and excess incidence of parents on cash benefits). Among the statistically significant factors shaping the post-separation parenting in 1999 are also partner violence, and problems with alcohol and drug abuse. Subsequent analysis of the data set suggests that these stressful causes for divorce tend to fade as the child ages (Ottosen, 2004).

The other two time intervals included in the analysis run from 1999–2003 (from when the child was 3–7 years old) and 2003–07 (from when the child was 7–11 years old). They exhibit a parallel pattern: on the one hand, there is no interaction between how fathers used leave for childcare and the post-separation organisation of parenthood. The general lack of commitment observed among Danish fathers to these family policy measures should probably be taken into account when explaining the insignificance of this factor. On the other hand, the bivariate statistics present a clear interaction between the social practices of fathering before and after family dissolution: fathers who participated in the everyday life care tasks while in intact families were much more inclined to be legal custody holders, have extended visitation schemes with the child and increased cooperation with the mother of their child than the fathers who were not involved in such activities. Thus, these findings indicate a relatively strong relationship between the social practice of intact family and the organisation of post-separation fatherhood. Judged from the bivariate tables, these

Table 12.4: Descriptive statistics. Associations between father involvement in the nuclear family and parameters for access to the child after family dissolution. Short-term and long-term effect

| | Parenting after family breakup, short term | | | | | | Parenting after family breakup, long term | | | | | | |
| | W2: dissolved 1996–99 | | | W3: dissolved 1999–2003 | | | W4: dissolved 2003–07 | | | W5: dissolved in 2011 | | | |
	Custody	Contact	Cooperation	Custody	Contact	Cooperation	Custody	Contact	Cooperation	Custody	Contact	Cooperation	Social significance
Father involvement (intact families)													
WAVE 1: 1996													
Paternity/parental leave	*	ns	***							***	ns	ns	*
Childcare for new born child	ns	ns	ns							ns	ns	ns	ns
Childcare for infant (4–5 months)	ns	ns	ns							*	**	**	**
WAVE 2: 1999													
Fathers took leave for childcare				ns	ns	ns				ns	ns	ns	ns
Paternal involvement in childcare tasks				**	***	*				***	***	***	**
WAVE3: 2003													
Fathers took leave for childcare							ns	ns	ns	ns	ns	ns	ns
Paternal involvement in childcare tasks							***	**	**	***	***	***	***

Note: P = *<0.05; **<0.01; ***<0.001

correlations appear to persist even in the long run, that is, after the child has turned 15.

Using logistic regression, the next step in the analysis is to test whether there is evidence of a long-term impact (in 2011) of paternal involvement in the intact family. Parallel to the regression analysis above, the various indicators of the involvement of fathers are collapsed into four variables. Four models are carried out: the probabilities in relation to legal custody, contact arrangements, parental cooperation and the father's social significance as experienced by the 15-year-olds themselves. These models also control for a number of socio-demographic and interpersonal variables, which may affect the organisation of fathering at age 15 (2011), including parents' past marital and socio-economic status, child's age at family break-up, current family relationships, geographical proximity, the presence of family law disputes and a variety of interpersonal divorce causes (according to the mother).

The results (see Table 12.5) indicate that neither the father taking paternity/parental leave nor childcare leave is associated with paternal status when the child is 15. However, the social practices of the intact family life seem important: a traditional gendered division of caring for the infant reduces the likelihood of extensive parental cooperation. Similar trends are observed regarding the father–child contact and father's social significance, but these associations do not pass the 95 per cent significance level. The variable 'father's lack of participation in childcare tasks' (ages 3 and 7) reduces the probability of joint legal custody and extended contact with the 15-year-old child.

Parallel to the analysis given earlier, results also show, first, that the likelihood of separated/divorced fathers holding legal custody decreases if the mother was young when giving birth or if the parents split when the child was very young (<4 years). Short-term cohabitation apparently results in less commitment toward shared parental responsibility. Second, the children of unmarried, cohabiting parents rarely tend to become the subjects of joint legal custody. For children born in 1995 to unmarried parents, the decision regarding the legal custody arrangement was of a more optional nature, unlike today, where joint legal custody is automatic.

Third, regarding new family formations, the analyses suggest – somewhat surprisingly – that the presence of a step-father (in the mother's household) increases the likelihood of separated/divorced fathers having extensive parental cooperation as well as being recognised as a significant person, according to the young people

Table 12.5: Regression. Probability of fathers having joint legal custody, extended father–child contact, extensive parental cooperation, (not) being a significant other to the child. Children aged 15, having ever experienced family dissolution

Variables	Model 1: Joint legal custody		Model 2: Extended father-child contact		Model 3: Extended parental cooperation		Model 4: (No) Social significance	
	P <	Odds Ratio	P <	Odds Ratio	P <	Odds Ratio	P <	Odds Ratio
No paternity/parental leave during first 6 months, 1996 (ref. at least 2 weeks)	0.9991	1.000	0.5229	1.147	0.5134	1.118	0.9763	0.995
Father not participating in early childcare (0–6 months), 1996 (ref. equal parenting)	0.6426	0.923	0.0595	0.713	0.0043	0.666	0.0680	1.315
Father not participating in childcare task (1999/3 years; 2003/7 years) (ref. involved)	0.0014	0.468	0.0007	0.239	0.2211	0.759	0.9598	0.989
Father did not take childcare leave (1996–2003)	0.4923	1.427	0.2124	0.508	0.0836	0.478	0.6397	1.212
Mother <25 years at child's birth (ref. =>25 year)	0.0185	0.596	0.3709	0.798	0.7558	1.061	0.1809	1.308
Parents never married (2011)	<0.0001	0.056	0.0978	0.526	0.2164	0.729	0.6978	1.106
Mother lives with new partner, 2011	0.5425	1.113	0.6503	1.087	0.0025	1.561	0.0129	0.677
Father lives with new partner, 2011	0.2525	1.235	0.0149	0.635	0.0692	0.761	0.3548	1.158
Legal conflicts about custody or contact (ever)	<0.0001	0.273	0.3202	0.796	<0.0001	0.246	0.0024	1.694
Parents live close to each other (<30 min), 2011	0.1111	1.331	<0.0001	3.897	0.0002	1.788	0.0278	0.706
Joint legal custody while being intact family	<0.0001	29.531	0.0723	2.086	0.8778	1.043	0.5857	0.859
Child < 4 years, when parents divorced	<0.0001	0.361	0.0648	0.622	0.1763	1.292	0.5850	1.112
Nuclear family dissolved, due to violence, abuse	0.0286	0.646	0.0046	0.483	<0.0001	0.387	<0.0001	2.593
Nuclear family dissolved due to disagreements about child rearing	0.6061	0.889	0.0928	0.646	<0.0001	0.436	0.0410	1.500
No. of observations	1.059		946		1.059		949	

Notes: Other factors included in the models were: Child firstborn, mothers' and fathers' education levels, cash benefits, infidelity caused divorce. None of these were significant, nor were the dummies for missing cases included in the table.
Source: DALSC 2011

themselves. In contrast, the presence of a step-mother (in the father's household) reduces the probability of extended father–child contact.

The analyses include a number of interpersonal factors, which are assumed to influence the configuration of the 'involved separated/divorced father'. Results show, fourth, that the presence of family law disputes in childhood generally weakens the father's position (except for contact arrangements, which are under the control of the family law authorities). The same is true if the family broke up due to stressful circumstances, such as violence or abuse problems. Moreover, family dissolution caused by disagreements concerning childrearing reduces the likelihood of fathers having extensive parental cooperation and being considered as a significant person by their 15-year-old child.

The analytical framework presented in the introduction to this chapter distinguished between the framework of parenthood arising out of family policy regulation and the content, understood as the social practices of the families. On the background of this analysis, it can be concluded that the family policy framework relating to leave for fathers does not appear to influence the relationship between separated/divorced fathers and their 15-year-old children in Denmark. In contrast, the framework given by family law, that is, the legal ties between members of the intact family in terms of marriage and legal custody, appear to be significant for the legal relationship between divorced fathers and their 15-year-old children. Within the context of this analysis, however, the social practices of the intact family seem to have the greatest explanatory power for understanding the configuration of the 'involved divorced father'. Nevertheless, one should note that early father involvement is not directly linked to the children's own perception of their father as a significant person.

Socio-demographic characteristics of socially included and marginalised (divorced) fathers in 2011

This last section focuses on the social characteristics of the men who end up being socially included (that is, still involved) in their role as a father, and those who tend to be marginalised (that is, absent) from fatherhood.

The DALSC data set offers no survey-based information from non-resident biological parents themselves, but the personal code number of the children provides the opportunity to link register-based data from Statistics Denmark to the survey. The focus is on the biological father's recent family situation, employment and educational status in 2011 (that is, wave 5). Two indicators of paternal involvement, one objective and one subjective, are included: the contact arrangement in 2011 and the 15-year-old's experience of their father as a significant person.

As Table 12.6 shows, it appears as though the father's current family status is less important, although single men have lost contact with their child(ren) slightly more often than men living with a new partner. In contrast, the educational and employment status unveil a clear polarisation trend: while approximately 31 per cent of the fathers positioned in the top of the occupational hierarchy have considerable contact (extended contact and equal shared residence) with their 15-year-old child and have very rarely lost contact (3 per cent), the inverse pattern is roughly true for fathers outside of the labour market. A parallel pattern, albeit not quite as pronounced, is observed regarding educational status. Consequently, the 15-year-old children more frequently perceive their unemployed and/or less educated fathers as 'less important'.

Conclusion

This chapter has examined the possible impacts of a modern father role for family stability and for how post-separation fathering develops. The study has demonstrated that a lack of paternal involvement in terms of non-use of leave or absence in everyday care tasks is associated with the risk of family dissolution. The efforts (or lack thereof) of the father in the first months of his child's life can be traced to the risk of family break-up until the child is 15 years of age.

The analysis provides material for discussing how the observed correlations should be interpreted. Are we to believe that the involvement of fathers in childcare itself would consolidate the intact family structure? Possibly, but not necessarily. Although the DALSC data suggest[5] that severe disagreements about childrearing or the division of household labour may contribute to divorce in some families, and that other interpersonal and socio-demographic factors can come in to play to increase or reduce the risk of family breakdown, this study has shown that there might still be a number of unobserved yet relevant factors that have not been captured in this analysis. The patterns of analysis suggest that among Danish families with young children, there are normative expectations of fathers about taking the short paternity leave (albeit not parental leave or leave for childcare). Similarly, fathers doing their share of the work related to daily care appears to be part of the Danish family project. In this context, it is worth keeping in mind those who deviate from the norm, that is, the fathers who did not deliver what was expected of them. What could be at stake in these families? The findings

Table 12.6: Socio-demographic characteristics of divorced men who are marginalised versus included as fathers to a 15-year-old child

	N =	Contact with child in 2011 (aged 15)						Social significance according to child, aged 15			
		No contact	Limited	Weekend	Extended	Equal shared	p<	Less important	Great importance	Very great importance	p<
FAMILY STATUS, 2011							**				ns
Father has no new partner	574	17	41	20	15	7		33	30	37	
Father living with new partner	414	12	39	29	13	7		33	35	32	
OCCUPATIONAL STATUS, 2011							***				***
Top managers and highly skilled employees	147	3	31	33	26	7		25	37	38	
Employees, medium-level skills	118	8	42	26	14	9		26	39	35	
Employees, basic-level skills	277	11	43	24	13	8		34	29	37	
Self-employed	78	5	42	26	18	9		25	33	42	
Other employees	169	14	34	28	16	8		35	31	35	
Cash benefits, early retirement, outside labour market	120	31	48	13	5	3		50	23	27	
FATHER'S HIGHEST EDUCATION, 2011							***				**
Basic school	228	19	46	22	7	5		44	26	30	
Student (upper secondary)	51	2	47	20	22	10		34	30	36	
Vocational	423	11	39	25	16	9		31	31	37	
Further, short	56	7	39	30	16	7		30	36	34	
Further, medium	88	11	36	22	23	8		21	46	33	
Further, long	67	3	34	39	18	6		24	34	43	

Note: *<0.05; **<0.01; ***<0.001
Source: DALSC, 2011 and register-based data

here may not only refer to the specific participation in childcare; they might also reflect a lack of 'commitment' to the nuclear family project among some of the families that later split up. From this point of view, one might therefore interpret 'paternal involvement' as an indicator of a broader commitment to the family.

Regarding the connection between early paternal involvement in the intact family and the likelihood of maintaining a close post-separation relationship to the child, this analysis leaves a more mixed picture, since it cannot demonstrate any impact of family policy measures, that is, leave to care for the child. In contrast, the legal ties between the members of the intact family appear to be important for the subsequent parental construction. Additionally, indicators of the social practices of everyday life serve to explain why separated/divorced fathers end up with joint legal custody, extended contact and parental cooperation. But these factors are not associated with the child's own perception of the father as a significant person. From this finding, it cannot be concluded that the deeds of fathers are subordinate to their position from the perspective of the child. First, the pattern of findings suggests that the 15-year-old's perception of their father follows the same track as the extent of parental cooperation (and may be affected by this). Second, one should bear in mind that from the perspective of a 15-year-old, completely different factors may be more essential for the perception of the father as a significant person than the early father–child interaction.

This study has also shown that factors other than involvement in childcare contribute to including or excluding the separated/divorced father. Specific attention was drawn to the significance of the paternal socio-economic resources, which contribute to consolidate the intact family structure. As suggested, this study has also observed a social selection when it comes to those who become excluded and those who remain included in the role as father following family break-up. These correlations suggest that social classes are masked in the construction of modern fatherhood, not least when the family dissolves.

Notes

[1] For children born up until 2002.

[2] Including analyses based on the DALSC data (Ottosen, 2000).

[3] A subsample of 611 children by immigrant mothers from selected countries was also undertaken, but due to low response rates from these respondents by the subsequent waves, this second data set suffers from poor quality; we have therefore omitted the subsample in this analysis.

[4] The results cover more than 21 tables of percentage distributions, which appear to be too complex to illustrate in a full version for this context.

[5] In all five waves, separated mothers were asked directly about the reasons for divorce/separation.

References

Amato, P.R. (2010) 'Research on divorce: continuing trends and new developments', *Journal of Marriage and Family*, vol 72, pp 650-66.

Amato, P.R. and Gilbreth, J. (1999) 'Nonresident fathers and children's well-being: a meta-analysis', *Journal of Marriage and the Family*, vol 61, pp 557-73.

Amato, P.R. Kane, J.B. and James, S. (2011) 'Reconsidering the "good divorce"', *Family Relations*, vol 60, pp 511-24.

Amato, P.R., Meyers, C.E. and Emery, R.E. (2009) 'Changes in nonresident father–child contact from 1976 to 2002', *Family Relations*, vol 58, pp 41-53.

Andersson, G., Kreyenfelde, M.M. and Mika, K.K. (2009) *Welfare state context, female earnings and childbearing*, WP-2009-026, Rostock: Max Planck Institute for Demographic Research.

Becker, G.S. (1981) *A treatise on the family*, Cambridge, MA: Harvard University Press.

Bonke, J. (2009) *Forældres brug af tid og penge på deres børn* [*Parents' use of time and money on their children*], Odense: University Press of Southern Denmark.

Christoffersen, M.N. (1998) 'Growing up with dad: a comparison of children aged 3-5 years old living with their mothers or their fathers', *Childhood*, vol 5, pp 41-54.

Duvander, A. and Andersson, G. (2006) 'Gender equality and fertility in Sweden: a study on the impact of the father's uptake of parental leave on continued childbearing', *Marriage and Family Review*, vol 39, pp 121-42.

Duvander, A. and Jans, A.C. (2009) 'Consequences of fathers' parental leave use: evidence from Sweden', in *Finnish Yearbook of Population Research*, Special Issue of the 16th Nordic Demographic Symposium in Helsinki, 5-7 June, pp 51-62.

Duvander, A. and Lammi-Taskula, J. (2011) 'Parental leave', in G.B. Eydal and I.V. Gíslason (eds) *Parental leave, childcare and gender equality in the Nordic countries*, Copenhagen: Nordic Council of Ministers, pp 29-62.

Esping-Andersen, G. (2009) *The incomplete revolution: Adapting welfare states to women's new roles*, Cambridge: Polity Press.

Familiestyrelsen [Division of Family Affairs] (2011) *Evaluering af forældreansvarsloven* [*Evaluation of the Act of Parental Responsibility*], Copenhagen: Familiestyrelsen.

Jensen, A.M. and Clausen, S.E. (2003) 'Children and family dissolution in Norway', *Childhood*, vol 10, no 1, pp 65-81.

King, V. and Sobolewski, J.M. (2006) 'Nonresident fathers' contributions to adolescent well-being', *Journal of Marriage and Family*, vol 68, pp 537-57.

Liefbroer, A. and Dourleijn, E. (2006) 'Unmarried cohabitation and union stability: testing the role of diffusion using data from 16 European countries', *Demography*, vol 43, no 2, pp 203-21.

Oláh, L.S. (2003) 'Gendering fertility: second births in Sweden and Hungary', *Population Research and Policy Review*, vol 22, pp 171-200.

Ottosen, M.H. (2000) *Samboskab, ægteskab og forældrebrud. En analyse af børns familieforhold gennem de første leveår* [*Cohabitation, marriage and family break-ups. An analysis of children's family relationships during the first years of life*], Copenhagen: SFI – The Danish National Centre for Social Research.

Ottosen, M.H. (2001) 'Legal and social ties between children and cohabiting fathers', *Childhood*, vol 8, no 1, pp 75-94.

Ottosen, M.H. (2004) *Samvær til barnets bedste. Om regler og praksis på samværsområdet* [*Contact in the best interest of the child. On legal rules and practices*], Copenhagen: SFI – The Danish National Centre for Social Research.

Ottosen, M.H. (2011) 'Research on the Danish longitudinal survey of children (DALSC) at the Danish National Centre for Social Research', *Scandinavian Journal of Public Health*, vol 39, no 7 (suppl), pp 121-5.

Ottosen, M.H. and Stage, S. (2011) *Dom til fælles forældremyndighed. Evaluering af forældreansvarsloven* [*Order to joint legal custody. Evaluation of the Act of Parental Responsibility*], Copenhagen: SFI – The Danish National Centre for Social Research.

Ottosen, M.H., Stage, S. and Jensen, H.S. (2011) *Børn i deleordninger* [*Children in shared living arrangements*], Copenhagen: SFI – The Danish National Centre for Social Research.

Parsons, T. and Bales, R. (1956) *Family, socialization and interaction process*, London: Routledge and Kegan Paul.

Plantin, L. (2001) *Mans foraldraskap. Om mans upplevelser och erfarenheter av faderskapet* [*Men's parenting. On men's experiences of fatherhood*], Gothenburg: Department of Social Work, Gothenburg University.

Sarkadi, A., Kristiansson, R., Oberklaid, F. and Bremberg, S. (2007) 'Fathers' involvement and children's developmental outcomes: a systematic review of longitudinal studies', *Acta Paediatrica*, vol 97, no 2, pp 153-8.

Theme 4:
Caring fathers and paid parental leave policies

The coming and going of the father's quota in Denmark: consequences for fathers' parental leave take-up

Tine Rostgaard and Mette Lausten

Introduction

The pursuit of gender equality is said to constitute one of the main characteristics of the Nordic welfare model, in the labour market and private sphere alike, as well as one of the primary societal values. As Ellingsæter and Leira (2006, p 7) write, 'gender equality is integral to Scandinavian citizenship.' Gender equality is perceived as being not only equality of opportunity, but also equality of outcome, and the gendered division of unpaid and paid work is particularly central. The gender equality model is therefore also the model which is predominantly presented and promoted in Nordic parenthood policies (Leira, 2006), as exemplified in the parental leave scheme, which is dominated by the effort to reconstruct gender and gender relations towards more active fatherhood.

Apart from extending the provision of childcare (see Eydal and Rostgaard, 2011), the Nordic countries (Denmark, Finland, Iceland, Norway and Sweden) have consequently all geared their leave policies towards the inclusion of fathers in the rearing of young children by introducing paternity and parental leave schemes. Four of the countries (Denmark, Iceland, Norway and Sweden) also introduced a father's quota in the late 1990s-early 2000s, which is an individual, non-transferable entitlement to a number of weeks of parental leave based on the 'use-it-or-lose-it' principle, in order to encourage fathers to take leave, while Finland instead introduced a gender bonus leave, recently converted into a fully fledged father's quota. In this manner, the Nordic countries followed the common path of political fatherhood policies, and had the most progressive state policies regarding gender equality and active fatherhood worldwide at the dawn of the new millennium, rendering the Nordic case unique and an exemplar for the generation and implementation of gender equality policies (Eydal and Rostgaard, 2012).

But not all countries still belong to what Lister (2009, p 242) calls 'the Nordic Nirvana of gender equality'. As of 2002, the Danish father's quota was eliminated for the sake of (again) allowing the family the decision of which parent should take the parental leave. Danish fathers still hold individual but transferable entitlement to take parental leave, but no longer with the strong and efficient incentive for take-up constituted by the father's quota (Haas and Rostgaard, 2011). Instead, the labour market agreements between the Danish labour market partners, consisting of employers and labour movement representatives, as well as local workplace agreements, have secured the rights for some groups of fathers to a father's quota, but with very diverse entitlements; in other words, the men in some labour market segments are not entitled to a father's quota.

This development could be claimed, first, to work against the principle of gender equality as previously outlined. Second, it could also appear to work against another of the constitutive elements of Nordic society: the principle of universalism (Anttonen et al, 2012), both for the fathers enjoying different rights as well as their children, some of whom have less opportunity to spend time together with their father in their early years due to institutional differences in leave entitlements and gender equality incentives.

The aim of this chapter is twofold: first, to investigate how the Danish father's quota situates itself in the Nordic agenda of gender equality and what have been the political arguments for and against the father's quota in the political process in Denmark. And second, what have been the consequences of the father's quota for the gender equality balance in how men and women share leave in Denmark, particularly the consequences for the variation in leave take-up among men of different socio-economic backgrounds. After having presented the theoretical framework for the analysis of policy change, the chapter thus presents an overview of the father's quota in the Nordic countries, and a more elaborate account of the policy background for the introduction and elimination of the father's quota in Denmark. This is followed by a description of the data sources used in the final section of the chapter, where a quantitative analysis of the changes in Danish fathers' take-up of leave as a consequence of the reforms is presented. The chapter concludes that although there is cross-party support for the father's quota, within the present centre/left-wing coalition government this is a politically risky project, especially when equality policies are of a more symbolic nature, as seems to be the case in Denmark. Looking into the consequences of the elimination of the father's quota in Denmark, an increasing discrepancy among fathers has taken place over time, in those who take leave and those who do not. Today, it is the more resourceful fathers – typically with a labour market entitlement to a father's quota – who take the leave.

Institutional and cultural factors explaining take-up

With this twofold analytical approach, the analysis takes into account both the political process surrounding the introduction of the father's quota and how it may contribute to or be inspired by changing norms and perceptions of gendered leave take-up, as well as examining the construction of the leave in terms of timing and policy instruments.

In this approach, the chapter leans on the theoretical perspective of historical institutionalism and the underlying understanding that the institutions, consisting of formal or informal rules, procedures, routines, norms and conventions embedded in the organisational structure of the welfare state, affect the behaviour of individuals (see, for example, Hall and Taylor, 1996; Thelen, 2002). Institutions offer a moral and cognitive pattern for the interpretation of what is the right action, and also influence the identity, self-images and preferences of the actors. Individuals are believed to respond instrumentally and strategically to the institutionally given opportunities and constraints in order to maximise the attainment of their goals given by a specific preference function, and in this specific case, how the leave arrangements are structured and which incentives, penalties and enforcements are built in, such as a father's quota. Historical institutionalism also brings forward the role of actors for institutional development, in conceptualising group conflicts as the main basis of change. In this analysis, the role of political parties is considered.

But the chapter also draws on the works of Pfau-Effinger (2005), who argues that the cultural system should be taken into account in addition to the institutional system, as it co-determines the development of welfare state institutions and the structuring of individual behaviour. The cultural system consists of values, ideas and ideals, which are collectively constructed and reproduced as meanings through the social practices of social actors – in the case of the father's quota, what is the dominant cultural orientation over time towards fathers taking leave.

With the combined focus on institutions and culture, the mere construction of leave policies is thus believed to contribute to newly institutionalised practices and roles as well as norms and preferences, and in this case, thus positively or negatively also affects leave take-up.

According to Olsen (2000), leave schemes contribute to the social construction of motherhood, fatherhood and parenthood, thereby contributing to our conception of what constitutes 'normal' gender roles. In addition to allowing parents to spend time with their children, leave schemes also create norms about what it means to be a 'good' parent. Changes in gender relations at the institutional level may thus change gendered practices of work–family reconciliation as well as workplace cultures (Haas, 2003) and individual family negotiations (Olsen, 2000). Consequently, overall gender equality in society may be affected. A father's quota might therefore create or consolidate the norm that fathers can and should take time off to care for their children, and may function as 'a manifestation of society's aim to induce into fatherhood more than the roles of breadwinner role and authority figure' (Björnberg, 1994, p 37). By creating better opportunities for fathers to argue for their take-up of leave with their partners, colleagues and employers, it also places fathers in a different and enabled position. Experiences from Norway thus suggest that the introduction of the father's quota may pressure the father somewhat to take leave; at the same time, it sends a signal to employers that fathers must prioritise childcare. In terms of the partner, the fact that women must now surrender some of the leave to the father also has a certain effect (NOU, 1995:27). In this way, it possibly exemplifies how 'gender relations are inscribed in social provision, patterning women's and men's social rights and their utilization of benefits' (Sainsbury, 1999, p 94). How policies are structured might therefore reflect the norms of parental relations between men and women and with their children.

Towards shared parenthood in the Nordic countries

It has been claimed that comprehensive childcare policies are a fundamental element in the social democratic welfare model in the Nordic countries (see, for example, Gornick and Meyers, 2003; Kangas and Rostgaard, 2007). This 'Nordicness' is also in the parental leave policies, which provide relatively extensive and generous support for taking time out from the labour market and include individual rights for both parents. The political arguments for generous paid parental leave have involved a combination of efforts to facilitate men and women's opportunities to both work and care, as well as to promote children's well-being and becoming (Eydal and Kröger, 2009). In recent years, however, active fatherhood in particular has been on the common Nordic agenda towards promoting a model of more equal parenthood and ensuring that the child–father relationship has the best possible start; and it is apparent that the Nordic countries have followed common goals and learned from each other's respective policy practices (Eydal and Rostgaard, 2012).

Consequently, all five Nordic countries have introduced policies including various incentives for fathers to become involved in childrearing. Parental leave with individual rights for both the father and mother was thus introduced in the 1970s and early 1980s in all of the countries, with Sweden as the forerunner in 1974, as a means to ensure that the father participates in the rearing of the young child. And within a relatively short period of time (1977-84), they had all introduced paternity leave for the father, to be taken at the birth of the child, with Iceland as the latecomer, paternity leave first introduced here in 1998 (see Table 13.1).

Four of the countries (Denmark, Iceland, Norway and Sweden) went further in the 1990s-2000s, also introducing so-called 'father's quotas'. To be precise, this is more a 'parent's quota' in Iceland, Norway and Sweden, as there are quotas for both mothers and fathers.[1] Finland introduced its own version of gendered incentives, which were transformed in 2013 into a father's quota (see Table 13.1).

The reason for introducing the father's quota has partly been the low parental leave take-up by men in the Nordic countries in the 1970s and 1980s, but more so because shared parental leave was considered to strengthen gender equality in general and the child–father relationship in particular (Eydal and Rostgaard, 2012).

The introduction of the father's quota has resulted in a considerable increase in fathers' take-up of parental leave, in Norway from 1 per cent of parental leave days in 1993, to 17.8 per cent in 2011 (see also Chapter Six, this volume). In Sweden, we also witness an increase in

Table 13.1: Father's leave: year of introduction, weeks of father's quota and take-up, Nordic countries

	Denmark	Finland	Iceland	Norway	Sweden
Parental leave	1984	1985	1981	1978	1974
Paternity leave	1984	1978	1998	1977	1980
Father's quota	1997	2013	2000	1993	1995
Length of father's quota (2013)	0 weeks	6 weeks	13 weeks	12 weeks	8 weeks*
Fathers' share of parental leave, % (2011)	7.4	8,3	29.0	17.8	24.5

Note: *Gender equality bonus.

Sources: Eydal and Rostgaard, 2012; Duvander and Lammi-Taskula, 2012. NOSOSCO: Nordisk statistisk årsbog, 2013.

father's leave take-up following the introduction of the father's quota, from 10.9 per cent of parental leave time in 1994 to 24.5 per cent in 2011. And following the introduction of the father's quota in 2000, Iceland succeeded in increasing father's parental leave uptake from 3.3 per cent of all parental leave days in 2000 to 29.0 per cent in 2011 (see also Chapter Fifteen, this volume). In Finland a bonus leave was introduced in 2003, giving the father the right to two weeks' (four since 2010) extra parental leave if he took two weeks of the shared parental leave period, although this required the mother's consent (Duvander and Lammi-Taskula, 2012; see also Chapters Fourteen and Sixteen, this volume). Here, the increase in parental leave take-up is less steep among fathers – from 0.8 per cent of total parental leave days in 2002, to 8.3 per cent in 2011 (see Table 13.1 for 2011 figures for all countries).

Denmark: longer and low-paid leave instead of gender equality incentives for the father

Turning to the Nordic father's quota outlier, Denmark – where the father's quota has come and gone – the gender equality agenda was less dominant in the early 1990s. Overall, gender equality as an ideological foundation constitutes the underlying rationale for policy developments less in Denmark than in the other Nordic countries. According to Borchorst and Dahlerup (2003), then, as now, gender equality policies have been of a more symbolic nature, with general – although somewhat unenthusiastic – acceptance among politicians of the need for action, but little being done. Where Denmark has since the 1960s been in the forefront in regards to the expansion of childcare – today providing for the highest share of children under three years among the Nordic countries (Borchorst, 2008; Eydal and Rostgaard, 2011), and thus facilitating women's take up of labour – Danish policies on parental leave have been less advanced in regards to the promotion of gender equality.

Unlike the Norwegian and Swedish cases, the Danish Social Democrats (Socialdemokraterne) were less ambitious in the 1990s in terms of promoting gender equality through leave scheme reforms. On the contrary, when the Social Democrats were able to return to power in 1993 together with centrist party coalition partners (Centrum-Demokraterne, Det Radikale Venstre and Kristeligt Folkeparti) they did not propose a father's quota. Instead, a so-called childcare leave of 13-26 weeks, depending on the age of the child, was introduced in January 1994 to supplement the 10-week parental leave which was already in place. The gender equality potential of the childcare leave was moderate, as the cash benefit was 80 per cent of the social security benefit – later to be reduced to only 60 per cent – thus primarily appealing to mothers, who usually have the lesser of the two household incomes[2] (Olsen, 1993). This leave scheme was part of a general strategy to reduce unemployment, which also included education and sabbatical leave arrangements.

The childcare leave was to be taken at the end of the parental leave, extending the total right to leave to 63 weeks from the birth of the child (right to 26 weeks before the child turned one year and 13 weeks thereafter, in all 39 weeks; in addition, each parent could negotiate with the employer up to a total of 52 weeks of childcare leave each). Parents thus had the right to each take up 13 or 26 weeks childcare leave as well as the 10-week parental leave (with 100 per cent of social security benefits, around €335 weekly), and full wage compensation for most public sector employees (there was also a four-week maternity leave for the mother before birth, 14-week maternity leave following the birth, and two-week paternity leave for the father to be taken within the first 14 weeks after the birth, all with 100 per cent social security benefits) (see Figure 13.1, prior to 1998).

Mothers usually took the childcare leave. Despite the original intention of the leave reform (also) being to increase labour market mobility, it was considered a failure from a gender equality perspective (Hjort Andersen, 1997). Campaigns to encourage more fathers to take leave were unsuccessful, prompting the then Minister of Social Affairs, Jytte Andersen, to address fathers directly in a 1997 statement, declaring that she found it 'shameful that fathers do not prioritize their children higher' (in *Jyllandsposten*, quoted in Olsen, 1997; author's translation).

The father's quota in Denmark

The time was therefore ripe to be inspired by the gender equality incentives implemented in neighbouring countries. In 1997, a coalition government consisting of the Social Democrats and centrist Social Liberals (Radikale Venstre) introduced a two-week father's quota. As in Sweden and Norway, the earmarked weeks were additional weeks, added to the existing leave. The introduction of the father's quota was argued on the basis of the relatively low parental leave take-up by men at that time (around 4 per cent of fathers), the hope being that a two-week quota would give fathers further opportunity to spend time with their children (*Lovforslag* 121, 1997-98 [Danish Bill for extension of paternity leave]).

Figure 13.1: Right to leave, mother and father. Weeks and level of compensation.

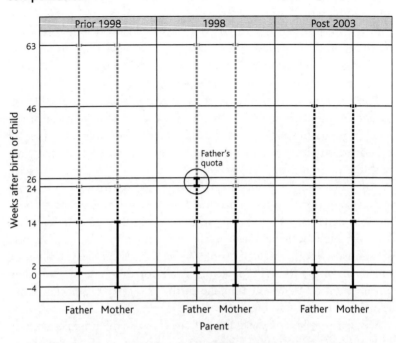

Compensation: Full ——— 60% ———
Shareable: No ——— Yes ·······

The introduction of the quota was hardly a response to public outcry for more gender-egalitarian leave rights in the media or from fathers' groups, nor was it a subject of lengthy parliamentary disagreement – less than one month passed from its proposal to being passed, a relatively short period of time for the Danish *Folketing* (Parliament). Although right-of-centre opposition parties criticised the proposal, the opposition mainly questioned the need for the quota, as fathers seemed little interested in taking leave, reference being made to the cost of adding extra weeks (Rostgaard, 2004; Cederstrand, 2011).

As of April 1998, Danish parents could now share 10 weeks of parental leave together with the 39-week childcare leave, and fathers were entitled to an additional two-week father's quota (in addition to the already existing maternity and paternity leave). The father now had a strong incentive to take leave following the parental leave, in weeks 25 and 26 (see Figure 13.1, 1998–2002). Apart from the childcare leave, the leave period was compensated with benefits on a par with social security benefits and, as mentioned, several labour market agreements provided better compensation.

Eliminating the father's quota

In Denmark, however, the father's quota only had a four-year life span. When a new bourgeois government consisting of the Conservatives (Konservative) and Liberals (Venstre) came into power in 2001, it picked up on earlier election promises to favour families with children. While arguing that voluntary workplace agreements were sufficient for ensuring the father's right to take leave, the new government extended the parental leave period from 10 to 32 weeks as of July 2002. In return, the father's quota was eliminated, as was the childcare leave (Rostgaard, 2002).

With the changes, parents now had an individual right to a 32-week parental leave, but only a right to compensation for 32 weeks in total (together with the already existing maternity and paternity leave), meaning that the total leave time was considerably shorter (see Figure 13.1, post-2002). Now, parents could also take leave at the same time. From a gender equality perspective, the father might not be holding primary responsibility for childcare, but he might well be 'assisting' the mother to a greater degree.

Although the changes actually constituted a considerable cut to the total leave time available, there was – perhaps surprisingly – no public debate as to whether this change would have a negative impact on families with children. One reason was that parents were now effectively secured full social security benefits for the entire leave period, or, as was the case for public employees, full wages. This represented an improvement on the 60 per cent of benefits paid as part of childcare leave.

The reform was therefore presented – and regarded – as an improvement of leave rights, although the fathers' individual right was in fact curbed. As Bloksgaard describes in this volume (Chapter Seven), in contrast to mothers, fathers must negotiate parental leave take-up with their employer. The main argument behind the reform was thus the higher benefit together with the newly introduced opportunity to take part-time leave. Perhaps more important was the re-introduction of the freedom to choose when to take leave. In Denmark, the choice agenda had now been taken over by the bourgeois parties, their argument being that the father's quota constituted state coercion in relation to what ought to be a private decision about how to share leave time between men and women (Rostgaard, 2004), and this remains dominant today whenever reserved parental leave time for the father is debated.

Interestingly, labour market partners representing employees and employers have been pushing for the introduction of a father's quota since the elimination of the original father's quota in 2002. In 2003, for example, the financial sector agreed to a fully paid four-week father's quota to be taken within the first 14 weeks of the birth of the child and three months of parental leave for each parent with full pay in the remaining period. In 2008, fathers working in the public sector gained an equivalent right to a four-week father's quota, and fathers working in the hotel and restaurant branch in the private sector received a one-week fully paid quota. Within the public sector, employees working in the central state or in municipalities have a fully paid six weeks father's (or mother's) quota.

Re-installing the father's quota?

Generally speaking, the father's quota currently separates the Danish political parties, the right-wing parties favouring individual choice and being against 'coercion', whereas the left-wing and centrist parties favour a quota from the perspective of gender equality, although it is not always so straightforward: The coalition government consisting of the Social Democrats, Social Liberals and Socialist People's Party (Socialistisk Folkeparti), who have formed the government since October 2011, originally intended to introduce a 12-week father's quota inspired by the other Nordic countries (Statsministeriet, 2011). As of September 2013, however, the government somewhat surprisingly announced that it had abandoned any such plans, most likely moved by numerous unfavourable opinion polls.[3] Instead, the plan is to introduce a gender equality bonus similar to the Swedish scheme, regardless of this having proven inefficient (see Chapter Sixteen, this volume), the argument being that a father's quota creates inequality: as many men working in the private sector will not take leave, these leave weeks will therefore be lost for the family.[4]

However, the question becomes whether the father's quota is in fact not creating more equality in fathers' take-up across occupational sectors as well as other socio-economic differences. The second part of this chapter investigates this by analysing the development in leave take-up among fathers with different backgrounds since 1998.

Data and methods

For the analysis of the changes in how fathers take leave, register data is applied, covering the entire population of couples becoming parents in the period of interest. The sample is chosen on the basis of the birth of the child; there were 1,006,237 fathers in total (see Table 13.2).

Data are available from 1990 to 2007, including data for days of parental leave and childcare leave take-up. Due to lack of data, however, the childcare leave take-up for the period April–December 1994–95 is not covered.

The sample includes fathers who are registered as having taken leave (either receiving unemployment benefits or earning full wages). This excludes those outside the labour market, such as students and homemakers, who are not entitled to benefits. Between 10-13 per cent of all parents with a newborn child did not receive a leave benefit (Statistics Denmark, 2012), and were therefore not included in the sample. The period of maternity leave prior to birth and the two-week paternity leave following the birth of the child were excluded in the analysis, as the interest is only in the impact of the reforms on how fathers take parental leave. Data on leave take-up covers a two-year period beginning with the birth of the child. This excludes the number of fathers postponing leave possibly until after the child's second year, as the 2002 reform made possible. According to Olsen (2007), 4 per cent of the fathers in her survey postponed leave until after the child's first year. This analytical strategy is chosen in order to ensure that leave is related to the birth of the child as far as possible and not a subsequent child; however, 8 per cent of fathers in the sample have another child within the two years.

The data set also includes socio-demographic information such as age, number of children in the family, gender, level of education, minority ethnic background, disposable individual and household

Table 13.2: Fathers taking parental leave or not in Periods 1, 2 and 3

	Fathers not taking parental leave	Fathers taking parental leave	Total
Period 1: 1990–97	391,533 (89.6%)	45,592 (10.4%)	437,125
Period 2: 1998–2001	164,065 (69.8%)	70,826 (30.2%)	234,891
Period 3: 2002–06	243,038 (72.7%)	91,183 (27.3%)	334,221
Total	798,636 (79.4%)	207,601 (20.6%)	1,006,237

Note: Including parental leave and before 2002 also childcare leave, not including paternity leave.

income and whether leave is being taken for the first or subsequent child.

Unfortunately, the data does not include information on the public/private sector division of work, only information on the occupational sector, which for analytical purposes is grouped into *private sector occupations*: (1) manufacturing, construction and farming; (2) wholesale, retail trade and services; and *public sector occupations*: (3) transportation and tele-communications; (4) financing and insurance activities; (5) public administration; (6) education, human health, and social work activities; and (7) miscellaneous services.

For the analysis of the impact of the leave reforms, the following cutting points were selected (corresponding to the three periods in Table 13.2):

1. The period 1990–September 1997, which includes fathers taking parental leave in the weeks 15–24 following the birth of the child, and from 1995 onwards also childcare leave.
2. The period from September 1997[5] to December 2001, which includes the parental leave take-up in the weeks 15–24 and/or weeks 25 and 26 (father's quota), and the take-up of childcare leave.
3. The period beginning in January 2002, including the 32-week parental leave period to be taken from week 15 and onwards.

The take-up data are presented as monthly averages. Regression analysis was applied to investigate the socio-economic variation in leave take-up among men. It should be mentioned that when studying related consequences of reform changes it could be argued that parents may attempt to take advantage of coming reforms by anticipating the conception of their child. In a Norwegian study and on the basis of fertility rates, however, Cools et al (2011) found that this did not seem to be the case.

The impact of leave structures on fathers' leave take-up

If we start by examining the share of fathers taking leave, there appears to be a general impact from the leave reforms on men's uptake of parental leave. Figure 13.2 illustrates the percentage of fathers taking parental leave during 1990–2008. It appears as though more fathers do take leave over time, but with a significant increase following the introduction of the father's quota in 1998.

The different leave schemes are marked in Figure 13.2: before 1995: no father's quota and no childcare leave, but parental leave in the

Figure 13.2: Percentage of fathers taking parental leave in Denmark, 1990–2008

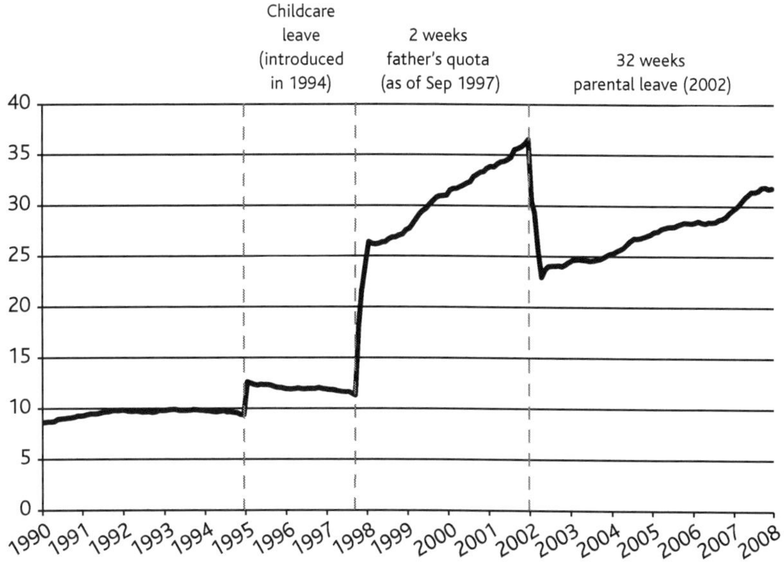

Note: According to the birth month. Before September 1997: Fathers taking parental leave (weeks 15–24) and from 1995 also data on childcare leave. September 1997 and after: Fathers taking parental leave and/or father's quota (weeks 15–24 and/or weeks 25 and 26) and childcare leave. 2002 and after: Fathers taking parental leave (32 weeks leave).

Source: Statistics Denmark, register data.

weeks 14–25; 1995–98: parental leave weeks 14–25 and a 26-week childcare leave (introduced in 1994 and taken by fathers, but register data is only available from 1995); from September 1997: as well as a two-week father's quota in weeks 25 and 26; and from 2002: 32 weeks of parental leave from week 15 onwards, but no father's quota and no childcare leave.

The introduction of the father's quota initially sparked increased uptake of parental leave among fathers, from 12 per cent of those becoming fathers in 1997 to 36 per cent of fathers in 2001, when at its height. From 2002, with the elimination of the quota, there is a drop to 22 per cent of fathers, but then the number begins to increase again. This development suggests that fathers increasingly take parental leave, regardless of whether or not there is a legislated father's quota. The hypothesis is that this is partly due to the introduction of father's quota arrangements in some of the labour market agreements, which started to set in as of 2003 (see also Chapter Seven, this volume). Several analyses have shown that leave take-up in recent years is particularly high among men in sectors with extensive leave protection, such as the banking and municipal sectors (Finansforbundet, 2012; KL, 2012). These sectors have witnessed a significant increase in leave take-up among fathers, for example, in the financial sector, from an average of 21 days of leave to 37 days in the period 2003-08 (Finansforbundet, 2012). Fathers working in the hotel and restaurant business display a similar increase in leave take-up from, on average, 15 days in 2004 to 26 days in 2008 (Bloksgaard, 2011). Another reason is believed to be the cultural shift in (male) attitudes to fatherhood and in men's role in childcare for the young child, which the introduction of the father's quota may have encouraged or at least supported.

Figure 13.3 illustrates this increase in leave take-up, showing that fathers' share of total days of leave in Denmark has generally been on the increase, especially since the introduction of the father's quota and childcare leave (data from 1995). The elimination of the father's quota in 2002 is followed by a slight drop in the fathers' share, which has since increased; once again, this possibly reflects the increasing number of fathers who have gained a right to a father's quota through collective agreements as well as changing norms.

Figure 13.3: Fathers' percentage share of total days of leave, 1990–2008

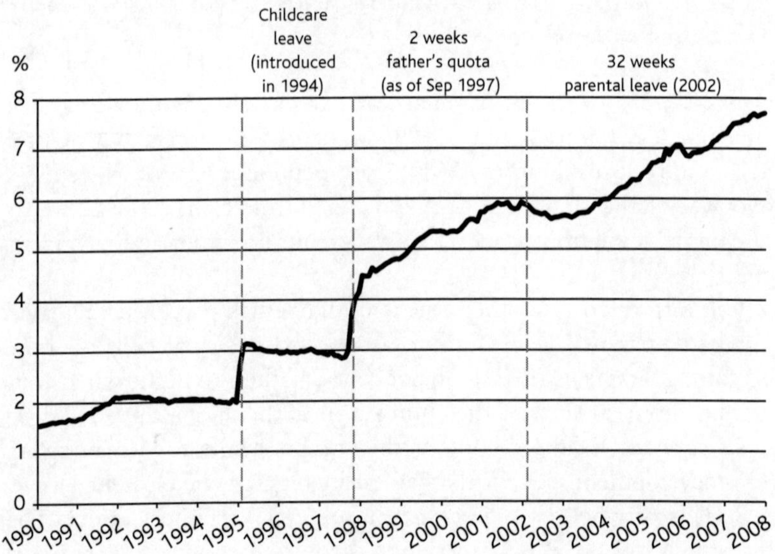

Note: Before September 1997: Fathers taking parental leave (weeks 15–24) and from 1995 also data on childcare leave. September 1997 and after: Fathers taking parental leave and/or father's quota (weeks 15–24 and/or weeks 25 and 26) and childcare leave. 2002 and after: Fathers taking parental leave (32 weeks leave).

Source: Statistics Denmark, register data.

Figure 13.3 shows a much smaller decline in the share of total leave days following the elimination of the father's quota than was the case in Figure 13.2, showing the percentage of fathers taking leave. This is believed to be due to the father's quota having a special effect on certain groups of fathers, ensuring that the average number of days increased overall.

Leave take-up among different groups of fathers

Scrutinising this further by analysing the consequences of the reforms for the variations in the share of men taking leave depending on different socio-economic backgrounds, this section investigates which fathers take leave depending on various socio-demographic variables. Before applying a regression analysis, Figures 13.4–13.6 present the differences over time in a selection of variables, as the reforms have affected fathers' entitlement to leave.

While Christoffersen (1990) found in the late 1980s that a Danish father's educational level did not influence his leave uptake, Figure 13.4 indicates that educational background now appears influential, with the fathers with the highest education taking leave, and with

Figure 13.4: Percentage of fathers taking leave, according to educational level of the father, 1990–2007

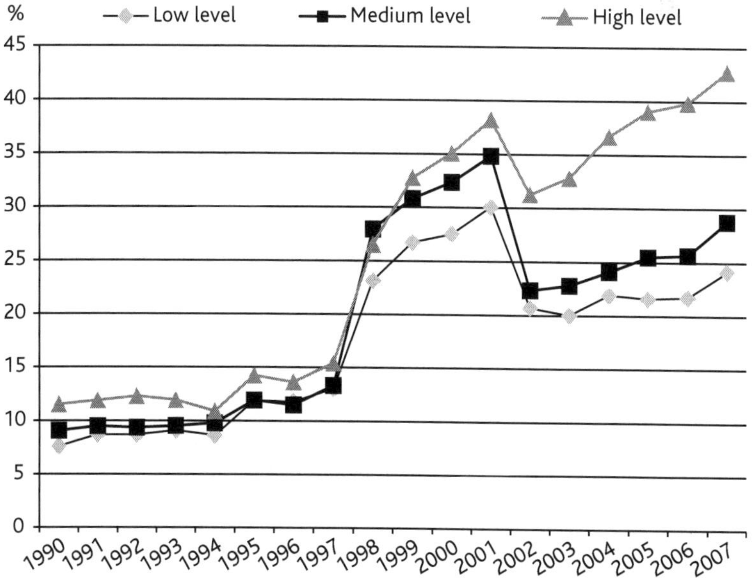

Source: Statistics Denmark, register data

increasing variation over time. With the reform changes, the least educated fathers are increasingly less likely to take leave. This variation in leave uptake according to education is well known from other Nordic research (see, for example, Danielsen and Lappegård, 2003), and possibly reflects norms about the role and practice of the father in the family. However, a recent Danish population survey on the support for a three-month (or more) father's quota found general support among men across the educational divide.[6] Moreover, slightly more men without a qualifying education expressed that they would have taken longer leave if the legislation provided time reserved for the father (DJØF, 2012). This suggests that there is general support across the educational divide for reserving time for the father as well as actual interest in taking leave, but also suggests that fathers with lower education have a harder time fulfilling such desires.

Much research also points to the mother's education level as possibly the most decisive factor determining a father's use of leave (see, for example, Nyman and Petterson, 2002). Figure 13.5 confirms that the mother's education level may indeed influence her partner's leave take-up. It underlines how fathers are more likely to take leave in families where the mother has a higher education. This is possibly due

Figure 13.5: Percentage of fathers taking leave, according to education level of the mother, 1990–2007

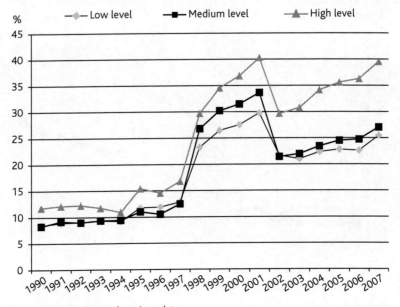

Source: Statistics Denmark, register data

to women in such families being more likely to return early to the labour market after giving birth, but possibly also a more traditional division of paid and unpaid work in families where the father has the highest education.

Turning to the workplace, Figure 13.6 illustrates the share of men taking leave in various occupations. It reveals an increasing difference after the elimination of the father's quota between fathers working in typical public sector occupations such as public administration, education, human health (hospitals and practitioners) and social services compared to fathers working in typical private sector occupations, such as manufacturing, construction and farming, as well as fathers employed in wholesale, retail trade and other services.

Figure 13.6: Percentage of fathers taking leave, according to occupational branch of the father, 1990–2007

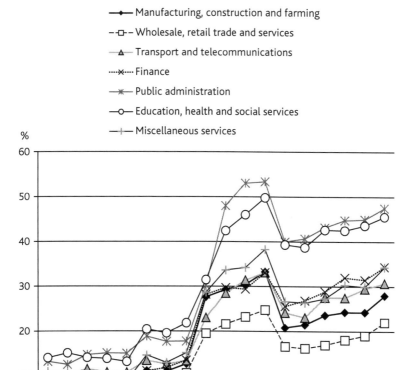

Source: Statistics Denmark, register data

Fathers employed in the public sector occupations with the most extensive additional parental leave rights, such as education, health and social services, as well as in public administration, are increasingly taking parental leave.

The final step in the analysis takes all of the aforementioned factors plus a number of other indicators into account in a simple logistic regression analysis, analysing the probability of fathers taking leave. This logistic analysis compares the fathers taking parental leave with those who do not (see Table 13.3). Table 13.3 shows the odds ratios of the probability of fathers taking leave in the three time periods, the first comparing the effect of introducing a father's quota (Period 2), in comparison to not having a father's quota (Period 1). Next, the model compares the effect of eliminating the father's quota and childcare leave (Period 2), which were replaced by the 32 weeks of parental leave (Period 3). The odds ratio analysis shows the likelihood of fathers taking leave when all other factors remain constant. It expresses the increase in likelihood that a certain event will happen given a certain factor, for example, that a father in Period 2 is almost four times more likely to take leave than a father in Period 1 (odds ratio = 3.81, Table 13.3, Model 1, first line). This indicates that fathers in Period 2 are generally more likely to take parental leave because of the introduction of the father's quota, compared to Period 1, where there was no specific quota for fathers. Comparing the fathers in Periods 2 and 3, fathers are less likely to take leave in Period 3, where there was no father's quota (odds ratio = 0.82).

Fathers to second or higher-order children are less likely to take parental leave (odds ratio = 0.65). This is true for all of the periods, indicating that fathers are typically more involved in the parental care of their first child than subsequent children. The same is true for fathers with a minority ethnic background compared to fathers with a Danish background. Minority ethnic fathers are less likely to take parental leave, something that is also witnessed in other studies (see, for example, Huerta et al, 2012).

Looking at Model 1, fathers with low and high education levels, compared to fathers having vocational training or short-term further education, are significantly less likely to take leave. At the same time, fathers with a partner with a medium or long-term education are more likely to take parental leave (odds ratio = 1.21), suggesting a different gender perspective on housework and parental leave in couples where the mother has a high education, or indicating that the mothers with a high education are more eager to return to work after maternity leave and therefore more interested in sharing parental leave. The same

Table 13.3: Odds ratios from logistic regressions on the probability of father's taking leave, comparing Periods 1 and 2 and Periods 2 and 3

	Model 1 comparing Periods 1 and 2	Model 2 comparing Periods 2 and 3
Dummy for taking leave in Period 2 (1998–2001) compared to Period 1 (1990–97)	3.81*	–
Dummy for taking leave in Period 3 (2002–08) compared to Period 2 (1998–2001)	–	0.82*
Father having first child (baseline)	–	–
Father having second child	0.65*	0.72*
Father having third or more child	0.60*	0.62*
Father ≤35 years (baseline)	–	–
Father >35 years	1.03*	0.99(*)
Father with Danish background (baseline)	–	–
Father with ethnic minority background	0.92*	0.83*
Education level of fathers and mothers:		
Father – education level only primary or secondary school	0.83*	0.80*
Father – vocational training and short-term further ed. (baseline)	–	–
Father – medium- and long-term further education	0.92*	1.07*
Mother – educational level only primary or secondary school	0.93*	0.93*
Mother – vocational training and short-term further ed. (baseline)	–	–
Mother – medium- and long-term further education	1.21*	1.23*
Disposable income in the household:		
Mother higher disposable income than father (baseline)	–	–
Father higher disposable income than mother	0.83*	0.82*
Low level of disposable household income (baseline)	–	–
Medium level of disposable household income	1.07*	1.18*
High level of disposable household income	0.94*	1.13*
Father – unemployment throughout the birth year of the child:		
Low level of unemployment through year (baseline)	–	–
High level of unemployment through year	0.51*	0.49*
Trade sector:		
(1) Manufacturing, construction and farming (baseline)	–	–
(2) Wholesale, retail trade & services	0.69*	0.69*
(3) Transport & telecommunications	1.11*	1.14*
(4) Financing and insurance activities	1.04*	1.12*
(5) Public administration	1.74*	2.02*
(6) Education, human health and social work activities	1.71*	1.81*
(7) Miscellaneous services	1.21*	1.22*

Note: * indicates statistically significant at 1% level, whereas (*) indicates statistically significant at 5% level.

The odds ratio is the ratio of the odds of fathers taking leave in one group (for example fathers having second child) compared to the baseline group (for example fathers having first child). An odds ratio greater than 1 indicates that fathers are more likely to take leave in the group. And an odds ratio less than 1 indicates that fathers are less likely to take leave in the first group than in the baseline group.

is true when examining Model 2 for Periods 2 and 3, where fathers with a high education are also slightly more likely to take leave (odds ratio = 1.07).

If the fathers have a high level of unemployment throughout the year of the birth of their child, meaning that the fathers are unemployed more than six months in that specific year, they are much less likely to take leave (odds ratio in Model 1 = 0.51, odds ratio in Model 2 = 0.49). This is a consequence of the benefit for parental leave being lower than the unemployment benefit for most of these fathers. As unemployed fathers were present at home anyway for most of the years in the data period, the unemployment period can be a kind of hidden parental leave with higher benefits.

Comparing fathers in different trade sectors, we see that fathers employed in the private sector (that is, manufacturing, construction and farming; and wholesale, retail trade and services) are much less likely to take parental leave than fathers employed in public sector occupations, where the odds ratios are 1.04 or higher for all sectors. In particular, fathers in the sectors (5) public administration (odds ratio = 1.74 in Model 1 and 2.02 in Model 2) and (6) education, human health and social work activities (odds ratio = 1.71 in Model 1 and 1.81 in Model 2) are much more likely to take leave than others. This can be partly due to specific and extensive leave protection schemes for these sectors, whereas part of it is caused by the composition of fathers in these sectors, that is, fathers with a higher education level.

To conclude on the simple logistic regression analysis from Table 13.3, there is a significant change in fathers' parental leave take-up due to the changes in the parental leave legislation, but also a compositional change in terms of more fathers taking leave, although the father's quota was eliminated in 2002. As also pictured in Figures 13.2 and 13.3, although there are fewer fathers taking leave after the 2002 reform, fathers' percentage of total days on parental leave are continuously increasing, indicating a growing interest among fathers to take parental leave. In contrast to, for example, Ellingsæter's findings (2012), however, which show that the introduction of the father's quota in Norway has helped reduce class differences in terms of which fathers take leave, such differences have only increased in Denmark since eliminating the father's quota.

Conclusion

In recent decades, all of the Nordic countries have been at the forefront in the generation and implementation of gender equality policies. Consequently, the Nordic countries had the most progressive state policies for gender equality and active fatherhood worldwide at the turn of the millennium. Early on, the institutional framing of active fatherhood has thus supported fathers in these countries taking parental leave, not least since the introduction of the father's quota, which constitutes a strong incentive for fathers to take leave.

As the Danish case illustrates, however, when gender equality policies are less institutionally rooted and of a more symbolic nature, the introduction of the father's quota becomes politically problematic. Despite the original intention and against basic ideology, even Social Democratic ministers may decide to let free choice rule when the public perceives a father's quota policy as being 'coercion'. Despite the path dependency of a two-week father's quota in the period 1998–2002, recent policy development indicates that the father's quota in Denmark remains a long way off, but only in regards to statutory policies. Danish labour market partners have gone further, and some fathers have earned the right to a father's quota in several labour agreements. Other fathers still have only their sharable right to parental leave.

Consequently, we witness an increasing discrepancy among fathers over time, in those who take leave and those who do not. The introduction of the father's quota triggered a significant increase in fathers taking leave, which dropped when the father's quota was eliminated. As the analysis suggests, the labour market agreements, together with a cultural shift, appear to have invoked an increase since then. However, it is now more the well-educated fathers, working in public sector occupations, with well-educated partners who take parental leave, presumably because they stand in a better situation in the labour market – they may have secured better leave rights and may also have a partner who is more eager herself to return to the labour market. As the analysis shows, there is growing interest among fathers in taking leave – and across the education divide – but this is more a consequence of the cultural change in the perception of fatherhood, and not the result of institutional support. As such, the institutional legacy of the father's quota in the period 1998–2002 may have contributed to a more gender-equal distribution of leave take-up. The present composition of statutory leave entitlements positions fathers differently, however, thus working against the Nordic principle of universalism.

Notes

[1] Although the quota is thus gender-neutral, it is referred to here as a father's quota in order to underline the political intention behind the scheme, which is to encourage fathers to take leave.

[2] Some municipalities (13 per cent in 1998), however, provided a maximum annual local supplement to the leave benefit of DKK 35,000.

[3] See http://bm.dk/~/media/BEM/Files/Dokumenter/Publikationer/2013/ Barsel_rapport%20pdf.ashx, attachment C

[4] For example, see http://politiken.dk/politik/ECE2067724/mette-frederiksen-ja-vi-gaar-imod-regeringsgrundlaget

[5] Although the father's quota was first introduced in April 1998, September 1997 is used as the cut-off point in order to include all of the fathers with a child aged 24-25 weeks as of April 1998.

[6] Forty-three per cent among those with no qualifying education, supported the proposal, 37 per cent of those with vocational training and 40 per cent of those with a higher education, that is, short-, medium-, and long-term education ($n = 1,000$).

References

Anttonen, A., Häikiö, L. and Stefánsson, K. (eds) (2012) *Welfare state, universalism and diversity*, Bristol: Edward Elgar Publishing.

Björnberg, U. (1994) 'Family orientation among men. Fatherhood and partnership in a process of change', in J. Brannen and M. O'Brien (eds) *Childhood and parenthood*, London: Institute of Education and University of East London.

Bloksgaard, L. (2011) *Mænd, barselsrettigheder og brug af barsel – en interviewundersøgelse blandt mandlige medlemmer i 3F* [*Men, leave entitlement and leave use*], Working Paper No 76, Aalborg: FREIA, Feminist Research Center in Aalborg, Aalborg University.

Borchorst, A. (2008) 'Woman-friendly policy paradoxes? Childcare policies and gender equality visions in Scandinavia', in K. Melby, C.C. Wetterberg and A.-B. Ravn (eds) *Gender equality and welfare politics in Scandinavia: The limits of political ambition?*, Bristol: Policy Press, pp 27-42.

Borchorst, A. and Dahlerup, D. (2003) 'Dansk ligestillingspolitik – diskurs og praksis: Konklusioner' ['Danish gender equality policy – discourse and practice: Conclusions'], in A. Borchorst and D. Dahlerup (eds) *Ligestillingspolitik som diskurs og praksis* [*Gender equality policy as discourse and practice*], Copenhagen: Samfundslitteratur, pp 185-205.

Cedstrand, S. (2011) *Från idé till politisk verklighet. Föräldrapolitiken i Sverige och Danmark* [*From idea to political reality. Parental politics in Sweden and Denmark*]. Doctoral Dissertation, School of Public Administration, University of Gothenburg, Umeå: Boréa.

Christoffersen, M.N. (1990) *Barselsorlov – mænds og kvinders erhvervsmæssige baggrund for at tage orlov* [*Parental leave – men and women's vocational backgrounds for taking leave*], Copenhagen: SFI – The Danish National Centre for Social Research.

Cools, S., Fiva, J.H. and Kirkebøen, L.J. (2011) *Causal effects of paternity leave on children and parents*, Discussion Paper No 657, Oslo: Statistics Norway.

Danielsen, K. and Lappegård, T. (2003) 'Tid er viktig når barn blir født – om ulik bruk av lønnet fødselspermisjon' ['Time is important when children are born – about unequal usage of paid maternity'], *Samfunnsspeilet* 5, Statistisk sentralbyra.

DJØF (2012) *Danskernes holdning til barsel* [*The Danes' position on parental leave*], Copenhagen: Epinion.

Duvander, A. and Lammi-Taskula, J. (2012) 'Parental leave', in I. Gíslason and G. Eydal (eds) *Parental leave, childcare and gender equality in the Nordic countries*, Copenhagen: Nordic Council of Ministers, pp 29-62.

Ellingsæter, A.L. (2012) 'Nordic Politicization of Parenthood: Unfolding Hybridization?', in M. Richter and S. Andresen (eds) *The Politicization of Parenthood*, Springer Science+Business Media B.V., pp 39-53.

Ellingsæter, A.L. and Leira, A. (2006) 'Introduction: politicizing parenthood in Scandinavia', in A.L. Ellingsæter and A. Leira (eds) *Politicising parenthood in Scandinavia: Gender relations in welfare states*, Bristol: Policy Press pp 1-28.

Eydal, G.B. and Kröger, T. (2009) 'Nordic family policies: constructing contexts for social work with families', in H. Forsberg and T. Kröger (eds) *Social work and child welfare politics through Nordic lenses*, Bristol: Policy Press, pp 11-28.

Eydal, G.B. and Rostgaard, T. (2011) 'Nordic child care – a response to old and new tensions?' in B. Pfau-Effinger and T. Rostgaard (eds) *Care Between Work and Welfare in Europe*, Houndsmills: Palgrave, pp 79-97.

Eydal, G.B. and Rostgaard, T. (2012) 'Towards a Nordic childcare policy: the political processes and agendas', in I.V. Gíslason and G. Eydal (eds) *Parental leave, childcare and gender equality in the Nordic countries*, Copenhagen: Nordic Council of Ministers, pp 147-78.

Finansforbundet (2012) 'Finansansatte tager mere orlov' ['Employees in the finance sector take more leave'] (www.finansforbundet.dk/da/Aktuelt/magasinetfinans/Magasinetfinansnr22010).

Gornick, J.C. and Meyers, M.K. (2003) *Families that work: Policies for reconciling parenthood and employment*, New York: Russell Sage Foundation.

Haas, L. (2003) 'Parental leave and gender equality: Lessons from the European Union', *Review of Policy Research*, vol 20, no 1, pp 89-114.

Haas, L. and Rostgaard, T. (2011) 'Fathers' rights to paid parental leave in the Nordic countries: consequences for the gendered division of leave', *Community, Work & Family*, vol 14, no 2, pp 177-95.

Hall, P. and Taylor, R. (1996) 'Political science and the three new institutionalisms', *Political Studies*, vol 44, pp 936-57.

Hjort Andersen, B. (1997) *Børns opvækstvilkår. En beskrivelse af første fase i en forløbsundersøgelse af børn født i 1995* [*Children's upbringing. A description of the first phase of a longitudinal study of children born in 1995*], Working Paper, Copenhagen: SFI – The Danish National Centre for Social Research.

Huerta, M.C., Adema, W., Baxter, J., Han, W., Lausten, M., Lee, R. and Waldfogel, J. (2012) *Fathers' leave, fathers' involvement and child development: Are they related? Evidence from four OECD countries*, OECD Social, Employment and Migration Working Paper No 140, Paris: OECD Publishing.

Kangas, O. and Rostgaard, T. (2007) 'Preferences or context: opinions of childcare', *Journal of European Social Policy*, vol 17, no 3, pp 240-56.

KL (2012) 'Kommunalt ansatte mænd er blevet vilde med barsel' (www.kl.dk/Momentum).

Leira, A. (2006) 'Parenthood Change and Policy Reform in Scandinavia, 1970s-2000s', in A.L. Ellingsæter and A. Leira (eds) *Politicising Parenthood in Scandinavia. Gender Relations in Welfare States*, Bristol: Policy Press, pp 27-52.

Lister, R. (2009) 'A Nordic Nirvana? Gender, citizenship and social justice in the Nordic welfare states', *Social Politics: International Studies in Gender, State and Society*, vol 16, no 2, pp 242-78.

NOSOSCO (2013) Nordisk statistisk årsbog, Nord 2013:001, Copenhagen: Statistics Denmark.

NOU (Norges Offentlige Utredninger) [Norwegian Official Report] (1995:27) *Pappa kom hjem* [*Daddy come home*], Oslo: Barne- og likestillingsdepartementet.

Nyman, H. and Petterson, J. (2002) *Spelade pappamånaden någon roll? Pappornas uttag av föräldrapenning* [*Did the father's quota play any role? Fathers' take-up of parental leave*], RFV Analyserar, Stockholm: Riksförsäkringsverket.

Olsen, B.M. (1993) 'Mens vi venter på far' ['Waiting for dad'], Dissertation, Copenhagen: Department of Sociology, University of Copenhagen.

Olsen, B.M. (1997) 'Orlov til børnepasning – en familiepolitisk revolution?' ['Parental leave – a revolution of family policy?'], *Tidsskriftet Kvinder, Køn og Forskning*, vol 2.

Olsen, B.M. (2000) 'Nye fædre på orlov – en analyse af de kønsmæssige aspekter ved forældreorlovsordninger', PhD -afhandlingsserien nr 14, Copenhagen: Sociologisk Institut.

Olsen, B.M. (2007) *Evaluering af den fleksible barselorlov - Orlovsreglerne set fra forældres, kommuners og arbejdspladsers perspektiv* [*Evaluation of the flexible maternity leave – Leave rules from the perspectives of parents, municipalities and workplaces*] *SFI report 29:07*, Copenhagen: SFI.

Pfau-Effinger, B. (2005) 'Culture and welfare state policies: reflections on a complex interrelation', *Journal of Social Policy*, vol 34, no 1, pp 1-18.

Rostgaard, T. (2002) 'Setting time aside for the father: father's leave in Scandinavia', *Community, Work and Family*, vol 5, no 3, pp 343-64.

Rostgaard, T. (2004) 'With due care: Social care for the young and the old across Europe', PhD Thesis, Odense: The Danish National Institute of Social Research/Southern Danish University.

Sainsbury, D. (1999) 'Gender and social-democratic welfare states', in D. Sainsbury (ed) *Gender and welfare regimes*, Oxford: Oxford University Press, pp 75-114.

Statistics Denmark (2012) *Dagpenge ved fødsel 2011* [*Benefits in connection with childbirth*], Nyt fra Danmarks statistik no 120, marts, Copenhagen: Statistics Denmark.

Statsministeriet (2011) *Et Danmark der står sammen* [*A Denmark that stands together*], Copenhagen: Statsministeriet (www.stm.dk).

Thelen, K. (2002) 'The explanatory power of historical institutionalism', in R. Maintz (ed) *Akteure – Mechanismen – Modelle. Zur Theoriefähigkeit makro-sozialer Analysen* [*Actors – Mechanisms – Models. Towards theoretical capability of macro-social analysis*], Frankfurt and New York: Campus.

FOURTEEN

Policy goals and obstacles for fathers' parental leave in Finland

Minna Salmi and Johanna Lammi-Taskula

Introduction

In Finland, as in all of the other Nordic countries, the improvement of gender equality has been one of the primary objectives of parental leave policy. Supporting working motherhood and emphasising caring fatherhood are the two sides of this endeavour (Ellingsæter and Leira, 2006). In recent decades, Finnish leave policy has also thus aimed to achieve a more equal sharing of parental leave by encouraging fathers to take more leave.

Despite this longstanding goal and policy redesign, Finnish fathers' take-up of parental leave has increased slowly compared to the other Nordic countries (see Chapters Six, Thirteen, Fifteen and Sixteen, this volume). In 2012, Finnish fathers took only 9 per cent of all parental benefit days. In this chapter, the focus is on the obstacles to a more equal sharing of parental leave in Finland: why do more fathers not take more parental leave?

The obstacles to more active leave take-up among fathers have generally been located as family finances, pressures of work and the tradition of a gendered division of labour (see Brandth and Kvande, 2006, 2012; see also Chapters One and Six, this volume). This chapter deals with these dimensions, but the main focus is on the policy process, on its role in the construction of leave schemes, and in the framing of fathers' use of parental leave. In Finland, leave policy development is part of a special working life policy design in which labour market partners have played a significant role over the past 40 years (Lammi-Taskula and Takala, 2009; Alaja, 2011). Central employer and employee organisations are involved in decisions concerning incomes and social benefits as well as working hours and work–family reconciliation. The state has often taken the initiative, but the actual negotiations have taken place in tripartite groups consisting of central employer and employee organisations and the government. Practically no parental leave legislation has been introduced without a unanimous decision in these tripartite negotiations.

In this chapter, the development of fathers' leave take-up is analysed as an issue of choice and change. The analysis is based on a combination of policy evaluation and survey data. The theoretical framing is in everyday life analysis, which interweaves the levels forming the context of fathers' choices to take or not take parental leave: the policy process which defines the available options; the different layers of everyday practices in the workplace and in the family together with the individual motivations constructed in these practices; and last, but not least, the understandings of gender constructed and reconstructed in the ongoing and changing practices. The everyday life approach makes it possible to combine an analysis of the social structures and processes – the tripartite policy process and policy goals behind the development of the parental leave scheme – and the individual practices among fathers.

After a short description of data and methods, the chapter begins with a description of the leave options available to Finnish fathers and how they exercise them. The theoretical framework of everyday life is then presented, followed by a description of the policy goals expressed in government documents, and how these have changed over the past 15-20 years. The special role of the policy process is then analysed, highlighting the influence of the tripartite negotiation system on leave policy. This is followed by a brief history of how the varying policy goals have been taken into account in the policy process, and how this has affected the policy measures taken to encourage fathers to take more leave. The chapter then illustrates the individual motivations and cultural perceptions among fathers using an analysis of the reasons they indicate for taking or not taking parental leave. In this context, the role of working life trends and attitudes in the workplace as obstacles to fathers taking leave is considered. Finally, the question as to why the current parental leave policy has not reached its objective of more fathers taking leave is discussed, examining the interplay between the different levels of obstacles.

The chapter concludes that the obstacles preventing fathers from taking parental leave and the reasons for their choices are to be found not only in gendered conceptions of the division of labour between women and men reflected at the individual level, but also in the structuring of leave schemes, which has failed to actualise the goal of improved gender equality. An important explanation for this is the Finnish tripartite policymaking process, whereby the schemes are developed as compromises between the negotiating parties.

Data and methods

In the chapter, qualitative and quantitative methods are applied. The policy analysis is based on an evaluation of government policy documents on parental leave from 1995 to 2011, originally reported in Lammi-Taskula et al (2009), and further text analysis.

The analysis of how parents take leave and the reasons given for sharing or not sharing the leave is based on Social Insurance Institution statistics and survey data from the authors' study on family leave and gender equality in working life. In the survey conducted in 2006, 1,058 fathers and 1,435 mothers of two-year-old children reported on their leave practices (Salmi et al, 2009). The fathers and mothers were selected from the Social Insurance Institution's register of leave benefit recipients. Every 20th mother was selected in the sample of mothers, the response rate being 48 per cent. The sample of fathers was a random sample including a quarter of the recipients of parental benefit and 3 per cent of recipients of paternity benefit; the response rate of fathers was 36 per cent. Both samples were weighted in order to be representative of the population. A problem with the data is that as the respondents are selected among leave benefit recipients, the data does not cover fathers who do not take any leave at all. Information on these fathers relies on mothers' reports.

Finnish fathers' leave options and take-up of leave

For a 10-year period until a change in the leave scheme in 2013, Finnish fathers were entitled to three types of leave. *Paternity leave*, usually taken immediately after the birth, was at most three weeks, and used while the mother is also on leave. The 26-week *parental leave*, starting after the mother completes her 18-week maternity leave, can be shared between the parents as they wish. Since 2003, if the father took the last two weeks of parental leave, he was entitled to an extra two-week bonus, lengthened to four weeks in 2010. This *bonus leave*[1] must be used within six months of the end of the parental leave period. Thus, the total length of maternity, paternity and parental leave was 44 weeks, with an additional four weeks of bonus leave for the father if he opted for the two last weeks of parental leave.[2] In other words, the transferable parental leave has constituted the main part of all forms of leave available to parents. However, the father's eligibility for any leave depends on whether he lives together with the child's mother. Moreover, as discussed later, the right to the father's bonus leave was, until 2013, contingent on the mother's consent.

During paternity, maternity and parental leave, the parent is entitled to an earnings-related benefit, on average 70 per cent of the previous income; there is no ceiling on the benefit level. For most employed mothers, collective agreements guarantee full pay for maternity leave, whereas full pay is guaranteed for one paternity leave week for 60 per cent of all fathers working in the private sector, and for all fathers working in the state sector. Parents without employment receive a minimum, flat-rate allowance (for further details, see Salmi and Lammi-Taskula, 2012).

Fathers' take-up of the different types of leave varies. The development of the leave take-up shows that changes in the gendered division of labour have taken place, but that this process has been quite slow. The oldest form of leave, paternity leave (since 1978), was primarily used in the past by well-educated men (Säntti, 1993), but is now taken irrespective of the parents' socio-economic backgrounds (Salmi et al, 2009). Taking paternity leave has thus changed from being an exceptional practice of 14 per cent of all fathers in 1978 to an 'everyman's mass movement' (Lammi-Taskula, 2007, p 70), including 84 per cent of all fathers in 2012.

Transferable parental leave has been available since 1980, but the proportion of fathers taking this leave has remained stable since 1995. Only 2-3 per cent of all fathers share the transferable parental leave with the mother by taking more leave than the father's bonus leave. Mothers take most of the transferable parental leave, and almost all the mothers take the leave.

The most recent addition to the leave schemes, the father's bonus leave, increased in popularity, with an increase in take-up from 4 per cent of fathers in 2003 to 32 per cent in 2012. The take-up of the bonus leave reveals a similar pattern as the paternity leave in the first decades: well-educated men with well-educated spouses have been more likely to take the bonus leave (Salmi et al, 2009).

Theoretical approach: everyday life connects policies, practices and change

Although in place for a number of years, the parental leave scheme in Finland has thus not resulted in a major transformation in how Finnish fathers take leave. Why is this so? The everyday life theoretical framework is applied here to understand how individual practices and social structures and processes interrelate and create or hinder opportunities for how fathers take leave.

Everyday life is understood here as a process whereby people transform the societal conditions of their lives into lived everyday life (Bech Jørgensen, 1988). Fathers are seen as actors whose choices are contextualised by multilayered factors: the policy measures made available to them and hence the policy process producing the measures; the demands of working life and the gendered understandings of parenthood in the workplace; and the fathers' individual motivation constructions in this multidimensional context together with negotiations between the spouses. All of these factors are situated in the social, cultural and ideological environment constructed by the deep-rooted traditions of a gendered division of labour, with the practices of care work being a core issue.

When defined as a process, everyday life is not understood as a separate individual life sphere as opposed to, for example, social structures, or an object to be defined or studied as such (Smith, 1988). Everyday life is constructed in a continuous movement between actors and structures. The decisions made by authorities and organisations at the structural level first reveal their actual meaning and consequences in the everyday practices of individuals. Likewise, problems between people's aspirations and structural conditions are revealed in everyday life. Hence, the everyday life perspective has a dual function: it analyses daily practices while also seeking to identify the formative role of social structures (Bech Jørgensen, 1988). Everyday life intermediates between individual practices and social structures and processes (Dahlström, 1987). For the policy process, a key issue is how adequately its actors are able and willing to recognise people's aspirations and to formulate policy measures to make room for them, and to acknowledge the consequences of the measures taken. Obviously, whose aspirations find a voice in the policy process is an issue of power. This chapter analyses how the structural conditions, for example, the leave schemes, are actualised in fathers' practices, and how the schemes acquire their form, that is, the policy process.

How does change come about – as in change in the division of labour between women and men? In their everyday practices, actors constantly make choices, which can be more or less significant and reflected. By these choices people create both continuity and change. Bech Jørgensen (1988) has developed the concept of 'self-evidences' to analyse how continuity and change can result from one and the same process of choice. 'Self-evidences' refer to symbolic orders in which everyday actions are culturally constructed as norms and traditions, for example, norms related to whether or not fathers should take parental leave and for how long. A small part of the self-evident is conscious and reflected, but most of the self-evident is produced unconsciously as people make choices towards the given and familiar options. But the non-self-evident is constantly present in the everyday situations as a possibility for choosing something other than the familiar. These new choices gradually connect with the self-evident, generating small cracks and shifts. A chain of such cracks can bring about a rupture. Thus, the choice between the self-evident and the non-self-evident forms a basis for both continuity and change.

Everyday life, care work and gender

Defining everyday life as processual movements between structures and actors relates to the idea of gendered and gendering practices (Acker, 1990; Rantalaiho and Heiskanen, 1997). Gender shapes the scope for action thought 'possible' or 'suitable' for men and women, as practices gradually produce and reproduce certain orders and differences between men and women, which come to be taken as unreflected self-evidences. Much active doing is involved in producing gender in everyday life; in organising one's activities according to what is understood as appropriate for one's sex category (West and Zimmerman, 2002). At the same time, choices made in everyday processes can also produce ruptures and changes in the conditions and ways of being women and men, and thus also in conceptions of gender.

Practices related to taking parental leave are closely connected to understandings of care work and its gendered character. Western philosophy has a long tradition of defining the physical care and maintenance of people as a dull routine in the sphere of everyday life, where people are not regarded as consciously reflecting actors (Salmi, 1997). This line of thought divides people's activities into two hierarchical areas: the sphere of the everyday particularity and the sphere of universal activities (Heller, 1984). Reasons for this hierarchisation can be found precisely in the division of labour between women and men (Smith, 1988). It leads to different ways of thinking, where men devote themselves to abstract thinking and women's everyday care work remains invisible to men. In this tradition, care work is devalued and belongs to women.

The division of labour between women and men – and parental leave take-up as a concretion of it – offers a good example of continuity and change in gendered practices and understandings of gender, as well as of the interaction between social structures and everyday practices and the power relations within them (see also Chapter Eight, this volume). Finnish women have been in the labour market since the 1920s (Salmi, 1996), and already in the 1950s half of all married women were employed (Keinänen, 1994). The division of labour in the home was much slower to change due to persistent cultural conceptions of the gendered character and value of care work (see Hobson and Morgan, 2002; see also Chapter Five, this volume).

However, what is considered 'natural', 'suitable' and 'possible' for women and men to do as regards childcare has changed considerably in the Nordic countries over the past 50 years. The power relations in families, based on these cultural conceptions as well as on women and men's positions and opportunities in the labour market, reflect on how care work is divided, and parental leave negotiated and shared between spouses (see also Morgan, 2002; Närvi, 2012). For their part, policy processes depend on power relations in the labour market; thus, policy processes and changes in the labour market have created both opportunities, demands and obstacles to changes in the gendered division of care. But gradual changes in women and men's practices and attitudes have also reflected in the development at the institutional level, even if this interaction is complex.

Goals of Finnish parental leave policy: gender equality or 'free choice'

To follow the development of Finnish leave policy at the institutional level it is necessary to know the expressed policy goals and how these have changed over time. The goals of Finnish leave policy have their roots in maternity protection. Maternity leave was introduced in 1964 to give the mother an opportunity to prepare for and recover from delivering her baby and to care for the newborn. After an active debate on gender equality in the 1960s and 1970s, several proposals from the parliamentary Council for Gender Equality and negotiations in tripartite groups, the leave schemes were developed to include paternity leave in 1978 and parental leave in 1980 (Lammi-Taskula and Takala, 2009). The goal of these schemes was to develop the father–child relationship and to give both parents an opportunity to care for a young child (Säntti, 1993; Vanhempainvapaatyöryhmän muistio, 2011).

For the past two decades, the promotion of gender equality has been the primary goal of leave policy in government documents. In the general societal debate, getting fathers to take more parental leave has been seen as necessary for improving gender equality from several perspectives. The leave is assumed to give the father an opportunity to create a relationship with his child, as well as to learn the practical chores related to childcare. More fathers taking more parental leave is also seen as one way to improve women's inferior position in the labour market (Salmi and Lammi-Taskula, 1999; see also Chapter Thirteen, this volume). Moreover, as the (male) chair of the parliamentary Council for Gender Equality puts it, 'if a man does not take parental leave, he leaves the power of decision as regards children and the home to his spouse' (Pennonen, 2012). This may backfire on the father if the parents break up and relations with the children must be rearranged (see also Chapter Twelve, this volume).

Flexibility entered the policy rationales at the beginning of 1990s with an explicit connection to fathers: the opportunity to take the short paternity leave in several spells was expected to motivate more fathers to take leave. Since then, flexibility has been one of the aims of leave reforms (Vanhempainvapaatyöryhmän muistio, 2011), and is closely connected with another, more recent, rationale: 'free choice'.

In Finland, the 'free choice of families' has been an argument in the debate on childcare policy (homecare versus daycare services) since the 1970s, but has gained a more pronounced position in connection with the leave options for fathers in the 1990s and 2000s (Salmi, 2006; Hiilamo and Kangas, 2009; Rantalaiho, 2010; Repo, 2010; Varjonen, 2011). The opposing ends of the argument are proposals of an individual father's quota – a non-transferable 'use-it-or-lose-it' entitlement not contingent on the mother's consent – as opposed to a policy of transferable parental leave where the parents make a 'free choice' regarding who takes the leave and for how long.

Actual policy measures have increasingly been based on the 'free choice' rationale. Accordingly, the leave scheme contains a long parental leave period, which the parents can share as they wish, but which in practice is taken almost exclusively by mothers. Thus, tension has developed between the 'free choice' rationale and the goal to promote gender equality. The seemingly gender-neutral transferable parental leave ignores that the supposed 'free choice' takes place in the context of the long history of the gendered division of labour which maintains an interpretation, both in families and in workplaces, of parental leave as the mother's domain (see Brandth and Kvande, 2012; see also Chapter Seven, this volume).

The negotiation system and governance of leave policy

Understanding the character of the Finnish leave schemes and the many but short steps towards fathers' individual leave entitlements requires some familiarity with the tripartite negotiation system through which the leave policy is developed.

The history of the tripartite decision making, with the central employer and employee organisations together with government representatives preparing proposals on leave policy, dates back to the beginning of the 1970s when the nationwide agreement on incomes policy included an agreement to lengthen maternity leave (Hiilamo, 2002). Paternity leave and parental leave were also introduced in tripartite incomes policy agreements in the 1970s (Hiilamo, 2002; Lammi-Taskula and Takala, 2009).

This tripartite negotiation system means that the interests of the central labour market organisations play an important role in the development of the leave schemes, and reforms are made only based on compromises, which these parties can reach. The tripartite groups are corporatist organs, and political interests and goals may come to play a minor role. As the decisions are compromises, development towards practical measures has been slow. Moreover, the compromises have led to complicated schemes, which are difficult to figure out (Lammi-Taskula et al, 2009).

The goal of promoting gender equality through a more equal sharing of parental leave is expressed in government documents, but it is not necessarily a prominent goal for the other two parties in the tripartite negotiations. The employer organisations want to avoid adding to any kind of absences from the workplace, so neither a longer leave period nor more parents on parental leave are in their interests. In their view, inequalities of women's position in the labour market related to few fathers taking leave do not give reason for a redesign of the leave schemes. In the employee organisations, opinions are divided (Lammi-Taskula and Takala, 2009). SAK, the industrial workers' organisation, has until recently been against long earmarked quotas for fathers, as they anticipate many blue-collar fathers would not use them, and hence the families would lose that period of leave; they see this as an equality problem, promoting transferable quotas instead. Academic and white-collar employees' organisations Akava and STTK, with many female members, stress the importance of promoting gender equality and propose longer, earmarked leave quotas for fathers (Vanhempainvapaatyöryhmän muistio, 2011).

Another challenge in the tripartite negotiation system is that the voice of the third party, the government, is constructed in a complicated manner not necessarily free of the opinions of the other two negotiating parties. The governance of leave policies is located in two ministries because the leave legislation is part of health insurance legislation as regards the benefits and part of employment contract legislation as regards leave entitlements. The ministry officials involved in the tripartite negotiations may have varying degrees of interest in and varying views on the leave issues. Basically, government programmes set the policy goals. But the policy definitions of government programmes are prepared in negotiations in which the central labour market organisations play an important role in the background lobby groups. Moreover, some political parties do not have an explicit leave policy of their own, relying instead on the policy definitions of the central labour market organisations. Thus, it is possible that the government representatives of the tripartite negotiations on leave issues do not have a clear stand of their own on which to build the compromises. Furthermore, the tripartite negotiation system leaves little room for the voice of different groups of citizens and non-governmental organisations (NGOs) or research to influence the policy process.

Gender equality and 'free choice' in the policy process: individual quotas or transferable leave

The role of the tripartite negotiations and the contradictory bearing of the two rationales, gender equality and 'free choice', present themselves in the recent history of the parental leave development. As the tripartite negotiations play a decisive role in the policy development, and as the opinions of the central labour market organisations regarding gender equality are divided, real steps towards improved gender equality in the sharing of parental leave have been short and slow (see also Lammi-Taskula and Takala, 2009).

Proposals of extended entitlements to fathers in 1999

The path towards the father's quota is a good example of this divided interest. In 1999, the Committee on Fatherhood, appointed by the Ministry of Social Affairs and Health, declared that 'the father has his own independent status as an equal and important parent for his child' (Committee on Fatherhood, 1999, p 1). To create the preconditions for the independent care responsibility of the father, the Committee proposed a father's quota to be introduced in the leave schemes, thus taking up a proposal made in 1989 by the Council of Gender Equality and initiatives made in Parliament during the 1990s (Lammi-Taskula and Takala, 2009). Having the position of the father in society in general on its agenda, the Committee was not a traditional tripartite group but was composed of broad expertise from research, administration and NGOs, and it only consulted central labour market organisations. Hence, it had a wider and more radical approach to leave policy. It proposed lengthening the parental leave by one month, which was to be earmarked as a quota for the father. The 1–3 weeks of paternity leave would remain intact, and both forms of leave could be used until the child turned three (Committee on Fatherhood, 1999).

The government that came to power in 1999 (Social Democrats, Conservatives, Swedish People's Party, Left Alliance and Greens) took up the challenge and wanted to review the possibilities to guarantee the father an individual one month's father's quota. In 2001, however, after considerable disagreement, a tripartite group instead proposed lengthening paternity leave to 25 working days (Lammi-Taskula and Takala, 2009). The fathers could take this leave either while the mother was on her maternity and parental leave, or immediately after the parental leave period ended. Thus, the proposal did not meet the original objective of providing an individual period of leave to the father, which was believed to serve the cause of gender equality. Instead, the justification was found in the flexibility rationale: the proposal was argued to give more flexibility to families to set the leave periods according to their needs.

The criticism of the tripartite group's proposal pointed out that it neither promoted the equal sharing of parental leave nor the right of fathers to participate in childcare. This critique brought together the Finnish Confederation of Professionals STTK from the employee side and the employer organisation representing the service sector, both suggesting a new 'bonus leave' model: the father would gain two extra, non-transferable weeks of leave if he at least took the two last weeks of the transferable parental leave.

Introduction of the Finnish father's bonus leave in 2002

The government took the initiative in 2002 by including the father's bonus leave model in its proposal for 'a family leave package' with several minor reforms prepared in the tripartite group (Varjonen, 2011). The goal was to make work–family reconciliation more flexible according to the needs of families, and to encourage parents to use family leave in a more equal fashion. Parliament passed the bill and the new 'bonus leave' came into effect in 2003.

The Finnish version of a father's quota – the father's bonus leave – was finally in place. The two bonus weeks were a non-transferable leave quota for fathers, but at the same time, the quota required the mother's consent for the father to take the last two weeks of parental leave. Thus, the father's bonus leave was a mix of new and old ideas: the new idea of independent father care and the old idea of the mother as the main caregiver.

However, the new bonus leave soon received criticism from a rapporteur nominated by the Ministry of Social Affairs and Health as well as from another tripartite working group appointed by the Ministry of Labour. The main object of their criticism was the inflexibility: the bonus weeks had to be taken immediately after the end of parental leave. This was thought to hinder fathers from taking the bonus leave in families where the mother planned to take child homecare leave after parental leave, as most mothers do. Survey findings from 2006 (Salmi et al, 2009) confirmed that this obstacle materialised in almost half of all families. Moreover, in the families in which the father did take the bonus leave, the lack of flexibility led to more than half of the mothers staying at home while the father was on leave. Due to the scheme design, the bonus leave did not achieve its aim of creating a period of independent childcare for the father. While flexibility was a popular rationale for leave reforms, it was not offered in this case when it would have been required to promote independent leave for fathers.

Revisions of the scheme 2007–13

A new tripartite working group was set up to draft the necessary reform to the scheme in 2005. But the compromise reached by the group provided limited flexibility, given that the average mother stayed on child homecare leave until the child turned two (Salmi et al, 2009): since 2007, the father's bonus leave could be taken within six months of the end of parental leave. Furthermore, the new government (Centre Party, Conservatives, Greens and Swedish People's Party) that came to power in 2007 decided to add two more weeks to the bonus leave as of 2010.

As the problems related to parental leave had not been solved, the new government also aimed to review the possibility of a more thorough reform of the parental leave schemes. A working group was appointed for the task in 2009, consisting this time not only of representatives from the central labour market organisations and the government, but also from family, child and youth NGOs and research. The working group members had varying views regarding the necessity of the reform, but there was agreement that the leave period with earnings-related benefits should be lengthened by extending the father's share. In its report from February 2011, however, the group did not reach agreement on any one model to redesign the leave schemes (for details, see Salmi, 2012).

The next government, which came to power in June 2011 (Conservatives, Social Democrats, Greens, Left Alliance, Swedish People's Party and Christian Democrats), did not take a stand on any of the proposals made by the parental leave working group. In its programme, the government wanted to increase the leave earmarked for fathers, but delegated the issue to be drafted in a tripartite working group. In the autumn of 2011, a frame agreement between the central employer and employee organisations and the government was drawn up on incomes policy and certain social policy schemes. It was agreed that from the beginning of 2013, the connection of the father's bonus leave to his taking the two last weeks of the transferable parental leave was to be dissolved. Since then, the father has an individual right to nine weeks of paternity leave (this term now covers all of the leave days earmarked to fathers), three weeks of which can be taken during the mother's maternity or parental leave. The reform also increased flexibility, as fathers are free to use their leave until the child turns two.

As of 2013, the Finnish father's quota is thus a true quota about which the father makes his own decision without requiring the mother's consent. However, the number of leave days for the fathers remained the same. Moreover, compared with the previous entitlements, the transferable parental leave is two weeks longer if the father uses his individual leave. Once again, the reform has both traits of efforts to promote independent fatherhood and traits of the predominance of the 'free choice' rationale with stress on transferable leave.

Fathers' individual motivations

As argued earlier in the theoretical approach, the realisation of the gender equality goal – or any change in people's practices – takes place in the interaction between structural conditions and individual action. Thus, the choice to be made by fathers as to whether or not to take leave is affected not only by the type of schemes determined in the policy process, but also by their varying individual motivations. Based on the 2006 survey data (Salmi et al, 2009), the reasons Finnish fathers indicate for taking or not taking parental leave are now analysed.

One of the structural characteristics framing the decisions made by fathers to take parental leave is the issue of 'free choice' and its emphasis on transferable leave. An underlying assumption in the 'free choice' rhetoric appears to be that the choices to share leave are based on rational arguments, which are weighed against each other. However, the survey findings applied in this chapter show that parental leave sharing is not necessarily discussed between the spouses at all. Discussion is even less common if the leave is not shared. Two thirds of the fathers discussed the issue with their spouses if the leave was shared, and less than a third if the leave was not shared (Salmi et al, 2009).

There are also situations in which the issue of leave sharing might not seem relevant for the spouses to discuss. On top of the obstacle caused by the inflexibility of the scheme discussed earlier, many families (20 per cent) were not even aware of the father's bonus leave option. Moreover, almost 10 per cent of the fathers could not take advantage of the bonus leave, as they were not employed.

The role of the family economy

One common explanation in the public discourse for fathers not taking parental leave is related to family finances. As men tend to have higher wages than women, it is often taken for granted that families cannot afford the father taking parental leave. This explanation did not prove to be very strong among the survey respondents, however, as only one in four families mentioned this.

Moreover, only one in three families had actually made calculations regarding the financial consequences of the father's leave. Calculations were made more often (50 per cent) if the leave was shared (Salmi et al, 2009). So it seems as though making the calculations convinced the spouses of the limited financial consequences of the father taking parental leave.

Perceptions of the division of labour between women and men

One of the reasons for the lack of discussion of leave sharing between the spouses might be that the traditional gender ideology remains strong. In families where the parental leave was not shared, almost half of the fathers and 30 per cent of the mothers considered men to be primarily responsible for the family's livelihood. Only an ample fourth of the fathers and one in ten mothers who shared the leave thought so (Salmi et al, 2009).

Views on the division of labour between women and men turned out to play a crucial role when parents make decisions on sharing the parental leave. When education level, spouse's education level, income level, employer sector and occupational group of fathers were taken into account, only the age of the father and his view on men as the main provider for the family predicted his take-up of parental leave. Fathers who think that men are mainly responsible for the family finances were less likely to take parental leave than other men (Salmi et al, 2009).

Pressures from work

Like family finances, job-related pressures are often assumed to contribute to the low motivation among fathers to take leave. Pressures from work may be of several kinds. First, the attitudes of superiors and colleagues may be so critical that they prevent the father from taking up the issue altogether. Second, the workload may be so massive or schedules so tight that either the father himself or his superior thinks it impossible to take leave. Third, fathers may suspect that taking family-related leave might have negative consequences for their professional skills or future career opportunities.

According to reports from Finnish fathers in 2006, attitudes in the workplace towards fathers taking parental leave are predominantly positive, even if superiors and colleagues make more negative comments about taking parental leave than paternity leave (Salmi et al, 2009). This survey did not cover fathers who had not taken any leave, however, so it does not provide information on how often negative responses in the workplace stop fathers from taking leave at all. Negative workplace attitudes are traced in some studies (Takala, 2005), and especially in qualitative interviews (Brandth and Kvande, 2012; Närvi, 2014; see also Chapter Seven, this volume).

Like financial reasons, pressures from work may include both real and supposed obstacles. Fathers who had taken parental leave were less likely (33 per cent) to consider it difficult to be away from work than fathers who had not taken leave (50 per cent). However, this experience was more common among leave-taking fathers in 2006 than in a similar survey from 2001 (Salmi et al, 2009). Assessing the absence to be a problem was unrelated to the father's occupational group, income level or employer sector.

Another kind of pressure from work may be an assessment that taking parental leave can be detrimental to professional skills or future career opportunities (Plantenga and Vlasblom, 2009). However, as fathers have taken quite short periods of parental leave in Finland – 29 days on average in the year of the survey – few Finnish fathers reported any such problems. The vast majority (84 per cent) of the fathers who had taken parental leave reported that the leave had no effect on their professional skills or any consequences for their position or future career opportunities (80 per cent) (Salmi et al, 2009).

Even if the fathers in the 2006 survey did not often refer to pressures from work as an obstacle for taking parental leave, work pressures may be a problem regarding longer periods of leave taken by fathers and the future development of leave take-up among fathers. Working life pressures have recently grown stronger as regards tight schedules and workplaces with undersized personnel (Lehto and Sutela, 2009). Together with increasing job insecurity, this development tends to be on the rise in the globalising economy, and will possibly lead to working life practices playing a more significant role as an obstacle to fathers taking leave.

Conclusion: 'free choice' and elusive gender equality

When examining the goals of Finnish leave policies in the light of the results that have been achieved, the conclusions are not very optimistic. Gender equality in leave take-up has progressed slowly, fathers still only take a small proportion of parental leave days, and the problem of the discrimination of women in the labour market because of their leave use remains acute (Lammi–Taskula et al, 2009).

This chapter has analysed the complexity of the reasons for the slow increase in Finnish fathers' leave take-up, aiming at recognising the multilayered character of the obstacles and their interplay. The analysis proves that the policy process, with its tripartite negotiation system, plays a considerable role in what kind of leave opportunities fathers have and how they actualise these opportunities, and why the changes have been so slow.

At the policy level, the goals – gender equality, 'free choice' and flexibility – are contradictory as such, but the contradiction has not been seen or acknowledged. Even if gender equality is declared to be the primary goal, leave schemes have been developed which do not realise this goal, the reason being that the schemes are formed in a policy process where the main interests of the parties involved are not necessarily the promotion of gender equality. The data presented on leave take-up shows that leave schemes based on the 'free choice' rationale, like the Finnish parental leave, do not contribute to the policy goal of improved gender equality, as they lead to fathers only taking the earmarked leave periods and mothers 'freely choosing' the transferable parental leave. Rather, the 'free choice' rationale reproduces the traditional gendered division of labour where mothers are seen as the primary caregivers.

It seems as though the 'free choice' rationale has walked over the goal to promote gender equality, even if this goal is repeated in every policy programme, and the main focus in the programmes has been to encourage more fathers to take more leave. Thus, one is tempted to ask whether the actual gender perception demonstrated in Finnish leave policy relies on the traditional division of labour between women and men, and whether gender equality is considered to be at a satisfactory level when fathers' share of parental leave take-up is small and grows only slowly.[3]

At the individual level, there has been a strong assumption in the public discourse that the family finances are the main obstacle for fathers' leave take-up. According to our findings, family finances are not such a major obstacle, and couples rarely make calculations regarding the financial consequences of the father taking leave. Instead, the findings indicate that attitudes towards the gendered division of labour are crucial. The main predictor of a father opting not to take parental leave is his view on men as the main breadwinners.

The impact of the structure of the leave scheme therefore becomes all the more important, and thus, in the Finnish case, the character of the policy process. If the policy process produces schemes in which the transferable leave period, in the name of 'free choice', plays the main role and the father's quota is quite short, the share of parental leave taken by fathers tends to remain small. Change in the actual take-up of parental leave is not possible if the scheme design does not support fathers' choices.

The impact of attitudes in the workplace on the choices made by fathers is difficult to find out using our data. However, the assessment that it is difficult to be away from work has grown more common among leave-sharing fathers in recent years. Qualitative research indicates that workplace attitudes are important, and recent working life developments and the prolonged financial crisis possibly accentuate this problem. Hence, it is all the more important that the structure of the leave scheme supports more active leave take-up among fathers to help develop the understanding of men as fathers in the workplace.

The Finnish leave policy and its realisation elucidate the interaction of structural conditions and the choices actors make in their everyday practices. The current leave scheme (with a long transferable period of parental leave and a short father's quota) and the decision-making process (with no clear room for political goals and debate) support mothers' and fathers' (more or less unconscious) choices towards the 'self-evident', that is, choices in line with the traditional gendered division of labour. For its part, a long quota for fathers would turn thoughts towards the non-self-evident, where the father is encouraged to ponder his significance as a parent and make an independent decision about whether or not to take leave. Through the father's quota, society would make its stand clear, expressed in several government programmes, that childcare concerns both men and women, and with this policy measure, support fathers in their choice towards the non-self-evident, and thus towards a change in the gendered understanding of care.

Notes

[1] The bonus leave was a non-transferable entitlement based on a 'use-it-or-lose-it' principle. Thus it had elements identical with the father's quota arrangements in the other Nordic countries (see Chapters Thirteen, Fifteen and Sixteen, this volume). However, it was not an individual right. Therefore, this entitlement is not called a father's quota but the term 'bonus leave' is applied, although this leave was called 'father's month' in the Finnish legislation.

[2] The Finnish leave system includes yet another entitlement, which falls beyond the present analysis. Parental leave ends when the child is 9-10 months old. At this stage, the child is entitled to daycare services, or either parent can take child homecare leave supported by a flat-rate homecare allowance until the child turns three. Almost all families (88 per cent) take advantage of the homecare allowance after parental leave for some period of time; in 97 per cent of these families, the parent taking care of the child is the mother (Salmi and Lammi-Taskula, 2012).

[3] In autumn 2013 the government decided that the homecare allowance period would be split evenly between mothers and fathers. Thus, the government took a major step away from the 'free choice' rationale by introducing a one-year father's quota to the homecare allowance. However, fathers hardly use their homecare allowance quota as the flat rate allowance is very low. In practice, this decision is a way to shorten the homecare allowance period by one year in order to raise the employment rate of mothers. No corresponding

motion to lengthen the paternity leave with an earnings-related benefit has been made.

References

Acker, J. (1990) 'Hierarchies, jobs, bodies: a theory of gendered organizations', *Gender & Society*, vol 4, no 2, pp 139-58.

Alaja, A. (2011) 'Tripartite political exchange and the Finnish social model', in V.-P. Sorsa (ed) *Rethinking social risks in the Nordics*, Jyväskylä: Foundation for European Progressive Studies, pp 147-66.

Bech Jørgensen, B. (1988) '"Hvorfor gør de ikke noget?" Skitse til teori om hverdagslivskræfterne og selvfølgelighedens symbolske orden' ['"Why don't they do anything?" A sketch to a theory of everyday life forces and the symbolic order of the self-evident'], in C. Bloch, L. Højgaard, B. Bech Jørgensen and B. Nautrup (eds) *Hverdagsliv, kultur og subjektivitet* [*Everyday life, culture and subjectivity*], Copenhagen: Akademisk forlag, pp 68-121.

Brandth, B. and Kvande, E. (2006) 'Care politics for fathers in a flexible time culture', in D. Perrons, C. Fagan, L. McDowell, K. Ray and K. Ward (eds) *Gender divisions and working time in the new economy: Public policy and changing patterns of work in Europe and North America*, Cheltenham: Edward Elgar Publishing, pp 148-61.

Brandth, B. and Kvande, E. (2012) 'Free choice or gentle force', in A.T. Kjørholt and J. Qvortrup (eds) *The modern child and the flexible labour market*, Houndmills: Palgrave Macmillan, pp 56-70.

Committee on Fatherhood (1999) *In search of a new kind of fatherhood*, Committee Report 1999, vol 1, Helsinki: Ministry of Social Affairs and Health.

Dahlström, E. (1987) 'Everyday-life theories and their historical and ideological contexts', in U. Himmelstrand (ed) *The multiparadigmatic trend in sociology*, Stockholm: Almqvist and Wiksell, pp 93-114.

Ellingsæter, A.L. and Leira, A. (2006) 'Introduction: politicising parenthood in Scandinavia', in A.L. Ellingsæter and A. Leira (eds) *Politicising parenthood in Scandinavia: Gender relations in welfare states*, Bristol: Policy Press, pp 1-18.

Heller, A. (1984) *Everyday life*, New York: Routledge.

Hiilamo, H. (2002) *The rise and fall of Nordic family policy? Historical development and changes during the 1990s in Sweden and Finland*, Research Report 125, Helsinki: Stakes.

Hiilamo, H. and Kangas, O. (2009) 'Trap for women or freedom to choose? The struggle over cash for childcare schemes in Finland and Sweden', *Journal of Social Policy*, vol 38, no 3, pp 457-75.

Hobson, B. and Morgan, D. (2002) 'Introduction', in B. Hobson (eds) *Making men into fathers*, Cambridge: Cambridge University Press, pp 1-21.

Keinänen, P. (1994) 'Perheet työelämässä' ['Families in working life'], in *Suomalainen perhe [Finnish family]*, Helsinki: Tilastokeskus, pp 10-28.

Lammi-Taskula, J. (2007) *Parental leave for fathers? Gendered conceptions and practices in families with young children in Finland*, Research Report 166, Helsinki: Stakes.

Lammi-Taskula, J. and Takala, P. (2009) 'Finland: negotiating tripartite compromises', in S.B. Kamerman and P. Moss (eds) *The politics of parental leave policies*, Bristol: Policy Press, pp 87-102.

Lammi-Taskula, J., Salmi, M. and Parrukoski, S. (2009) *Työ, perhe ja tasa-arvo [Work, family and gender equality]*, Selvityksiä 2009: 55, Helsinki: Sosiaali- ja terveysministeriö.

Lehto, A.-M. and Sutela, H. (2009) *Three decades of working conditions: Findings of Finnish quality of work life surveys 1977-2008*, Helsinki: Statistics Finland.

Morgan, D. (2002) 'Epilogue', in B. Hobson (eds) *Making men into fathers*, Cambridge: Cambridge University Press, pp 273-86.

Närvi, J. (2012) 'Negotiating care and career within institutional constraints: work insecurity and gendered ideals of parenthood in Finland', *Community, Work and Family*, vol 15, no 4, pp 451-70.

Närvi, J. (2014) *Määräaikainen työ, vakituinen vanhemmuus – sukupuolistuneet työurat, perheellistyminen ja vanhempien hoivaratkaisut [Temporary work, permanent parenthood – gendered careers, family formation and parents' care decisions]*, Helsinki: Terveyden ja hyvinvoinnin laitos.

Pennonen, A. (2012) 'Miehiä meidän makuun' ['Men of our taste'], An interview with the chair of the Council for Gender Equality, *Anna*, 10/2012.

Plantenga, J. and Vlasblom, J.-D. (2009) 'The economics of leave: Theoretical considerations and empirical evidence', Presentation in the 6th International Leave Policies and Research Seminar, Prague, 10-11 September (www.leavenetwork.org).

Rantalaiho, L. and Heiskanen, T. (eds) (1997) *Gendered practices in working life*, London: Macmillan.

Rantalaiho, M. (2010) 'Rationalities of cash-for-childcare: the Nordic case', in J. Sipilä, K. Repo and T. Rissanen (eds) *Cash-for-childcare: The consequences for caring mothers*, Cheltenham: Edward Elgar Publishing, pp 109-42.

Repo, K. (2010) 'Finnish child homecare allowance – users' perspectives and perceptions', in J. Sipilä, K. Repo and T. Rissanen (eds) *Cash-for-childcare: The consequences for caring mothers*, Cheltenham: Edward Elgar Publishing, pp 46-64.

Salmi, M. (1996) 'Finland is another world: the gendered time of homework', in E. Boris and E. Prügl (eds) *Homeworkers in global perspective*, New York: Routledge, pp 143-66.

Salmi, M. (1997) 'Home-based work, gender and everyday life', in E. Gunnarsson and U. Huws (eds) *Virtually free? Gender, work and spatial choice*, Stockholm: Nutek, pp 131-50.

Salmi, M. (2006) 'Parental choice and the passion for equality in Finland', in A.L. Ellingsæter and A. Leira (eds) *Politicising parenthood in Scandinavia: Gender relations in welfare states*, Bristol: Policy Press, pp 145-68.

Salmi, M. (2012) 'Leave policies development in Finland', in S. Parrukoski and J. Lammi-Taskula (eds) *Parental leave policies and the economic crisis in the Nordic countries*, Report 24/2012, Helsinki: National Institute for Health and Welfare, pp 37-42.

Salmi, M. and Lammi-Taskula, J. (1999) 'Parental leave in Finland', in P. Moss and F. Deven (eds) *Parental leave: Progress or pitfall?*, Brussels: NIDI CBGS, pp 85-121.

Salmi, M. and Lammi-Taskula, J. (2012) 'Finland: country note', in P. Moss (ed) *International review of leave policies and related research 2012*, (www.leavenetwork.org).

Salmi, M., Lammi-Taskula, J. and Närvi, J. (2009) *Perhevapaat ja työelämän tasa-arvo* [Family leave and gender equality in working life], Helsinki: Työ- ja elinkeinoministeriö.

Säntti, R. (1993) *Katsaus perhepolitiikan haasteisiin* [Overview on the challenges of family policy], Julkaisuja 1993: 8, Helsinki: Sosiaali- ja terveysministeriö.

Smith, D. (1988) *The everyday world as problematic: A feminist sociology*, Oxford: Open University Press.

Takala, P. (2005) 'Uuden isyysvapaan ja isän muiden perhevapaiden käyttö' ['Fathers' take-up of the new bonus leave and other forms of family leave'], *Sosiaali- ja terveysturvan selosteita 43/2005*, Helsinki: Kelan tutkimusosasto.

Vanhempainvapaatyöryhmän muistio (2011) [Report of the Parental Leave Working Group], *Selvityksiä 2011: 12*, Helsinki: Sosiaali- ja terveysministeriö.

Varjonen, S. (2011) *Äidin hoiva, jaettu vanhemmuus – ja vapaus valita. Perhevapaiden uudistamisen argumentointi 1970-luvulta 2000-luvulle* [*Mother's care, shared parenthood – and freedom to choose. Argumentation in Finnish parental leave reforms from the 1970s to the 2000s*], Helsinki: Kela.

West, C. and Zimmerman, D.H. (2002) 'Doing gender', in S. Fenstermaker and C. West (eds) *Doing gender, doing difference: Inequality, power, and institutional change*, New York and London: Routledge, pp 3-23.

FIFTEEN

Caring fathers and parental leave in prosperous times and times of crisis: the case of Iceland

Guðný Björk Eydal and Ingólfur V. Gíslason

Introduction

In Iceland, the legislation on paid parental leave from 2000 drastically changed the scene for parents, and put Iceland at the forefront of the Nordic nations in terms of quotas for fathers. The law provided each parent with non-transferable rights to a three-month paid leave of absence and an additional three-month leave that they are free to decide how (or if) to share between the parents. This chapter examines the origins of this – in a comparative sense – radical policy of de-gendering leave take-up. Second, the chapter discusses how Icelandic fathers capitalised on the new opportunities and how leave take-up differs between different social groups of fathers. Finally, the chapter follows the policy development and usage among fathers in the aftermath of the 2008 financial crisis, primarily in order to estimate if a crisis leads to a reversal or re-examination of the policies and practices introduced during economic boom years. The theoretical framework of the chapter considers the policy–practice interplay: how the policies on a father's quota, which has the declared aim of changing the division of unpaid labour between parents, have framed fathering practices; at the same time, however, it is assumed that the fathering practices and how the policies were perceived in general have also influenced the policymaking. Hence, the chapter investigates which social prerequisites are required in order for fathers to make use of parental leave.

The main results are that the origins of the policy are multifaceted, but the political agreement regarding the importance of non-transferable entitlement to parental leave seems firm. Paternal take-up is high, which seems to have facilitated development towards increased gender equality in society in general.

The policy–practice interplay

The task of examining the extent to which individual doings are the result of own decisions or the result of influences from social structures affecting individuals – that is, the agency–structure question – is at the core of sociology. In recent decades, influential scholars in family studies have emphasised the importance of individualisation and how individuals are now 'doing' families rather than 'being' families, meaning that families and family-making is not only prescribed by traditions and structures, but each individual decides for themself what kind of family they want to create, to an unprecedented degree in modern history (see, for example, Giddens, 1992; Beck and Beck-Gernsheim, 2002; Júlíusdóttir, 2009; Kjörholt, 2011). The theories on 'doing families' have also been applied in research on fatherhood, and underscore the importance of investigating the ideas and practices of fathers in order to understand the meaning men invest in their roles as fathers (see Chapter One, this volume). However, several scholars have questioned whether we are actually witnessing a major change from traditional ways of 'being families' to some sort of a post-modern freedom to 'do families' on the basis that they over-emphasise the role of agency. Duncan (2011) points out that:

> … empirically we find that people usually make decisions about their personal lives pragmatically, bounded by circumstances and in connection with other people, not only relationally but also institutionally. This pragmatism is often non-reflexive, habitual and routinised, even unconscious. Agents draw on existing traditions – styles of thinking, sanctioned social relationships, institutions, the presumptions of particular social groups and places, lived law and social norms – to "patch" or "piece together" responses to changing situations. Often it is institutions that "do the thinking".

The critics of the individualisation thesis point out the importance of keeping the strong influence of traditions, institutions and policies in mind when changes in fatherhood are examined. Thus, the theoretical framework of this chapter considers both policies and practices of fatherhood.

Governments interested in promoting gender equality and encouraging female participation in the labour market have increasingly turned their attention to the social roles of men, and fathers in particular. The main reason appears to be the insight that the eschewed division of labour regarding housework and childcare is a major hindrance for women in the labour market and their carrier since women shoulder the lion's share of the unpaid work. As outlined in this volume (see Chapters Seven, Eight, Fourteen and Sixteen) steps have therefore been taken in the Nordic countries, and across the European Union (EU) (Moss, 2013), to change the laws and regulations influencing the choices parents face in order to encourage a more equal division of labour. Father's quota policies are therefore intended to influence fathering practices. The idea is that more fathers being care takers in the first months of the lives of their children would reduce the disadvantages that children may constitute for labour market active women, since they will not be away for a long time, and employers can expect men and women alike to leave the labour market for similar periods of time to care for their children. Such policies must enjoy wide support in society in order to be effective, since the state can only provide certain structures and support, but cannot force fathers to use the entitlements. Thus, it is the dialogue between the policymaking and practice that is the fabric of the analytical perspective of this chapter, which investigates how policies on father's quotas have influenced practice and vice versa.

Data and methods

This chapter draws on existing Icelandic studies that have investigated the development of leave policies in the 2000s, surveys among parents investigating how fathers have exercised their leave entitlements, and qualitative interview studies with fathers in order to gain insights and understanding into fathering and the creation of fatherhood (Gíslason, 2005, 2007a, 2008; Eydal and Gíslason, 2008; Eydal, 2008, 2011).

In order to investigate the impact of the financial crisis that hit Iceland severely in 2008, we draw both on previously collected and newly generated data. First, the Maternity/Paternity Leave Fund provided statistics on take-up during the period 2008–11. Second, in order to see if public attitudes to parental leave legislation from 2000 had changed, surveys were conducted among a representative sample of 600 Icelanders aged 17 and older in 2003 and 2012. Last, but not least, parliamentary documents were examined in order to trace the changes in legislation of paid parental leave during the aftermath of the crisis. Thus, various data sets were used in order to answer the questions raised in this chapter.

Equal rights of both parents to paid parental leave

Explicit family policy was not a political issue in Iceland until the 1990s, and public spending on family policy measures as a proportion of GDP was smaller in Iceland than in the other Nordic countries. Left-of-centre political parties, labour unions, employers and the women's movement called for increased consideration of family policy and gender equality issues during the 1990s, and the work–life balance gained widespread attention from policymakers. In 1997, the Icelandic Parliament, Alþingi, formally recognised the need for an explicit public family policy in passing a parliamentary resolution on family policy, emphasising the importance of ensuring both parents equal opportunities with respect to work and care (Eydal and Gíslason, 2008).

During the 1980s and 1990s, female labour market participation was encouraged; for example, by increasing daycare service volume, institutions entrusted with the task of promoting gender equality were established and gender-discriminating laws abolished. Mothers increased their labour market participation, but fathers continued working long hours. Male participation in housework and childcare increased, but continued to lag behind the number of hours women spent on these tasks (Eydal and Gíslason, 2008). At the same time, Icelandic fertility rates were considerably higher than in the other Nordic countries (see Chapter One, this volume). Research on Icelandic families in the early 1990s revealed that the parents of young children were under great financial and time pressure (Júlíusdóttir, 1993). Thus, the discussion on how to create policies encouraging fathers to take greater part in childcare grew in Iceland as in the other Nordic countries (Duvander and Lammi-Taskula, 2011).

Increased pressure to provide fathers with their own entitlements to paid parental leave

Historically, Iceland was a latecomer among the Nordic countries regarding rights to paid parental leave, first enacting universal rights to three months' paid parental leave as late as 1980. According to that law, fathers could take 30 days of leave, but only if the mother resigned her entitlements to the father. In 1987, the parental leave period was gradually extended to six months, but nothing was stated in the legislation about the (possible) division between parents, only that both parents held this right (Eydal and Gíslason, 2008). Statistics show that very few fathers used the entitlement to paid parental leave. In the years 1993–98, between 8 and 17 fathers annually received some payments for parental leave, or about 0.3 per cent of the number of mothers receiving payments (Staðtölur almannatrygginga, 2001). In the 1990s, this was considered to be a problem by various governments, political parties and labour market organisations. Public committees were appointed (in 1989 and 1995) to seek solutions, but to no avail. In 1995, a Committee on the Gender Role of Men (established by the Council for Gender Equality) introduced the first proposal on individual non-transferable entitlements for fathers to paid parental leave, a father's quota, suggesting that fathers should have the right to a four-month quota of a total of 12 months (Gíslason, 2007a). These ideas influenced the members of parliament, and members from the Women's Alliance and the People's Alliance (a leftist party) presented bills on the issue in the Alþingi, albeit unsuccessfully (Eydal and Gíslason, 2008).

The issue also caught on outside the Alþingi: in opinion polls prior to the 2000 legislation, Icelandic men clearly indicated that they wanted to work less, spend more time with their families, and that they were prepared to take parental leave. Trade unions discussed the issue, and made recommendations regarding a father's quota, and the Confederation of Icelandic Employers publicly voiced support for changes that would, among other things, entail the linking of payments during parental leave with a salary. Furthermore, local authorities discussed the need for increased paternal involvement in childcare, and the municipality of Reykjanesbær entitled all of their male employees to two weeks' paid paternity leave in 1996. Reykjavík City Council even initiated a social experiment in 1996, where eight men working for the municipality received three months of paternity leave with full pay on the condition that the experience would be documented on television and in a sociological study. The aim of the project was to raise awareness, change attitudes and '… contribute to legislative reform of parental leave through the constitution of an individual, non-transferable right of fathers to paternity leave' (Einarsdóttir, 1998, p 4).

Generally speaking, a broad political and social agreement that changes were called for was establishing itself, and the idea of the equal right of both parents to quotas won increased support. In 1997, the Minister of Finance took the next step by giving all publicly employed fathers the right to two weeks' paid paternity leave. Finally, the Alþingi enacted laws proposed by a coalition government of the Progressive Party (a centre party) and the Independence Party (centre-right), that came into power in 1995, giving all fathers the right to a two-week paid paternity leave to be used within the first eight weeks after the birth of the child (Eydal and Gíslason, 2008).

This development reveals the interplay of practices and wishes by fathers on the one hand, and the changing policies of most social actors aimed at accommodating and encouraging the development already underway. The stage was set for a radical new step.

The 2000 legislation: the equal right of both parents to paid parental leave

In the run-up to the 1999 parliamentary election, all of the political party programmes emphasised the importance of increasing opportunities available to fathers to take parental leave (Gíslason, 2007a). The centre-right coalition government that came into power in 1995 continued after the election, proposing new legislation on parental leave in 2000 ensuring both parents the same non-transferable entitlements to paid parental leave: a three-month father's quota, three-month mother's quota and three months for the parents to divide between them at will.[1] The quota was only transferable if either parent passed away before fully using their leave. It is important to note that all parents, regardless of whether they held custody or shared residence with their child, were entitled to paid parental leave. In cases where the parents did not share custody, the custodial parent must give their consent with respect to the visiting rights/access (Act on Maternity/Paternity and Parental Leave no 95/2000; see Chapter Four, this volume).

The stated aim of the 2000 legislation was twofold: to ensure that children enjoyed the care of both parents, and to enable women and men alike to coordinate family life and work outside the home (Act on Maternity/Paternity and Parental Leave no 95/2000). In other words, the policy was meant to actively encourage fathers to participate in the care of their young children by earmarking part of the parental leave for fathers and to improve the labour market position of women. The Bill argued that the traditional mother–father division of labour had often resulted in fathers being deprived of opportunities to be with their children, and references were made to research that showed that a majority of Icelandic men claimed that they wanted to be able to reconcile labour market participation and childcare to a greater extent. It stated that the equal rights to parental leave and the quota played an essential role in ensuring that both parents had the opportunity to reconcile work and family life (Eydal and Gíslason, 2008).

The parliamentary debates revealed that further hopes were attached to these changes. The Minister of Social Affairs mentioned that he hoped this would have the added impact of reducing the gender pay gap, and the chair of the Left–Green Movement voiced similar expectations. References were also made in the debate to different agreements within the EU and that one of the goals of the legislation was to adopt the Directive on Parental Leave (96/34/EC) as a European Economic Area member state (Gíslason, 2007a). The law increased the flexibility of parental leave, and parents were free to choose to exercise their rights full or part time or to take leave simultaneously in the first 18 months of their child's life. Fixed payments were replaced by 80 per cent of previous wages during parental leave and, quite extraordinarily compared to all other Nordic countries, the original law had no benefit ceiling, even though this was introduced in 2004. Parents who were not active in the labour market or working 25 per cent or less were entitled to a flat-rate benefit, and students were also entitled to a fixed birth grant, but twice as high as those who were labour market inactive (Act on Maternity/Paternity and Parental Leave no 95/2000; Eydal and Gíslason, 2008).

The three-month father's quota was not the only important change to the paid parental leave scheme; the total period of leave was gradually extended from six to nine months. This is believed to have promoted the widespread acceptance of the legislation, since nothing was 'taken from' the mothers (Eydal and Gíslason, 2008; Einarsdóttir and Pétursdóttir, 2009). Last, but not least, a special fund was established to administer the payments. This fund received its income as part of the insurance levy already paid by employers. Part had been used to finance the unemployment insurance fund, but part of that was now allocated to the Maternity/Paternity Leave Fund (Act on Maternity/Paternity and Parental Leave no 95/2000). A win-win situation had therefore been created; everybody was better off after the change, with no added costs to either employer or employee (Gíslason, 2007a). The Icelandic scheme was unique when it was implemented. According to Moss and O'Brien (2006, p 22), 'this scheme contains one of the most generous "father-targeted" leave entitlements so far developed in modern economies in terms of both time and economic compensation.'

It soon became apparent, however, that the cost estimates for the leave scheme had been far too low. In 2004, the Minister of Social Affairs proposed changes to the Maternity/Paternity Leave Act, simultaneously increasing revenues for the fund and cutting expenses; there was a ceiling on the payments from the fund, meaning that maximum payments were limited to IKR 480,000 per month. The fund data show that less than 3 per cent of parents had incomes over this ceiling, meaning this change had no effect on take-up rates. Some trade unions paid (part of) the difference from the 80 per cent from the parental leave fund to full salary, or had an agreement with their employers, such as the Confederation of Icelandic Bank and Finance Employees, that they would compensate for this (Eydal and Gíslason, 2008).

As stated above, the Bill on paid parental leave was introduced by a centre-right coalition. The left-of-centre parties had proposed similar policies and supported the Bill, and it was passed unanimously in the Alþingi. The social partners also supported the Bill. Furthermore, the Act enjoyed general support in the populace. Gallup polls, conducted in 2003, showed wide acceptance particularly among women (90.8 per cent), but also among men (80.3 per cent) (Eydal and Gíslason, 2008). There was widespread support for the Bill, and agreement on the need for non-transferable entitlements for fathers to paid parental leave and, as the next section shows, Icelandic fathers proved eager to exercise their new rights. In the Nordic context, it may seem surprising that a centre-right government would introduce a quota of this magnitude. Right-wing political parties have rather tended to emphasise 'choice' for families, both regarding the division of parental leave and whether they want homecare allowances or daycare (see, for example, Ellingsæter and Leira, 2006; Eydal and Rostgaard, 2011).[2] It is difficult to view this as anything but a genuine commitment to gender equality from this Icelandic government. At the same time, it provided parents with considerable flexibility with respect to part-time leave and both parents taking leave at the same time. Indeed, there was hardly any mention of the importance of choice when the issue was discussed. Instead, there was broad agreement in the Alþingi and society in general concerning the importance of enabling fathers to take their share of paid parental leave by providing the three-month father's quota, thereby ensuring children care from both parents.

How did fathers in Iceland receive their father's quota?

Icelandic society had been moving towards gender equality for a number of years prior to the passing of the parental leave legislation. This is apparent in the increased number of women in politics, increased female labour market participation and higher numbers of women in university education. Similar tendencies were also emerging in family life, perhaps most obviously in the increasing number of parents opting for shared custody of their children after separation or divorce, up from 23 per cent in 1994, when joint custody was legalised, to 83 per cent in 2010 among divorced parents and 94.3 per cent among separated unmarried couples (Statistics Iceland, nd). Similarly, books and periodicals intended for parents shifted from an exclusive focus on mothers towards addressing both parents, and emphasising the importance of sharing care (and housework) (Gíslason, 2007b). Furthermore, there was a trend among fathers to take a leave of absence in connection with the birth of their children despite the lack of any right to paid parental leave. A study conducted among all parents to a first-born child born in 1997 found that 13.4 per cent of the fathers took a leave of absence from work in the first month after their child was born without any financial compensation from the state (Eydal, 2008). Some Icelandic fathers had therefore already changed their practices before the law was enacted – thus the policies supported these new practices.

At the same time, the uneven sharing of care work and household chores was considered an obstacle to increased gender equality. Research showed, for example, that having a child had very gendered effects on fathers and mothers; fathers worked more to make ends meet, while mothers worked less to be able to better attend to the family (Statistics Iceland, 2001; Gallup, 2006).

Over 80 per cent of fathers made use of their right the first year after the law came into force (Fæðingarorlofssjóður, nd). Table 15.1 shows how the increases in take-up rates follow the increase in entitlements from 2001, when the fathers had a single month, to 2003, when the third month was added. In the 2003–07 period, most fathers used their three-month entitlement. In the vast majority of cases, the mothers used more of the joint period than the fathers. In 2007, 21.2 per cent of the fathers used more than their basic three months, as compared to 93.1 per cent of the mothers. Thus, Icelandic fathers follow the same pattern as fathers in other countries, mainly using their quota entitlements (Bruning and Plantenga, 1999; Armeniaa and Gerstel, 2006; Ray et al, 2008; Moss and Kamerman, 2009; Duvander and Lammi-Taskula, 2011; see also Chapter Sixteen, this volume).

According to the statistics, the proportion of fathers not making full use of their rights increased by around 5 per cent for each month that was added to their right, reaching 14.2 per cent in 2003 and 19.5 per cent in 2005. After that, it began to fall to 16.4 per cent in 2007. Similarly, the proportion of fathers using (some of) the sharable time was 14.5 per cent the first year, rising steadily until reaching 19.5 per cent in 2005, and remained around that level in 2006 and 2007. The Icelandic results are in line with what has been noted in other Nordic countries; in most cases, parents make use of their own parental leave quota. The difference between mothers and fathers is that the former

Table 15.1: Fathers' and mothers' uptake of paid parental leave in Iceland, 2001–07

	2001	2002	2003	2004	2005	2006	2007
Mothers (n)	4054	4070	4167	4291	4302	4417	4555
Applications from fathers as % of mothers	82.4	83.6	86.6	89.8	88.2	88.6	88.5
Average number of days used by fathers	39	68	97	96	99	99	101
Average number of days used by mothers	186	187	183	182	184	185	181
% of fathers using more than their basic rights	14.5	13.9	16.1	17.1	19.5	19.7	21.2
% of mothers using more than their basic rights	94.2	93.4	90.9	90.5	89.7	90.3	93.1
% of fathers using less than their basic rights	5.1	10.1	14.2	17.9	19.5	18.5	16.4
% of mothers using less than their basic rights	0.9	0.8	1.0	1.1	0.1	0.3	1.5
% of fathers taking all of the leave in one package	45.2	21.2	17.9	15.0	25.8	25.7	25.7

Sources: Eydal and Gíslason, 2008; Fæðingarorlofssjóður, nd

use most of the shared entitlements that parents can divide among themselves (Duvander and Lammi-Taskula, 2011; see also Chapters Thirteen, Fourteen and Sixteen, this volume).

A 2007 survey among parents of first-borns born in 2003 showed that many fathers (60 per cent) take leave during the first few weeks after the birth, when the mothers are also on leave (Eydal, 2008). In a survey among parents in 2006 (Jónsdóttir and Aðalsteinsson, 2008), 76.3 per cent of parents said that, at some point in time, they had taken leave at the same time as their spouse, and 32 per cent of the respondents said they spent a total of four weeks together with their spouse on leave. According to Eydal (2008), the most usual pattern is that after the first month, when the parents have both taken some weeks, the mother continues on leave, and the father then takes the remainder of his leave once the mother's leave is over. Results from other studies further show that fathers are more likely than mothers to divide their leave into a number of shorter spells (Gíslason, 2007a; Jónsdóttir and Aðalsteinsson, 2008). Scholars have pointed out that when fathers divide their leave into shorter spells, it becomes more likely that the father takes on the role of reserve, rather than independent, carer (Brandth and Kvande, 2003a, 2003b; Pétursdóttir, 2004; Gíslason, 2009).

What characterises the fathers taking paid parental leave and those who do not? Research from the other Nordic countries has found considerable differences between various groups of fathers regarding how they use their entitlements. Swedish research (see, for example, Haas, 1992; Näsmann, 1992; Duvander, 2002) found a positive correlation between the level of education, employment security and the take-up rate of parental leave for fathers. Sundström and Duvander (2002) show that fathers with incomes above the population's mean are more likely to take advantage of their parental leave than those who do not. Swedish fathers were also less likely to take parental leave if both parents had a low income. More recent studies have also shown that lower-income fathers take shorter leave periods than other groups (Duvander and Lammi-Taskula, 2011).

A study by Eydal (2008) compared Icelandic fathers who took paid parental leave to those who did not in order to see if they somehow differed in terms of age, family status, education, employment status and income. The results showed a significant difference between income groups – that is, the higher the household income, the greater the proportion of fathers taking parental leave, which is in line with the Nordic research results noted above. Similar results were obtained by analysing applications to the fund, that is, better-off fathers are more likely to take leave – and more days of it (Gíslason, 2007a).

Finally, the 2007 study of parents of first-borns showed the greatest difference in the take-up figures being between fathers living with the mother and those not doing so, as shown in Table 15.2. This finding is important, since the law provides entitlements to all parents regardless of whether they share residency or custody.

Table 15.2 shows how fathers who have never lived with their child have the lowest take-up rates (73 per cent take no leave), followed by fathers who have ended cohabitation or divorced the mother during the first three years of their child's life (32 per cent). Fewer fathers who have started cohabiting or married the mother after the birth of the child take paid parental leave than fathers who have been living with the mother since the child's birth. The parental relationship is therefore of vital importance for the likelihood of the father using his entitlements. Parents not living together have generally been neglected in research on parental leave (see, for example, Kiernan, 2005, 2006; O'Brian, 2007). This is also the case in Iceland, and very little is known about the situation of lone fathers and how they experience their right to paid parental leave. A qualitative study conducted in Iceland in 2008 provides insights into the obstacles and hindrances that parents, who do not know each other well, face when forming

Table 15.2: Family status of parents of children born in 2003 and fathers' paid parental leave take-up

Length of leave	n = 855	No leave	<3 months	≥3 months
Cohabiting (no changes from birth)	343	7%	12%	81%
Married (no changes from birth)	310	10%	12%	78%
Cohabiting/married after the birth of the child	26	19%	12%	69%
Parents have never lived together	70	73%	3%	24%
Parents have terminated cohabitation or divorced after the birth of the child	106	32%	18%	50%

Source: Figures from Eydal, 2008.

a parental relationship and learning to trust each other. The parents in the study called for more counselling and education (Eydal and Ragnarsdóttir, 2008).

Fatherhood in the aftermath of financial crisis

In 2008, the Icelandic currency, IKR, fell sharply in value. In October of that year, three of the country's major banks collapsed and were taken over by the state. Iceland was hit by a severe economic recession (Jónsson, 2009). The government was forced to cut welfare costs, and even though all of the political parties had expressed their will to extend the length of the paid parental leave before the parliamentary elections in the spring of 2007, it was clear that the scheme would suffer cuts (Eydal, 2011). Table 15.3 shows the austerity measures taken in relation to the paid parental leave.

In December 2009, the government proposed that one month of the paid parental leave should be postponed until the child had reached three years of age, and used before the child reached age five. There was powerful opposition from the labour unions against the idea of postponing this month, the result being that the Alþingi instead proposed further cuts to the financial compensation, and the payments ceiling was further lowered. Neither government therefore changed the main characteristics of the scheme nor the quota entitlements of both parents (Eydal and Gíslason, 2013).

The financial compensation ceiling affected 45.7 per cent of fathers and 19 per cent of mothers in 2010 (Fæðingarorlofssjóður, 2010). When the ideas about the cuts were presented, representatives from the fund declared their worries that the cuts would have a negative impact on the uptake rates, particularly among fathers, and such worries were also aired in the Alþingi (Eydal and Gíslason, 2013).

Table 15.3: Laws on paid parental leave: changes during the aftermath of the 2008 crisis

Government	Year	Changes
A coalition of the Social Democratic Alliance and the Independence Party	December 2008	The ceiling of payments lowered from 480,000 IKR to 400,000 IKR
A coalition of the Social Democratic Alliance and the Left–Green Movement	June 2009	The ceiling of payments lowered from 400,000 to 350,000 IKR and the period that the parents could use their leave extended from 18 months to 3 years
Same government	December 2009 (Law came into force 1 January 2010)	Ceiling of payments lowered to 300,000 IKR, and parents with more than 200,000 IKR will receive 75% of previous income instead of 80%

Source: Eydal and Gíslason, 2013

Fathers' leave take-up after the crisis

Figures on parental leave use have yet to reflect any major reduction in the uptake of fathers in the aftermath of the crisis as shown in Table 15.4. Since the period parents have to make use of their rights was extended to three years, it is too early to tell if a major reduction in take-up will occur, but so far the main statistics do not indicate that. However, according to personal communications with the executive director of the Maternity/Paternity Leave Fund, the major change appears to be that fathers are exercising their rights later in their children's lives than before and for even shorter spells; obviously this is not in accordance with the aims of the law.

The change of the period that parents can use the parental leave, from 18 to 36 months, possibly also increases opportunities for fathers who do not live with their children to take paid parental leave, as lone mothers might feel more comfortable with accepting their children staying with their fathers for longer when they are older. As mentioned above, the full effect of the changes remains to be seen.

Attitudes towards paid parental leave for fathers

Surveys were conducted in 2003 and 2012 among a representative sample of Icelanders aged 17 and older to measure the support to paid parental leave for fathers. The support for the rights of fathers to 3–6 months' paid parental leave was extensive in 2003, and had increased significantly in 2012, as shown in Table 15.5.

Table 15.4: Paid parental leave take-up in Iceland, fathers' applications as % of total applications by mothers, and number of days used by fathers/mothers and fathers as % of mothers

Year	% of total applications	Average number of days of fathers	Average number of days of mothers	Days used by fathers as % of mothers
2006	88.6	99	185	53.5
2007	88.5	101	181	55.8
2008	90.9	103	178	57.8
2009	96.6	99	178	55.1
2010	95.3	92	179	51.4
2011*	92.2	86	179	48.0
2012*	89.6	79	179	44.1

*The figures for 2011 and 2012 are preliminary

Source: Fæðingarorlofssjóður, nd

Table 15.5: What is your opinion of fathers using their right to 3–6 months paid parental leave? Results from 2003 and 2012

	2003	2012
Very positive	69.4	73.7
Rather positive	16.0	14.9
Uncertain	3.7	6.6
Rather negative	5.9	2.6
Very negative	5.1	2.3

Source: Gallup, 2003; Survey conducted for the authors by Capacent Gallup, 2012 among representative sample of respondents 18+, Chi-Square value 19,2, p < 0.001

Both surveys found significantly more support among women, younger respondents, and people in employment ($p<0.05$). In 2012 similar patterns emerged. Women, younger people and employed people were significantly more supportive to paid parental leave for fathers ($p<0.05$). All respondents aged 18–24 ($n = 72$) were very or rather positive compared to 81 per cent among those aged 55 and older. Women were more supportive than men – 91 per cent of the female respondents were positive compared to 85 per cent of the men. Employees were more supportive than employers – 88 per cent of the full-time employed were positive compared to 81 per cent among employers.

Policies during the aftermath of the crisis

Both 'post-crisis' governments clearly stated with each cut that the measures were temporary and would be reversed once state finances had improved. The left-wing government coming into power after the mass demonstrations had brought down the sitting government in spring 2009 stated that the scheme would be restored as soon as possible. Furthermore, the government policies emphasised that the financial crisis should not endanger gender equality. In December 2012, the same government introduced a Bill proposing an extension to the leave period to 12 months to be gradually implemented by 2016, proposing a 4+4+4 division. Furthermore, the Bill proposed the restoration of financial compensation by raising the monthly ceiling from 300,000 IKR to 350,000 IKR (Eydal and Gíslason, 2013).

The Bill was introduced in the Alþingi on 30 November 2012 and referred to the Welfare Committee for review. After receiving external reviews and working with the Bill, the Committee suggested the division of the 12 months to be 5+5+2, which was unanimously accepted on 22 December 2012. The law would thus provide each parent with five months' paid parental leave and an additional two months to share between them, receiving up to 80 per cent of their previous salaries while on leave. The ceiling is to be raised to the pre-2008 level. The original Bill proposed that the leave could be used within an 18-month period, but the Welfare Committee changed this to two years (Eydal and Gíslason, 2013).

The Alþingi accepted the reformed Bill unanimously, which renders Iceland a very different case from the other Nordic countries, where parental leave quota issues tend to be disputed (Eydal and Rostgaard, 2011). All interest groups and organisations supported it, but it attracted limited media attention and stimulated little public debate. There are many reasons for this, one being the timing of the legislation – in December, people did not follow the Alþingi news in detail – and the other main reason might be the fact that many big issues were discussed in the Alþingi in December to which the media paid more attention.

The new law from 2012 shows how the restoration of the paid parental leave scheme was prioritised above other important issues, such as restoring the purchasing power of social security benefits. Extending the leave period had been high on the political agenda before the crisis, so there was a political agreement about the need to extend the nine-month leave to 12 months. The fact that the Alþingi opted for a 5+5+2 division reveals how the quota system has been institutionalised – the entitlements have been largely individualised, and there was no discussion about the need for free choice for families. The fact that Icelandic fathers used their three-month entitlements to such a high degree has probably been the main reason for this development; thus, the practices influence the policies.

The parliamentary elections in 2013 led to a major change in the political landscape when a right-of-centre coalition came into power. The new government deemed that the state's finances were in such a shape that austerity measures were necessary and extensions of the parental leave were not a priority. Consequently, the extension of the parental leave period adopted (unanimously) in December 2012 was revoked.

Conclusion

The origins of the policy of non-transferable rights to parental leave for fathers are to be found, on the one hand, in the Icelandic state's ongoing efforts to increase gender equality, and, on the other, in the expressed wishes of Icelandic men to be able to participate more fully in family life and particularly in childcare. The 2000 reform has been a massive success in terms of usage by fathers, and has contributed to a more equal sharing of work between men and women. The financial crisis was a major test for the system but seems to have ridden the storm, and the Alþingi had even decided to continue to build on the successful model by extending the leave to 12 months, dividing it so that each parent had five months and could share the additional two months as they like, even though the law was abolished before it was enacted.

One of the arguments for enacting the law on the father's quota in 2000 was that surveys among fathers had shown that they wanted to be able to take parental leave. The Icelandic experience confirms the findings in other Nordic countries, namely, that once fathers are provided with non-transferable rights to parental leave, with financial compensation that ensures that the family economy is not jeopardised, they use their entitlements. These are the main social prerequisites needed if fathers are to take parental leave.

The non-transferability is important for two interrelated reasons. First, it strengthens the bargaining position of the father vis-à-vis his employer if there is a period of parental leave that he alone can use. It is his social right, not a sharable one, not something that can be transferred to the mother. The second reason is similar: the mother does not have to defend her decision to 'allow' the father in to the caring of the young children on her return to work. It appears obvious that the 'good mother' idea is fairly strong in Iceland, meaning a mother who prioritises her children in every aspect of life, and spends as much time as possible with them. So earmarking allows both parents to share in the care taking and paid labour by being able to point out that the social rules are constructed with that in mind. The father 'must' use his right, since it cannot be used by the mother, and the mother 'cannot' extend her time away from the labour market, since it is now the father's turn at home.

The second prerequisite is almost a truism. It goes for men and women alike that the family economy is of the utmost importance. Traditionally, the father has been obliged to see to it that the growing family has what it needs in terms of material goods. If he is to be given the chance to become more involved in caring for his child(ren), then the economy must be solid, and wage-related financial compensation for both parents is required.

Thus, when enabling support structures meet fathers who want to practise fatherhood as caring fathers, change becomes almost inevitable. Icelandic fathers were willing and able to participate more in childcare and family life. But the Icelandic experience also shows that there are somewhat different responses in different family situations, and the fathers who are least likely to take leave are those who are not living with the mother.

The other group that seems to call for special attention are the low-earning households. It is not entirely clear why fewer fathers in this group exercise their right. At least four explanations seem plausible. One is that their financial situation is so vulnerable that parents cannot afford the father only bringing home 80 per cent of his salary for some months. Second, if the labour market is uncertain, there is a greater danger of losing one's job for taking parental leave. Third, the mother possibly sees the birth as a welcome escape from a drab and dreary job – or even escape from the labour market altogether. And finally, traditions might have a stronger hold on these parents, perhaps coupled with insecurity among the fathers regarding their ability to interpret and meet the needs of an infant, that is, some sort of essentialism regarding fathers and mothers, men and women. Thus, the practices might change at different paces among different groups of fathers (see also Chapter Six, this volume).

All in all, this somewhat radical social experiment appears to have been successful in most aspects, showing that policies can affect powerful changes in practices and gender relations. At the same time, it seems clear that the practices of fathers have also contributed, both to the making of the original policies and the institutionalisation of the fathers quota. The high take-up rates and increased participation in childcare after the paid parental leave have been key elements in this development, together with the general societal support that the father's quota policies have enjoyed.

Construction of fatherhood is an ongoing project to which each generation contributes. The long-term effects of the father's quota and practices of Icelandic fathers in the first decade of this century have yet to be investigated fully, but the available data on the outcomes of the policies support the notion that a father's quota is the right policy instrument to reach the twofold goals of the legislation: to ensure children's rights to care from both parents and to enable both parents to earn and care.

Notes

[1] The two-week paternity leave immediately after birth was abolished, but fathers could use their quota simultaneously with the mother if they wished.

[2] Homecare allowances exist in Iceland on the local level, but legislation on such payments has never been presented in the Icelandic Parliament (Eydal and Rostgaard, 2011).

References

Armeniaa, A. and Gerstel, A.N. (2006) 'Family leave, the FMLA and gender neutrality: the intersection of race and gender', *Social Science Research*, vol 35, pp 871-91.

Beck, U. and Beck-Gernsheim, E. (2002) *Individualisation*, London: Sage.

Brandth, B. and Kvande, E. (2003a) *Fleksible fedre* [*Flexible fathers*], Oslo: Universitetsforlaget.

Brandth, B. and Kvande, E. (2003b) '"Home alone" fathers', *NIKK magasin*, vol 3, pp 22-5.

Bruning, G. and Plantenga, J. (1999) 'Parental leave and equal opportunities: experiences in eight European countries', *Journal of European Social Policy*, vol 9, no, pp 195-209.

Duncan, S. (2011) 'Personal life, pragmatism and bricolage', *Sociological Research Online*, vol 16, no 4, 13 (www.socresonline.org.uk/16/4/13.html).

Duvander, A. (ed) (2002) *Couples in Sweden: Studies on family and work*, Stockholm: Swedish Institute for Social Research.

Duvander, A. and Lammi-Taskula, J. (2011) 'Paid parental leave', in I.V. Gíslason and G.B. Eydal (eds), *Parental leave, childcare and gender equality in the Nordic countries*, Copenhagen: Nordic Council of Ministers, pp 31-64.

Einarsdóttir, Þ. (1998) *Through thick and thin: Icelandic men on paternity leave*, Reykjavík: Jafnréttisnefnd Reykjavíkurborgar.

Einarsdóttir, Þ. and Pétursdóttir, G.M. (2009) 'From reluctance to fast track engineering', in P. Moss and S. Kamerman (eds) *The politics of parental leave policies: Children, parenting, gender and the labour market*, Bristol: Policy Press, pp 175-91.

Ellingsæter, A.L. and Leira, A. (2006) 'Introduction: politicising parenthood in Scandinavia', in A.L. Ellingsæter and A. Leira (eds) *Politicising parenthood in Scandinavia: Gender relations in welfare states*, Bristol: Policy Press, pp 1-25.

Eydal G.B. and Ragnarsdóttir R.S. (2008) *Hvernig haga einstæðir foreldrar fæðingarolofi? Rannsóknarritgerð* [*How do lone parents organize their paid parental leave?*], Working Paper, Reykjavík: Þjóðmálastofnun.

Eydal, G.B. (2008) 'Policies promoting care from both parents – the case of Iceland', in G.B. Eydal and I.V. Gíslason (eds) *Equal rights to earn and care: The case of Iceland*, Reykjavík: Félagsvísindastofnun, pp 111-48.

Eydal, G.B. (2011) 'Childcare policies at a crossroads: the case of Iceland', in A.T. Kjörholt and J. Qvotrup (eds) *The modern child and the flexible labour market: Early childhood education and care*, Houndmills/Basingstoke: Palgrave, pp 38-55.

Eydal, G.B. and Gíslason, I.V. (eds) (2008) *Equal rights to earn and care: The case of Iceland*, Reykjavík: Félagsvísindastofnun.

Eydal, G.B. and Gíslason, I.V. (2013) *Iceland 2012: Revised law on paid parental leave*, Reykjavik: Þjóðamálastofnun. (http://thjodmalastofnun.hi.is).

Eydal, G.B. and Rostgaard, T. (2011) 'Gender equality re-visited: changes in Nordic child-care policies in the 2000s', *Social Policy & Administration*, Regional Issue, vol 45, no 2, pp 161-79.

Fæðingarorlofssjóður (2010) *Samantekt yfir tölulegar upplýsingar Fæðingarorlofssjóðs 2001-2009* [*Statistical information from the Maternity/Paternity Leave Fund 2001-2009*], Reykjavík: Vinnumálastofnun.

Fæðingarorlofssjóður (nd) Unpublished data from the Maternity/Paternity Leave Fund.

Gallup (2003) 'Fæðingarorlof karla og kvenna nýtur viðtæks stuðnings' ['Paid parental leave of men and women enjoys wide support'], *Fréttatilkynning*, Apríl.

Gallup (2006) *Viðhorfsrannsókn* [*Value survey*] (www.capacent.is).

Giddens, A. (1992) *The transformation of intimacy: Sexuality, love and eroticism in modern societies*, Cambridge: Polity Press.

Gíslason, I.V. (2005) 'Feður sem taka lengra fæðingarorlof' ['Fathers who take longer parental leave'], in Ú. Hauksson (ed) *Rannsóknir í félagsvísindum VI [Social research VI]*, Reykjavík: Félagsvísindastofnun Háskóla Íslands, pp 293-304.

Gíslason, I.V. (2007a) *Parental leave in Iceland: Bringing the fathers in. Development in the wake of new legislation in 2000*, Akureyri: Jafnréttisstofa.

Gíslason, I.V. (2007b) 'Maskulinitet eller sociala möjligheter' ['Masculinity or social possibilities'], in Ö.G. Holter (ed) *Män I rörelse. Jämställdhet, förändring och social innovation i Norden [Men in movement. Gender equality, change and social innovation in the Nordic region]*, Riga: Gidlunds förlag, pp 75-117.

Gíslason, I.V. (2008) 'You are regarded as weird if you don't use the paternity leave', in G.B. Eydal and I.V. Gíslason (eds) *Equal rights to earn and care, the case of Iceland*, Reykjavík: Félagsvísindastofnun, pp 87-109.

Gíslason, I.V. (2009) 'Gender changes in Iceland: from rigid roles to negotiations', *Arctic and Antarctic*, vol 3, no 3, pp 121-49.

Haas, L. (1992) *Equal parenthood and social policy*, Albany, NY: State University of New York Press.

Jónsdóttir, B. and Aðalsteinsson, G.D. (2008) 'Icelandic parents' perception of parental leave', in G.B. Eydal and I.V. Gíslason (eds) *Equal rights to earn and care: The case of Iceland*, Reykjavík: Félagsvísindastofnun, pp 65-86.

Jónsson, Á. (2009) *Why Iceland? How one of the world's smallest countries became the meltdown's biggest casualty*, Columbus, OH: McGraw-Hill.

Júlíusdóttir, S. (1993) *Den kapabla familjen i det isländska samhället. En studie om lojalitet, äktenskapsdynamik och psykosocial anpassning [The capable family in Icelandic society. Study about loyalty, dynamics in marriage and psycho-social adaption]*, Gothenburg: University of Gothenburg.

Júlíusdóttir, S. (2009) 'Family-focused social work: professional challenges of the 21st century', in T. Kröger and H. Forsberg (eds) *Social work and child welfare politics: Through Nordic lenses*, Bristol: Policy Press, pp 11-28.

Kiernan, K. (2005) *Non-residential fatherhood and child involvement: Evidence from the Millennium Cohort Study*, London: Centre for Analysis of Social Exclusion, London School of Economics and Political Science.

Kiernan, K. (2006) 'Non-residential fatherhood and child involvement: evidence from the Millennium Cohort Study', *Journal of Social Policy*, vol 35, no, pp 651-69.

Kjörholt, A.T. (2011) 'The modern child and the flexible labour market: an introduction', in A.T. Kjörholt and J. Qvotrup (eds) *The modern child and the flexible labour market: Early childhood education and care*, Houndmills/Basingstoke: Palgrave, pp 1-18.

Moss, P. (2013) *International review of leave policies and research 2013*, Leave Policy Research Network (www.leavenetwork.org/fileadmin/Leavenetwork/Annual_reviews/2013_complete.6june.pdf).

Moss, P. and Kamerman, S. (eds) (2009) *The politics of parental leave policies: Children, parenting and the labour market*, Bristol: Policy Press.

Moss, P. and O'Brien, M. (eds) (2006) *Employment relation research*, Series no 57, International Review of Leave Policies and Related Research, London: Department of Trade and Industry.

Näsmann, E. (1992) *Parental leave in Sweden – a workplace issue?*, Stockholm Research Reports in Demography 73, Stockholm: Stockholm University.

O'Brien, M. (2007) 'Fathers, work and family life', *Community, Work & Family*, vol 10, no 4, pp 375-86.

Pétursdóttir, G.M. (2004) '"Ég er tilbúin að gefa svo mikið". Sjálfræði, karllæg viðmið og mótsagnir í lífi útivinnandi mæðra og orðræðum um ólíkt eðli, getu og hlutverk' ['"I am prepared to give so much". Independence, masculine norms and contradictions in the lives of working mothers and discourses on different nature, abilities and roles'], Unpublished MA thesis, Reykjavík: Háskóli Íslands, Félagsvísindadeild.

Ray, R., Gornick, J.C. and Schmitt, J. (2009) *Parental leave policies in 21 countries: Assessing generosity and gender equality*, Washington, DC: Center for Economic and Policy Research.

Staðtölur almannatrygginga [Social Security Statistics] (2001) Reykjavík: Tryggingastofnun Ríkisins.

Statistics Iceland (nd) *Mannfjöldi [Population]* (www.hagstofa.is).

Statistics Iceland (2001) Labour Force Survey, Reykjavik: Statistics Iceland.

Sundström, M. and Duvander, A. (2002) 'Family division of childcare and the sharing of parental leave among new parents in Sweden', in A. Duvander (ed) *Couples in Sweden: Studies on family and work*, Stockholm: Swedish Institute for Social Research, pp 1-28.

SIXTEEN

Parental leave use for different fathers: a study of the impact of three Swedish parental leave reforms

Ann-Zofie Duvander and Mats Johansson

Introduction

Fathers' increased parental leave use has been an objective in Sweden since the introduction of parental leave in 1974. Various strategies have been pursued to reach the goal, and numerous reforms have been introduced. In 1995, one month of parental leave was reserved as a quota[1] for each parent, meaning that the month was forfeited if not used by the same parent. In 2002, another month of quota was reserved for each parent, and a so-called 'gender equality bonus' was introduced in 2008, that is, a tax credit for parents who share the leave equally. Almost 90 per cent of Swedish fathers now take parental leave, but even if fathers' leave has increased substantially over the last decades, the three reforms have had an impact on the number of parental leave days taken by fathers and mothers differently (Duvander and Johansson, 2012a). This study is aimed at going beyond the average number of parental leave days taken by fathers, and determines which fathers contributed to the changes (and non-changes) in leave use after the reforms in question. During the time between the first and last reforms, the expectations and rhetoric around fatherhood also changed considerably, more emphasis being placed on active fatherhood (Klinth, 2008). These expectations possibly differ between groups of fathers, however, as the norms for how to behave as fathers differ. None of the reforms mentioned are directed at specific groups of fathers, and all fathers are entitled to parental leave. Nevertheless, these reforms may involve varying incentives to increase the leave use for different groups of fathers.

This chapter focuses on the effectiveness of such incentives by investigating which groups of fathers responded positively, thereby acting as forerunners by increasing their leave lengths. In addition, are there other groups of fathers lagging behind and remaining unaffected by the reforms? Even if Sweden has seen a trend towards increased sharing of leave between mothers and fathers, presumably together with increased paternal involvement in the care for the child, Swedish fathers are not a homogeneous group, and fathers are likely to respond to policy reform differently. This chapter focuses on the leave use among fathers with different education levels, in different work sectors, and fathers in families of different birth origins. These groups of fathers represent fathers with different situations in the labour market, and it can be assumed that fathers therefore have different opportunities for taking leave. Thus, different responses to the reforms can be expected, depending on the individual father's situation and opportunity to take parental leave. The results will provide insights into how different policy instruments affect the development of shared parenthood in Sweden, which is also important for other countries that are currently debating the development of their family policy. The results may provide keys for how to remove hindrances for leave usage among fathers. The study finds that the relative difference between fathers with different characteristics is changing over time, especially after policy reforms. It is therefore important to consider the differences in leave usage as changing over time and in relation to a certain policy context. As the study includes the evaluation of three policy reforms to the parental leave system, it is also possible to compare how these reforms may vary in impact on fathers with different characteristics.

Swedish register data is used to analyse the reforms, and the reforms may be considered as representing natural experiments, as the regulations are different for parents with children born within days of each other. Existing national studies indicate an increase in fathers' usage of parental leave after both quota months, but more so for the first reserved month of quota and not at all for the gender equality bonus (Duvander and Johansson, 2012a; Ekberg et al, 2013). The approach in this study differs from previous studies, as the effects of all three reforms are analysed at the same point in time: 24 months after the introduction of each reform. In the majority of cases, parents' use of parental leave after their child's second birthday is for shorter periods, for example, to extend summer holidays (Ekberg et al, 2013). Analysing the effect of the reforms after the same duration, with the same sample selection and with the same control variables, may thus provide insights into how reforms operate and affect parents' patterns of parental leave use.

In the following, the Swedish parental leave is introduced after which factors related to how the fathers took leave are reviewed. After a section on data and methods, the results are presented and discussed. The main result of the study is that the first quota month influenced the leave use of all fathers, but especially the ones using few days before the reform. The result was a more equal leave use, both between groups of fathers and fathers and mothers. The second quota month also influenced the leave use, but the number of fathers taking advantage of the policy change was more limited. The fathers with limited education, outside the labour market, and fathers where both parents are foreign-born showed no change in leave use. As other groups of fathers with high education and high income increased their use, the result was remaining or increasing differences between groups of fathers. The gender equality bonus did not seem to have had an impact on the leave patterns of any of the groups of fathers.

Swedish parental leave over time

In 1974, Sweden introduced parental leave with earnings-related benefits paid for six months after childbirth, entitling parents to share leave as they preferred. Sweden was thus the forerunner in the Nordic countries (and the entire world). Over time, the parental leave benefit in Sweden and elsewhere has been extended. The leave has also become individual, especially as quotas are specifically reserved for the mother and father. The parental leave insurance is one of many social reforms introduced during a period of Social Democratic Party dominance of Swedish politics (Chronholm, 2009). The specific aim was to facilitate the combination of work and caring for children for both men and women. The question of fathers taking leave was part of the political debate from the beginning (Klinth, 2002). The debate around the introduction of parental leave may be characterised as a turn to a gender-neutral policy, in contrast to, for example, the Danish debate at the same time, which focused on the protection of women (Cedstrand, 2011). Even if Swedish fathers received the right to leave, however, very few fathers exercised this right in the 1970s, and it took time for the share of fathers taking leave to increase.

In the 1980s, leave rights were gradually extended from 6 to 12 months, and an additional three months' leave with a low, flat-rate benefit was added. Cuts to the earnings-related benefits were made during the economic crisis in the 1990s to the current level of 80 per cent of earlier earnings. Parents with no previous earnings over the last eight months receive a low flat rate for the same number of benefit days (Swedish Social Insurance Agency, 2014), which provides a strong incentive to work before having children, especially for women.

In 1995, one reserved month of quota was introduced for each parent, meaning that the month would be forfeited if not used by the designated parent. This is referred to here as the father's quota, and there is also a mother's quota. At the same time, the leave was formally divided between parents, implying that the parent who wanted to use more than half of the leave required the consent (by signature) of the other parent. This change may have negligible practical implications but had the symbolic value of emphasising this as a gender-neutral and individual parental leave benefit. The reform applied to all parents with joint custody (see also Chapter Five, this volume), which is the absolute majority in Sweden, also for parents not living together. The reform was much debated publically, as some perceived it to be an intrusion into the private sphere (Cedstrand, 2011). However, the political debate was not a left–right divide, and opponents were found in most political parties. The reform was decided on by the Liberal–Conservative government, a decision that remained unchanged by the Social Democrats when they took over government six months later.

In 2002, the Social Democratic government extended the leave by one month to 16 months (including flat-rate leave) and provided an additional quota of one month for each parent. The main difference between the first and second quota reform is that in 2002 a month was added to the leave length, meaning that an increase in one parent's leave did not necessarily mean a decrease in the other parent's leave. This reform was less fiercely opposed, perhaps as norms around parental leave had changed and perhaps as it did not restrict the other parent's use of leave and thus posed no threat to the mother's time at home (Duvander and Johansson, 2012a).

In 2006, Sweden elected a new Liberal–Conservative government, which introduced a gender equality bonus in 2008. The gender equality bonus was a tax credit paid to the parents' tax account the year after the parental leave was taken. Essentially, for every day that the parents shared the leave more equally, or, in practice, for every day that the mother went back to work and the father used the leave, the mother would receive a tax credit of 100 SEK (approximately €10). The bonus did not apply to the quota months or the days with the low flat rate, and could thus be paid for a maximum of four-and-a-half months. Parents who had used the leave in a manner that might entitle them to the gender equality bonus received a letter from the Swedish Social Insurance Agency (*Försäkringskassan*) encouraging them to apply for the bonus. Parents then needed to prove that the parent

Table 16.1: Overview of reforms in the Swedish parental leave benefit

Year	
1974	Introduction of parental leave benefit for 6 months
1980s	Stepwise extension to 15 months parental leave
1995	First quota month to both father and mother
2002	Second quota month to both father and mother and extension to 16 months parental leave
2008	Gender equality bonus

not on leave had been at work or studying, a requirement aimed at increasing labour force participation. The rules have been perceived as complicated, and were simplified in 2012 (see www.forsakringskassan. se). Payments now come without delay and without application.

Parental leave usage

The parental leave policy allows for very flexible usage, something that is often utilised (Eklund, 2004). Most of the leave, however, is taken up during the child's first two years. For the samples in the present study, parents used on average between 79-96 per cent of the leave days they were entitled to in the course of the child's first two years.

The fathers' share of parental leave usage has increased over time, from 0.5 per cent of all parental leave days in 1974 to 24.4 per cent in 2012 (Swedish Social Insurance Agency, 2013a). Perhaps the most dramatic shift in men's use came in 1995 with the introduction of the father's quota, as only about half of all fathers took any leave previously, whereas almost 90 per cent of the fathers of children born since 1995 have taken leave (Duvander and Lammi–Taskula, 2012). Compared to the other Nordic countries, Swedish men are on parental leave for a long time. Even if the Icelandic fathers take a larger share of the leave, Swedish fathers take more days (Duvander and Lammi–Taskula, 2012; see also Chapters Thirteen and Fifteen, this volume). Notably, the proportion of parents sharing the leave equally, defined as somewhere in the range of 40–60 per cent, has now increased to around 13 per cent of all parents. At the same time, however, the group of fathers not taking any leave appears stable (Swedish Social Insurance Agency, 2013b).

Which fathers take leave?

As exemplified above, Sweden has seen a trend towards fathers taking more leave, which is accompanied by a shift towards more involved and active fathers (Johansson and Klinth, 2008; Johansson, 2011). Strong consensus on the importance of gender equality and paternal engagement is now in place (Klinth, 2008). In all European countries, and as pointed out in all of the chapters in this volume, active fatherhood is becoming part of how we define masculinity (O'Brien et al, 2007), but Sweden in particular in the 2000s has displayed a clear shift from fathers as secondary parents to an idea of the father as an equal parent with the same responsibilities for the child as the mother (Johansson and Klinth, 2008). Fathers' use of parental leave is often used as a measure of paternal involvement, and the increase in fathers' leave usage has been marked by considerable variation between groups. These differences may be explained by attitudes and norms as well as variations in structural constraints and incentives for different groups to take leave (see also Chapters Thirteen, Fourteen and Fifteen, this volume). Structural constraints can include economic constraints and obstacles in the workplace (see Chapter Seven, this volume). Fatherhood is also perceived differently according to class (Plantin, 2007; Stefansen and Farstad, 2010; Stefansen and Skogen, 2010; see also Chapter Six, this volume). Other studies have shown that this must be understood in the intersection of the potential structural constraints associated with, for example, race, however, as shown in US studies (Glauber and Gozjolko, 2011), perhaps best translated to immigrant status in the Nordic countries. Thus, the internal homogeneity within class should not be exaggerated (Irwin and Elley, 2011). Differences in parental leave usage may thus originate from structural constraints, which at times may be difficult to disentangle from attitudes, at least analytically. The most notable example is possibly the measure of education level, which is associated with attitudinal differences as well as different income levels and positions in the labour market (Geisler and Kreyenfeld, 2011).

Other factors, such as workplace characteristics, are found to be important predictors of the sharing of parental leave (Bygren and Duvander, 2006), including employers' attitudes to leave (Haas and Hwang, 2009). Fathers employed in a female-dominated workplace are more likely to take longer leave, and fathers in the public sector take more leave, possibly because these employers are more open to temporary exits from the labour market. Multiple fathers at the same workplace taking leave seem to increase the likelihood of yet other fathers taking leave (Bygren and Duvander, 2006; see also Chapter Seven, this volume). When asked, parents usually claim that financial considerations or work are the most important reason for how they have divided the leave between them (Duvander and Berggren, 2003).

Moreover, large-scale register studies show that both parents' incomes are important for how they divide the leave (Sundström and Duvander, 2002). Mothers with higher income commonly use less leave and fathers with higher income commonly use more leave, although it should be stressed that also in households where women have the highest income they still use the majority of the leave (Swedish Social Insurance Agency, 2013b).

Country of origin is also found to be influential, as fathers with immigrant origin are less prone to take leave, although the immigrant fathers who take leave seem to do so for a longer period (Duvander and Eklund, 2006). It is worth pointing out that the parental leave benefit mirrors the parents' position in the labour market. As the leave benefit is income-related and immigrant parents more often have a weak position in the labour market, many immigrant parents receive a much lower benefit than Swedish-born parents. This is important in Sweden, as a relatively large share of the population is born abroad (about 13 per cent), a figure which is even higher among men and women of childbearing age.

Another factor is the birth order of the child, as men and women alike take longer leave with their first child (Sundström and Duvander, 2002; Hobson et al, 2006). The regional variation in leave usage is also pointed out, as a more gender-equal division of leave is found in northern Sweden (Almqvist et al, 2011). One possible reason for this is that the labour market situation and opportunities to find work differ markedly in the different regions in Sweden. The north, for example, is characterised by high unemployment.

The lower usage among fathers with low education and income is possibly explained by economic constraints (Sundström and Duvander, 2002), together with attitudes and various meanings attached to fatherhood (Plantin, 2007). These differences may cause concern, as they may lead to variations in fathers' investments in their children (O'Brien et al, 2007). A growing number of studies indicate a correlation between leave usage and long-term child involvement (Nepomnyaschy and Waldfogel, 2007; Eydal, 2008; Haas and Hwang, 2008; Duvander and Jans, 2009; Chapter Twelve, this volume).

The differences in how fathers take leave might also be affected by reforms in the leave system. Different groups of fathers might be expected to respond differently to the quota months and the gender equality bonus, as the reforms affect them differently. The first quota month was aimed at fathers who did not previously take leave and now have an incentive to take one months' leave. The second quota month was aimed at increasing fathers' leave use to two months, while the bonus was aimed at getting fathers to take more than two months. The reforms are thus likely to target different groups of fathers with different levels of use. For example, the fathers who are outside the labour market and only receive the flat rate have less reason to be concerned about the quota months, as they would only get a low benefit if taking leave. The bonus requires two parents in the labour market for it to be worthwhile and is thus directed at dual-earner couples.

The expectations for the different groups of fathers are therefore that the first quota month primarily affects the fathers who formerly used less than one month of leave, but that those outside the labour market (or with a vulnerable labour market situation) remain unaffected. The second quota month is likely to affect those already taking leave and merely need a 'nudge' to take more, while those already taking two months or more are more likely to remain unaffected. The gender equality bonus may influence the fathers already taking a large share of the leave to take even more. As earlier studies have shown no aggregated effect of the bonus, however, the expectations for changed patterns should be modest.

Data and methods

The analysis builds on national register data from the Swedish Social Insurance Agency, data assembled from records obtained from local insurance offices and covering the entire Swedish population. They contain detailed information on the starting date of parental leave, number of days (parts of the day if not a full day) and the amount of benefit per day. They also include parents' individual characteristics, such as gender, date of birth, birth order of the child, geographical location, income, education level and country of birth (see Appendix A at the end of this chapater for variables that are not self-explanatory).

Empirically, the study makes use of the fact that all three reforms were introduced for children born after a specific date. The first quota month is applicable to children born on or after 1 January 1995, the second quota month to children born on or after 1 January 2002, and the gender equality bonus to children born on or after 1 July 2008. Children born within a few days of one another are treated under different regulations, thus rendering all three reforms examples of natural experiments (Angrist and Krueger, 1999; Rosenzweig and Wolpin, 2000).

From the register data, all parents with children born from two weeks before to up to two weeks after each reform were sampled, and subsets of parents of children born before (control group) and after (treatment group) each of the reforms were constructed. The analysis was conducted by comparing the use of parental leave in the control and treatment groups. To control for potentially unobservable differences between parents who gave birth in different months and seasonal variation in the use of parental leave, a difference-in-difference approach was applied, including parents with children born one year before the introduction of each of the reforms in the statistical analysis.

As the reforms only affect the children of parents with joint custody, children whose parents did not have joint custody during the entire period of observation were excluded from the sample (for discussion about non-custodial parents, see also Chapter Four, this volume). Multiple births, foreign-born and adopted children were also excluded from the analysis, as there are special regulations for these children. As this chapter focuses on the division of parental leave between women and men, same-sex parents were also excluded – these parents are obviously too few to study separately with the method used in this chapter. Finally, children who died or emigrated during the period of study were excluded from the sample. The final samples consisted of 10,000-14,000 children for each reform studied (for more details, see Duvander and Johansson, 2012b). The leave use was followed for the child's first 24 months, thus excluding possible short periods of leave use after the initial long period of leave.

The average number of parental leave days taken was estimated using linear regression models (OLS [ordinary least square] models). In these models, estimates of the parental leave days taken were conducted when taking into account the differences between groups in a range of demographic and socio-economic variables. In all of the models, the effect of being in the treatment group is captured by a dummy variable indicating treatment or control group.

The analyses capture the immediate response to the reforms for the first parents who were affected by the reform. If a reform changes behaviour gradually but nevertheless initiates a change, it may be overlooked if we focus on the first parents to meet the reform (see a similar argument in Ferrarini and Duvander, 2010). Thus, the long-term effect of the reforms of parents gradually changing their behaviour may be different from the immediate response covered here. However, it is plausible that the results presented in this chapter capture the general direction and provide a hint of the magnitude of the reforms.

Fathers' response to reforms

Table 16.2 presents the average use of parental leave days for children born immediately before and after each reform. This is not the final use of parental leave days, but only the days taken during the first 24 months of the child's life. Moreover, only earnings-related days are counted and not the three months paid at a flat rate. The flat rate days were included in an earlier study which followed parents 18 months after the reforms (M. Johansson, 2010), and they did not influence the results, probably as they are often used for occasional days off work during the child's pre-school years. The first quota month had a major impact on how both fathers and mothers took parental leave days. Fathers' usage increased from an average of about 25 days for the fathers of children born immediately prior to the reform to 35 days for the fathers of children born immediately after the reform. Mothers' use of parental leave instead declined, from almost 320 to 294 days for children born immediately before and after the reform. The obvious explanation is that the first reserved month restricted the maximum days any of the parents could use by 30 days.

The introduction of the second quota month also shows a significant effect on how fathers take parental leave. The reform increased fathers' use of leave by on average about seven days during the first 24 months. As the parental leave was extended by 30 days when the second month of quota was introduced, mothers also took more days after the reform.

In contrast to the changes related to the first and second months of quota, there are no statistically significant changes in the parental leave days taken after the introduction of the gender equality bonus.

Table 16.2: Mean number of parental leave days taken before and after reforms

	Control group	Treatment group	Difference
First quota month 1995			
Fathers	**25.5**	**35.6**	10.0
Mothers	**320.0**	**295.2**	−24.8
Second quota month 2002			
Fathers	**41.5**	**47.8**	6.3
Mothers	**269.8**	**279.5**	9.7
Gender equality bonus 2008			
Fathers	57.9	56.3	−1.5
Mothers	286.4	283.5	−2.9

Statistically significant differences between control and treatment groups marked in bold.

Table 16.2 also indicates a general trend of more days of parental leave taken by fathers and fewer days for mothers, a trend that is also visible between the reforms. The mean number of days taken by fathers increased by about six days between 1995 and 2002 (from 35.6 to 41.5 days) and also between 2002 and 2008, while the mothers' mean numbers of days decreased by over 20 days. Leave usage would thus appear to be changing independently of the reforms studied here, although at a slow pace.

The question addressed in this chapter is how these changes of different magnitudes affected different groups of fathers. As already mentioned, the effects for various groups of fathers are reported when other characteristics of the mother and father are considered. The estimated effects for all of the factors are found in Appendix B at the end of this chapter, while the focus in this section is on the fathers' education level, work sector and parents' country of origin. All of the tables and figures present the predicted number of parental leave days taken by fathers. Changes in the predicted number of days used for a certain group of fathers are thus changes controlled for other characteristics.

Figure 16.1 shows the number of days of leave fathers took before and after the three reforms when grouped according to level of education. Education level is categorised into primary, secondary and tertiary education the year before the child is born. The fathers enrolled in education when becoming fathers were categorised at the level they had already completed. A dramatic development over time is visible for all groups, but the different groups obviously developed differently. The first bar for all groups shows the number of days before the first reserved month was introduced in 1994. The fathers with primary education took on average about 20 parental leave days at the time, and their usage was increased most by the first reform. The increase was smaller for fathers with higher education, yet had taken more days before the reform.

Between the introduction of the first and second quota month, the leave usage increased especially for fathers with tertiary education. The fathers with secondary education seem to have reacted most to the second reform, especially more than those with primary education, the former taking almost 10 more days of leave after the reform. Fathers with tertiary education also took more leave, while the fathers with primary education fell behind.

The second quota month thus seemed to have increased the differences between fathers with primary education and those with higher education. Figure 16.1 also clearly illustrates how the differences

Figure 16.1: Number of parental leave days taken according to fathers' education level

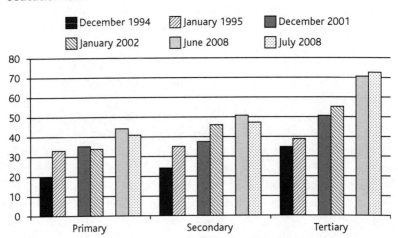

increased over time after the second reserved month. By the time the gender equality bonus was introduced, all of the groups were taking more leave, but while fathers with primary education took on average 44 days, fathers with tertiary education took 70 days of leave. The bonus did not seem to affect the usage in any of the educational groups.

When turning to the fathers' work sector in Figure 16.2, it becomes obvious that fathers in the public sector took more leave than fathers in the private sector before the introduction of the first quota month. Fathers outside the labour market took less leave than the other groups of fathers; they obviously had less incentive to take leave, as they would receive a low benefit. The relative difference between different work sectors and non-working fathers, on the whole, was unchanged by any of the reforms, but all groups of fathers took more parental leave after the reform was introduced. The second quota month seemed to have mattered most for the fathers working in central government, but also in local government and the private sector. The usage among fathers outside the labour market was significantly decreased by the reform. By the introduction of the gender equality bonus in 2008, it becomes clear that the fathers outside the labour market have fallen behind even more, as the working fathers all increased their usage up to 2008. However, none of the groups were affected by the gender equality bonus.

In Figure 16.3, the fathers are divided according to the birth origins of both parents. The largest group is obviously the group where both parents were born in Sweden, while the groups where one of the parents is foreign-born were small, and the results should be interpreted

Figure 16.2: Number of parental leave days taken according to work sector

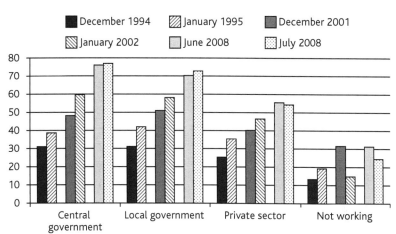

with caution. About 5-6 per cent of the sample belongs to the group with one foreign-born parent and 9-12 per cent to the group with two foreign-born parents (Duvander and Johansson, 2012b). Before the first reserved month was introduced, foreign-born fathers took fewer parental leave days on average than Swedish-born fathers. If the mother was also foreign-born, fathers' usage of parental leave increased dramatically after the introduction of the first reserved month. The usage differences between fathers of different birth origin were not

Figure 16.3: Number of used parental leave days according to parents' birth origin

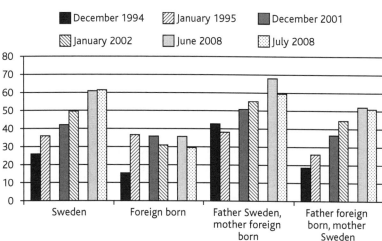

very large after the introduction of the first quota month. However, differences between families with two Swedish-born parents and those with two foreign-born parents increased until the introduction of the second reform. The differences also seemed to increase after the introduction of the second reserved month, as Swedish-born fathers increased their usage even more, while fathers in families where both parents were foreign-born remained on average unaffected by the reform. Swedish-born fathers also increased their leave usage between 2002 and 2008, when the gender equality bonus was introduced, while fathers where both parents were foreign-born did not change their usage. The gender equality bonus did not change the usage of any group, but it became clear by 2008 that Swedish-born fathers took much more leave than foreign-born fathers. These changes in behaviour are controlled for other differences between the groups, for example, in income.

In Appendix B, patterns similar to those described here are also found for other factors. Fathers' and mothers' individual income levels, as well as mothers' education levels, were found to be associated with the leave usage similar to fathers' education levels. The general pattern is that before the first quota month, there were considerable differences between groups of fathers. These differences decreased after the introduction of the first reform, but then tended to increase over time up to and by the second quota month. Leave usage increased for most groups of fathers up to 2008, but more for some groups than others. While Swedish-born and well-educated fathers largely took more leave, foreign-born fathers and fathers with little education and no employment hardly took more leave. The gender equality bonus did not seem to have any impact on leave usage for any of the groups of fathers.

Conclusion

The 'participating father' has become part of the general notion of fatherhood in Sweden, but it is important to distinguish this idea of fatherhood from gender-equal parenthood (Bekkengen, 2002). Even if most fathers share the leave, they remain nowhere near using half of the period. Many families still have large obstacles to a more equal sharing of the leave, both practical (for example, financial and work-related) and obstacles related to power structures, traditions and values. The result of the reform impact in this study should be interpreted not just as being contingent on the individual characteristics of the father, but also on the societal climate and economic circumstances at the time of introduction.

This study shows that the fathers who changed their behaviour in relation to the first reserved quota month were those who took little or no leave before 1995. The fathers who already took one month of leave did not change their usage to the same extent. Perhaps the most striking observation is when comparing fathers with different education levels; fathers with only a primary education increased their use of leave dramatically by almost two weeks, while fathers with tertiary education hardly changed their usage at all. When comparing various subgroups of fathers, the conclusion is that the differences in parental leave usage between fathers after the first reform were much less than before the reform. It therefore seems as though the first quota month was part of creating a new fatherhood for all fathers. It also seems as though the fathers who may have had more difficulties taking leave – financially and because of a vulnerable labour market situation – still did so. Reserving time for fathers will clearly help parents overcome other obstacles to sharing the leave, and the reform may be thus interpreted as a success.

When the second quota month was introduced, fathers who could benefit financially from the reform took more leave. For example, all of the employed fathers took more leave, but those who were without employment did not. As the leave is income-related, the fathers with no work would have received a very low benefit. While a low replacement mattered less for the first reserved month, increasing the quota to two months was perhaps too high a threshold for financially vulnerable groups. The results from the second quota month also indicate increasing differences between fathers with primary and higher education, groups that are typically situated differently in the labour market. Thus, while the first month reduced the differences between groups of fathers, the second month increased the difference between the fathers in a more vulnerable situation (no income, low education, foreign-born) and the rest of the fathers. The increasing differences are in line with how Haas and Hwang (2009) find that white-collar fathers receive more formal and informal support to take leave than blue-collar fathers. It is also parallel to other developments in society whereby fatherhood is seen as important, but how to practise it is the family's choice (Klinth, 2008). This study focuses on the increase in leave usage, but the share of fathers taking leave at all is obviously crucial to this measure (for details, see Duvander and Johansson, 2012b). The second month may also be seen as a success, as it did increase fathers' leave use on an aggregated level, but the effect obviously varied between groups.

There are no effects so far on leave usage for any group of fathers from the gender equality bonus, but the differences between groups of fathers tend to increase over time – also up to the point of the introduction of the gender equality bonus. It is especially important to point out which fathers fall behind and do not use the leave to the same degree. These are currently foreign-born fathers, fathers with little or no income, fathers with little education and fathers with no labour market position, characteristics that overlap in many cases. For example, there is a larger proportion of foreign-born fathers than Swedish-born fathers outside the labour market. As the parental leave insurance is meant to cover income loss for temporary exits from the labour market, the results are hardly surprising. As fathers without work have little to gain financially from taking leave, they will not make use of it. The leave usage among fathers in Sweden is becoming increasingly polarised, and the obvious question may be why fathers with high education and income do not take leave in an even more gender-equal manner. Another question is whether fathers would take more leave if they all had a better chance of a stable labour market position and decent income. It is important to point out the close connection between work and family life as well as family and labour market policies. As long as structural constraints such as vulnerable labour market positions remain, it seems less likely that information and campaigns that encourage fathers' parental leave will be successful. It is also important to point out that the parental leave insurance is still directed at families with two parents, and single parents (mothers and fathers alike) will have greater difficulty taking advantage of the reforms discussed in this chapter. This especially applies to the gender equality bonus. In Sweden currently, alternatives to the bonus are being discussed and there are strong voices lobbying for a longer father's quota.

One may also question the objective of fathers' increased parental leave as a state policy regulating childcare in a way that makes middle-class behaviour the norm, failing to recognise other ways of understanding shared parenting (Gilles, 2005). The questioning of shared leave is mainly done in Sweden by emphasising the family's right to decide over parental childcare, and less with a social class perspective in focus. Moreover, parental childcare might obviously be provided without being on leave, and leave can be taken without having the primary responsibility for the child. The Nordic countries have different regulations, and, for example, it is common in Norway for the mother to remain home while the father is on leave (Brandth and Kvande, 2003; see also Chapter Six, this volume). Unemployed fathers and students are also likely to be at home during the mother's leave. This calls for a combination of qualitative and quantitative studies on how parental leave is used for various groups of parents in Sweden, and a more critical eye on how shared parental leave may have an impact on shared parental childcare.

In the current Swedish debate, the quota months are not under strong critique, unlike the case in Norway (see Chapter Thirteen, this volume). The direct effects are known, and the more indirect effects are increasingly discussed. The effects on other areas of society are difficult to measure, especially as influences are likely to be gradual. There are scientific attempts to relate leave to other areas of gender equality, such as income development (see, for example, E.-A. Johansson, 2010). When drawing conclusions from such studies, one should bear in mind that the influence from fathers taking more leave may take time.

This chapter has accounted for how three reforms have had a varying impact on fathers with different characteristics. These have clearly had different impacts on different groups of fathers, and thus have had an impact on the relative differences in usage between groups. An important conclusion is therefore the importance of being cautious when forecasting a potential effect of a reform from an earlier introduced reform. Despite this caution, an informed guess is that quotas are more efficient than tax bonuses in terms of changing parents' behaviour.

Note

[1] The definition of father's quota applied in this book is that it is a non-transferable, individual right to a part of the parental leave, based on the 'use-it-or lose-it' principle.

References

Almqvist, A.-L., Sandberg, A. and Dahlgren, L. (2011) 'Parental leave in Sweden: motives, experiences and gender equality amongst parents', *Fathering*, vol 9, no 2, pp 189-206.

Angrist, J.D. and Krueger, A.B. (1999) 'Empirical strategies in labor economics', in O.C. Ashenfelter and D. Card (eds) *Handbook of labor economics*, vol 3, part A, Amsterdam: North-Holland, pp 1277-366.

Bekkengen, L. (2002) *Man får välja – om föräldraskap och föräldraledighet i arbetsliv och familjeliv* [*One has to choose – parenthood and parental leave in work and family life*], Malmö: Liber.

Brandth, B. and Kvande, E. (2003) *Fleksible fedre* [*Flexible fathers*], Oslo: Universitetsförlaget.

Bygren, M. and Duvander, A. (2006) 'Parents' workplace situation and fathers' parental leave use', *Journal of Marriage and Family*, vol 68, pp 363-72.

Cedstrand, S. (2011) *Från idé till politisk verklighet: Föräldrapolitiken i Sverige och Danmark* [*From idea to political reality: Family policy in Sweden and Denmark*], Umeå: Boréa Bokförlag.

Chronholm, A. (2009) 'Sweden: individualization of free choice in parental leave', in S.B. Kamerman and P. Moss (eds) *The politics of parental leave policies*, Bristol: Policy Press, pp 227-41.

Duvander, A. and Berggren, S. (2003) *Family assets: Time and money: Social insurance in Sweden 2003*, Stockholm: National Social Insurance Board.

Duvander, A. and Eklund, S. (2006) 'Utrikesfödda och svenskfödda föräldrars föräldrapenninganvändande' ['Foreign-born and Swedish-born parents' parental leave use'], in P. de los Reyes (ed) *Om välfärdens gränser och det villkorade medborgarskapet* [*The limits of welfare and the conditions of citizenship*], SOU, vol 37, pp 33-68, Stockholm: Fritzes.

Duvander, A. and Jans, A. (2009) 'Consequences of fathers' parental leave use: evidence from Sweden', in *Finnish Yearbook of Population Research*, Special Issue of the 16th Nordic Demographic Symposium in Helsinki, 5-7 June, pp 51-62.

Duvander, A. and Johansson, M. (2012a) 'What are the effects of reforms promoting fathers' parental leave use?', *Journal of European Social Policy*, vol 22, no 3, pp 319-30.

Duvander, A. and Johansson, M. (2012b) *Ett jämställt uttag? Reformer inom föräldraförsäkringen* [*Equal use? Reforms within the parental leave*], Report 2012, vol 4, Stockholm: Inspectorate for Social Insurance.

Duvander, A. and Lammi-Taskula, J. (2012) 'Parental leave', in I. Gíslason and G.B. Eydal (eds) *Parental leave, childcare and gender equality in the Nordic countries*, Copenhagen: Nordic Council of Ministers, pp 29-62.

Ekberg, J., Eriksson, R. and Friebel, G. (2013), 'Parental leave: a policy evaluation of the Swedish "Daddy Month" reform', *Journal of Public Economics*, vol 97, pp 131-43.

Eklund, S. (2004) 'Flexibel föräldrapenning: hur mammor och pappor använder föräldraförsäkringen och hur länge de är föräldralediga' ['Flexible parental leave: how mothers and fathers use parental insurance and how long they are on parental leave'], *RFV Analyserar 2004*, vol 15, Stockholm: National Social Insurance Board.

Eydal, G.B. (2008) 'Policies promoting care from both parents: the case of Iceland', in G.B. Eydal and I.V. Gíslason (eds) *Equal rights to earn and care: Parental leave in Iceland*, Reykjavik: University of Iceland, pp 111-48.

Ferrarini, T. and Duvander, A. (2010) 'Earner-carer model at the crossroads: reforms and outcomes of Sweden's family policy in a comparative perspective', *International Journal of Health Services*, vol 40, no 3, pp 373-98.

Geisler, E. and Kreyenfeld, M. (2011) 'Against all odds: fathers' use of parental leave in Germany', *Journal of European Social Policy*, vol 21, no 1, pp 88-99.

Gilles, V. (2005) 'Raising the "meritocracy": parenting and the individualization of social class', *Sociology*, vol 39, no 5, pp 835-51.

Glauber, R. and Gozjolko, K.L. (2011) 'Do traditional fathers always work more? Gender ideology, race, and parenthood', *Journal of Marriage and the Family*, vol 73, pp 1133-48.

Haas, L. and Hwang, P. (2008) 'The impact of taking parental leave on fathers' participation in childcare and relationships with children: lessons from Sweden', *Community, Work and Family*, vol 11, no 1, pp 85-104.

Haas, L. and Hwang, P. (2009) 'Is fatherhood becoming more visible at work? Trends in corporate support for fathers taking parental leave in Sweden', *Fathering*, vol 7, no 3, pp 303-21.

Hobson, B., Duvander, A. and Halldén, K. (2006) 'Men and women's agency and capabilities to create a worklife balance in diverse and changing institutional contexts', in J. Lewis (ed) *Children, changing families and welfare states*, Cheltenham: Edward Elgar Publishing, pp 267-96.

Irwin, S. and Elley, E. (2011) 'Concerted cultivation? Parenting values, education and class diversity', *Sociology*, vol 45, no 3, pp 480-95.

Johansson, E.-A. (2010) *The effect of own and spousal parental leave on earnings*, IFAU Working Paper 2010, vol 4, Uppsala: IFAU (Institute for Labor Market Policy Evaluation).

Johansson, M. (2010) 'Jämställdhetsbonusen: en effektutvärdering' ['Gender equality bonus: an evaluation of effects'], *Social Insurance Report*, vol 5, Stockholm: Swedish Social Insurance Agency.

Johansson, T. (2011) 'Fatherhood in transition: paternity leave and changing masculinities', *Journal of Family Communication*, vol 11, no 3, pp 165-80.

Johansson, T. and Klinth, R. (2008) 'Caring fathers: the ideology of gender equality and masculine positions', *Men and Masculinities*, vol 11, no 1, pp 42-62.

Klinth, R. (2002) *Göra pappa med barn. Den svenska pappapolitiken 1960-1995* [*Make fathers have children. Swedish fatherhood politics 1960-1995*], Umeå: Boréa Förlag.

Klinth, R. (2008) 'The best of both worlds? Fatherhood and gender equality in Swedish paternity leave campaigns 1976-2006', *Fathering*, vol 6, no 1, pp 20-38.

Nepomnyaschy, L. and Waldfogel, J. (2007) 'Paternity leave and fathers' involvement with their young children: evidence from the American Ecls-B', *Community, Work and Family*, vol 10, no 4, pp 427-53.

O'Brien, M., Brandth, B. and Kvande, E. (2007) 'Fathers, work and family life: global perspectives and new insights', *Community, Work and Family*, vol 10, no 4, pp 375-86.

Plantin, L. (2007) 'Different classes, different fathers? On fatherhood, economic conditions and class in Sweden', *Community, Work and Family*, vol 10, no 1, pp 93-110.

Rosenzweig, M.A. and Wolpin, K.I. (2000) '"Natural" natural experiments in economics', *Journal of Economic Literature*, vol 38, pp 827-74.

Stefansen, K. and Farstad, G.R. (2010) 'Classed parental practices in a modern welfare state: caring for the under threes in Norway', *Critical Social Policy*, vol 30, no 1, pp 120-41.

Stefansen, K. and Skogen, K. (2010) 'Selective identification, quiet distancing: understanding the working-class response to the Nordic daycare model', *The Sociological Review*, vol 58, no 4, pp 587-603.

Sundström, M. and Duvander, A. (2002) 'Gender division of childcare and the sharing of parental leave among new parents in Sweden', *European Sociological Review*, vol 18, pp 433-47.

Swedish Social Insurance Agency (2013a) *Social insurance in figures*, Stockholm: Swedish Social Insurance Agency.

Swedish Social Insurance Agency (2013b) 'De jämställda föräldrarna. Vad ökar sannolikheten för ett jämställt föräldrapenninguttag?' ['Gender equal parents. What factors increase a gender equal parental leave use?'], *Socialförsäkringsrapport 2013*, vol 8, Stockholm: Swedish Social Insurance Agency. Swedish Social Insurance Agency (2014) *Social insurance in figures*, Stockholm: Swedish Social Insurance Agency.

Appendix A: Description of variable definitions (for more information, see Duvander and Johansson, 2012b)

Variable	Explanation
Flat rate, father, mother[a]	Parent has earnings below the flat rate compensation at the time of each reform (60 SEK/day at the time of the introduction of the first and second reserved month, and 180 SEK per day for the gender equality bonus)
Low, father, mother[a]	Parent has earnings over the flat rate compensation and up to 5 price base amount
Medium, father, mother[a]	Parents' earnings are over 5 price base amount but below the highest compensation rate at the time of each reform (7.5 price base amount at the time of the introduction of the first and second reserved month, and 10 price base amount for the gender equality bonus)
High, father, mother[a]	Parents' earnings are above the ceiling of the parental leave benefits
Central government, father, mother	Parent employed in government sector
Local government, father, mother	Parent employed in municipal authority or county council
Private sector, father, mother	Parent works in private sector
Unknown sector, father, mother	Parent is not working
Cities[b]	Municipalities with a population of over 200,000 inhabitants and municipalities where more than 50% of the nocturnal population commute to work in another area. The most common commuting destination is one of the metropolitan municipalities
Larger towns[b]	Municipalities with 50,000-200,000 inhabitants and more than 70% of urban area
Rest of Sweden[b]	Municipalities in which more than 40% of the nocturnal population commute to work in another municipality and municipalities with fewer than seven inhabitants per km² and fewer than 20,000 inhabitants and municipalities where more than 40% of the nocturnal population aged between 16-64 are employed in manufacturing and industry (SNI92) and municipalities that do not belong to any of the previous categories and have a population of more than 25,000 and municipalities that do not belong to any of the previous categories and have a population of 12,500-25,000 and municipalities that do not belong to any of the previous categories and have a population of less than 12,500

Notes:

[a] Parents are divided into four groups according to their annual earnings. Earnings are expressed in price base amounts the year before each reform (1994 for the first reserved month, 2001 for the second reserved month and 2007 for the gender equality bonus). The price base amount follows the price trend in Sweden each year and is set by government. The amount is used for calculating different kinds of benefits. The amount of benefit changes automatically when the price base amount is changed. The price base amount was 35,200 SEK (approx €3,520) in 1994, 36,900 SEK (approx €3,690) in 2001 and 40,300 SEK (approx €4,030) in 2007.

[b] The regional breakdown is based on the division made by the Swedish Association of Local Authorities and Regions (Sveriges kommuner och landsting, SKL). For a detailed description, see SKL's homepage at www.skl.se

Appendix B: Parental leave days for various groups of fathers before and after reforms in the parental leave insurance (OLS regressions)

	First reserved month		Second reserved month		Gender equality bonus	
	Control	Treatment	Control	Treatment	Control	Treatment
Gender						
Boy	24.7***	35.2***	41.0**	48.4**	57.5	56.4
Girl	26.3***	35.9***	42.0***	47.1***	58.2	56.3
Age						
<30, father	23.7***	33.0***	40.5**	47.1**	56.6	53.5
31-35, father	27.6***	37.6***	43.5	46.5	60.7	61.5
36+, father	26.9***	38.5***	40.4***	50.3***	55.9	53.2
<30, mother	25.5***	35.9***	39.9***	46.7***	55.7	52.9
31-35, mother	25.2***	35.7***	43.3**	48.8**	61.1	60.6
36+, mother	26.1*	32.7*	44.2	50.0	57.3	58.5
Country of birth						
Both parents Sweden	26.0***	35.9***	42.0***	49.6***	60.9	61.4
Both parents abroad	15.4***	36.6***	35.8	30.9	35.7*	29.6*
Father Sweden, mother abroad	42.7	38.1	50.8	55.2	68.0	59.5
Father abroad, mother Sweden	18.6*	25.9*	36.5	44.6	52.0	50.9
Birth order						
First child, father	28.9***	37.7***	45.3***	53.6***	65.7	64.2
Second child, father	23.2***	33.1***	37.8**	43.2**	53.1	51.4
Third+ child, father	23.0***	35.6***	38.2	40.5	47.4	45.1
Earnings						
Flat rate, father	6.9***	17.4***	20.0	18.9	39.5	36.4
Low, father	20.3***	34.6***	37.7	41.2	48.8*	42.5*
Medium, father	32.0***	40.0***	42.1***	49.2***	60.0	56.8
High, father	34.5	36.0	44.5***	56.8***	61.1	64.3
Over ceiling, father			45.7	45.0	61.2	61.0
Flat rate, mother	40.2*	50.1*	48.3	49.8	61.0*	52.5*
Low, mother	23.2***	32.6***	38.3	41.7	46.6	43.2
Medium, mother	28.2***	39.9***	39.7***	48.8***	57.1	58.8
High, mother	23.3***	41.2***	54.4	59.5	76.3	74.3
Over ceiling, mother			68.9	71.1	79.7	78.9

(continued)

A study of the impact of three Swedish parental leave reforms

	First reserved month		Second reserved month		Gender equality bonus	
	Control	Treatment	Control	Treatment	Control	Treatment
Sector						
Central government, father	31.0**	38.6**	48.1**	59.6**	76.0	77.0
Local government, father	31.1***	42.0***	51.0	58.1	70.2	72.8
Private sector, father	25.3***	35.4***	40.2***	46.4***	55.5	54.3
Not working, father	13.3	19.2	31.5***	14.9***	31.3	24.5
Central government, mother	28.1***	40.2***	51.3	52.0	76.1	73.7
Local government, mother	24.1***	35.7***	38.2***	48.8***	56.4	58.4
Private sector, mother	25.9***	34.6***	40.4***	47.2***	57.7	57.0
Not working, mother	26.7*	35.4*	50.4	41.9	48.2**	36.5**
Living location						
Cities	27.7***	37.8***	45.2**	50.6**	64.4	62.7
Larger towns	26.8***	35.7***	42.2	45.3	58.7	57.4
Rest of Sweden	22.8***	33.7***	37.3***	46.8***	49.7	48.2
Education						
Primary, father	19.8***	33.0***	35.2	33.8	44.3	40.9
Secondary, father	24.1***	35.1***	37.5***	46.0***	50.8	47.2
Tertiary, father	34.7	38.9	50.6*	55.2*	70.6	72.6
Unknown, father	3.9**	19.3**	29.6	29.8	37.2	27.2
Primary, mother	21.7***	31.1***	37.5	36.7	44.0	40.1
Secondary, mother	21.9***	32.8***	34.9***	42.3***	46.0**	41.2**
Tertiary, mother	33.7***	43.1***	51.4***	58.4***	70.2	72.3
Unknown, mother	32.5	36.3	44.1	36.5	43.4	36.6
Observations	12,440		10,371		14,467	
R2	0.0623		0.0722		0.1046	

Notes:
***Significant difference (1% level) between control and treatment groups;
**Significant difference (5% level) between control and treatment groups;
*Significant difference (10% level) between control and treatment groups.

Theme 5:
International reflections on findings

SEVENTEEN

Parental leave and fathers: extending and deepening the knowledge base

Janet Gornick

Introduction

In recent decades, social scientists from numerous disciplines in the Nordic countries and abroad have turned their attention to the study of gender disparities in paid work and, in tandem, gender divisions of labour at home. A second voluminous literature has addressed social policies that facilitate reconciling parenthood and employment – often referred to as 'family-friendly' policies. Researchers tackling these policy questions have also come from multiple disciplines, and they have employed diverse analytic methods, both quantitative and qualitative; some have worked from a gender or feminist perspective while others have not.

These two large bodies of scholarship have converged in recent years around the study of leave policies, that is, policies enabling parents to take temporary breaks from paid work – with job protection, remuneration or both – to care for young children. That these groups of scholars are interested in leave is hardly surprising given that leave policies are intended to affect outcomes in both paid and unpaid work, and they are a core component of the work–family reconciliation policy package. It is also not surprising that this literature is heavily cross-national (albeit largely limited to affluent countries), because policy designs vary sharply across countries. Perhaps more remarkable is the recent and sustained swell of research focused squarely – or even exclusively – on leave policies and fathers.

In this brief chapter, I first focus on key conclusions from the existing fathers-and-leave literature – drawing substantially on my own past work. Following that, I highlight the conclusions and lessons emerging from the studies in this innovative volume.

Lessons learned until now

Research on fathers and leave has generally tackled three large, intertwined questions:

1. What leave rights and benefits are actually granted to fathers in the world's affluent countries?
2. What policy features encourage or incentivise fathers to take up the leave and benefits to which they are entitled?
3. To what extent – and where – are leave policy designs the most and least gender-egalitarian?

Several conclusions have emerged from this body of scholarship. First, as scholars have assessed the existing leave provisions for fathers – across countries – they have had to grapple with the fact that these schemes not only vary widely, but that they are also remarkably complex. Leave is often provided to fathers via father-only paternity leave schemes (which are relatively straightforward). In many countries, however, some or all of the leave granted to fathers is embedded in parental leave policies, such policies often being famously complicated. Parental leave schemes typically combine job protection and wage replacement (with durations that may not coincide); they often grant combinations of paid and unpaid time off; and each parent's entitlement may depend on the other parent's eligibility or actual usage. Moreover, leave policies frequently include features allowing flexibility in the timing of take-up (across days, weeks, months or years), and many schemes rely on diverse – and sometimes overlapping – funding streams. Finally, some schemes reserve periods of parental leave specifically for either of the parents, typically the father. Leave reserved specifically for fathers – that is, individual rights to non-transferable periods of leave – are intended to increase male take-up of parental leave, and thus more gender-egalitarian leave outcomes. In this book, these periods of leave are referred to as a 'father's quota'.

That said, fathers' leave entitlements vary markedly across affluent countries. In their 2010 study, Ray, Gornick and Schmitt compared 21 public parental leave schemes on several dimensions, including the generosity of the leave granted to mothers and fathers as of 2009. Obviously, leave generosity can be measured in countless ways. Ray et al captured the total number of weeks available to fathers, in couples, including both paid and unpaid leave. Their indicator – reported in Figure 17.1 below – includes only portions of leave entitlements available for fathers; it excludes any periods that could be taken by mothers. Thus, this figure captures periods of leave granted only to fathers (paternity leave), other periods granted to individuals (including fathers), and periods of leave set up as the father's quota – this measure captures, in essence, the minimum paternal entitlement. Given the social and economic pressures acting on fathers, the paternity leave and the father's quota are often the only days that fathers take. (Figure 17.1 reflects these policies as they existed in January 2009.)

On the high end, a handful of countries offer fathers (unpaid) job-protected leave in excess of one year, including both Sweden and Norway. The vast majority of countries offer much less, however, and four countries offer nothing at all to fathers (Australia, Canada, Japan and Switzerland).

Overall, *paid* leave available for fathers is remarkably limited. As of 2009, Sweden offered fathers the most such leave; Norway offered substantially less; Finland and Denmark even less (Ray et al, 2010, unfortunately did not include Iceland). Ten countries, including the US, provided neither paid paternity nor paid parental leave reserved for fathers.

Second, recent research suggests that fathers appear to be more likely to take up the leave to which they *are* entitled under certain circumstances – specifically, when the effective wage replacement rate is high, when some or all of fathers' rights cannot be transferred to

Figure 17.1: Total and FTE (full-time equivalent) paid leave for fathers in couples, in weeks, 2009[1]

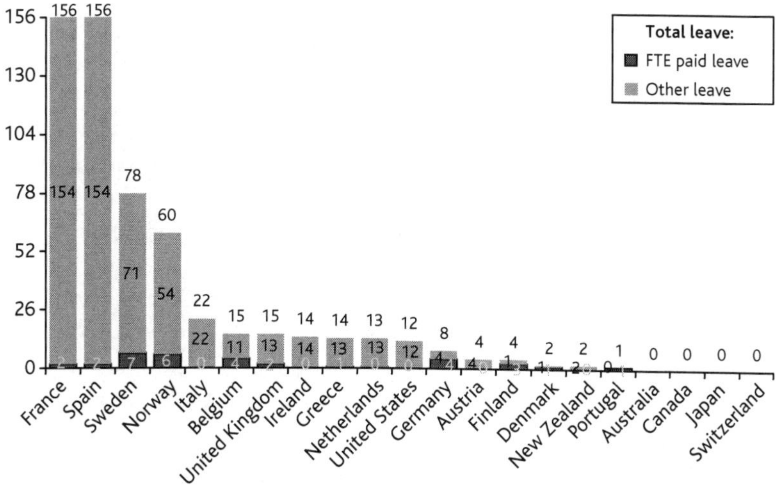

Source: Figure 3 in Ray, Gornick, Schmitt 2010

their (usually female) partners, and when leave can be taken flexibly (for example, part-time, intermittently).[2]

Even though most parental leave schemes in high-income countries are now designed on a gender-neutral basis (outside of a brief health-related period reserved exclusively for mothers), the progress in many countries has been slow in getting fathers to take any parental leave, let alone an equal share. In countries such as Germany, France and Austria, 2 per cent of fathers participate in leave compared to 90 per cent of mothers, reflecting, in part, 'traditional norms' and beliefs that 'parental leave continues to be a women's affair' (de Henau et al, 2007, p 80). Women are not only more likely to take leave, but they are also usually the sole participants in leave (de Henau et al, 2007).

These enormous gender differences in leave take-up have prompted several studies aimed at identifying the most successful practices for encouraging fathers' take-up (Bruning and Plantenga, 1999; Leira, 1999; Björnberg, 2002; Pylkkänen and Smith, 2004; Deven and Moss, 2005; Eriksson, 2005; O'Brien, 2005; Duvander and Andersson, 2006; de Henau et al, 2007; Eydal and Gíslason, 2008; Jónsdóttir and Aðalsteinsson, 2008).

One country, Portugal, has made five days of paternity leave obligatory (on the same principle that new mothers must take 90 days leave around the time of the birth of their child), leading to a steep increase (although not universal take-up) in the use of the obligatory portion, and also in the proportion of men making use of additional leave entitlements (Wall and Leitao, 2008). Beyond such measures, specific design features of policies also have an impact. Men's leave take-up is much more sensitive to wage replacement levels than is the case with women, with countries with higher reimbursements often having more father take-up, leading researchers to see replacement rates at 80-100 per cent as a step toward universal father take-up (Deven and Moss, 2005). In Luxembourg and Norway, where income replacement rates are high, use of paternity/parental leave by men is very high (de Henau et al, 2007). In Slovenia, two thirds of all fathers take the portion of paternity leave paid at 100 per cent of wage replacement, but the uptake of additional leave paid at a much lower rate of wage replacement drops to a few percentage points (Stropnik, 2008). Where wage replacement is below 100 per cent, few parents in couples are able to afford a simultaneous reduction in income for both of them. Pre-existing differences in earnings, with male jobs typically paying more than female jobs, also tend to reinforce a traditional division of care work, with women making use of leave and men continuing in full employment.

Yet even in countries with high wage replacement levels, women have been the majority of leave takers, and policymakers have reacted by increasing incentives for a more equal share of leave by providing portions of leave to each parent on a non-transferable ('use-it-or-lose-it') basis, meaning that unless the father takes leave, leave is lost to the family. Research predating this volume from Iceland, Norway and Sweden revealed increases in fathers' use of leave with the introduction of the non-transferable father's quota (Leira, 1999; Björnberg, 2002; Eriksson, 2005; Duvander and Andersson, 2006; see Ray et al, 2010, for a detailed discussion of non-transferability). As can be expected, this policy design feature receives sustained attention in this volume.

In addition, a strong preference for leave flexibility among fathers has been noted in several countries. Where fathers do take leave (in addition to paternity leave, which must usually be taken close to the birth or adoption of a child), they are much more likely than mothers to make use of flexible arrangements allowing them to take leave as a reduction in working hours rather than as full-time leave. In Belgium, all employees are entitled to a 12-month job-protected career break, which can either be taken in a single block or spread out over a longer period by reducing the weekly workload, up to a maximum of five years at 80 per cent. Although women proportionately continue to be three times as likely as men to take such leave to care for children, take-up among men has grown rapidly (albeit from a low base), and men have been particularly likely to choose the 80 per cent option (Vandeweyer and Glorieux, 2008). Likewise in the Netherlands, on average, fathers who took parental leave (Dutch fathers have a comparatively high take-up rate, at over one fifth of men entitled to leave) took it as a 20 per cent reduction in the usual working hours (Greonendijk and Keuzenkamp, 2008, p 261). In Germany, a policy reform introduced in 2001, making it possible to combine parental leave with up to 30 hours of weekly part-time work, resulted in a tripling of the proportion of fathers taking parental leave, although the overall numbers remain limited (Bundesregierung Deutschland, 2004, p 18).

Third, the extent to which the underlying architecture is gender-egalitarian – in practice – varies from country to country. Ray et al (2010) constructed a 15-point gender equality scale and applied it to the same 21 countries (noted above). This index consists of three components: the portion of a couple's leave that is available to fathers (worth 9 points), the wage replacement rate during the father's leave (worth 5 points), and additional incentives or disincentives for fathers to take parental leave (worth 1 point, positive or negative) (see Ray et al, 2010, for details).[3] The results are reported in Figure 17.2 below.

Figure 17.2: Gender Equality Index, 2009

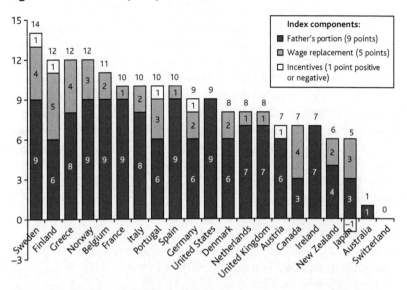

Source: Figure 4 in Ray, Gornick, Schmitt 2010

These results indicate that, as of 2009, Sweden earned the highest score on this index, with 14 points. Finland, Greece[4] and Norway each earned 12 points, and Belgium followed, with 11 points. France, Italy, Portugal and Spain each received 10 points. Germany and the US fell at the median of nine points. Denmark, the Netherlands and the UK trailed closely behind at 8 points. Austria, Ireland and Canada each earned 7 points, and four countries scored fewer than 7 points: New Zealand (6), Japan (5), Australia (1), and Switzerland (0) (again, Ray et al, 2010, unfortunately, did not include Iceland).

In a final analysis (not shown here), Ray et al (2010) combined measures of leave generosity with scores on this gender equality index. In short, four countries fell among the five most generous with respect to paid leave *and* among the five most gender-egalitarian. These four countries included three Nordic countries – Finland, Norway and Sweden – and Greece. Each of these countries provides couples with six months or more of fully paid leave and scores 12 or more points on this gender equality index. Taken as a group, then, these four countries have policy features that appear to go the furthest in promoting both generosity and gender equality.

Caring fathers in the Nordic countries: further lessons

Despite this substantial amount of accumulated knowledge to date, the literature on fathers and leave has remained incomplete in many ways. *Fatherhood in the Nordic welfare states: Comparing care policies and practice* offers a wealth of new research on fathers and fathering practices in the five Nordic countries – both deepening and broadening the knowledge about fathers and leave.

Few questions are asked of comparative leave scholars, especially in Anglo-Saxon settings, more often than this one: 'If the Nordic countries have such well-developed and gender-egalitarian leave policies, why does men's take-up so substantially lag behind women's?' Several studies in this volume shed light on the answers to that question.

In the remainder of this brief chapter, I highlight three illuminating findings, which recur throughout this collection and extend current knowledge, especially about the barriers to gender-egalitarian leave usage.[5] While some of these 'new' findings may not be especially new to Nordic analysts, they are relatively new, or at least under-emphasised, in the larger body of leave scholarship.

First, a range of results reported in this volume underscore that gendered expectations regarding paid and unpaid work remain powerful and consequential – 'even' in these notoriously (relatively) gender-egalitarian Nordic countries. Despite the strong signal sent by the state, indicating that father-provided care is valued, many men and women adhere to traditional gendered role allocation – they 'do gender', if you will – which in turn constrains the power of the structural innovations embedded in the leave laws.

For example, in their study of obstacles to fathers' leave-taking in Finland, Salmi and Lammi-Taskula highlight the persistence of gendered role-taking:

> Views on the division of labour between women and men turned out to play a crucial role when parents make decisions on sharing the parental leave. When education level, spouse's education level, income level, employer sector and occupational group of fathers were taken into account, only the age of the father and his view on men as the main provider for the family predicted his take-up of parental leave. (Chapter Fourteen, this volume)

Stunningly, Salmi and Lammi-Taskula report that only one in three families actually made calculations regarding the financial consequences of the father's leave. Prior notions about who should take leave were often (apparently) unaffected by the financial realities that policy designers believe to be so central to family decision making.

Clearly, despite dramatic shifts in gender roles in recent decades, many men and women in the Nordic countries still 'do gender'. Part of this practice includes, *ceteris paribus*, allocating work and care responsibilities according to gender. While the mere existence of gendered role allocation is not unexpected, the magnitude and power of 'gendering' as a continued obstacle to fathers' leave-taking – a recurring theme throughout this volume – may surprise (and disappoint) many readers.

Second, workplace actors and practices remain another substantial barrier to more extensive use of leave by fathers. Findings reported in this collection indicate that – in many cases – employers and places of employment continue to impede fathers' leave-taking. That constraint interacts with stubbornly gendered expectations, further undermining the potential of policy design elements aimed at shoring up men's take-up.

While many chapters address this, workplace constraints (intertwined with gendered expectations) are treated in the greatest detail in Bloksgaard's chapter on negotiating leave in the Danish workplace.[6] About her three workplace study, Bloksgaard concludes:

> This chapter has shown that highly gendered expectations
> for women and men as parents/leave-takers and workers/
> providers, respectively, exist in the three workplaces studied.
> These findings confirm earlier Danish workplace studies....
> the sharable and assumed gender-neutral Danish parental
> leave is perceived as being 'for mothers'. This finding
> supports research in the other Nordic countries showing
> that the mother usually takes all of the sharable leave
> entitlement and the father only the elements earmarked
> specifically for fathers.... In Denmark, there is neither a
> strong cultural ideal of 'the present father' as one who takes
> leave nor a legislative father's quota setting limits for fathers'
> work–life and legitimising leave as 'appropriate behaviour'
> for fathers in the workplace. (Chapter Seven, this volume)

Third, the research presented in this volume brings into relief how fathers' leave-taking is 'classed': for multiple reasons, constraints on leave usage are more severe among lower-earning, lower-income and/or less educated men. In addition to suppressing men's leave-taking in the aggregate, the existence of class gradients raises the spectre of hidden forms of inequality among fathers and their families as well as the possibility that leave policies might inadvertently worsen some forms of inequality (prior to this volume, several scholars assessed the class gradient in women's access to and use of leave, but much less has been known about how men's leave is 'classed').

A recurring theme in this volume is the diversity of experiences seen among men. Rostgaard and Lausten sum this up in reference to the Danish case:

> Consequently, we witness an increasing discrepancy among fathers over time, in those who take leave and those who do not…. [It] is now more the well-educated fathers … with well-educated partners who take parental leave, presumably because they stand in a better situation in the labour market – they may have secured better leave rights and may also have a partner who is more eager herself to return to the labour market…. The present composition of statutory leave entitlements positions fathers differently, however, thus working against the Nordic principle of universalism. (Chapter Thirteen, this volume)

Obviously, the evidence of class effects is not limited to Denmark. Duvander and Johansson find (possibly increasing) class-related disparities in Sweden: '… and the result was thus remaining or increasing differences between groups of fathers.' Eydal and Gíslason, referring to Iceland, report that one 'group that seems to call for special attention is the low-earning households', adding that it 'is not entirely clear why there are fewer fathers in this group that make use of their right.' Brandth and Kvande's rich and nuanced study of 'classed fathering practices' in Norway concludes that care 'is reconciled with norms of masculinity' in both the working and middle classes; it 'may, however, proceed at different speeds and along rather varied roads.'

In conclusion, this methodologically diverse, rich, broad and innovative volume sheds invaluable light on the contemporary state of fathers and parental leave in the Nordic countries. Three key findings are likely to 'jump out' at leave scholars – especially from outside the Nordic countries. In short, (1) gendered expectations about work and care still matter (and they matter a lot); (2) workplaces present constraints (in part by cementing the gendered practices that still guide many families' decision making and behaviour); and (3) fathers' leave-taking is 'classed', meaning that effective access to, and use of, leave remains disparate across groups of men. Nordic scholars, policy advocates and policymakers still have plenty of work to do – as they continue to strive for societies characterised by gender-egalitarian parenting and the principles of universalism.

Notes

[1] Editors' note: For an overview of available leave periods in the Nordic countries as of 2013 see Chapter Thirteen.

[2] This section, on policy features associated with men's take-up, is drawn from a literature review on the impact of work-family policies, prepared for The World Bank (forthcoming) by Janet C. Gornick and Ariane Hegewisch.

[3] Ray et al (2010) recognised that a more comprehensive index would have included a component capturing flexibility, but it was outside the scope of their study.

[4] While a large body of prior literature has reported that the Nordic countries have social policies in place that support gender equality, earlier research had not painted Greece as a high performer in this area. At the same time, it is important to stress that while the Greek law has gender-egalitarian design elements, its impact may be comparatively limited. Greece – even before the severe crisis – had much higher shares of self-employment and informal employment than these three Nordic countries and a higher share than most of the rest of the sample as well. High rates of self-employment and informality reduce the effective coverage rates for parental leave policies.

[5] Although issues related to leave are laced throughout this volume, I direct most of my remarks to Chapter Six, on classed fathering practices in Norway, Chapter Seven, on negotiating leave in the Danish workplace, and on the four chapters in the final section: Chapter Thirteen, about gendered incentives in Denmark, Chapter Fourteen, about obstacles in Finland, Chapter Fifteen, that focused on the Icelandic case and Chapter Sixteen, on Swedish reforms.

[6] It is important to note that Denmark is something of a Nordic outlier inasmuch as workers must negotiate their own leave rights and options. In that sense, the Danish case provides the most intense look at the constraints that come into play when fathers must negotiate individually – as is the case in many non-Nordic countries.

References

Björnberg, U. (2002) 'Working and caring for children: family policies and balancing work and family in Sweden', in A.H. Carling, S. Duncan and R. Edwards (eds) *Analysing families: Morality and rationality in policy and practice*, London and New York: Routledge, pp 93-100.

Bruning, G. and Plantenga, J. (1999) 'Parental leave and equal opportunities: experiences in eight European countries', *Journal of European Social Policy*, vol 9, pp 195-209.

Bundesregierung Deutschland [Government of Germany] (2005) *Bericht der Bundesregierung Deutschland 2004. Unterrichtung der Bundesregierung: Bericht über die Auswirkungen der §§15 und 16 Bundeserziehungsgeldgesetzes* [*Communication of the Federal Government: Report about the effects of para 15 and 16 of the Federal parental/educational leave law*], Prepared by BMFSFJ, German Parliament, 15th Election cycle, Drucksache 15/3400; 17 June.

de Henau, J., Meulders, D. and O'Dorchai, S. (2007) 'Parents' care and career: comparing parental leave policies across EU-15', in D. del Boca and C. Wetzels (eds) *Social policies, labour markets and motherhood: A comparative analysis of European countries*, Cambridge: Cambridge University Press, pp 63-106.

Deven, F. and Moss, P. (eds) (2005) *Leave policies and research: Reviews and country notes*, CBGS-Werkdocument 2005/3, Brussels: Centrum voor Bevolkingsen Gezinsstudie (www.cbgs.be).

Duvander, A. and Andersson, G. (2006) 'Gender equality and fertility in Sweden: a study on the impact of the father's uptake of parental leave on continued childbearing', in S.K. Wisensale and L. Haas (eds) *Families and social policy: National and international perspectives*, New York: The Haworth, pp 121-42.

Eriksson, R. (2005) *Parental leave in Sweden: The effects of the second daddy month*, Working Paper Series 9/2005, Stockholm: Swedish Institute for Social Research.

Eydal, G.B. and Gíslason, I. V. (2008) 'Paid parental leave in Iceland – history and context', in G.B. Eydal and I.V. Gíslason (eds) *Equal rights to earn and care: Parental leave in Iceland*, Reykjavik: Félagsvísindastofnun Háskóla Íslands, pp 15-44.

Gornick, J.C. and Hegewisch, A. (forthcoming) *The impact of 'family-friendly policies' on women's employment outcomes and on the costs and benefits of doing business*, Commissioned report for The World Bank.

Greonendijk, H. and Keuzenkamp, S. (2008) 'The Netherlands', in P. Moss and M. Korintus (eds) *International review of leave policies and related research 2008*, BERR Employment Relations Series No 100 (www.berr.gov.uk), pp 256-69.

Jónsdóttir, B. and Aðalsteinsson, G.D. (2008) 'Icelandic parents' perception of parental leave', in G.B. Eydal and I.V. Gíslason (eds) *Equal rights to earn and care*, Reykjavik: Félagsvísindastofnun Háskóli Íslands, pp 65-86.

Leira, A. (1999) 'Cash-for-child care and daddy leave', in P. Moss and F. Deven (eds) *Parental leave: Progress or pitfall?*, Brussels: NIDI/CBGS Publications, pp 267-92.

O'Brien, M. (2005) *Shared caring: Bringing fathers into the frame*, Working Paper Series No 18, Manchester: Equal Opportunities Commission (www.uea.ac.uk).

Pylkkänen, E. and Smith, N. (2004) *The impact of family-friendly policies in Denmark and Sweden on mothers' career interruptions due to childbirth*, IZA Discussion Paper No 1050, Bonn: Forschunginstitut zur Zukunft der Arbeit GmbH (17A)j (http://papers.ssrn.com).

Ray, R., Gornick, J.C. and Schmitt, J. (2010) 'Who cares? Assessing generosity and gender equality in parental leave policy designs in 21 countries', *Journal of European Social Policy*, vol 20, no 3, pp 196-216.

Stropnik, N. (2008) 'Slovenia', in P. Moss and M. Korintus (eds) *International review of leave policies and related research 2008*, BERR Employment Relations Series No 100, London: Department for Business, Enterprise, and Regulatory Reform (BERR) (www.berr. gov.uk), pp 300-7.

Vandeweyer, J. and Glorieux, I. (2008) 'Men taking up career leave: an opportunity for a better work and family life balance?', *Journal of Social Policy*, vol 37, no 2, pp 271-94.

Wall, K. and Leitao, M. (2008) 'Portugal', in P. Moss and M. Korintus (eds) *International review of leave policies and related research 2008*, BERR Employment Relations Series No 100, London: Department for Business, Enterprise, and Regulatory Reform (BERR) (www.berr. gov.uk), pp 291-99.

EIGHTEEN

Nordic fathers: tracking diversity and complexity

Margaret O'Brien

> In a rapidly changing world, we will continue
> witnessing the growing momentum and
> recognition of the importance of men for
> gender equality, reconciling work–family life
> and impacting the future of their children.
> (UN, 2011, p 49)

Introduction

The Nordic countries have been a global touchstone for policymakers and academics concerned with encouraging the greater participation of fathers in childcare and gender equality. They have led the way in devising work–family policy innovation, and attempts to emulate (under the banner of taking a 'Nordic turn') are occurring across Europe (Erler, 2009) and in other regions of the world (Chin et al, 2011). This collection represents a very welcome addition to the international scholarship on fathers, because, despite over half a century of pioneering research (Haas and Hwang, 2013), there have been few books solely devoted to Nordic fathers, and none representing the full range of Nordic countries: Denmark, Finland, Iceland, Norway and Sweden. The breadth and depth of new knowledge about the state of contemporary Nordic fathers is impressive; there is insight into the institutional context in which fathers shape their personal, family and working lives together with specific studies of men's experiences as fathers.

This brief chapter focuses on a common theme cutting across many chapters – the growing diversity and complexity of the household and family relationships of Nordic men with partners and children. While all Nordic governments promote a dual earner/dual carer social democratic welfare state model emphasising the active participation of fathers in childcare, variations in policy and family practices exist. Differences are connected to historical and cultural legacies within and between the five countries, but wider international factors are also driving diversity. The impact of migration on fathering practices is a source of diversity addressed by some of the authors. Similarly, how post-separation fatherhood is managed and negotiated in Nordic families reveals challenges to a shared parenting ideal. Finally, the qualitative studies of gay fathers and role-reversal heterosexual fathers offer insights into 'doing' Nordic fatherhood in diverse contexts.

Migration and moving from homogeneity

Over the last 20 years, as international migration has increased, the Nordic region has become an affluent receiving destination for many families following political unrest in Africa and Asia (Haour-Knipe, 2011). Any new environment provides opportunities and constraints, new sets of values, beliefs and standards and new norms which may change the balance of authority within the family. In her Danish qualitative study, Anika Liversage, in Chapter Ten, portrays how first-generation migrant fathers may feel a post-migratory loss of authority moving to a country where the need for a providing male head of household is less clear in light of a responsible welfare state: 'The assistance offered by the welfare state, including help to single mothers and youth, can also be felt as pulling the carpet out from under the formerly powerful male heads of households' (see Chapter Ten, this volume).

Interviews suggest that, within the Danish labour market, it can be difficult for even highly educated first-generation migrant fathers to regain their former occupational status. Liversage argues that the resulting financial hardship and family strain can have a deleterious influence on second-generation sons who may lose respect for their fathers.

This study and others in the volume testify to the problems with a theory of change in the institution of fatherhood from a patriarchal past to an equal present. A future challenge as Nordic countries become more multi-ethnic and multi-faith is to explore if gender equality can co-exist with different ways of 'doing' fathering and mothering. Forging hybrid parenting practices and identities wherein elements of country and heritage of origin can be weaved together with the new host country with its distinctive cultural ideals is going to become more pressing for future generations.

Post-separation fatherhood

A further source of diversity expressed in this volume is the increase in separation of consensual unions, divorce and re-partnering, all key demographic changes shaping contemporary Nordic fatherhood and indeed other post-industrial societies across the world. Throughout their life course, fathers are now more likely than in previous generations to experience more than one family type, and in the process, fathers typically cease to reside with the children of their first relationship, increasing the potential for marginalisation in family life. Coltrane (2004, p 224) has characterised the simultaneous trends of greater father involvement and increased paternal marginality, especially through relationship breakdown, as constituting the 'paradox of fatherhood' in modern times.

Post-separation fatherhood is difficult to investigate from the perspective of all the parties, particularly the non-resident father. Mai Heide Ottosen's chapter, Chapter Twelve, provides unique insight into the characteristics of non-resident fathers from the perspective of children using a nationally representative longitudinal study of Danish children born in 1995. By the time the children reached 15 years of age, 31 per cent of them had parents who had separated. Cross-checking the children's survey data with the national, register-based records for the non-resident father revealed that contact levels were much higher when non-resident fathers were in high-status occupations. Only 3 per cent of the non-resident fathers working in top management or highly skilled occupations had no contact with their child – according to the child – and most had regular contact. The pattern was reversed when the non-resident father was unemployed and, worryingly, there was a tendency for the children of these marginalised fathers to regard them as being 'less important'. A recent British study has also found that poor socio-economic resources, such as insecure work and housing, hinder contact between non-resident fathers and their children (Poole et al, 2013). Social inequalities can exacerbate paternal marginality in post-separation fatherhood, showing once more the importance – even in Nordic countries – of situating modern fatherhood in a socio-economic and social class context.

Legal codification of diverse fatherhood

This book provides new insights into how Nordic legislators have both responded to and shaped the diverse roles of fathers in recent years. Hrefna Friðriksdóttir, in Chapter Three, shows how Nordic countries have generally accepted an inclusive definition of 'the family' not privileging heterosexual marriage, and more recently are developing legal systems to regulate new forms of fatherhood, such as 'contractual fatherhood', formed in cases of reproductive technologies. Although the Nordic countries were world leaders in legally recognising same-sex relationships in the late 1980s and 1990s, the access of gay couples to parenthood through adoption or reproductive technologies was not enshrined until the mid-2000s.

In all five Nordic countries, there has been debate about whether the introduction of sharing responsibilities contravenes the best interests of the child principle. Somewhat controversially, perhaps, Friðriksdóttir suggests that after separation, Nordic fathers have especially benefited from the United Nations (UN) Convention on the Rights of the Child (UNCRC 1989), specifically Article 18, which advocates the sharing of parental responsibilities. Under Article 3 of the UNCRC, the best interests of the child are deemed paramount in contact decisions over any concept of parental or gender rights to a child. However, the UNCRC also enshrines contact with parents as a basic human right for children (Article 9), and advocates the sharing of parental responsibilities (Article 18) as well as listening to and respecting the views of children (Article 12). These principles are difficult to implement when there are conflicts about contact between a residential parent (usually the mother) and non-residential parent (typically the father). Fathers' lobbyists often complain that courts tend to underplay their childcaring competencies, whereas mothers' lobbyists declaim fathers' desires for contact without responsibility.

In response to these challenges, Nordic law has recently been stepping back from legal presumptions of shared care, giving parents space to negotiate on a case-by-case basis within a framework of ensuring child well-being. The consequences for active, post-separation fatherhood are far from clear:

> There are clear indications that Nordic family law is adapting in this area by taking certain steps back from presumptive legal solutions and focusing more on actual care and the welfare of each child to protect its harmonious development. It remains to be seen how these latest reforms will affect the status of fathers and resonate with their realities. (Chapter Three, this volume)

Doing fatherhood in diverse contexts

Arnfinn Andersen's chapter on gay men making space for fatherhood (Chapter Eleven) and Steen Baagøe Nielsen and Allan Westerling's chapter on heterosexual fathers who provide the main care for the children (Chapter Nine) are strong exemplars of discovery-led qualitative studies. Both resonate with Badinter's (1981) classic observation that, 'After centuries of the father's authority or absence, it seems that a new concept has come into existence – father love' (p 315), and that 'fathers should not be regarded merely as alternative mothers' (Richards, 1982, p 57). The informants in both studies provide accounts of how men in diverse fathering contexts create intimacy with their children through everyday negotiations and routine practices around food and space. Scholars are increasingly aware that if we only study those fathers who are co-resident, married and presumed biological, we may be generating theory and concepts on an increasingly selective, albeit still a majority, group. In depicting the lives of non-normative fathering, their work contributes towards extending the sampling frame of what it means to be a Nordic father.

In summary, this tremendous collection tells the story of the trials and tribulations involved in being a father in the Nordic region of the world. It shows that Nordic fatherhood is not a singular institution or experience, occurring instead across a rich set of diverse and complex kin and family alliances, household and economic contexts, bounded by historical and cultural legacies. The research evidence suggests that caring fatherhood is culturally embedded, but that the processes of de-traditionalisation are still under way and incomplete.

References

Badinter, E. (1981) *The myth of motherhood*, London: Souvenir Press.

Chin, M., Lee, J., Lee, S., Son, S. and Sung, M. (2011) 'Family policy in South Korea: development, current status and challenges', *Journal of Child & Family Studies*, vol 21, no 1, pp 53-64.

Coltrane, S. (2003) 'The paradox of fatherhood: predicting the future of men's family involvement', *Vision 2003: Contemporary Family Issues*, Minneapolis, MN: National Council on Family Relations, pp 35-43.

Haas, L. and Hwang, P. (2013) 'Fatherhood and social policy in Scandinavia', in D. Schwalb, B. Schwalb and M. Lamb (eds) *Fathers in cultural context*, New York: Routledge, pp 303-30.

Haour-Knipe, M. (2011) *Fathers, migration and families United Nations: Men in families and family policy in a changing world*, New York: United Nations (http://social.un.org).

Erler, D. (2009) 'Germany: taking a Nordic turn?', in S. Kamerman and P. Moss (eds) *The politics of parental leave*, Bristol: Policy Press, pp 73-85.

Poole, E., Speight, S., O'Brien, M., Connolly, S. and Aldrich, M. (2013) *What do we know about non-resident fathers?*, ESRC Briefing Paper (www.modernfatherhood.org/wp-content/uploads/2013/11/Briefing-paper-Non-resident-fathers.pdf).

Richards, M.P. (1982) 'How should we approach the study of fathers?', in L. McKee and M. O'Brien (eds) *The father figure*, London: Tavistock, pp 57-71.

UN (United Nations) (2011) *Men in families and family policy in a changing world*, New York: UN (http://social.un.org/index/Family/Publications.aspx).

Conclusions

Conclusions:
'What is constructed can
be transformed'[1]

Guðný Björk Eydal and Tine Rostgaard

The aim of this book has been to provide an insight into the contemporary policies and practice of fatherhood in the five Nordic countries of Denmark, Finland, Iceland, Norway and Sweden. Authors from all five Nordic countries have written about fatherhood, how fathers in the Nordic countries practise fatherhood and, how such practices are framed by policies.

The book and its themes have been framed by the particular geographic setting in which it takes place. As the Nordic countries are known for their welfare model and extensive support to families, this book has investigated those policies that set out to support fathers in caring for their children, and asks if the outcomes of such policies are consistent with the goals outlined in Nordic family and gender equality policies. In addition to family law and policies on family benefits, the book has investigated fathers' right to individual entitlements of paid parental leave, otherwise known as the 'father's quota'. Furthermore, the book has investigated how Nordic fathers practise fatherhood in diverse family settings. Thus, the book offers an understanding of the complexity in constructing fatherhood: how it is shaped in the interaction between policies, cultures and the daily practices of fathers, highlighting both similarities and differences within the Nordic region, and addressing the diversity among the Nordic populations, including ethnicity, class, sexual orientation and parental status.

The book has addressed new fathering practices. As other studies have shown, the international trend indicates that fatherhood is gaining a higher status, and fathers are becoming more preoccupied with finding time to spend with their children (O'Brien and Shemilt, 2003; Gauthier and DeGusti, 2012). Nevertheless, in Chapter Two, Rostgaard and Møberg find that Nordic fathers have more relaxed attitudes towards the importance of fatherhood in comparison with other European fathers. This includes the value they place on fatherhood as a condition for adulthood, and whether they accept voluntary childlessness as well as which age is the right age to have children. The results indicate that Nordic fathers show a tolerance towards the variety of choices other men can make in adulthood. The analysis also finds that such relaxed attitudes are associated with childlessness and having fewer children. Therefore, as the chapter underlines, in times of political focus on low fertility rates, ideational factors are important to include in the understanding of what frames male fertility.

While Nordic fathers may be more relaxed in their attitudes when it comes to the importance and timing of fatherhood, they have clearly increased their participation in their children's care over time. These results are also reflected in the two chapters on fathers' time use based on a full account of fathers' time involvement relative to mothers. Both studies find that over time Nordic fathers spend more time with their children, indicating that while Nordic fathers may be tolerant towards other men's choices, they are serious about their own involvement in family life. Chapter Five by Ylikännö, Pääkkönen and Hakovirta confirms such developments in the fathers' involvement. Here, we learn that Finnish fathers now spend considerably more time with their children than was the case two decades ago. The authors also show a clear trend towards a less gendered division of care responsibilities in Finnish families. In Chapter Eight on time use, Nordenmark compares Nordic and Southern European gender policy regimes with regards to fathers' time use. Besides the above-mentioned common trend in spending more time with children, his study confirms that there is a relationship between gender policy regimes and the amount of time fathers invest in their families and homes, where Nordic fathers are more time-involved, but mainly with respect to housework. Interestingly, Nordic fathers only stand out comparatively in their contribution to housework, but not in regards to time spent on childcare. The driving factor for the fathers' involvement in both housework and caring appears to be attitudes. Regardless of policy regime, fathers who are more inclined to gender equality are more likely to spend time on housework and childcare in both the Nordic and Southern European countries. Nordenmark's results suggests that if gender equality is to be achieved with respect to family responsibilities, it would be well worth the investment in welfare policies that support more egalitarian attitudes among fathers.

As both chapters on time use indicate, there are changes taking place, and many chapters in the book investigate such changes in fatherhood practices. For instance, their results support the conclusions of Brandth and Kvande (2002, 2003) that fatherhood practices are never solid and static, but rather fluid as they are continuously being constructed and negotiated in relation to different structures in society, such as fatherhood ideals, work–life demands and policies including parental leave entitlements. As the results in this book have shown, Nordic fathers create their practices in concordance with social structures and institutions, resulting in varying fatherhoods. The results of Brandth and Kvande in this volume show how these practices can be class-specific and how, if policies that define the father's quota are class-blind, it could result in the different take-up of leave among various classes. However, they find that while middle-class fathers may make more use of their entitlements compared to working-class fathers, working-class fathers might use the opportunity that the father's quota represents to transform their gendered (and class-based) fathering practices (see Chapter Six). Furthermore, the conclusions of Ottosen's study of fathers' involvement in care post-divorce (Chapter Twelve) show that if the father is not involved in the care of the young child, there is not only a greater risk of family dissolution, but that if a divorced father belongs to the top of the occupational hierarchy, his involvement in caring for the young child also increases his likelihood of remaining in contact with the child post-divorce. This suggests that social classes are masked in the construction of modern fatherhood, not least when the family breaks up. Such class-based outcomes are also supported by the results presented in other chapters, for example, Rostgaard and Lausten (Chapter Thirteen), who point out that the abolishment of the father's quota in Denmark has left Danish fathers in a different position regarding their possibilities for taking parental leave, so that Danish fathers' ability to take leave now depends on their socio-economic status.

Likewise, in her account of minority ethnic fathering practices, Liversage, in Chapter Ten, points out that fathering possibly has an ethnic dimension. She finds that minority ethnic fathers are more inclined to understand the roles of fathers as complementary rather than equal to the mother, contrary to the dominant view in Denmark, and ethnic fathers may feel challenged as their children steer towards family and gender practices that are very different from their own. Such findings regarding class and/or ethnicity pose challenges to the Nordic welfare states, since it shows that, despite the same legal entitlements, fathers from different socio-economic and cultural backgrounds do not have the same opportunities to use their rights due to class or cultural constraints.

The results of Andersen's analysis of gay parenthood (Chapter Eleven) also provide insights into the challenges that gay fathers must overcome when negotiating their fatherhood practices in those cases where their child has two homes and when living with two mothers.

His results shows how a whole new set of rules and arrangements must be created. These results can nevertheless be applied to all fathers who are negotiating their space regardless of their family status. Nielsen and Westerling, in Chapter Nine, focus on those fathers who have taken long-term paid parental leave, or in other ways differ from mainstream father practices, thus they are pioneering and highly committed in their care roles. Their study shows how these fathers have had to find and negotiate new ways of 'doing fatherhood', revealing the learning processes necessary for fathers who lack role models. These fathers have had to carve out their space for fatherhood in different settings, including their workplace, as Bloksgaard's study shows clearly in Chapter Seven. In her investigation of how fathers negotiate their leave rights in three Danish workplaces in the private sector, she finds that despite seemingly identical entitlements for fathers and mothers, only fathers must negotiate with their superior when to take their leave. She also shows how the cultures of the workplaces can create hindrances for fathers' take-up of leave despite their formal rights to leave. These results are also supported by the conclusions of other authors in the book; Salmi and Lammi-Taskula, as one example (Chapter Fourteen), point out the importance of workplace attitudes towards paternal leave.

The book has also addressed the policies and legal frameworks of families and fatherhood in several chapters. The results show that despite a long-term emphasis on the equal rights of parents to earn and care consistent with the dual earner/dual carer model, the policies are not entirely gender-neutral, and that the Nordic welfare states still have a way to go in this respect. Friðriksdóttir (Chapter Three), who accounts for the contemporary development in family law in all five Nordic countries, concludes that there are inconsistencies in Nordic family law regarding the rights to be a legal father and the juxtaposing of marriage and cohabitation with regards to legal fatherhood and parental responsibilities. The results of the policy analysis conducted by Hakovirta et al (Chapter Four) on how the Nordic welfare states support fathers in providing economically for their children through cash and fiscal family benefits shows that only Swedish, and to some extent Norwegian, family policies provide the same rights for both parents independent of their family model. Thus, by applying the fatherhood perspective, it revealed that Nordic welfare policies need to be improved in order to better ensure the rights of the child to care from both parents.

Several of the chapters show how the father's quota has provided an efficient policy means with which to increase the number of fathers on parental leave and their share in the care of their children (see

Chapters Six, Thirteen, Fourteen, Fifteen and Sixteen). However, as Rostgaard and Lausten, and Salmi and Lammi-Taskula point out, the Nordic countries have taken quite different paths in this regard. While Iceland, Norway and Sweden have ensured both parents 8–14 weeks' leave, Denmark abolished the father's quota following a short period in the early 2000s, and Finland has provided fewer rights for fathers compared with the other Nordic countries.

Salmi and Lammi-Taskula provide an insight into the mechanisms at play when the father's quota was initially debated in Finland. They conclude that the goals of gender equality, 'free choice' and flexibility can be contradictory, and that this contradiction has not been acknowledged within policymaking where it can have the effect of creating less equality even when the pronounced aim is gender equality. Their data on leave take-up shows how leave schemes in Finland based on the 'free choice' rationale, 'do not contribute to the policy goal of improved gender equality, as they lead to fathers only taking the earmarked leave periods and mothers "freely choosing" the transferable parental leave' (Chapter Fourteen, this volume). Thus, they conclude that the 'free choice' rationale does not promote equal care from both parents. On the contrary, it reproduces the traditional gendered division of labour where mothers are seen as primary caregivers. The main conclusions of Salmi and Lammi-Taskula are consistent with the conclusions of other authors in the book that examine the father's quota, that change in the actual take-up of parental leave is not possible if the scheme design does not support a father's ability to choose.

Despite the clear results regarding the outcomes of the father's quota, such policies have been critically debated in all five Nordic countries in recent years, with the exception of Iceland, where despite the severe implications of the economic crisis, the characteristics of the scheme have remained unchanged. In fact, as Chapter Fifteen by Eydal and Gíslason shows, the long-term goal to increase the father's and mother's quota to five months for each parent over time was enacted into law in 2012. Even though the state budget did not allow implementing the increase at this time, it signals a future political promise that would ensure that the Icelandic fathers' position would be better than that of fathers in any other Nordic and non-Nordic country so far. The results of Eydal and Gíslason's chapter regarding the effects of the cuts to the benefit amount and the influences of the crisis are a reminder of the importance of considering the level of benefit payments. None of the Nordic countries have managed to bridge the gender pay gap, and the dependency on the male wage means that fathers are in a more precarious situation than mothers, and if the father wants to take leave, it could result in a severe reduction in household income.

The international scholars kind enough to comment on this typescript and share with the readers their views and conclusions from a non-Nordic perspective, Janet Gornick and Margaret O'Brien, both emphasise the importance of the support generated by Nordic family and gender policies. Gornick, in Chapter Seventeen, points out in her comment on the conclusions and lessons emerging from the book, in particular the book's contributions to the research on parental leave, that gendered expectations continue to be functioning at both the micro and meso levels in the West, and this includes the Nordic countries. O'Brien points out that while all Nordic governments promote a dual earner/dual carer social democratic welfare state model, great variations in the policy and family practices exist between the countries, and she continues by emphasising the challenges that migration, separation and sexual orientation pose for both practice and policies. Hence, their conclusions support our understanding that despite the obvious success of the Nordic policies in enhancing gender equality, these countries are still faced with further challenges as their societies become more diversified.

Thus, this volume contributes to the critical discussion of the remaining hindrances and challenges facing Nordic fathers when entering fatherhood. While the overall results confirm that the goal of policies on gender equality, families and the labour market are the equal rights of both parents to earn and to care, structural and cultural hindrances remain that need to be recognised and defined in order to eliminate these obstacles. At the same time, the volume shows that fathers in the Nordic countries construct a variety of fatherhoods that are built on their cultural heritage, and at the same time, these fathers are innovating new practices. Finally, this volume will hopefully serve as a reminder of the need for further research, as many important issues have been left out. One of the lessons learned was the importance of increasing interdisciplinary research, such as a collaboration of scholars from health, human and social sciences. Hopefully the results have also inspired research on the issues discussed in this book that are not yet fully understood, for example, the complex interplay of mechanisms in the family and workplace.

Note

[1] Quoted from Porter (2013); originally from the South African gender activist Dumisani Rebombo.

References

Brandth, B. and Kvande, E. (2002) 'Reflexive fathers: negotiating parental leave and working life', *Gender, Work and Organization*, vol 9, no 2, pp 186-203.

Brandth, B. and Kvande, E. (2003) *Fleksible fedre. Maskulinitet, arbeid, velferdsstat [Flexible fathers]*, Oslo: Universitetsforlaget.

Gauthier, A. and DeGusti, B. (2012) 'Time allocation to children by parents', *Europe International Sociology*, vol 27, no 6, pp 827-45.

O'Brien, M. and Shemilt, I. (2003) *Working fathers: Earning and caring*, Manchester: Equal Opportunities Commission.

Porter, A. (2013) '"What is Constructed can be Transformed": Masculinities in Post-Conflict Societies', *Africa International Peacekeeping*, vol 20, no 4, pp 486-506. DOI:10.1080/13533312.2013.846137

Index

Page references for tables and figures are in *italics*; those for notes are followed by n